The "Greek Crisis" in Europe

Studies in Critical Social Sciences Book Series

Haymarket Books is proud to be working with Brill Academic Publishers (www.brill.nl) to republish the *Studies in Critical Social Sciences* book series in paperback editions. This peer-reviewed book series offers insights into our current reality by exploring the content and consequences of power relationships under capitalism, and by considering the spaces of opposition and resistance to these changes that have been defining our new age. Our full catalog of *SCSS* volumes can be viewed at https://www.haymarketbooks.org/series_collections/4-studies-in-critical-social-sciences.

Series Editor
David Fasenfest (SOAS University of London)

Editorial Board
Eduardo Bonilla-Silva (Duke University)
Chris Chase-Dunn (University of California–Riverside)
William Carroll (University of Victoria)
Raewyn Connell (University of Sydney)
Kimberlé W. Crenshaw (University of California–LA and Columbia University)
Heidi Gottfried (Wayne State University)
Karin Gottschall (University of Bremen)
Alfredo Saad Filho (King's College London)
Chizuko Ueno (University of Tokyo)
Sylvia Walby (Lancaster University)
Raju Das (York University)

The "Greek Crisis" in Europe

Race, Class and Politics

Yiannis Mylonas

Haymarket Books
Chicago, IL

First published in 2019 by Brill Academic Publishers, The Netherlands.
© 2019 Koninklijke Brill NV, Leiden, The Netherlands

Published in paperback in 2020 by
Haymarket Books
P.O. Box 180165
Chicago, IL 60618
773-583-7884
www.haymarketbooks.org

ISBN: 978-1-64259-193-4

Distributed to the trade in the US through Consortium Book Sales and Distribution (www.cbsd.com) and internationally through Ingram Publisher Services International (www.ingramcontent.com).

This book was published with the generous support of Lannan Foundation and Wallace Action Fund.

Special discounts are available for bulk purchases by organizations and institutions. Please call 773-583-7884 or email info@haymarketbooks.org for more information.

Cover design by Jamie Kerry and Ragina Johnson.

Printed in United States.

10 9 8 7 6 5 4 3 2 1

Library of Congress Cataloging-in-Publication Data is available.

Did there remain in his nation even a small soul, something he could work with in order to bring about general happiness? Or had everything there been so worn away by suffering that even imagination, the intelligence of the poor, had entirely died? Chagataev knew from childhood memory and from his education in Moscow that any exploitation of the human being begins with the distortion of that person's soul, with getting their soul so used to death that it can be subjugated; without this subjugation, a slave is not a slave.

    PLATONOV, 2013: 103

To be underdeveloped is not merely to be robbed or exploited: it is to be held in the grip of an artificial stasis. Underdevelopment not only kills: its essential stagnation denies life and resembles death.

    BERGER & MOHR, 2010: 36

Contents

Preface XI
Acknowledgements XVI
List of Figures and Tables XVII

1 Introduction: the Study of the Greek Economic Crisis in Europe through the Media 1
   1.1 Contextual Issues, Critical Political Economy and Cultural Studies 3
   1.2 European Mass Media as the Empirical Material of the Study 6
      1.2.1 *A Brief Excursion on Liberalism and its Discontents* 8
      1.2.2 *Greek, Danish and German Mainstream News Media* 10
   1.3 On Method: Thematic Analysis, Discourse Theory Analysis, Critical Discourse Analysis 14
      1.3.1 *The Relevance of Discourse Theory* 15
      1.3.2 *Critical Discourse Analysis Perspectives* 18
   1.4 The Analytical Pillars: Race, Class, Politics 20
      1.4.1 *On Race* 20
         1.4.1.1 Colonial Remainders: An "Eternal" Greece 23
      1.4.2 *On Class* 30
         1.4.2.1 Dismantling Class Privilege 35
      1.4.3 *Theorizing (Post)Politics* 39
   1.5 An Outline of the Chapters to Follow 45

2 Greek Crisis, Eurozone Crisis, Global Capitalist Crisis 48
   2.1 Setting the "Greek Crisis" in Perspective 48
   2.2 A Crisis of Capitalism and Capitalist Crises: A Brief Excursion into Marxian Analyses 56
   2.3 Crisis and Restructuring: Neoliberalism, Globalisation, Financialisation 63
   2.4 The Greek Crisis as a Symptom: Centre (Core) and Periphery Divisions 69
   2.5 The EU, the Euro, and Austerity 73
   2.6 Debt, Austerity and Primary Accumulation 78
   2.7 Concluding Remarks: Understanding Capitalism as Religion 85

3 The "Greek Crisis" in the Media: Hegemony, Spectacle and Propaganda 87
   3.1 Media Aspects 87

3.2　Political Communication and the Public Sphere　88
3.3　Understanding Hegemony　92
　　3.3.1　*The "Greek Crisis" in the Media: A Critical Overview*　93
　　3.3.2　*Hegemony, Propaganda and Biopolitics*　97
3.4　Spectacular Dimensions of the "Greek Crisis"　105
3.5　Concluding Remarks: Interpellating and Disciplining the Working Class　110

4　A Cultural Failure: Reification, Orientalism, Nationalism　113
4.1　Introduction: (I)liberal Uses of Culture　114
4.2　Hegemonic Constructions of the (Occidental) Self and the (Oriental) Other　115
4.3　Greece as a non/quasi-European Other　120
　　4.3.1　*The Culturalisation of Greece and its Crisis*　121
　　4.3.2　*Greece as a Commodity: Media Rituals to Sustain Ideological Myths*　134
　　4.3.3　*Nationalism, Narcissism, Anxiety: Europe as a Panopticon and a Benchmark*　140
4.4　Concluding Remarks: The Occident, the Orient and the Liberal Meritocracy Cult　150

5　Under a Middle-Class Gaze　153
5.1　Governing Inequality　153
5.2　The Middle-Class Gaze and the Media　154
5.3　"The Loser" as a Master Class Frame　156
5.4　The Greek Crisis and the Construction of "Losers"　158
　　5.4.1　*The Irrational: Ignorant, Irresponsible, and Frustrated*　160
　　5.4.2　*The Immoral: Lazy, Profligate, Deceitful and Bankrupt*　164
　　5.4.3　*The Threatening Other: Resentment, Spite, and Loath*　170
　　5.4.4　*Idealising the Bourgeois; the Enduring Myths of a Peripheral Upper Class*　176
5.5　Concluding Remarks: Reaction, Diversion, Division　179

6　Exceptionalising the Crisis, Normalising Austerity　183
6.1　Technocratic Politics　183
6.2　Establishing the Crisis and Austerity in Depoliticised Terms　184
　　6.2.1　*The Eurozone Crisis as an Apocalyptic Spectacle: Mediatised States of Exception*　185

  6.2.2 *Naturalising Austerity; the Only Solution (Without an Alternative)* 191
  6.2.3 *The "Extreme Center" and Constructions of "Realism"* 199
 6.3 Concluding Remarks: Authoritarian Capitalism with Fascist Dispositions 209

7 **Conclusions: Context, Politics, Negativity** 213
 7.1 Reinventing Critique, Reinventing Politics 213
 7.2 Debunking Hegemony's Crisis' Myths 215
 7.3 The Making of Regimes of Entitlement: Class is at the Heart of the Matter 219
 7.4 Capitalism is Apocalyptic: Politicising the Crisis, Austerity, the "Free Market", and the (Capitalist) Economy 221
 7.5 Negativity and Utopia 223

Bibliography 229
Index 251

Preface

Offended Lands[1]

The so-called "Greek crisis" officially started at the end of 2009. At that time, I was defending my Ph.D. thesis at the Humanities Faculty of Copenhagen University, after having moved to Denmark in early 2006, to pursue a Ph.D. degree there.

A year prior to the crisis, I attended a public presentation in Copenhagen, which attempted to analyze the recent "December 2008" events in Greece – an upheaval sparkled by the cold-blooded murder of a teenager named Alexis Grigoropoulos by a far-right policeman. What to me and others (Vradis & Dalakoglou, 2011) was a class and generation-based revolt – related to the cumulated contradictions of late capitalism in a peripheral European state – to the Danish scholar it seemed to be yet another case of Greek exceptionality. Under an indignant tone, the presenter stressed common liberal arguments that place issues such as gerontocracy and a male-dominated political system at the core of Greece's problems. However true these dimensions may be (although not exclusive to Greece), this approach showed a limited understanding of the system's flaws. Following the presenter's line of thought, one can even assume that young neoliberal "centrists" like the banker Emmanuel Macron in the French Presidency, or, neoliberal, right-wing, conservative women like Angela Merkel (or, Margaret Thatcher to this regard), are presumably "solutions" or signs of political health.

In 2010, a "Greek-crisis" publicity emerged with Greece entering the global news agendas on a nearly daily basis, which soon took a very malicious turn particularly during 2011 and 2012. The Greek crisis popular narrative was conceptualised through various pre-existing demeaning stereotypes deployed to viciously attack the Greek people as a whole, but in reality, aiming especially at those of the middle and the lower social strata. A selection of fragmented bits of negative information that sought to "expose" the reality of Greece, often presented in a highly detailed manner, was spectacularly exhibited to publics across the European Union (EU) (and beyond), sequenced in a way that proved the "Greek scrounger" thesis on one hand, and the "self-inflicting" character of the Greek crisis on the other. Demeaning stereotypes and prejudices over Greece pre-existed in the Western world. One can argue that the media and the "Greek crisis" publicity only amplified what already was in place,

---

[1] Pablo Neruda in Mike Davis (2017: v)

preying on racist "gut feelings" on what Greece "really is", while tapping on general anxieties and creating a moral panic around the Greek crisis theme. The subtle bigotry of culture and class emerged in unprecedented ways, intensified by an economic emergency policy framework. The media's amplification and repetition of such new racist tropes legitimised their everyday uses, serving the formation of a popular consensus around the imposition of harsh austerity regimes in Greece that were soon to be implemented in other crisis-struck Eurozone states too. This publicity created a regime of entitlement to address the Greek people in demeaning terms, objectifying them and demanding the implementation of policies that bared no democratic legitimacy. Built on upper-class knowledge regimes and marked by a general ignorance towards the periphery and its context, this sense of entitlement produces consensus over austerity, depoliticises the crisis and curbs the development of solidarities, while intensifying nationalism and a market-orientated understanding of the world.

Between 2010 and 2012, I was employed by Lund University in Sweden, to work as a post-doctoral scholar in media sociology. In 2010, and 2011 in particular, the Greek/Eurozone crisis' publicity intensified an assemblage of micro (and major) aggressions that the Greeks living in the North/West were exposed to daily. I can recall numerous occasions of unprovoked aggression coming from a variety of people in the countries I worked at and resided then, notably Denmark and Sweden, ranging from co-workers in the academia to students, policemen, bank clerks, bartenders, and to be sure, mere acquaintances and encounters. Such stories are common among many Greeks living abroad during those years. Unsurprisingly, acts of aggression also came from citizens of peripheral EU states like, for example, Poland, whose large migrant waves across Europe have experienced equivalent racist degradation to those that the Greeks have. Migrants from non-EU states also exhibited similar anti-Greek sentiments. Possibly, citizens of peripheral states saw in the Greek crisis publicity a further possibility to identify with the West/North European norm and thus "integrate" further in their host countries. "Ordinary people", of middle and working-class backgrounds, even self-designed "leftists" felt entitled to express their loath openly. A sense of joy, indeed, seemed to follow the iteration of discriminatory and shaming remarks (particularly mild ones, made to pass as "humorous"), which confirmed a habitus of supremacy, which in the North passes largely uncontested. The "Greek crisis" political management and publicity by the liberal dominant class became a source of what Deleuze and Guattari call micro-fascisms in the terrain of everyday life.

In times of high uncertainty, the publicity of the "Greek crisis" produced a bitter result, corroding the relations of people and undermining the emergence of possibilities of solidarity. In fact, the EU's conservatives and neoliberals colonised the word solidarity itself, creating a rather false, "newspeak" version of it, associated with "no-alternative" policy agendas. Hence, they named solidarity the flow of loans forced to Greece in the no-alternative crisis-policy context. These "bailout loans" augmented Greece's debt, so as not to cancel it as odious at the expense of private creditors, such as German, French and American banks who were exposed to the Greek public debt. The bailout loans legitimised the pursuing of austerity and privatisations in Greece, which severely undermined the living standards of the Greek people and the state of the Greek democracy itself. So much for "help"; or, to use some Danish irony, "tak for hjælpen!"

The escalation of the "Greek crisis" spectacle probed me to the study of the hegemonic crisis and austerity discourse, as represented in mainstream mass media. The reason for that was to deploy critical theory in a coherent and systematic way to criticise and challenge the hegemonic neoliberal ideology, as it unfolded in Europe and the Eurozone crisis context. Most importantly, I focused on the media because it was the media that endlessly propagated the demeaning and fictitious themes enunciated by influential European politicians. The media were caught in a process of destruction of local contexts and subjective experiences that capitalist restructuring requires. This means the erasing of modes of life, meanings and social relations viewed as not economically productive, from the public sphere.

After publishing my first critical analysis of the German media representations of the Greek crisis in June 2012, a German colleague wrote back to me that "Bild is already known" for what it is, implying that my analysis was offering nothing really new. She then pointed towards the existence of the more serious German media that supposedly approached the crisis in more actual and objective terms. Further, I was also told in a reassuring fashion that "it is not as bad" (probably as I wrote in my analysis that it was), as if this knowledge was somehow held by natives like her better than myself and others, potentially "complaining" and exaggerating Southerners living in the North. Nevertheless, it seemed like my critique had touched upon a sensitive nerve, challenging a white/bourgeois sense of entitlement to point the finger to *others,* without accepting any critique back.

While in Madrid in March 2014, following the "New abduction of Europa: debt, war, democratic revolution" conference, and during a visit at Prado museum, I had the chance to view Francisco Goya's "Black paintings". What struck me the most was his "Fight with cudgels", which was later chosen as the cover image of this book. There, two men that both seem to be equally ordinary, are viciously striking each other with clubs, appearing grounded in a standstill, at what gives the impression of a deserted space. The painting seemed to represent the position of the oppressed people of Greece, especially after the rise of the neo-nazi party of the Golden Dawn into a parliamentary force during the crisis years. But on a further level too, Goya's painting also seemed to represent the position where the entire world's oppressed are today, immersed in competition norms, and generally lacking counter-hegemonic perspectives, identities, and strategies. In short, during social crises, the lack of a widely shared vision for the making of a better world that can be more just, equal, and joyful, is substituted by social cannibalism. In his excellent book "On Artists", John Berger notes that, besides being a graphic artist, Goya was also a commentator. For Berger (2015: 173), Goya's underlining theme of commentary has to do with "the consequences of Man's neglect of his most precious faculty, Reason". Reason, however, often appears to be constitutive of mainstream liberal repertoires. For instance, in the "Greek crisis" context, a public call to reason has been deployed to serve the ends of the "no alternative" to austerity thesis, blocking critique and counter-hegemonic politics. To this regard, in their first volume of "Capitalism and Schizophrenia", Deleuze and Guattari (1977) note that it is not the sleep of reason that breeds monsters but instead, monsters are bread by the sleepless reason itself, submerged in the structures of power and conformity of the modern capitalist societies. Therefore, the idea of reason is also a site of contestation between competing practices, ideologies, and interests. The developing of a critical form of reason though remains an important dimension to understand the systemic nature of the problems that the world faces today and to counter the widespread tendencies of inertia, regression, fragmentation, and pessimism.

Despite the ghastly rise of inequality today, where the 1% of the wealthiest people control 50% of the world's wealth, or, the rapid catastrophe of the natural environment caused by an industrial civilisation based on the acceleration of production and consumption of commodities, no political formation currently exist to "reach for the emergency brake" in Walter Benjamin's (1974) sense, and halt capitalism's catastrophic course. Instead, there is a widespread faith in capitalism, strongly shared by the dominant classes, and also followed by the lower ones. Potentially, this proves the religious dimension of capitalism, as perceived by Walter Benjamin. Nevertheless, bright and courageous minorities from across the world were the ones expressing solidarity to the symbolic and material plight of Greece, particularly during the most crucial, first crisis years, and addressing the crisis and austerity in political terms. It seemed that such minorities kept alive a sense of collective humanity that is burdened by the same problems and is marked by the same universal emancipatory aspirations. As capitalism is today – despite its grotesque signs of decadence – possibly stronger than ever before, the introducing of counter-hegemonic concepts and critical analyses may estrange what passes as "common sense", and trigger the imagination for the crafting of critique and politics that can escape the margins and become popular and mass.

Acknowledgements

This book is the outcome of a long study and research process that conventionally started in 2011.

Various people have offered invaluable help while conceptualizing and developing this study. Here, I wish to express my gratitude to a few of them:

Firstly, I wish to thank my parents, Konstantinos Mylonas and Eleni Skonderikli Mylonas, and my brother Panagiotis Mylonas for their continuous support. Sincere thanks to my colleagues and friends, notably Panos Kompatsiaris, Matina Noutsou, Stamatis Messinis, Theodora Vetta, Stergios Valioulis, Vangelis Poulios, Jaka Primorac, Dimitris Christoforidis, Niki K., and also the Crisis Mirror group in Copenhagen, for inspiration, extended conversations, reflections and intellectual exchanges on theory, politics, society and culture. Special thanks to Professor Ilya Kiriya, to Elena Rhimanova, to the School of Media and the National Research University Higher School of Economics in Moscow, for offering a generous, stimulating and overall excellent work environment, vital for the completion of this book. To this regard, I also wish to thank Brill Publications and the editors of this book, Jennifer Obdam, Professor David Fasenfest, and Judy Pereira.

Last and foremost, warm thanks to Elena Zamkova, for brightening this journey.

Figures and Tables

Figures

1. Voucher used instead of money to pay productivity bonuses. Source: Photo by author.   61
2. "Extraction brings illness and death" – Social Dispensary of Thessaloniki. Posters against the Canadian "Eldorado Gold" mining activities at Chalkidiki. Source: Photo by author, Thessaloniki, April 2018.   83
3. Small businesses closed during the crisis years. Source: Photo by the author, central Thessaloniki, April 2018.   84
4. The monument of the destruction of the Cretan village Kandanos by the Wehrmacht. Source: Photo by the author.   127
5. The crisis falsehoods: OECD (2017) charts on average annual work hours   138

Tables

1. The Greek sovereign debt before and after the bailout programs   50
2. Constructions of Europe and Greece in the German and the Danish liberal press   116
3. Constructions of "European Greece" and "Oriental Greece" in the Greek liberal media   117

CHAPTER 1

Introduction: the Study of the Greek Economic Crisis in Europe through the Media

As is generally known, the latest major economic crisis of global proportions started in the USA with the credit crunch of 2007–8. Ten years later, in 2018, critics note that the crisis is far from fully resolved, with a new – and potentially more serious – one pending (Roos, 2018b). Along with the economic crisis, a broader and multifaceted crisis with harsh political, ecological and social dimensions is advancing, with capitalism being the root cause of it (Feldner & Vighi, 2015).

In the 2010's, a growing scholarly literature developed, tackling the various political, cultural and social dimensions of the aforementioned economic crisis. The study of the media is one important dimension in the analysis of the crisis, its politics, and its culture. The media play a crucial political role in the ways that the crisis is perceived and managed. In today's liberal democratic states, it is through the mass media that the policies predicated to alleviate the crisis are publicly explained and legitimised in order to be applied.

The media have also been caught in the economic crisis and the restructuring process that societies have been undergoing for several years now. The economic crisis and the cuts introduced by austerity policies have had severe effects in the media industries as well. Most importantly, the general neoliberal framework preceding the crisis had already seriously compromised the political-democratic role of the media and, along with that, their independence. Economic pressures turned the media into entertaining and marketing businesses, focusing mostly in the production of popular content so as to compete more effectively in a global media market that is nowadays dominated by few oligopolistic media conglomerates (Mosco, 2009: 133).

Studies have shown that the media heavily relied on the official version of the economic crisis, as articulated by the leading politicians of the most influential states, as well as by technocrats and economists. Furthermore, as the crisis developed over time, the media seemed to forget their own crisis explanations and to constantly adopt different ones, in what Laura Basu (2018) described as "media amnesia". For instance, during the initial stages of the US credit crunch, the media paid attention to the role of finance and banking in the development of the crisis, but in the Eurozone crisis context, the media heavily relied on cultural and class stereotypes to explain the causes of the crisis, while dropping their earlier focus on deregulated finance. In this regard,

Greece, the Eurozone crisis' epicentre, was mercilessly targeted by mainstream media, and received highly negative, and largely misleading, publicity over its sovereign debt crisis. What was soon understood as a "Greek-bashing" process (Bickes, Otten & Weyman, 2014), grew out of a sensualistic "Greek crisis" media spectacle, in which the Greek people (mostly the working class) were deemed guilty of cheating a supposedly benevolent European Union (EU) (Gkintidis, 2018) and their (ostensibly innocent) "fellow Europeans", so as to enjoy a lavish and excessive consumeristic lifestyle, presumably in an endless vacation.

Often enough, the so-called Greek crisis was represented in even more crude forms that included biology-based hints and metaphors, rendering Greeks as Europe's "Other". To give an example, in July 2015, after the so-called "Greferendum" that occurred in Greece with regards to the continuation or not of austerity policies in the country, the Dutch "centre-left" *De Volkskrant* newspaper showed its discontent with the Greek referendum's results and the sweeping victory of the anti-austerity vote by publishing a sketch of a supposedly stereotypical Greek figure. This image featured a man with a degrading form (ugly, dark, obese, middle-aged, bald, poorly dressed and grumpy), who occupied a standard tourist landscape and posed with one hand giving the finger (to the Dutch/European reader) and with the other begging. In line with the mainstream tropes about the Greek crisis, in which Europe "helps" but Greece deceives, this particular sketch also carried sharp affinities with Nazi propaganda in its portrayal of what the Nazis described as the "eternal Jew" (sic), through a stereotypical figure created by the Nazis that also displayed equivalent degrading features (dark, ugly, grumpy, etc.), who subtly begged with one hand while holding a whip with the other.[1]

The spectacular bashing of the Greek people, and especially its working class, paved the way for austerity to unleash an unprecedented assault on the Greek citizens' social, political and human rights while plundering public and private wealth under the pretext of repaying the debt. Jerome Roos (2019: 240) mentions that "the Greek program included about 22.5 structural measures to be applied per year, compared to 8.5 per year in 2010 in the IMF programs" amounting to the 18% of gross domestic product (GDP) during the crisis years, when Germany's total austerity was at 2% and Ireland's to 9%. The rapid loss of the GDP, the rise of unemployment and the mass decline of living standards that the politics of crisis and austerity brought to Greece have been analogous to circumstances faced by countries during war or revolution. At a public level, austerity took on a punitive form for appeasing the "hard-working Europeans". Simultaneously, austerity was also presented as not just rightful, but also, most

---

[1] Both pictures can be seen here: https://pbs.twimg.com/media/CJYVhQXUMAApgjV.png (accessed 17/09/2018).

significantly, the only available policy doctrine to overcome the crisis. As it will be argued in the following chapters, the iteration of racist and classist stereotypes by the mass media has been integral to the public legitimation of austerity in Greece.

In this introductory chapter, I present the research approach developed in this study through a review of specific socio-political readings that offer critical concepts to scrutinise the Greek crisis' publicity in Europe, as it was covered by the popular mainstream media. Overall, the research includes newspapers, journals, as well as news and lifestyle websites from the EU countries of Greece, Denmark, and Germany. As will be further explained, these countries represent main core-periphery dichotomies in the EU. Their study can highlight major socio-political trends that currently shape the EU's political culture. I focus on conservative and liberal media because they represent the most dominant voices in the national public spheres of Europe, iterating and reproducing the prevailing crisis' explanations. The chapter will also present the analytical methodology followed. This is a qualitative, thematic form of textual analysis, displaying the central themes expressed in the mainstream "Greek crisis" media representations. In particular, the analysis is based on three interrelated themes: race, class and post-democratic politics. These main themes are further developed through the relevant critical theoretical advances and are analytically disclosed through discourse analysis perspectives.

1.1   Contextual Issues, Critical Political Economy and Cultural Studies

The book advances a critical understanding of the public meanings ascribed to the economic crisis and to austerity with a focus on Greece. Greece and its modern socio-political history are hardly known outside Greece, and thus the Greek socio-historical context and its repercussions are poorly (if at all) understood, particularly in the West. Instead, Greece is usually overdetermined by the prevailing consumerist fantasies cultivated by popular culture and the tourist industry, along with enduring colonial themes that prioritise ancient Greece at the expense of modern Greece.

As Fredrik Jameson (2015: 123) writes:

> Modern Greek history is far less familiar than that of other Western countries. Greece has gone through a collective experience of which most other modern nations have only known bits and pieces: revolution, fascism, occupation, civil war, foreign intervention, Western imperialism, exile, parliamentary democracy, military dictatorship, and after the sixties, a ringside seat at the horrendous violence of the new Balkan wars, with

their flood of refugees recalling Greece's own refugee experience after being driven out of Ionia at the end of World War I.

Since 2010, the economic crisis has been another destructive event occurring in a country "overburdened with history", to use the words of the British historian Mark Mazower (2000). The study aims to contextualise the "Greek crisis" while showing the poor and deeply problematic representation of it by the Western liberal-bourgeois media and the dominant politico-economic interests with which they are connected. Drawing on the art theorist John Roberts (2015) and his account of the contemporary Russian avant-garde group Chto Delat, I argue that, just as with the Russian case which he studies through the critical work of Chto Delat, the focus on the Greek hitches and context provides a set of questions to address the current international situation and affairs, which are inscribed in the Greek pitfalls themselves as joint and reciprocally defining problems. Thus, quoting Roberts (2015: 174), with this work I intend to "resist the pitfalls of nationalist reflection while rejecting the notion that an internationalism of the periphery can speak without resource to its national voices and context".

Studies show that any social crisis – such as a major economic crisis – produces symptoms of social disintegration like pauperisation, anomie, apathy, depression, political regression or polarisation, among others (Dimitriou, 2016). The so-called structural adjustment reforms that, since the advent of neoliberalism in the 1970s, emerged as the sole and mandatory economic crisis' resolution doctrine have escalated such phenomena of socio-political degradation to a broadening pool of countries across the world (Matza, 2018). Neoliberalism is an authoritative system that impels a totalistic view of social life based on the capitalist market framework. The example of the current state of Ukraine, as Yurchenko (2018) has persuasively demonstrated in a stimulating study, expresses all the aforementioned effects that crisis and austerity bring. Indeed, Greece, too, after nine years of crisis and austerity, shows signs of such symptoms as well. The rise of fascist tendencies, nationalism and authoritarianism, the escalation of depression, everyday acts of aggression, suicides, the dilapidation of the urban and the natural environment, the rise of precarity and exploitation in the workplaces, and the escalation of wealth inequality are all important consequences of both the capitalist crisis and neoliberal austerity in Greece, just like elsewhere.

Leading EU politicians along with various economists and "experts" maintain that neither the crisis nor the (austerity) reforms are political in themselves. Instead, they usually establish a causal, "common sense" explanation for the economic crisis, that is often explained through medical or housekeeping metaphors (Varoufakis, 2017; Maesse, 2018). As far as neoliberal austerity is concerned, they make a procedural case for it, presenting it as a mere technical form for the economic crisis' management, which comes as the crisis' "natural" remedy.

In contrast to the mainstream and dominant accounts, a review of relevant and up-to-date critical political economy perspectives demonstrates the global and systemic character of the crisis and the highly political nature of austerity policies. Critical political economy analyses situate the Eurozone/Greek crisis in a global capitalist crisis framework (Harvey, 2014; Roos, 2019). Austerity reforms are perceived to be capitalist restructuring policies. In this study, I deploy a Marxian analysis of the Eurozone/Greek crisis as a symptom of the capitalist crisis of accumulation and reproduction, understanding austerity as a neoliberal restructuring doctrine. This is combined with a cultural studies approach, focusing on a discourse analysis of the semiotic systems of the crisis and austerity and the ways that these are publicly circulated through the mass media. In this sense, the economy is not separate from society and culture (Maesse, 2018b: 4). Sum and Jessop (2013: 141) argue that semiosis is crucial "in construing, constructing and temporarily stabilizing capitalist social formations at least within specific spatiotemporal fixes and their zones of relative stability".

What Sum and Jessop (2013: 1) describe as the cultural political economy analysis is a method that "combines the analysis of sense- and meaning-making with the analysis of instituted economic and political relations and their social embedding". The fixing of the crisis and austerity's meanings publicly is crucial for the achieving public consensus about the policies that such meanings are connected with. Public meanings are inherently ideological in the sense that they do not have any objective, natural or ontological essence. Rather, they are constructed through hegemonic interventions related to material interests and value systems associated with dominant social groups. Simultaneously, these meanings are not "produced from scratch". Instead, their edifice is based on "construals" (Sum & Jessop, 2013: 473), that is to say, on sedimented forms of knowledge (Carpentier, 2017: 46), established institutions, social relations and material components that have obtained a seemingly fixed, normative and institutionalised character over the course of time.

Maintaining that capitalism is at the root of all world's problems and crises today, this book aims to put forth a narrative that places class conflict at the centre of crisis and austerity politics. Class conflict, as Raymond Williams (2015: 135) argues, is the condition of the capitalist social order. Williams does not identify class conflict with class struggle, as the latter is something that can emerge through the political activity of the working class. Williams' statement remains relevant for the present economic crisis context because austerity policies' prime focus is the restructuring of the work and the living conditions of the working people, pursuing the intensification of economic productivity at the expense of the living standards of the many. To use a recent example from March 2018, the Greek daily *Kathimerini*, one of the newspapers studied here, published a review of the Greek entrepreneurs who received the "businessman of the year" award for investing in innovation. In this review, one entrepreneur emphatically argues that "the country (Greece) will exit the crisis when we all (sic) begin to pursue riches; for there is nothing shameful in being rich, because poverty is what one should be ashamed of" (*Kathimerini*, 29/03/2018). Class is central to understanding the dominant logic of the crisis, austerity and their mainstream public construction. The study of the media is an inquiry into the experience of the capitalist crisis and neoliberal austerity, linked to the ways that common meanings and descriptions are generated and communicated, together with patterns of learning, describing and persuading. These dimensions, related to the culture of the crisis and austerity, are equally fundamental entities in the perception of the crisis and austerity otherwise, through the demonstration of their profound political character. The focus on the crisis' public meaning, through the study of mass media, concerns the understanding of the ideology and politics of the Eurozone crisis and the ways that public consensus dominant policy discourses and strategies are achieved in the EU.

1.2 European Mass Media as the Empirical Material of the Study

The understanding of media that is followed in this research is connected to critical approaches that stress the media's political function as important institutions that produce social consensus and sustain a given form of social order (Herman and Chomsky, 1988; McChesney, 2009). This is usually related to the material interests, ideologies and value systems of dominant societal groups. In this study's context, the mass media reproduced the dominant views of the crisis and austerity, stressing a need for economic growth as a universal condition of prosperity, while turning a blind eye to the unevenness of capitalist growth, its exploitative character and the detrimental effects that it has on society, polity and the natural environment.

The decision to study German and Greek media while analysing the culture and the politics of the crisis and austerity in the EU may be rather obvious. Germany has a leading position in today's EU, directing the development of ordoliberal austerity to indebted Eurozone countries such as Greece (Streeck, 2016). The German government's outline of the Eurozone/Greek crisis and its public narratives are hegemonic across Europe and elsewhere (Ojala &

Harjumieni, 2016). Greece in that sense is chosen for being the crisis' epicentre in the EU. The main interest in studying Greece is to see how the crisis and austerity meanings generated in Germany and in the EU are appropriated and domesticated in the Greek public sphere, and how consensus over austerity policies is being pursued this way. Although Denmark is not a Eurozone member, it is part of the capitalist North European core. Denmark makes a good case in seeing how other capitalist core countries respond to the crisis of the Eurozone and to calls for austerity.

The critical study of the German and the Danish media cultures aims to contest popular ideas about the North as broadly progressive, egalitarian, tolerant and democratic, maintaining that such conditions are only historical-political possibilities, susceptible to change and potential decline, rather than essentialist and permanent features. For example, *Time* magazine declared Angela Merkel to be 2015's "person of the year" with a cover image of her oil-painted portrait (suggesting her premature monumentalisation), under a headline proclaiming her to be "The Chancellor of the free world" (sic). Such a problematic claim was further amplified by the liberal media across the globe in the dawn of Donald Trump's election to the US presidency. As critics explained (Berezin, 2014), Merkel's conservative government has normalised the political right in the EU, turning right-wing conservativism into a somewhat "centrist", "responsible" or "realistic" position that further stabilised the advance of German Ordoliberalism in the EU's policymaking framework (Dardot & Laval, 2014). Similarly, although Denmark is often proclaimed to be one of the "world's happiest nations", particularly due to its well-functioning social-democratic institutions and norms, it is also a country that, in its recent history, has been gradually developing into a very xenophobic state where, as Bolt (2011) emphasised, "'foreigners' are smeared and mocked on a daily basis" in the Danish public sphere and in daily life contexts, and at the same time "actual race-based laws against immigrants and asylum seekers" are being established. Scholars have noticed the escalation of a "liberal intolerance" (Lindekilde, 2014; Yilmaz, 2016) in Denmark, fuelled by regressive laws and the cultivation of negative popular attitudes towards non-Westerners, the working class and the poor.

The empirical material that the research draws from is popular media such as newspapers, journals and news and lifestyle websites from the three EU states chosen for this study, Greece, Denmark, and Germany. The book brings together in a comprehensive manner the findings of previously published research (Mylonas, 2012, 2014, 2015, 2017, 2017b, 2017c, 2018, 2018b, 2018c, 2018d; Mylonas & Kompatsiaris, 2013, 2019 (forthcoming); Mylonas & Noutsou, 2018). Overall, the study focuses on the coverage of selected political events of high importance for the Eurozone/Greek crisis, which occurred between the end of

2009 and the middle of 2015, such as the national elections in Greece and in Germany, the voting of austerity measures in Greece, the passing of the bailout loans by the German parliament and the Greek referendum of July 2015. Different keywords have been deployed for the study of the media presented here, which reflect distinct local realities and temporal contexts regarding the various events surrounding the crisis. Most importantly, all the media chosen as empirical cases reflect common ideological predispositions. Thus, I concentrate on the liberal news media, both progressive and conservative, because liberalism shapes the most dominant voices in the national public spheres of Europe, reproducing the prevailing crisis' explanations and advocating austerity reforms.

1.2.1 A Brief Excursion on Liberalism and its Discontents

Arguably, liberalism is the current hegemonic ideological framework on a global scale, emerging after the demise of the state socialist bloc in the late 20th century (Vincent, 2010: 54). In historical terms, liberalism is contingent to various political mores and trajectories, from both the right and the left (Crouch, 2011: 3); "across and within scholarly discourses, liberalism is construed in manifold and contradictory ways: as an embattled vanguard project and constitutive of modernity itself, a fine-grained normative political philosophy and a hegemonic mode of governmentality, the justificatory ideology of unrestrained capitalism and the richest ideological resource for its limitation" (Bell, 2014: 683). The notion of liberalism has different meanings in the North American and in the European context. While in the US liberalism is mostly connected to political progressivism and even to some socialist ideas, in Europe it is more associated with centrist positions that generally abstain from socialism (Vincent, 2010: 25). In this work, I understand liberalism from a perspective that is connected to Continental political thought and critical theory in particular.

Broadly put, the prevailing current of liberal thought is associated with notions, institutions and practices related to the representative, parliamentary democracy, which pay particular attention to the development and protection of individual liberties and rights. Private property and "free market" activity in a capitalist economic framework are central features of the liberal philosophy, constituting the substance of individual rights and freedoms. Critics of liberalism focus on its philosophical, political and economic predispositions. Karl Polanyi (2001) criticized the liberal notion of "self-correcting" free markets, a prevailing 19th century philosophical idea and political practice. For Polanyi, what initially emerged as a counter-bureaucratic idea was later developed into a religious dogma. This occurred to respond to the organisational demands of a market economy, which required establishments such as a labor market, the gold standard, and "free" trade (Polanyi, 2001: 141). "Free markets" are neither natural, nor universal. Instead, they are historical and political developments, aggressively pursued by specific social groups, politicians and intellectuals, with dangerous outcomes for society as a whole. On his part, Domenico Losurdo (2011: 52) underlined the inherent Western-centric focus of liberalism. In Losurdo's sense, this has undermined the development of an equal understanding of the non-Western Other, who is viewed in inferior terms through the lens of the liberal civilisation standards that are attributed to the West. Herbert Marcuse (2009) pointed out the existence of elements of totalitarianism within liberal thought. He demonstrated the affinities between liberal and totalitarian – namely, fascist – intellects and politics, which can even lead to tactical political alliances during exceptional events such as crises and revolutions. As Marcuse explains, liberalism develops a private rationalisation of social life. This turns reason into a privatised realm, lacking a general end that would rationalise the overall goals that the system sets. Arbitrary forces, such as nature, and the capitalist economy's hypothetical "natural essence" in particular, are left to constitute the order and the structure of society (Marcuse, 2009: 18).

The changing demands that the development of capitalism imposes on society and its political organisation tend to nullify liberalism's most progressive elements because they create obstacles for capitalist accumulation, growth and reproduction. The end of the 20th century saw the predominance of a market-oriented, "pure" form of liberalism that became increasingly influential as a policy-making doctrine and an individual mode of conduct. This "pure" form of liberalism, generally known as "neoliberalism", responded to capitalism's demands for economic restructuring that proved to be incompatible with civil and social rights and institutions that generally characterise a progressive liberal framework, connected to the social-democratic, welfare capitalist condition of the mid-to-late 20th century in the West (Slobodian, 2018). Thus, neoliberalism is what defines the leading form of liberalism today (Dardot & Laval, 2014: 28).

Nancy Fraser (2017) notes two branches of existing neoliberalism: a progressive and a conservative one. Progressive neoliberalism stands for individual freedoms, consumer lifestyles and gender rights (all within an individualist framework corresponding to prevailing bourgeois myths of the thriving, entrepreneurial and self-made individual), while conservative neoliberalism stresses more austere values connected to property, savings, traditional social, racial and gender hierarchies, religion and hard work. Progressive neoliberalism in particular, is associated with the decline of progressive social demands and movements with socialist aspirations, and their assimilation by "third way" politics, as represented by the governments of Tony Blair in Britain and Bill Clinton in the USA during the 1990's (Fraser, 2017: 282).

Although conservativism may appear to be incompatible to specific neoliberal traits related to individual freedoms, conservative ideological themes are also regularly reproduced today in different ways with neoliberalism in the background, in order to produce a shared attitude towards the crisis and austerity. Class-related themes are sidestepped by both conservative and progressive neoliberals, as the idea of competitiveness, which is a foundational theme of neoliberal ideology and policy-making, marks both positions today (Davies, 2014: 117). Likewise, policing, militarisation and claims for a "strong state" are frequently promoted as solutions for the anomie triggered by socio-economic crises of global proportions (Vincent, 2010: 81). While commenting on recent anti-immigration trends in the EU, the director of the British-based Institute of Race Relations, Liz Fekete (2016: 5), proclaims that

> Neoliberalism and the promise of abundant riches and freedom no longer provide a plausible script, particularly as systemic corruption is becoming institutionalised within the political process. Hence the comfort of the sticking-plaster of nationalism and the narrative of anti-multiculturalism and anti-immigration. Mainstream politicians in Hungary, Poland and Slovakia speak the tired old language of authoritarianism, ethnic nationalism and the nation state, with nineteenth- century style Social Darwinism and racism providing pitch and tenor.

1.2.2   *Greek, Danish and German Mainstream News Media*

The empirical research of selected articles on the Greek crisis that appeared in the German, the Greek and the Danish media, cover different moments of the Greek crisis and the ways that it developed between 2010 and 2015. The study works in a rather synthetical and comparative manner, using specific theretical concepts and methods of discursive and textual analysis to highlight common ideologico-discursive patterns apparent to all media, while also looking at their respective differences. Although the research is often concerned with material covering different events of the crisis, the study of various crisis-related events across different mainstream media underlined by common political and economic structures and trends, allow us to gain a broader picture of the ways that the media function during the prolongued and indefinite timespan of the Eurozone crisis, and to foreground main and enduring ideological and political tendencies that involve the media.

INTRODUCTION

As far as Germany and its media are concerned, an obvious pick for the study has been *Bild*, a conservative and nationalist tabloid newspaper (Klein, 1998), which is Germany's most popular daily. *Bild* belongs to the Axel Springer publications, Europe's largest publishing corporation.[2] The German dimension of the study also includes *Der Spiegel*, a weekly journal.[3] Unlike *Bild*, *Der Spiegel* is generally considered to be a credible popular journal with a progressive reputation, producing investigative journalism. Nevertheless, as research has shown, *Der Spiegel's* views on the crisis were very similar to those of *Bild*, reflecting the neoliberal nationalism of Germany and the EU's core cultural racism towards the "Southerners". In her own study of the Eurozone crisis coverage by *Bild* and *Der Spiegel* from a postcolonial perspective, Ervedosa (2017: 150) shows that these seemingly different media even employed the same contributors, such as a certain Nikolaus Bloeme, author of many polemical articles targeting Greece, while using various racist cultural tropes; "Nikolaus Bloeme's

---

2   The latest search on *Bild* was conducted on the 18/04/2018 at *Bild's* website (www.bild.de) with the keywords "Griechische-Krise" ("Greek crisis"). This search produced 309 articles, published between the 11/12/2009 and the 08/08/2012. The specific research period corresponds to the (official) beginning of the "Greek crisis", up until the country's June 17, 2012 national elections where a conservative coalition government came to power. This period concerns the initial financial markets' devaluation of the Greek economy, which lead to the signing of the first "Memorandum of Understanding" (MoU) and the formation of the supervising mechanism known as "the Troika", during Spring 2010. At that point, an immense loan (proclaimed to be the biggest public loan ever given to a state) was conditioned to Greece so as to continue to serve its public debt. In exchange for that, the Greek government agreed to advance "structural adjustment reforms" -generally known as austerity. The year 2011 included major acts and events of civil unrest across Greece, against the signing of a second MoU that included more loans and more austerity reforms; the end of the same year also witnessed the assigning of an unelected technocratic government in Greece, headed by a former European Bank vice president named Lucas Papademos. From a German perspective, the voting of Germany's share in the so-called Greek bailout funds, and the public negotiation of Germany's leading position in the handling of the Eurozone crisis were central issues discussed in *Bild* during the period of the study.

3   With regards to *Der Spiegel*, the keywords "Finanzkrise-in-Griechenland" produced were deployed in December 2017 for a search at *Der Spiegel's* websites (http://www.Der Spiegel.de and www.spiegel.de/international/europe/). A total of 183 articles were gathered, published between 10/12/2009 and 17/01/2015. The search includes the beginning of the Greek crisis (as mentioned above) and continues through the reign of a conservative coalition government in Greece, up until Greece's January 25, 2015, national elections that brought a left-wing, Syriza-led coalition into power. *Der Spiegel's* study concerns the period that the conservative Antonis Samaras government reigned in Greece, supported by Merkel to pursue the implementation of the second MoU. In 2014, this government presented a –largely fictitious- "success story", according to which "recovery" was slowly emerging. Simultaneously, a nationalist, law-and-order agenda was advanced by Samaras. A central event of this period also traced by the study is the German national elections of September 2013, sustaining Merkel's reign.

nomination in *Der Spiegel* and articles of his such as 'The Raged Greek' (*Der Wutgrieche*) are symptomatic of the tabloid and neoliberal character that this magazine has assumed in recent years" (Ervedosa, 2017: 153). *Der Spiegel* may generally be understood as media that represents progressive neoliberalism, connected to the expression of support for gender and individual rights while advocating for a market-centric, but somehow fairer, wealth distribution (Wood, 1999; Fraser, 2017).

In relation to Denmark, two popular conservative dailies were chosen, *Jyllands Posten* and *Berlingske*, which are two of the three most widely sold dailies in Denmark.[4] *Jyllands Posten* is owned by the JP/Politikens Hus A/S, a multimedia and publishing company, owning various popular newmedia in Denmark and Sweden. *Berlingske* is owned by Berlingske Media, a company also owning different media in Denmark. *Jyllands Posten* acquired negative world fame in 2005 and 2006 when it reproduced a series of provocative illustrations that ridiculed the Prophet Mohamed (Žižek, 2006) on the basis of "freedom of speech" (sic). As for *Berlingske* (previously called *Berlingske Tidende*), first published in 1749, it is the oldest Danish daily and one of the world's oldest newspapers. *Berlingske* is an established, conservative newspaper that also offers an extensive business/finance-centred reporting. While *Jyllands Posten* can be considered a daily read by a conservative, lower-middle-class readership, *Berlingske* is read more by an upper-middle-class group of Danish conservatives.

For the Greek side of the research, Greece's largest and oldest conservative and liberal daily, *Kathimerini,* was chosen,[5] and along with it, two

---

4   The Danish part of the study captures what is probably the peak moment of the Syriza-led government in Greece during its first period in office, while it attempted to challenge austerity within the EU/Eurozone limits. In a joint research project done by the author and the historian and translator, Matina Noutsou, we collected from Copenhagen libraries a total of 165 articles published in the Danish dailies *Jyllands Posten* and *Berlingske*. These were articles that covered the Greek referendum (so-called "Greferendum") and were published between the 27/06/2015 and the 28/07/2015. This referendum was about the acceptance or not of the EU's proposal for continuing austerity regimes in Greece (Varoufakis, 2017).

5   Coming to the Greek media, the research on *Kathimerini* was done online (http://search.kathimerini.gr/) during the last months of 2013. The study focused on *Kathimerini*'s construction of the crisis, austerity and the opposition to them (Mylonas, 2014). Different keywords were used in the Greek language. These were «δημοκρατία» (democracy), «Δεξιά» (the right), «ακροδεξιά» (the far right), «Ευρώπη» (Europe), «Αριστερά» (the left), «άκρα» (extremes), «κίνημα αγανακτισμένων» (indignant citizens' movement) and «λαϊκισμός» (populism). The research focused on articles published by *Kathimerini* between three distinct periods in time. The first one, between 1 December 2009 and 31 May 2010, concerned the moment of the crisis' emergence until the signing of the first MoU by the time's Papandreou government. The second period (between 15 May 2011 and 30 October 2011), corresponded to the signing

popular liberal news and lifestyle websites were also studied: *Protagon* and *AthensVoice*.⁶

Founded in 1919, *Kathimerini* belongs to the Alafouzos companies that are related to a ship-owning family, which also owns the Skai group – one of Greece's prime media groups. In 2014, when the study was done (Mylonas, 2014), *Kathimerini's* average daily sales (including subscriptions) was 140,761, making it one of the most widely sold newspapers in the country (considering the loss of sales that all newspapers experienced due to the crisis). In general, *Kathimerini* is frequently read abroad through its online, English-speaking version and enjoys the status of a "credible" source (Pleios, 2013). *AthensVoice* is a popular weekly free-press paper published in Athens by "Plus Athens Publishing". During the time of the study (in 2016), its website (which offers regular daily content updates) ranked as the 95th most visited website in the Greek cyberspace (www.alexa.com, 18/01/2016). *AthensVoice* was founded by Fotis Georgeles, an active journalist and writer in the Greek media since the 1980s, who contributed to popular lifestyle magazines of the 1980s and 1990s such as the infamous *Klik* (Sevastakis, 2004) and the counter-cultural *Babel*. *Protagon* (which ranked 153 on the Greek cyberspace [www.alexa.com, 18/01/2016]) is a

---

of the second MoU (by the unelected government of Lucas Papademos) and the rise of the Indignant Citizens' movement followed by mass protests across Greece. The third period captures the time between 1 April 2012 and 30 November 2012. During this period national elections occurred (as mentioned above) bringing a conservative coalition to power. Besides that, the neo-nazi party of the "Golden Dawn" (GD) gained electoral power and enters the Greek parliament (Kompatsiaris & Mylonas, 2015). *Kathimerini's* searches produced numerous results that I had to cut down in order to develop a manageable corpus of empirical material for a qualitative study. In that sense, I picked indicative articles from each period of the events described.

6   As for *AthensVoice* and *Protagon*, a 30/10/2015 search using the keyword «Διαφωτισμός» (Enlightenment) delivered 113 relevant articles for *AthensVoice* and 86 for *Protagon*, making a total of 199 articles studied. These were authored in different moments between 2007 and 2015. They were written by various contributors ranging from writers to academics, journalists, or economists. The specific search term was deployed so as to inquire further on the Greek liberals own culturalist and moralist diagnoses of the fundamental errors of the Greek society and its people, which (supposedly) triggered the crisis and brought the country to the fringes of Europe. A perceived Enlightenment deficit has been a persisting explanatory framework of the Greek crisis among Greek liberals. Such liberal media concentration the attention of a mainly middle-class pool of citizens in favor of the Euro-currency, mainly for lifestyle reasons, as Streeck (2014: 157) notes. This discourse marks the Greek liberals' (and through them, the Greek bourgeoisie's) distinct contribution to the Greek crisis and austerity hegemonic narratives, in a self-orientalizing and self-bashing fashion. To be sure, this discourse is deeply classist, as it targets the working-class and the poor of Greece, attempting to force them to concede to austerity through the cultivation of guilt and inertia.

news and opinions' website, founded by Stavros Theodorakis – a journalist and currently a politician with the "centrist" party called "to Potami" (the River) – and other journalists. This site served as a rather pluralistic forum, dominated by liberal progressivist voices. The economist Yanis Varoufakis was also a regular contributor to the website. The course of the crisis, and the political engagement of several of Protagon.gr founders or contributors (such as Stavros Theodorakis and Yanis Varoufakis, who both got involved into party politics), also saw the steady decline of *Protagon's* popularity.

1.3 On Method: Thematic Analysis, Discourse Theory Analysis, Critical Discourse Analysis

The analytical approach toward the corpus of the media texts gathered for this study is qualitative; it reflexively draws on thematic analysis (Saldaña, 2009), on post-structuralist, discourse theory analysis (De Cleen & Carpentier, 2007; Carpentier, 2011, 2017), and on critical discourse analysis (CDA) (Fairclough, 2003; Van Leeuwen, 2008). This section will explain how these analytical frameworks are used and how they can be combined despite their theoretical differences. This section will briefly discuss the main ideas of discourse theory and CDA and the ways that they relate to this study. The qualitative processing of a large corpus of data requires broader theoretical concepts to advance the analysis in a consistent manner. Discourse theory provides us with concepts that enable the deconstruction of key hegemonic ideas that appear in the media texts, showing the political character of common-sense frames, while foregrounding the importance of identity constructions in hegemonic interventions and during socio-political antagonisms. CDA then enables us to go deeper into the media texts, and to study how discursive constructions are textually produced. Selected textual excerpts are used to exemplify this purpose.

To handle a large amount of texts, a thematic analysis helps to categorise the empirical material into specific themes, addressing the media's meaning constructions with group associations. Therefore, the selected media texts were read and coded according to the prevailing thematic categories that were common to all texts studied (Saldaña, 2009: 3). The overarching thematic categories are composed of "pattern codes" (Saldaña, 2009: 152), which are meta-codes explaining the key ideas expressed in each theme. The analytical themes developed are also understood as media frames in the sense that they denote specific meanings for the object that they display. Media framing produces particular ways of viewing at things and offers the conceptual bases to make sense of social realities, related to the media producers' take on the matter: "to frame is to select some aspects of a perceived reality and make them more salient in a communicating text, in such a way as to promote a particular problem definition, causal interpretation, moral evaluation, and/or treatment recommendations for the item described. Typically frames diagnose, evaluate, and prescribe" (Entman, 1993: 52).

1.3.1 *The Relevance of Discourse Theory*

Maintaining that the crisis and austerity are political issues, with politics being a central variant defining the social world, discourse theory (Laclau & Mouffe, 1985; Laclau, 1996) and its advances (Stavrakakis, 1999; Glynos & Howarth, 2007; Carpentier, 2011, 2017; Phelan, 2014; Dahlberg, 2014) allow us to approach media representations from a political point of view. Discourse theory advocates an understanding of society as a contingent field dominated by power relations and shaped by historical contexts and political interventions. Anything appearing as objective is only an outcome of successful hegemonic practices, which construct a common social imaginary, in other words, a common understanding of what is normal and a common approach to making sense of the world. By prioritising the political as the main constitutive force of reality, discourse theory takes any apolitical public explanation of social phenomena as inherently ideological, developed by hegemonic interventions that are connected to established social hierarchies and powerful material interests.

Laclau's discursive ontology of the social is often noted to downplay the materialistic side of things, by favouring the discursive as the founding dimension of all aspects of the social world. Discourse theory, though, does not negate materiality. Rather, it constitutes the discursive as material, with material entities obtaining substance through meaning-making (Schou, 2016: 302). Thus, discourse theory can also be seen as advancing a materialistic understanding of discourse. In his latest work, the media scholar Nico Carpentier (2017: 4) proposes viewing the discursive and the material as mutually constitutive entities that are not commensurable with each other. One cannot privilege either the material or the discursive, but instead they should be seen as "knotted" entities, defining the complexity of social processes that can be marked by both "incessant change and deep sedimentation".

Additionally, scholars argue that there are many common theoretical as well as political parameters between critical theory and post-structuralism. These allow both currents to function in a symbiotic and even complementary manner (Howarth, 2018). After all, Marxism itself has been a rather heterogeneous entity. The stressing of the non-essential character of social phenomena does not deny their stability, endurance and power. Instead, it emphasises their role as historically contingent entities, susceptible to changes. Therefore, while approaching specific empirical phenomena that are part of the political economy, discourse theory analysis can show how capitalism reproduces itself discursively (Beetza & Schwab, 2018).

Laclau's theory is also part of a post-modern endeavour that emerged in a period when the idea of the social class started to become somehow obsolete. Postmodern thought foregrounded the notion of identity instead. Identity was understood to be a more inclusive framework to perceive oppression on the one hand and counter-hegemonic politics on the other. Identity and identity politics, however, have also proven to be compatible with the neoliberal capitalist agendas. Particularity and difference work profitably for the production of value in the flexible, post-Fordist regime of capitalist accumulation (Shi, 2018). Furthermore, the latest development of the so-called identarian movements of white supremacists in Europe and the US suggest that identity politics are deployed by far right and racist agendas as well, a case with deep historical roots.

Class subjects and identities are the outcomes of the capitalist accumulation and reproduction process. Class is also a position that people can identify with. Various institutions (such as the education system and the media) interpellate people into preferred subject positions, which in the capitalist world correspond to the upper-class viewing of things. As Laclau though stresses, interpellation is never complete since people may identify with a variety of subject positions simultaneously (Rear, 2013). Furthermore, a prevailing upper-class viewing of things does not automatically make all people adopting such a view to become upper-class. Nevertheless, it legitimises the existing class hierarchy and reproduces the social imaginary of the bourgeoisie. The material dimension of class makes specific discourses that are associated with upper-class values and are more buoyant than others.

A problematisation of the notion of identity through the lens of political economy may allow us to inquire into the ways that the structures and norms of bourgeois society produce, interpellate and overdetermine diverse social groups and fractions under a shared – yet upper-class – worldview. It is in this theoretical context where the culturalist explanations of the Eurozone's crisis can also be seen as dimensions of a class-based hegemonic intervention to stabilise the established form of social and geopolitical order, which was ruptured by the latest economic crisis. Class in this sense underlines the uses of cultural identity, while the negation of politics by economic technocracy works for the progression of upper-class interests. Cultural, nationalist and moralist topics can substitute class in hegemonic public interventions. Maintaining that class interests lie at the core of the hegemonic strategy for the neoliberal restructuring of society (through austerity policies), the analysis of class hegemony can be reintroduced in the general study of the politics of crisis and austerity, while exhibiting the inherently political act of undermining and discrediting working-class identities, lifestyles and cultures in the mainstream media, along with the naturalisation of upper-middle-class values. Class in this way becomes part of the analysis of the hegemonic crisis and austerity constructions. According to Schou (2016: 301), Laclau did not object to the overdetermination of identity traits such as ethnicity or race by class; although Laclau deemphasises class, he does not discount class relations.

Laclau's work offers sophisticated ideas to analyse how hegemony is achieved, transformed, maintained and challenged. As will be explained in the chapters that follow, concepts such as nodal points, floating signifiers, discursive articulations, identities and chains of equivalence, myths, social imaginaries and discursive logics are deployed in the analysis of the hegemonic discursive constructions that appear in the media. To this regard, the notion of discursive logics provides us with useful categories for an in-depth analysis of meaning-making constructions. The political theorists Jason Glynos and David Howarth (2007) developed three interrelated categories of discursive logics for social research: the social, the political and the fantasmatic logic. The social logics refer to objectified, "sedimented" forms of meaning that pass as natural, self-evident and objective, where ideology remains hidden. The political logics relate to the political aspect of reality and to the processes of constitution, contestation and legitimation of "political frontiers" (Glynos & Howarth, 2008: 16). The fantasmatic logics are associated with the category of affect and the category of pleasure, and derive from Lacanian psychoanalysis. Further, the idea of the myth in particular is crucial in the analysis to unpack the ideological structure of the various claims appearing in the media, which relate to the worldviews and political choices of powerful social groups. Moments of crisis, in which hegemony is ruptured, generate myths to suture the crisis and sustain hegemony. Laclau's understanding of the term myth concerns the attempts of specific social forces to achieve social hegemony through the making of a world-view that is widely accepted as common sense. The prevalence of a myth and the establishment of its meanings as common sense and as "objective" makes what Laclau describes as a social imaginary (Rear, 2013). As the analysis will show, ideological myths form the basis of the legitimation of various claims made by the media.

1.3.2 *Critical Discourse Analysis Perspectives*

CDA is a text-based analytical framework that is associated more with the broader critical theoretical endeavour of this study and has a more rigid understanding of the discursive and the material world as different entities (Chouliaraki & Fairclough, 2005). For Fairclough's (2003) CDA approach, discourse mainly constitutes identities, social relations and systems of belief. In that sense, the understanding of discourse from a CDA point of view is more limited in comparison to discourse theory perspectives. Nevertheless, it has been noted that discourse theory and CDA have common political and social theoretical aims and perspectives, related to the deepening of democracy in particular (Carpentier & De Cleen, 2007: 275).

CDA allows us to perform in-depth analyses of media texts by looking at the uses of the language, and other forms of semiosis. CDA's categories of interdiscursivity and intertextuality – regarding the ways that various discursive constructions circulate through a variety of contexts and texts – provide us with the theoretical links to connect discourse to media texts (Rear, 2013). With the use of selected examples from the empirical material gathered, CDA tools demonstrate how the economic crisis is transformed into a cultural and a moral issue, and how neoliberal austerity is objectified as both a common-sense and a scientific imperative. CDA helps us to understand how exactly the capitalist crisis and neoliberal austerity are represented in a seemingly depoliticised manner by the media, and how questions related to economic injustice, inequality and exploitation are effectively excluded from the media's economic crisis coverage.

The basic structure of Fairclough's CDA consists of a threefold analytical paradigm, which includes the interrelated categories of text, discursive practice and social practice (Jørgensen & Phillips, 2006: 68). Discursive practice concerns issues of text production, distribution, and consumption, while social practice is connected with social processes external to the text. At the first level, the analysis attempts to describe and to interpret the given text, its content and its textual genre (e.g. a news report found in a yellow press newspaper). On the second level, the analysis looks at issues of textual production and consumption (e.g. who produced a particular text and in which structure, what is its intended audience and what kind of semiotic configurations are deployed). On the third level, the analysis looks at the broader societal level in which the text is situated, including its processes and events, and provides theoretical explanations of the phenomena studied through the analysis of texts.

In this study, the main issues examined through CDA are the ways that the media texts evoke identity constructions and manifest specific social relations in the Greek/Eurozone crisis context. Media production presupposes specific identity traits and subject positions in the objects it represents. Media production also targets a favourable audience, to which it also attributes specific characteristics (e.g. national or class ones). Semantic exclusions occur when the media' favours particular views as being more plausible than others. In this regard, the analytical category of nominalisations (Fairclough, 2003: 145) is central to the study. Nominalisations are textual constructions that subsume broader social processes in reduced forms, represented by nouns, clauses and grammatical constructions (e.g. the use of the passive voice to undermine agency in practices and processes, or the development of metaphorical schemes to displace a given issue and, for instance, transform it from a political and economic one to a cultural one) that simplify and potentially obscure things without adequately explaining them. As will be shown, forms of semantic exclusion, particularly through derogatory stereotyping, are frequent and persistent in the making and sustaining of the "Greek crisis" narrative.

CDA also shows how discursive legitimation is produced over the claims and the knowledge regimes that the media construct and reproduce. This is helpful in preceiving the cultural and moral construction of the crisis and the support of austerity regimes (Doudaki, 2015, 2018). The CDA scholar Teo Van Leeuwen (2008: 106) provides us with four main categories of discursive legitimation: moral evaluation, authorisation, rationalisation, and mythopoesis. To put in brief, moral evaluation concerns the legitimation of claims based on references to value systems; authorization is the legitimation by reference to authority symbols and figures (such as laws, traditions, the state authorities and different kinds of experts); rationalization is the legitimation process that emerges by references to instrumental goals set, as well as by references to theoretical forms of knowledge that are considered to be "natural" or common sense (Van Leeuwen, 2009: 113); mythopoiesis, finally occurs through storytelling practices, such as different sorts of moral tales, cautionary tales, and stories that produce different forms of institutional frameworks in symbolic terms, so as to provide a "mythical model of social action" (Van Leeuwen, 2009: 119) and to draw a simple and meaningful scheme of otherwise highly abstract processes. The analysis deploys all of these categories to highlight the ways that the hegemonic economic crisis and austerity discourse is publicly articulated, justified, explained and defended by the media. The study shows that all of these legitimation patterns are in use across the media studied, with mythopoesis and authorisation having the most regular patterns that legitimise the hegemonic constructions of the Greek crisis in the media. Additionally, the analytical category of rhetorical topoi makes an important contribution in the analysis of legitimacy construction (Wodak & Boukala, 2015: 94), allowing us to emphasise central ideas that the media refer to so as to establish particular claims and truth regimes. Topoi show us how particular arguments and claims are warranted as acceptable. They concern the underlining logics and recurrent themes. The implications of authoritative voices, principles and values, along with the evocation of common-sense patterns, constitute frequent topics of claims made by the media studied.

1.4 The Analytical Pillars: Race, Class, Politics

Informed by critical socio-political theory, the main thematic categories that structure the analysis of this study are the following: race, class and politics. These are theoretical categories deployed to critically elaborate the main analytical themes found in all the media studied. The Greek crisis has generally been covered through the development of culturalistic, moralistic and technocratic claims and arguments. From a critical point of view, these themes largely depoliticise the capitalist crisis and neoliberal austerity, and represent profound racist, classist and apolitical/antidemocratic positions. Despite their depoliticising character, these positions are still political though. To put in another way, neoliberal hegemony naturalises capitalism, warrants technocratic politics as the only realistic and truly democratic policy-making option, and views culture, class and, as well will see, local political institutions and oppositional politics, as the true sources of the economic crisis and the overall problems deriving from it. In this sense, neoliberal reforms (like austerity) are meant to resolve the given crisis according to the ways that hegemony configures it. Race, class and politics are critical terms deployed to denote the deeply problematic character of cultural, moral and technocratic meaning regimes that dominate the public discussion of the Greek crisis and to demonstrate their inherently political character that corresponds to capitalist restructuring processes. Race, class and politics form distinct analytical sections (presented in separate chapters) of the media's representation of the Greek crisis in its different dimensions and national and temporal contexts. These three central analytical categories are developed as umbrella themes that include several other "minor" codes associated with each category.

1.4.1 On Race

As scholars of the phenomenon agree (Garner, 2010; Back & Solomos, 2009), race is a political construction that developed in the Western world during the rise of capitalist modernity. The category of race was developed to label and objectify different human populations, placing the Western white person as superior to all others. As a system of knowledge and organisation, racism developed along with colonial expansion and the governmental imperatives of colonial administration through a variety of formal and informal practices. Racism is a politico-historical construction with no actual substance or consistency, connected to the military and economic dominance of Western powers around the globe and to the institution of their political and cultural hegemony in the colonised populations of capitalism's periphery. The rise of modernity itself and the Enlightenment were key in providing a (pseudo) scientific framework for the construction of race, due to the different forms of classification that the positivist understanding of the world created, including the invention of categories for the splitting of people into a hierarchy of different races that emphasised not just physical, but also cultural, economic and political differences, which were constructed as "natural" (Garner, 2010: 68).

The establishment of the nation-state has also been central in the reproduction of forms of racial classification to establish the common cultural and institutional grounds of population control and effective governance. While discussing the origins of racism in the US, the French political theorist Pierre Rosanvallon (2011: 157) argues that racism can be understood as a structural constituent of liberal democracy itself, rather than a distortion of it. This idea is also shared by critics of liberalism, arguing that racism marks the limits of liberalism (Losurdo, 2011). Racial divisions allowed for the development of certain ideas of equality that only concerned the white Americans. In continental Europe, too, racism has been constitutive in the making of national bonds, despite existing wealth inequalities within those deemed as national siblings. Racialised others have historically played the role of the scapegoat to ease class anxieties and to sustain an alliance between the lower and the upper classes (Rosanvallon, 2011: 149).

Racism is a constantly developing entity, taking different forms, deploying different vocabularies, and launching various constitutive myths that attempt to legitimise the idea of race as a (biological) "fact", other than a practice of discrimination and an expression of hate (Ahmed, 2000; Lentin & Titley, 2011). Often enough, racism is proclaimed to be a thing of the past, and in this way its presence as an enduring and contemporary phenomenon, inherent in institutional structures of the nation-state, is denied (Lentin & Titley, 2011: 17). Despite formally denouncing it, particularly after the Holocaust, Western countries remain deeply racist (Ahmed, 2000: 10; Lentin & Titley, 2011: 49). In this regard, Sara Ahmed stresses the persistence of colonialism today by foregrounding the continuous hegemony of the West as a geopolitical, economic and cultural entity, dominating the world and constructing it according to its own imperatives. In a critical account of the "postcolonial" idea, which implies the withering away of colonialism's racist culture, Ahmed (2000: 11) argues that

> Colonialism, as an encounter, involves not only the territorial domination of one culture by another but also discursive forms of appropriation: other cultures become appropriated into the imaginary globality of the colonizing nation.

Consequently

> Racism expresses itself through displacement, through denial, through the capacity to say two contradictory things at the same time, the surface imagery speaking of an unspeakable content, the repressed content of a culture.
> HALL, 1992: 15

Undeniably, a shift from biological to cultural racism is evident today (Ahmed, 2000: 117; Skeggs, 2003: 138). Issues of culture and identity have come to be essential markers of distinction and difference, replacing former racist tropes connected to physiology, blood and skin colour. For instance, recently multiculturalism and migration have become central political issues for many Western states, problematised by leading politicians who are also fervent advocates of free-market policies and socially conservative agendas. Angela Merkel is known for proclaiming that "multiculturalism in Germany has failed" (Lentin & Titley, 2011: 1). This "failure" is generally attributed to the supposed differences of culture, putting aside the structural questions over the various problems associated with the position of migrants and refugees in Western capitalist states.

Often enough, racism is attributed to an alleged lack of knowledge. Critics suggest, though, that racism is actually based on specific (pseudo) knowledge regimes: "the stranger is produced through knowledge" (Ahmed, 200: 16). The non-Western Other is racialised through coercion, but also through knowledge, consumption and performance practices (Ahmed, 2000: 115). The "bodily and cultural capital" (Ahmed, 2000: 34) of the non-Western Other is crucial for his/her estrangement. The Other's features are objectified by Occidentalist worldviews, which establish dominant forms of seeing and being seen. The gaze reproduces racist knowledge regimes on a daily basis. For Mirzoeff (2011: 196), "all visuality was and is imperial visuality, the shaping of modernity from the point of view of imperial powers" with "imperial visuality being an intensified and abstracted means of ordering biopower". The Western subject reproduces the (structural) difference that separates him/her from the Other (Ahmed, 2000: 125). The gaze is a crucial process performed by the subject towards the object of observation. The racial gaze constructs and reproduces the objectified stranger while sustaining the supreme identity of the subject that is able to define and remain undefined. The technique of the gaze is "informed by access to cultural capital and knowledge embedded in colonial and class privilege which give the dominant subject the ability to move and in which the stranger is assumed to be knowledgeable, seeable and be-able" (Ahmed, 2000: 133).

Dependent on the socio-temporal context, the Other represents different things, ranging from fears of threat and danger to fantasies of joy. In this regard, the metaphors that Zygmunt Bauman (2011: 78) uses to describe what he frames as the liquid modern condition, the tourist and the vagabond, are relevant to discuss the construction of the non-Western Other. For Bauman, the tourist is an archetype that marks the contemporary, "liquid" modern condition. On the antipode of the tourist lies the vagabond and the refugee, representing the exceedingly unwanted and potentially threatening humanity. The tourist is wanted and admired because s/he is wealthy and able to experience the world, while "vagabonds are travelers refused the right to turn into tourists" (Bauman, 2011: 93). The tourist may have more "positive" encounters with the Other mainly through the market framework. Here, privilege is exercised through the consumerist potentials that the Other, his/her habitus and his/her culture, entail. The white, middle-class subject is able to "reconstitute the space of the Other through the hegemonic self", assuming it, approximating it and even performing it through a fetishistic relationship with the Other's culture, as advanced by consumerism (Ahmed, 2000: 132). As Bauman (2004, 2013) notes, however, the Other in his/her vagabond form, rejected as useless by the capitalist society and not fully appropriated by consumer culture, forms a disturbing sign of what the tourist may become due to the radical instability and insecurity that characterises late modernity. This insecurity fuels racism, intersecting it with class issues.

1.4.1.1 Colonial Remainders: An "Eternal" Greece

Both the US financial crisis and the Euro crisis were largely constructed in moral, cultural and technocratic terms, which undermined the mainstreaming of broader systemic explanations of the economic crisis that could highlight its global dimensions and its historical continuities with previous economic crises (Fairclough & Fairclough, 2012: 7; Basu, 2018: 139). According to such narratives, the economic crisis was an event produced by the excessive and avaricious activities of immoral professionals and individuals (e.g. specific greedy bankers), or a problem caused by dysfunctional, "non-competitive" states and problematic local cultures. As the Eurozone crisis' epicentre, Greece was addressed in both moral and cultural ways (Stavrakakis, 2013), following the hegemonic liberal-conservative narrative. The structural explanations provided where partial at best, as they did not address the global dimension of the crisis, as well as the power imbalances and the deep contradictions of the capitalist economy. Instead, they only amplified the most problematic aspects of the governance of peripheral countries like Greece, making out of them a sui generis case. Greece was presented as a non- or quasi-European state because it was (allegedly) poor, bankrupt, idle, corrupt, irresponsible and traditional, and stood on the antipode of Europe, which was rich, industrious, hard-working, responsible, honest and secular.

Research has shown that such distinctions are rarely rigid and dichotomous, since the "pre-modern" always emerges in the modern and vice-versa (Triantafyllidou, Gropas, and Kouki, 2013: 14). In this regard, the conceptual framework of Orientalism is useful to critically address the ways that Greece, along with it the European periphery – the South of Europe and Ireland in particular – was constructed as Europe's Other. Orientalism is here understood as a flexible, historically developing, discriminatory discursive framework, eligible to include anything departing from the politico-economic and cultural cannons and imperatives of the West:

> The new European orientalism is a derivative or correlates of a phenomenon covered by such concepts as globalisation, the expansion of multinational capital, flexible capitalism, transgressions, migrations, transnationalism or the media-covered global village. With these changes, the meaning of orientalism acquires entirely new dimensions [...] in a sense that covers not only Saidian distinction into orient and occident, but also into capitalism and socialism, civility and primitivism, and class distinction into elites and plebs.
> BUCHOWSKI, 2006: 465–466

Orientalism is a product of a Western-centric, Occidentalist culture that is based on a self-proclaimed supremacy of European culture over others, a condition that was historically imposed primarily through military means. In his analysis, Samir Amin (2009: 166) presents Eurocentrism as composed of the following characteristics:

> This construct [Eurocentrism], like the analogous Orientalist, construct: (1) removes Ancient Greece from the very milieu in which it unfolded

and developed – the Orient – in order to annex Hellenism to Europe arbitrarily; (2) retains the mark of racism, the fundamental basis on which European cultural unity was constructed; (3) interprets Christianity, also arbitrarily annexed to Europe, as the principal factor in the maintenance of European cultural unity, conforming to an unscientific vision of religious phenomena; and (4) concurrently constructs a vision of the Near East and the more distant Orients on the same racist foundation, again employing an immutable vision of religion. These four elements combined in different ways at different times. Eurocentrism is not, properly speaking, a social theory, which integrates various elements into a global and coherent vision of society and history. It is rather a prejudice that distorts social theories. It draws from its storehouse of components, retaining one or rejecting another according to the ideological needs of the moment.

Although Greece was never a Western colony, it was imagined by Western colonial powers as the Occident's symbolic centre (Carastathis, 2014: 2). This image triggered some support for the Greek struggle of independence from the Ottoman Empire. The emergence of a New Greek state after a popular revolt, though, was followed by heavy interventions from the leading world powers, resulting in the decision to install a Bavarian royal descendant (named Otto) who, at the age of 17, was brought to Greece to become the country's king.[7] Moreover, the New Greek state became indebted to European banks in 1823 (Roos, 2019: 97), only two years after the struggle for independence begun.

Thus, constitutive elements of subtle colonisation are evident in the development of modern Greece, politically, economically and ideologically. In his work, the archaeology professor Yannis Hamilakis (2015; 2016) talks about the underlining crypto-colonial themes in the constitution of Greece since the 19th century that define Greece's relationship to Western powers. While the sovereignty of Greece was seriously undermined by imperial powers through debt and military coercion, the identity of modern Greece was also overdetermined by the Western notions of classical antiquity. Under the Western gaze

---

7   In a critical review of the modern Greek history, the late, antifascist Resistance fighter and public intellectual, Kyriakos Simopoulos (2001), rhetorically wondered why a revolution against autocracy (such as the 1821 struggle for Greece's independence) was succeeded by the establishment of a new autocrat sent from abroad, instead of the development of a democratic state. Simopoulos argues that through their participation in the revolutionary tasks, the people showed impressive capacities of self-organising. Among other things, Simopoulos also discusses the Bavarians' discontent over the Greek people, who did not match their fantasies of Greece.

and the knowledge assumed about Greece, modern Greece constantly fails to live up to its classical heritage (Hamilakis, 2016: 238). With classical antiquity being at the heart of the national Greek identity, many Greeks have proven receptive to the recurring, disciplinary uses and manipulations of classical antiquity by the West. To give an example from the media studied, in an article published on 6 March 2010 in *Bild*, one reads the following title: "What we owe to the *Ancient* Greeks". The word "Ancient" purposefully appears in italics in *Bild*, so as to create an emphatic distinction between the modern and the ancient for *Bild*'s readers. According to Susan Buck-Morss (1987: 210–211)

> The study of early and particularly classical Greece is the example par excellence of the reconstruction of history as a political act – an act of racism, sexism, and cultural imperialism, in which Western Europe robbed Greece of its historical heritage, claiming itself to be the legitimate heir.

Following a political economy approach in one of his earlier works, the Greek sociologist Nicos Mouzelis (1979) emphasises the imperial pressures exercised on Greece and the Balkans during the 19th and the 20th centuries by Western states and empires. Western imperialism perceived Greece as an underdeveloped country. Because the geopolitical region that Greece belonged to (the Ottoman Empire) did not develop the capitalist mode of production that was advanced in the West, its regions were tied to the demands Western capital by being the main suppliers of raw materials and by providing markets for goods. Mouzelis (1979: 29) notes that the competition launched by Western capital in the economic formations of the Balkan lands, along with military and political interventions, did not allow the development of local industrial sectors based on the specificities of the region and its needs.[8]

---

8 The Danish historian Mogens Pelt (2006: 15) also explains that Germany has a long tradition of expansion towards the south-east. More specifically, Germany managed to gain noteworthy economic influence in Greece during the 1930s, which was resumed after the Second World War, through the US's effort to constitute Germany as the main pillar against the Soviet Union and the "Eastern bloc" in Europe – the writing off of Germany's First World War debts in 1953 was part of this strategy. Greece's right-wing government also participated in this agreement by accepting to write off its share of Germany's First World War reparations and to freeze its demands for war reparations from Germany for the Second World War. The enduring politico-economic influence of Germany on Greece meant Greece's withdrawal from its rightful Second World War reparation demands, and even Greece's halting of the persecution of German war criminals (Fleischer, 2008).

Liberal intellectuals stress the role of the Orthodox Church in Greece's alleged underdevelopment, the conservative role of the Greek family structure, or, a supposed hegemony of the left in the country (Koliopoulos & Veremis, 2003; Triantafyllou & Ioakeimoglou, 2007; Kalyvas, 2015). The Orthodox Church is understood as a conservative force against the West and against the Enlightenment that casts its influence over the whole society while sustaining its Oriental (Byzantine/Ottoman) traits. Mitralexis (2017: 126) shows that liberal intellectuals (notably, Nikiforos Diamantouros), created a simplistic and popular hermeneutic schema, according to which modern Greece is divided between an Ottoman-Byzantine-Orthodox based, "underdog culture", and a European-orientated, "reforms culture". For such authors, the underdog current (which is passive, inert and complaining) is the prevailing one, stalling progress, while the reformist (which is industrious and entrepreneurial) is the guarantor of progress. Mitralexis explains the neo-orientalist underpinnings of such schemas and demonstrates their penetration in the public sphere due to the credibility of their enunciators. As the analysis to follow will also show, in such narratives, the dichotomies between the Enlightened/Non-Enlightened, the Occident/Orient or the modern/unmodern appear fixed, clear and resolute. Furthermore, the process of modernity itself also appears reified as a de facto positive entity that constantly progresses in a linear fashion. Critical theory has challenged such binary understandings of historical processes and problematised modernity. Adorno and Horkheimer (1989) showed the emptying of modernity's Enlightening and the emancipatory potential in the instrumental rationality of positivism and the competitive and self-referential attitude of the leading modern bourgeois subjectivity. In this way, the Enlightenment was turned into a new mythological belief system and modernity into an arrangement of subjugation and violence. Adorno (2004: 34) notes that "the ratio becomes irrational where [...] it runs counter to the meaning of thought by hypostasizing its products, the abstractions. The commandment of its autarky condemns thinking to emptiness, and finally to stupidity and primitivism".

In the same critical spirit, Zygmunt Bauman (1998: 87) indicated that "the Holocaust did not just avoid the clash with the norms and institutions of modernity. It was these norms and institutions that made the Holocaust feasible. Without modern civilisation, there would be no Holocaust". The Holocaust was materialised by modernity and all features characterising a society (like that of Germany) as a modern one: industrialism, efficiency, bureaucracy, advanced technology, mass communications and social conformity. Instead of being an exception, the Holocaust is a possible trajectory of modernity (Bauman 1998: 7). Consequently, modernity, the Enlightenment and industrialisation, among other historical developments related to notions of progress and civilisation, are not fixed but elusive entities that require constant problematisation regarding the broader contexts and political configurations as they emerge.

Mythological knowledge produces a fetishised relationship between the West and the East. Generally stated, the mythic understanding implies that nothing can ever change (Buck-Morss, 1991: 79). This has important political repercussions. In the Greek crisis context, it implies that the crisis is reified into a "tragedy", or a "drama" that is intrinsic to the "eternal nature" of (the Orientalised) Greece. The crisis' ruins, too, become naturalised for Greece, as the ancient ruins obtain an archetypical place in the popular fantasy of Greece. Along with other "hellenotropes" (Gumpert, 2017), the ruins form a regular crisis-trope in mainstream Greek crisis discourses across the globe, turning the current ruining of Greece into an ahistorical locus, away from systemic understandings of decline.

In principle, the culturalisation of the problems and the crises that the (non-Western) Other faces has been central in the justification and the public legitimation of colonial and imperial conquests. Usually, these are explained through modernising and developmental discourses, in which interventions are framed as civilisational boosts carried out by "benign" Western forces. Colonial exploitation and imperialist aggression were often construed as "civilizing missions" for helpless or "failed" peoples (Said, 1977: 107; de B'béri & Louw, 2011: 336; Vetta, 2017; Ervedosa, 2017). Such demeaning assessments of the periphery are ignorant of the contextual issues and local/global power hierarchies. They also undermine local struggles that could advance a democratic form of modernity across the globe. As Chibber (2013) maintains, the general rise of the living standards in Western countries occurred through (nowadays largely forgotten) working-class struggles, and not due to any kind of upper-class generosity or Occidentalist wisdom.

Greece's Oriental construction today is situated within the broader neoliberal assemblage of governance, which is "mobilized to justify austerity" (Bozatzis, 2016: 49; Kompatsiaris, 2017: 361). In this regard, the idea of debt in both symbolic and material terms is crucial for understanding the colonial and imperial legacies that produced Greece as an eternally lagging locus, whose authentic (classical) legacy is best represented by the West. Greece is thus symbolically indebted to its ancestors (as defined by the West), whom it needs to deploy as benchmarks for it to reach their greatness and achieve a historical continuity in greatness. Simultaneously, Greece is also materially indebted to its (Western) creditors, whom it needs to pay off (through austerity, privatisations and neoliberal deregulation). These two dimensions of debt collide. For Hamilakis (2016), the (symbolic and material) imperatives of debt are both external and internal to Greece: there is the external financial debt owed to Greece's creditors, and there is also the internal debt Greece owes to its ancestors.

Orientalist discourses have a disciplinary function within Greece since they overdetermine the ways that the Greek people understand their identity and their position in the broader historical and geopolitical context. In this sense, a "self-Orientalising" process also occurs within the country, due to the effect of the Occidentalist views cast upon the country. This process is characteristic of many peripheral states. Studies in the European periphery also showed similar phenomena taking place there, connected to collective manifestations of inferiority:

> What is somewhat unique about the position of eastern Europe in the world today is that, as citizens of EU-member states, many inhabitants of the region perceive the European Union, rightly or wrongly, as a resource that offers them an opportunity to boost their "racial" credentials, that is, a chance to proceed "upward" on the scale of privilege in an obviously unequal, oppressive and discriminatory system.
> BÖRÖCZ & SARKAR, 2017: 314

The influential work of Franz Fanon sheds interesting insights to analyze the "self-orientalisation" (Streinzer, 2018) observed in the periphery. Drawing on psychoanalysis and Marxism, Fanon (2008: 2) argues that

> All colonized people, people in whom an inferiority complex has taken root, whose local cultural originality has been committed to the grave, position themselves in relation to the civilizing language: i.e., the metropolitan culture. The more the colonized has assimilated the cultural values of the metropolis, the more he will have escaped the bush. The more he rejects his blackness and the bush, the whiter he will become.

While Mouzelis (1979: 146), in his own analysis of the development of modern Greece (and its shortcomings), notes that

> Cultural imperialism goes hand in hand with economic imperialism in all peripheral social formations. But what was specific to Greece was the total lack of awareness or any serious resistance to that "cultural imperialism".

To conclude then with Samir Amin (2014: 98)

> That Greece is today at the heart of the conflict is both because Greece is part of the Eurozone and because its people hoped to escape the fate of

the ex-"socialist" peripheral Balkan countries [...] The Greeks thought (or hoped?) that having avoided the misfortune of being governed by "communists" (powerful in the heroic times of the Second World War) and that by grace of the Colonels (!),[9] they would not have to pay the price imposed on the rest of the Balkans. Europe and the Euro would work differently for them [....] The Greeks are stuck with the outcome of their naïve illusions. They should know now that the system will reduce their status to that of their Balkan neighbors, Bulgaria and Albania. For the logic of the Eurozone is no different from that of the European Union; on the contrary, it reinforces its violence. In a general fashion, the logic of capitalist accumulation produces an accentuation of the inequality among nations (it is at the source of the construction of the core/periphery contrast), and accumulation dominated by the generalized monopolies reinforces still more this immanent tendency of the system.

1.4.2 *On Class*

In its forms and guises, racism should be understood as a constitutive part of capitalist societies' disciplinary technologies of governance. Such governing technologies allow the effective division and organisation of labour, along with the reproduction of specific social relations, institutions, norms and hierarchies favourable to the interests of the bourgeoisie in all of its transformations and variants. Indeed, the ideology of racism itself is related to the rise of capitalism (Chibber, 2013: 37), its utilitarian understanding of the world, the geopolitical expansion of capital interests, the division of labour and the establishment of capitalist social relations in the colonies, with the subsequent destruction of previous forms of social and economic organisation (Davis, 2017).

Racism is thus also captured within other forms of social relations, particularly those concerning class and gender (Roediger, 2017). For instance, research (Back & Solomos, 2009: 15) has found that during the Victorian times, the middle classes would often express racial views blended into their class perceptions in England and elsewhere in Europe too. Wallerstein explains that capitalist accumulation both universalizes and divides. A universal ideology is central for the rationalization of the world and its effective organization according to the capitalist reproduction process. Competition and the division of labor though create social hierarchies that often result to racism. Racism is also an instrument to suppress labor costs and labor dissent. Class and race in that sense are entangled (Balibar & Wallerstein, 1991: 33). Skeggs (2003: 111) and

---

9 Samir Amin here refers to the infamous Dictatorship of the Colonels (1967–1974), which was backed by the USA so as to suppress the influence of the left in the country.

others (Jones 2016) argue that frequently today, the working classes and more generally the lower social strata (often called "the underclass") are publicly constructed in racial terms, shamed, ridiculed, estranged and misrepresented by the media of their respective countries. The capitalist crisis of the 1970s and the policies following it regarding the outsourcing of industry, the deregulation of trade and labour, the rise of financial activities and the reduction of progressive taxation, alongside the defeat of major working-class struggles (such as those of the striking miners in the UK during the 1980s), opened the way for what Jones describes as "the demonisation of the working class". The problems caused by capitalist restructuring related to unemployment or the abolishing of welfare were reframed as moral problems of the working class, related to its own ignorance, lack of motivation and irresponsibility.

For several years, class has been dismissed from mainstream social research, as well as from the conventional understandings of society, as a reductionist and outdated category (Shi, 2018). The sociologist Erik Ole Wright (2015: 139) writes that, during the 1990s and the 2000s, a debate took place among academics about the existence of social class as well as the relevance of the concept of class for understanding society. By focusing on the work of Pakulski and Waters entitled "The Death of Class" (1996), Wright (2015: 141) notes that the main critics of the Marxian-based class analyses perceived class to be not an existing social category, but a conceptual framework that emerges through four main propositions deriving from Marxist theory. These are a) the proposition of economism, b) the proposition of group formation, c) the proposition of causal linkage, and d) the proposition of transformative capacity. In his discussion of these propositions, Wright shows that Pakulski and Waters approached the Marxist class analysis as a case that is based on mere claims (and not facts). Without these claims, they argued, class analysis would have no substance at all. Fuchs (2015: 15) notes that in the work of Pakulski and Waters, social class has "collapsed and decomposed, replaced by lifestyles, consumption patterns, aesthetic preferences, cognitive arrangements, information flows, and value commitments". The post-modern approach to social life gives more emphasis to culture, identity and the contingency of meaning-making, instead of the material conditions that influence social life. In contrast to such a view, Wright (2015: 146) argues instead that class boundaries have not disappeared. Wright then summarises the characteristics of class relations in contemporary capitalist societies into three dimensions: property, authority and expertise (or, as he says, skills). These are further followed by more detailed subcategories. In addition, Wright stresses the enduring inequalities in the distribution of capital and their effects on social and individual life, the problems of labour extraction today and the effects of class location in the formation of individual subjectivity.

For her part, Beverly Skeggs (2003: 45) discusses the above-mentioned tendency of class negation to be occurring, not just in academia, but also in politics and in popular culture. What is remarkable is that this retreat from questions of class comes in times of burgeoning economic polarisation and inequality. Zygmunt Bauman (2013) argues that today's unprecedented inequality is tolerated due to ideological reasons. The neoliberal socio-political project was "winning the hearts and the minds of the people", according to one of its political zealots, Margaret Thatcher, by advancing as common sense the ideology of the ruling classes and spreading it to the subordinate ones. Moreover, neoliberalism also succeeded in assimilating or marginalising its enemies (such as labour parties and unions). Historical events like the fall of the socialist bloc and the subsequent victory of capitalism, the globalisation of the "free market" doctrine and liberal democracy and the general public discrediting of Marxist analyses, are key factors explaining the ideology in negating social class and its value in order to understand existing modern society.

Contemporary scholars of class emphasise the challenges that the transformation of work poses in the fluid and precarious context of neoliberal society. In a time understood to offer few opportunities for upward social mobility, these pressures are experienced not only by the poor but also by the middle class:

> Middle-class livelihoods are being scrambled and unsettled, re-arranged or re-calibrated in regard to long-term expectations. It is not just that the middle-class is being squeezed [...] It is more that there is a major revision of certain key features of the post-war social contract, which entailed universalistic modes of "redistribution" to the benefit of working-class and lower-middle-class people alike, in the form of welfare, social security, health, and education. These provisions were compensatory at that point in time when capital was keen to establish a more consensual relationship with labor, and they were also to an extent redistributionist, and thus egalitarian.
>
> MCROBBIE, 2016: 44

The predominance of the capitalist market as a supposedly neutral and efficient system constitutes the principal factor in the offsetting of class and its politics (Skeggs, 2003: 42). Usually, the term market "is a neutral way of speaking capitalism" (Skeggs, 2003: 62). In the capitalist framework, the market, as Wood (2017) explained, is a compulsory system that organises the social relations of economic activity based on exclusions, scarcities and rewards. In this way, particularly contradictory and dangerous ideas, like claiming that selfishness is in some way a virtue that may even benefit others, that greed is a good thing or that inequality is "natural", reproduce the ideology of the compulsory market system of capitalism. Hence, the poor and the excluded have only themselves to blame for their state by not trying "hard enough" or by making supposedly "wrong choices".

> The rich and the poor had somehow exchanged class positions (at least for the purposes of moral righteousness), a cliché repeated in management literature as well as more radical places such as Wired magazine [...] the fantasy of the market as an anti-elitist machine made the most sense when couched in the language of class.
> SKEGGS, 2003: 46

Skeggs argues that, along with the concept of identity, the notion of a "new individualism" became a prevailing sociological idea to explain subjectivity, social group formation and various other related social phenomena while abstaining from class concerns. Here, class emerged as a more static and monolithic concept, somehow unable to capture the contingency and mobility of the late modern world. Mobility appeared as more of a horizontal than a vertical process, presumably allowing more possibilities of social elevation for a variety of people irrespective of their economic, national or other position. This was claimed despite the fact that, in today's capitalism, as Bauman (2011) illuminated through his tourist and vagabond metaphors, few can actually benefit from mobility, while many are forced – rather than choosing – to be mobile.

Sociologists like Ulrich Beck (1999) and Antony Giddens (1991) coined the concepts of "individualisation" and "reflexive self" to speak about what they saw as the rise of new, post-class formulations of social agency. These processes were understood to be social transformations brought about by the dynamics and challenges of the globalised, late modern world. In the "late", "second" or "reflexive" modern era, class became a concept and a social characteristic of a different historical configuration, which was inadequate to capture the complexity of the present. Such theories foregrounded the importance of the individual in place of class, in which individuals are determined through their ability to reflect upon their own specific situation and to make personal choices about identity, belonging, profession, tastes and interests. In this sense, the individual can master his/her condition, author his/her own self-biography, without being determined by the collective attributes and constraints that characterise the class, gender or national backgrounds (Skeggs, 2003: 52). Politics in this context also assume a more individual and reflexive entity, beyond the realm of the class-based struggles and mass movements of the past, more connected to the Fordist era of capitalism and modernity. To this extent, Beck (1999) talks about subpolitics, while Giddens (1991) discusses "life politics", which are associated with rather intimate issues and concerns, and which correspond to particular social contexts; these are apt to be the decisions, judgments and actions of the individual.

Critics stress the middle-class character of such arguments, correlated to the general state of the unequal distribution of resources in contemporary society and the relatively privileged position that enables such reflexivity and freedom (Skeggs, 2003: 54). The "possessive individual", notably the upper/middle-class subject, who is able to own or to access resources and assets, is central to the configuration of the biographical self-individuality. On a political level, too, the focus on issues of the individual and identity matters enables the further establishment of neoliberalism and the decline of collective demands for redistribution and justice. As a result, accounts that highlight the individual as a more useful category than class to grasp the dynamics of the late modern society reinforce the middle-class locus as the ideal social position and affirm the centrality of the middle-class experience as the vantage point to assess social life. Therefore, Giddens and Beck's focus on the importance of the narrative self in late or reflexive modernity legitimises "the middle-class experience as a universal one" (Skeggs, 2003: 124).

The American political and media theorist Jodi Dean sees individualisation as a central process in the development of capitalism. Influenced by Althusserian theory and psychoanalysis, Dean (2016: 54) notes that capitalist institutions interpellate subjects to become individuals. The individuals are disconnected from the collective and at the same time disciplined to work, consume and live according to the requirements of capitalist reproduction. The individual is actually forced to develop "life tactics" (Sennett, 1998) in a highly competitive world, without institutional and collective safety networks. Individualisation is connected to the calculative and instrumental spirit of capitalism, optimising production under a strict life-discipline (Wendling, 2012). Here, the idea of time and the process of labour division are crucial. It is through time that labour and productivity are effectively measured, because, due to the division of labour in the industrial mode of production, labour cannot be measured by tangible objects. The intensification of production leads to the further compression of time as an entity that wealth production and profit is dependent upon. Poor time management in this regard comes to be seen as a character defect.

In the absence of welfare institutions protecting society from capitalism's demands for productivity, the proletarianised individual is powerless. Tied to the realm of necessity, this individual lacks the resources to cultivate a reflexive self and empower his/her position. Furthermore, the development of guilt, shame and the confessional cultures in Christianity and their contextualisation in capitalism, has been crucial in the effective control of the working class.

Control is well achieved particularly through self-monitoring (in the case of guilt) as well as through societal monitoring (in the case of shame). Confession came to be an important process for the rise of the individual as a "self-conscious person equipped with subjectivity and moral standards" (Skeggs, 2003: 120). The development of the self in the Western context relates to "a movement from outside to inside" (Skeggs, 2003: 122), with the self-being a resource to be mobilised for the presentation of knowledge and wittiness. The process of fictionalising life stories and initiating self-narratives enables the permanence of the self and connects to the making of character and personhood. Skeggs also makes a distinction between character and personality. The character appears to be a rather permanent feature, whereas personality is a changeable one, developed by access to material and symbolic resources. It is here where the class aspect emerges in the making of what Skeggs terms the "classed selves". This occurs because the working class lack access to resources that can allow its members to know and to tell their own story. Instead, the upper/middle classes are only capable of making and prescribing their own stories and biographies. The working class is overdetermined by the ways its story is fabricated by the upper classes, which constantly problematise it, so as to effectively control it and meet the demands of productivity.

1.4.2.1 Dismantling Class Privilege

Conceivably, property is the central bourgeois institution, connected to a sense of ownership and personhood as well. Property assumes an ontological entity in the bourgeois society as a natural right of the individual that is earned through work, which is to be safeguarded by the liberal state institutions. Besides its concrete material dimensions related to possession and consumption, the commodity form is also characterised by important symbolic attributes as an abstraction of display and exchange. Because ownership in the bourgeois society is connected to entities like money and time, property is extended to things that one has control over (Wendling, 2012: 51). The lack (or the possession) of property come to define the right to personhood in bourgeois societies and, along with it, the ways that the haves and the have-nots are treated by the liberal bourgeois state.

In this context, work is crucial for defining the qualities and the "essence" of individuals and groups (Wendling, 2012: 12). Work is also an important component to make property claims essential. In the capitalist world, hard work has always been valued as an important moral trait and a key to both success and happiness. Work produces and sustains possessions and wealth and constructs regimes of entitlement to exclusive forms of property (Wood, 2017: 157). As Hobsbawm (2000) showed in his "age of capital", however, the virtue of hard work principally emerges from the myth of the successful, talented and gifted, industrious, self-made, entrepreneurial bourgeois individual, who, despite hardships, is able to master his/her world through work and determination. Such a case ignores privilege and social hierarchy; it also overlooks the division of labour in capitalism and the normative and institutional regimes that enable the appropriation of the fruits of the labour of some, primarily those of the working class.

Often enough, the bourgeois self-perception is based on notions of individual exceptionality, talent and excellence (Sennett, 2006). This makes another enduring myth of bourgeois culture, associated with hard work and the regimes of entitlement deriving from it. Privilege in this sense takes a deserving perspective, as something rightfully earned and attributed to special people. Socio-economic hierarchy is in this way grounded on such constitutive individualist myths. The notion of the gifted individual is grounded not only in the idea of work, but also most importantly in natural and theological grounds. In that sense, nature, the family "genes" or God's prudence are what made someone deserve his/her privilege.

In an example brought from an ethnographical research on the Wall Street culture, Karen Ho (2009) foregrounds a "culture of smartness" cultivated among those working and seeking a career into finance in Wall Street, the world's epicenter of financial businesses. Here, a myth of cleverness is reproduced among those working in the Wall Street. Accordingly, those that wish to work hard so as to make a career in Wall Street are seen as "smart" ones. On the contrary, those that opt out or are "left behind" from Wall Street, are simply "not smart enough" to either take what is seen as the optimal career decision or, to actually be able to work for the Wall Street. In turn, this "smartness cult" puts enormous pressure on the employees of this industry to constantly multiply their productivity:

> The "culture of smartness" is central to understanding Wall Street's financial agency, how investment bankers are personally and institutionally empowered to enact their worldviews, export their practices, and serve as models for far-reaching socioeconomic change. On Wall Street, "smartness" means much more than individual intelligence; it conveys a naturalized and generic sense of "impressiveness" of elite, pinnacle status and expertise, which is used to signify, even prove, investment bankers' worthiness as advisors to corporate America and leaders of the global financial markets. To be considered "smart" on Wall Street is to be implicated in a web of situated practices and ideologies, coproduced through the interactions of multiple institutions, processes, and American culture at

> large, which confer authority and legitimacy on high finance and contribute to the sector's vast influence. The culture of smartness is not simply a quality of Wall Street, but a currency, a driving force productive of both profit accumulation and global prowess.
>
> HO, 2009: 40

Bourdieu's (2010)[10] seminal work, "Distinction", shows the importance of symbolic assets in achieving class hegemony. For Bourdieu, the dominant social classes sustain their power and privilege through their ability to define the cultural tastes of the lower classes. In this way, they become role models for the lower class rather than class antagonists. Besides economic and political capital, the affluent social classes also hold important cultural and social capital (Crossley, 2008: 89). Cultural capital concerns knowledge and taste regimes, while social capital includes social networks and connections. Combined, these features enable the upper classes to sustain their privileged social position and set the criteria that define the life goals and preferences of the lower classes. The upper class not only defines the problems of the working class, but also its aims. "To be socially dominating, a ruling idea must extend beyond the norms of the class to which its norms originate. Usually, this is used to illustrate the extension of the bourgeois[11] norms downwards, into the aspirations of the working class to achieve them to redeem a system" (Wendling, 2012: 21).

---

10   With his research set in the context of the French society during the 1960's and 1970's, Bourdieu (2010: 66) noticed a key division of the middle-class, between the intellectuals and the industrialists. In this context, the intellectuals were connected to the consumption of avant-garde forms of culture responding to high educational statuses, while opposing to the industrialists' rather hedonistic forms of cultural habits, related to expressions of conspicuous consumption. In their study of contemporary British middle-class culture, Bennett et al. (2009: 179) foreground a relatively united managerial and professional class not differentiated in terms of intellect (as in Bourdieu's case), and an intermediate class standing between the professional/managerial and the working-class. This research did not notice a division between an intellectual and a hedonistic cultural consumption, but a prevailing cultural omnivore tendency among the prevailing professional/managerial class. Education and a high engagement with different forms of cultural activities and products play here an important role in sustaining the privileged socio-economic position of the managerial and professional class members, prone to downgrading and exclusion by the constant processes of neoliberal restructuring. It is interesting to also note that Bennett et al. (2009) observed new variables of class formation in the development of neoliberal capitalism, noting new middle-class fractions as well.

11   Wood (2017) dissociates the idea of the bourgeois from that of the dominant class, emphasising that the meaning of the term bourgeois is more akin to that of the urban dweller, who is not necessarily a capitalist. Likewise, Wood also dissociates capitalism from modernity and from the Enlightenment, so as to disrupt the evolutionary narratives of

The French social theorist, Jacques Ellul (2008) argues that the idea of happiness is the main preoccupation of the bourgeois existence. Happiness here takes on an existential form and becomes a quest for having a fulfilled life. For Žižek (2011), the idea of happiness in capitalist society is overdetermined by commodity culture and substituted by the possessing of commodities. In this way, it becomes a never-ending task, constantly regenerated by marketing strategies that colonise human desire. The promise of happiness with its vague and general form may sustain an indefinite consumerist yearning. Placed in an antagonistic social realm, happiness takes the form of a compulsory command. Indeed, the theme of happiness is constantly evoked by consumer culture, blended with notions of individualism, success, work and entitlement.

Such upper-class myths as those mentioned above (individualisation, happiness through possessions, talent, exceptionality and smartness, or honest hard work associated with achieving social elevation, success and wealth), fail to consider the actualities behind work, wealth production, property regimes and privilege in capitalist society. These upper-class myths usually rely on inherited economic, social and cultural capital, and involve strong state interventions to advance and protect bourgeois interests. Different problems arise while looking deeper at the kind of work that the above bourgeois myths are concerned with. For instance, the manual-oriented, working-class labour is not entitled to diverse forms of property accessed by money. In the abstract and divided form of capitalist labour, the worker neither produces a full object nor is s/he entitled to it. Exploitation is the most central feature of work in capitalism, despite the bourgeois idealisation of work. As Marx (1992: 282) noted in his early political and economic writings:

> Wages are determined by the fierce struggle between capitalist and worker. The capitalist inevitably wins. The capitalist can live longer without the worker than the worker can without him. Combination among capitalists is habitual and effective, while combination among the workers is forbidden and has painful consequences for them. In addition to that, the landowner and the capitalist can increase their revenues with the profits of industry, while the worker can supplement his income from industry with neither ground rent nor interest on capital.

---

capitalism, equating it to a historical necessity leading to human progression. The term bourgeois is reflexively used in this work, taking Wood's arguments into consideration, but also maintaining the rhetorical power of the term and its historical connotations for an antagonistic working-class identity.

While the worker is tied to the realm of necessity, "freed" from any alternative means to make a living and forced to sell the only form of capital that s/he possesses, which solely concerns the labour potential of his/her manual or intellectual skills, the buyer of labour, is not driven by daily material constraints, scarcity and insecurity, but by aspirations of growth, power, wealth and success. Labour is sold for a price that the worker can barely control, while s/he is forced to compete among a mass of equivalent workers also constrained by the scarcities imposed by unequal regimes of private property.

For Marcuse (2009: 14), the universal dimension of the bourgeois ideology negates class and pursues a unification of class under the domination of one class within it. In this sense, "it constructs a classless society that is based upon the existing class society". In Marcuse's thought, the ideas of the folk community aspired by fascism are relevant here since historically fascism attempted to create this unity without disturbing privilege.

To conclude, the social relations of production as well as the cultural norms and their daily reproduction in capitalist societies produce classed selves. The upper classes sustain their power and privilege not only through state laws, but also through establishing cultural norms that make their own value systems and aspirations universal. Besides material privileges, the upper class has access to symbolic resources that allow it to develop its own self-understanding and narratives in ways that the working class and the poor cannot. This permits the upper class to effectively define the lower class and to interpellate it. Capitalist reproduction is based on individualisation, a prerequisite for the division of labour, which is also a precondition for capitalism to develop on a global scale (Slobodian, 2018). The individual emerges as an ideal subject in the late modern world, even though individualisation remains a rather illusionary process in the context of a mass society (Buck-Morss, 1991). In this way, the idea of the individual is connected to a middle-class position, which mediates the aspirations of the upper class most effectively, due to the middle-class potential of social elevation. In principle, the middle-class is a fundamentally conservative class striving to maintain its status quo and privileges. Some also note the dynamic character of the middle class in fostering social change by developing new and critical ideas and by participating in new social movements.

1.4.3 *Theorizing (Post)Politics*

In his political writings, the French philosopher Jacques Rancière (2007: 6) discussed a phenomenon he described as the "end of politics", which has been occurring in Western societies since the late 20th century. He explained this turn as being marked by an eclipse of "the art of politics as a program of liberation and a promise of happiness". In Rancière's sense, emancipatory demands were put aside by more "realistic" predicaments of the time's stakes. Simultaneously, ideological positions expressing anti-establishment and subvertive political visions were also dismissed as utopic or even extremist. The place was occupied by what is described as a "centrist" position that is supposed to reflect the spirit and the demands of the times more adequately.

Using Rancière's theoretical conceptualisation of the post-political era as a foundation, I will proceed by discussing various complementary approaches on the matter, so as to unpack its complexity. The idea of post-politics is a theoretical conceptualisation to describe particular tendencies occurring in the neoliberal age, related to the advent of technocracy as a mode of governance and the naturalisation of capitalism. The concept of post-politics is heuristically used to inquire on politics that attempt to pass as non-politics. Its use here does not imply the eclipse of politics per se, but the ways that the neoliberal hegemony abstracts its own political agendas, institutions and practices, and marginalises oppositional politics.

At the heart of the issue rest ideological as well as institutional factors and interventions that concern a kind of politics, associated with establishing and securing capitalist markets across the globe (Slobodian, 2018). The post-political problem discussed here thus concerns an anti-democratic and apolitical shift that is developing across the globe through policies and cultures that pursue a market-based constitution. This often occurs through the instrumental usage of the term "democracy" to potentially moralise the various financial and military forms of imperialist expeditions intensified by Western powers particularly after the collapse of the Soviet bloc.[12] Although the idea of democracy is sustained by this market-oriented regime of neoliberal politics, and consented by both the political left and the right, democracy in such a context also becomes an increasingly hollow entity that creates a political impasse (Dean, 2009b: 25).

In his work, the British political scientist Colin Crouch (2004, 2011), talks about the development of "post-democracy", caused by the decline of the post Second World War social consensus and related to the expansion of democratic rights to the working class within a welfare capitalist framework. This shift begun to occur after the 1970s world economic crisis and the deregulatory

---

12   In this regard, the Croatian scholar and member of the "Praxis" critical theory group, Predrag Matvejević (2013), used "democratism", rather than democracy, to describe the sort of regime imposed in the countries of the former Socialist bloc, with its empty democracy talk and its emphasis on the establishment of capitalist markets at the expense of literally everything else.

policies following it. Neoliberalism, in this case, is a central ideological-political dynamic fostering the post-democratic shift. The decline of economic growth, combined with worker demands for a larger share of capital profits, met with a political response that came at the expense of popular demands for redistribution, compromising the social and political rights enjoyed previously in core Western states.

An important ideological development was the prevalence of what Crouch (2004: 11) perceives as US-based concepts of democracy, focusing on limited government and unrestrained market activity across the globe, with democracy being reduced to the level of national elections mostly. Technocratic experts, such as professional politicians and economists, are to do the work of governance given that the general public lack of the relevant knowledge for such a highly complicated task in today's globalised world. In this sense, neoliberalism brought a depoliticised form of governance by prioritising the maintaining of economic growth. Depoliticisation is seen to bring civic disempowerment and a general public disengagement with politics (Beveridge, 2017: 591).

Post-democracy was also marked by a shift in the public discourse of civil rights from a positive rights formation, connected to welfare and state protectionism, to an emphasis on negative rights (Crouch, 2004: 13). While positive rights concern the right to participate in political affairs, the right to form civic organisations and the right to have accurate information, negative rights focus on the protection of the individual (and his/her assets and property) against others and against the state, and are generally associated with rights to property and entrepreneurship. Negative rights are linked with the negative freedom that emphasises the restrictions posed by other people or by the state institutions on one's freedom, rather than on the resources that may empower and enable one to pursue his/her freedom.

The kind of freedom advocated by neoliberals is a market kind of freedom (Harvey, 2005: 5), which is supposed to allow individuals to track and to safeguard their interests in the best way. Likewise, an interest-based understanding of human nature is generally advanced through this narrative. For neoliberals, freedom is not concomitant with political activity and notions of community and collectivism. According to Hayek, a highly influential neoliberal theorist, "an individual can be oppressed in a democratic system, just as he can be free in a dictatorial system. The highest value is therefore precisely individual liberty, understood as a faculty left to individuals to create a protected domain for themselves (their property), and not political liberty, as people's direct participation in selecting their rulers" (Dardot & Laval, 2013: 306). In this way, "liberty according to Hayek (1960) should be placed above all other values, including democratic ones. What matters for neo-liberalism is the equality of everyone before the law, not equality in the determination of the law" (Amable, 2010: 15).

David Harvey (2005: 19) perceived neoliberalism to be primarily an upper-class restoration project. In this sense, in the capitalist advanced, Western states in particular, neoliberalism was the capital's response to the threats it faced from social movements, socialist and communist parties, and trade unions when a new economic crisis erupted in the 1970s. Capitalism needs the state in order to suppress dissent through either consent or coercion. Hence, neoliberal politics are concerned with the advance of policy institutions that encase the capitalist economy on a global scale, through the naturalisation of the economy and the delegitimation of political interventions from below. Neoliberalism stabilised the capitalist social relations, achieved some capital growth (primarily through finance) and gained additional power for the politico-economic establishment of the bourgeoisie.

Neoliberalism is a doctrine that is meant to produce a strong state to safeguard the freedom of the economy, with competition as a foundational feature of this sort of "freedom". At the core of the neoliberal turn has been an ongoing effort to establish competition across all aspects of life, as a global governing rule and a universal norm (Dardot & Laval, 2013: 155). Such a goal is a deeply political one, as it functions both on an official political level in order to achieve reforms that would promote competition, as well as on a biopolitical level, to produce self-regulated competitive individuals. In this regard, the welfare state is usually targeted as costly and inefficient. Often enough, welfare is presented to be the main reason for inequality and poverty, because it supposedly passivises individuals and creates regimes of privilege. Taxation is also "unfair" and damaging to economic freedom. Budget "holes" resulting from the subsequent loss of tax revenues are instrumentalised by neoliberal pundits to attack welfare. A moralistic ideology connected to the bourgeois values of property, hard work and success, accompanied by traditional values (e.g. family and religious faith), denounces the welfare state. Instead of welfare, individual responsibility and personal life-choices become mandatory and are emphasised as the answer to (and the causes of) the problems of the politico-economic system. A micro-economic calculation of individual conduct is promoted to acclimate an individual to the risks and challenges faced in the "free market" society and to effectively adapt to it. Dardot and Laval (2013: 169) note that normalisation, discipline and control are interconnected dimensions of the ways that neoliberalism develops in society. The neoliberal turn of capitalism necessitates the general biopolitical reproduction of the neoliberal logic to society, in which citizens are meant to run their lives as a business and to compete with each other. As Michel Foucault (2008: 30) has demonstrated in his late work, the neoliberal society is a market society that is run by economic rationales and a biopolitical mode of governance grounded on the predominance of the market apparatus.

Neoliberalism itself is an ideology, a structure of governance that is linked to the political objectives of the capitalist economy, a mode of individual self-conduct, as well as a mode of capitalist production and accumulation.[13] Neoliberalism brings forth an economic form of politics, while branding such politics as "democratic" for purely instrumental reasons. In the neoliberal context, all aspects of life are subsumed by economic concerns. Democracy and citizenship are defined by consumerist choices and entitlements rather than from civic rights and popular sovereignty. Although the people's sovereignty has been the legitimising foundation of today's representative democracies, Rancière (2006: 73) and others (Ross, 2009), note an increasing discontent among the dominant politico-economic social groups over democracy as the rule of the people. In fact, throughout the 20th century, liberal intellectuals understood democracy to be a threatening entity to their own understanding of Western civilisation, which, in their view, was best defended by the expansion of capitalist markets globally (Slobodian, 2018: 16).

In a recent work (2018), the American historian Quinn Slobodian discusses neoliberalism as the defining current of liberal thought to emerge after the Second World War that shaped the world as it is today. For neoliberals, the people and their subversive political potential are perceived to be the root cause of a variety of today's problems, including the economic crisis itself. Slobodian (2018: 4) argues that the principal goal of the neoliberal project has been the defence of the "world economy" from democracy, whose globalizing trend in the 20th century produced challenges that classical liberals could never have predicted. Democracy is conditionally supported by neoliberals as a system that can maintain social and world peace, but this only has a functional use, which is to be constrained from its more subversive possibilities, so as to avoid disrupting the economy (Slobodian, 2018: 108). Ideally, the neoliberals strive for a consumer-based democracy regulated by economic institutions that safeguard "market freedom". For such reasons, neoliberal intellectuals (particularly those connected to the so-called Geneva School) have historically sought to develop policymaking doctrines and institutions and ally with business people

---

13   The anthropologist Aihwa Ong (2006: 4) understands neoliberalism as an assemblage of different rationales and practices that take shape in diverse contexts, underlined by economic principles. For the cultural theorist Stuart Hall (2011: 11), "neoliberalism is not one thing. It evolves and diversifies. Nevertheless, geopolitically, neoliberal ideas, policies and strategies are incrementally gaining ground, re-defining the political, social and economic model, governing the strategies and setting the pace".

and politicians, so as to "encase" the economy (Slobodian, 2018: 5). Beyond an economic discipline, neoliberalism is a discipline of law and governance, designed for the development and the maintenance of a global order to progress and to safeguard capitalism. Slobodian also stresses the global dimension of the neoliberal project, constructing an extra economic framework of transnational institutions and laws in order to diminish national sovereignty, neutralise workers' struggles and protect property rights and capitalist markets, while promoting competition.

In the neoliberal era, democracy is associated with "negative rights", safeguarding the "right" of (usually wealthy) individuals to pursue their interests without restrictions. At the same time, democracy assumes the role of an institution to sustain popular conformity for technocratic rationales and policy imperatives. The supposedly neutral authority of politico-economic experts to decide upon common affairs occurs precisely through the amalgamation of the market and the state. A market-conceived and market-organised society and polity are meant to be governed by experts preoccupied with the economy and the maintenance of social order (Rancière, 2006: 96).

In Rancière's terms, the political is a radically contingent entity, open to a variety of possibilities and visions that materialise through the activities of a sovereign people. In addition, other than a form of society or a form of constitution, democracy is more of "an anarchic title specific to those that do not have a title for governing than they have for being governed" (Rancière, 2006: 46). Democracy in this sense entails no essentialist entitlements that can establish hierarchies and privileges to few. The people, as a political subject bearing no entitlements (for instance, of kinship or wealth) to govern or to submit to be governed by a given form of power, are fundamental in legitimising decisions and actions deemed as egalitarian and democratic. Rancière's idea of politics is very much understood in this maximalist democratic framework. Contrary to this idea of politics, the kind of establishments and forms of social order that are run by powerful hierarchies are more akin to what Rancière describes with his use of the term "police". Rancière uses the term police to describe established, hierarchical forms of government and social order that have more authoritarian characteristics. In Rancière's sense, police and politics are antithetical concepts because the practices he frames as "police" circumvent the radical contingency that politics should entail. Likewise, for Rancière (2006: 53), in its current form, liberal representative democracy resembles more of an oligarchical form that represents specific powerful minorities "entitled to take charge of common affairs".

The US-based, Italian political theorist, Enzo Traverso (2017), points out that the neoliberal vision of the (free) market is an ideology that forms the only existing political religion today, in an era where political imaginaries and utopias are in decline. What he frames as the "idolatry of the market" concerns the elevation of the market into a political value that is not to be challenged. The market is thus a taboo that is not to be contested by the mainstream right or left on a policy-making level. The market constitutes the fundamental doxa that policy-making is established today on national and transnational scales (Traverso, 2017: 148). For Jodi Dean (2012: 6) the decline of left-wing opposition to neoliberalism has more to do with the left's loss of Communism as a horizon from which new political movements can emerge. Dean (2009b: 20) sees the left's clinging to democracy as highly problematic, because, as explained, neoliberal hegemony has colonised the meaning of democracy and incorporated democratic demands such as diversity, inclusion, dialogue and participation. As Dean notes, the political right also uses democracy as a pretext to express various regressive claims. By sharing the same political horizon with its adversaries, the left is unable to project an adequate counter-hegemonic vision to society and to even adequately name an adversary.

1.5 An Outline of the Chapters to Follow

In what follows, Chapter 2 presents a critical political economy overview of the Eurozone/Greek crisis. Indebtment, restructuring, austerity, and finance are explained in systemic terms. A critical theoretisation of the crisis and its politics is crucial to seeing past the hegemonic crisis explanations that have been largely casual, moral and cultural. This overview draws on a) an up-to-date critical political economy approach to capitalism, the crisis and neoliberal restructuring, using the works of David Harvey, Wolfgang Streeck, Ellen Meksins Wood, Klaus Dörre, Stephan Lessenich and Hartmut Rosa; b) centre-periphery analyses influenced by Immanuel Wallerstein, Nicos Poulantzas and Samir Amin; c) critical approaches to neoliberalism, globalisation, debt and finance, as developed by scholars such as Quinn Slobodian, Cedric Durard, Jerome Roos, Pierre Dardot and Christian Laval.

Chapter 3 looks at the media and their political role in covering the Eurozone crisis, its policy-making processes and their contestation, and the advance of austerity reforms in the EU's periphery. A literature review of the relevant research is discussed, showing that the role of the mainstream EU media has been largely affirmative towards the hegemonic crisis' rationales. In this sense, mass media are approached here as propaganda machines (Herman & Chomsky, 1988), striving to achieve public consensus about austerity, while advancing the hegemony of the dominant political and economic classes of the core Eurozone countries. Furthermore, I argue that besides achieving public consensus over the crisis and austerity, the role of the media is also a biopolitical one. I return to the above mentioned Foucauldian-based critique of neoliberal governance. During the crisis, various ideas aimed at developing the self in the context of a market-dominated society, such as entrepreneurialism, mobility, competition and risk-taking; these ideas have been constantly iterated by the mass media to organise a collective-individual ethos to meet austerity's demands. Finally, the crisis and austerity representations are viewed as public spectacles, commodifying the crisis to increase circulation and visibility. In that respect, class and race stereotypes drawn from the entertainment and the tourist industries are crucial for both achieving consensus for austerity and for the making of profitable media content.

Chapters 4, 5 and 6 present the analysis of the selected media texts. Chapter 4 focuses on the analysis of the crisis' culturalist constructions. The analysis rests on a thematic, Laclau-based, discourse theory analysis (Carpentier & De Cleen, 2007) showing the identity constructions of the hegemonic, cultural-based construction of the Greek crisis. Post-colonial theory (Said, 2003; Ahmed, 2000; Chibber, 2013) is used to explain the structural and historical dimension of such new racist discursive articulations in the media. The analysis also stresses the dimension of the commodification of the Orientalised other through the crisis spectacle and its socio-political dimension in sustaining nationalist identifications and middle-class aspirations and lifestyles.

Chapter 5 explores the class dimension of the "Greek crisis" discursive construction. This involves the moral dimension of the crisis' lay explanations, which are defined by key bourgeois values. As mentioned, the media's iteration of similar value frameworks forms the biopolitical dimension of austerity's restructuring process. The Greek economic crisis is thus judged according to bourgeois principles to have occurred due to a failed people and a failed country. Although the "Greek crisis" narrative is supposedly addressing "all Greeks", it is the working class and the poor who are mostly blamed for it. In this respect, the idea of the "loser" is central to the class frames of the "Greek crisis" narrative. While exploring different aspects of the loser framework, various affective modalities also emerge. These concern the ways that the loser is constructed. Depending upon the temporal context, the loser is viewed as entertaining, as pitiful and also as dangerous, threatening "our" well-being, that is, the well-being of hard-working, European middle-class taxpayers. A prevailing upper/middle-class gaze is cast upon the subject-in-crisis, inspecting, ridiculing and assessing it. In political terms, the class gaze aims to alienate class identities and class solidarities, sustaining the social, political and economic logic of bourgeois society and developing nationalist themes.

Chapter 6 presents the political dimensions of the Greek crisis hegemonic discursive construction and their media representation. These concern the advance of overall anti-democratic and apolitical ideas and the discrediting of critique, deliberation, protest and other popular forms of opposition to austerity. This analytical section is divided into three interrelated topics that show how hegemonic politics surface in the representations studied. These topics include a) an Apocalyptic representation of the crisis as an unprecedented and eschatological event that requires exceptional policy responses, b) the naturalisation of austerity, as a painful – yet rational and just – solution to the crisis, and c) the media's display of a "realist" ideological position, often theorised through the "extreme centre" thesis (Ali, 2015). Together, these analytical subcategories are primarily concerned with hegemony's negation of political opposition and the normalisation of hegemonic meanings and politics.

The concluding chapter of the book summarises the key arguments and findings of the study. The critique is advanced through a negative stance towards both capitalism and Eurocentrism. The importance of the critique is defended on the grounds that it may be constitutive for the development of counter-hegemonic subjectivities and visions to constitute new, internationalist and socialist politics, for the 21st Century.

CHAPTER 2

Greek Crisis, Eurozone Crisis, Global Capitalist Crisis

2.1 Setting the "Greek Crisis" in Perspective

The economic crisis in Greece is in its 9th year in 2018. Along with it, an unprecedented and polyvalent socio-political crisis has also emerged (Tziovas, 2017). Estimations show that austerity may last for more than fifty years; the repayment of Greece's growing debt may take much longer. In 2017, after eight years of neoliberal austerity reforms, the Greek sovereign debt had reached a staggering 179% of GDP (Table 1) (which amounts to about 317 million Euros), with the International Monetary Fund (IMF) estimating that it will reach 275% by 2060 (Basu, 2018: 140). In 2009, right before the bailout program's start, the Greek sovereign debt was at a 126% of the country's GDP at the time (amounting to just above 301 million Euros). Besides the augmentation of Greece's sovereign debt, during the crisis years, the country's GDP also plummeted. Greece's unemployment also accelerated to over 20% of the total working population. Poul Thomsen, the notorious IMF's director of the "European Department" and its representative in Greece's "Troika" mechanism until 2015, stated in early 2017 that "it would take Greece twenty-one years to return unemployment to pre-crisis levels" (*Keep Talking Greece*, 2017). According to Eurostat data from 2017, 35.6% of the Greek population is at risk of poverty and social exclusion. In 2007, this number was at 20% (Eurostat, 2009). The so-called "structural adjustment reforms" imposed on Greece through the bailout programs produced an unprecedented economic, social, political and humanitarian decline in Greece.

Greece entered a prolonged economic crisis in late 2009, when the international financial rating agencies downgraded the Greek government bonds. Accordingly, its sovereign debt was assessed as "unsustainable". This meant that Greece had difficulty borrowing credit from financial markets at low interest rates. After revealing his predecessors' false statistics, the time's "socialist" Greek Prime Minister George Papandreou Jr., requested financial assistance from the EU, which created the so-called support mechanism headed by what came to be known as the Troika, an institutional framework consisting of the European Commission (EC), the European Central Bank (ECB) and the IMF. In return for a colossal loan provided by the Troika, Greece had to implement a series of budget cuts and privatisations of public assets through the implementation of "structural adjustment reforms", or what is generally known as austerity policies beyond the seemingly neutral and technical vocabulary of economists. Neoliberal austerity reforms were agreed through the signing of three "Memorandums of Understanding" (MoU) between the Troika and the different Greek governments that have been in power since 2010. These reforms were supposed to "correct" the Greek "irregularities" and to make Greece align better with the EU's core. However, these reforms worsened Greece's economic prospects. The first MoU's loan and the ones that followed after the signing of two more MoUs shrunk the possibility of Greece defaulting and cancelling the debt. Such a default would have been more of a blown to the private sector and less to state budgets (Roos, 2019: 37). Nevertheless, due to the state's reliance on credit and to the possible effects of such a default to the domestic economy and to the financial system overall, default was avoided, while Greece's debt was converted into a public one, owed to the creditor states of the EU.

The EU and the Greek politico-economic establishment publicly sketched a picture of the economic crisis of Greece as a self-inflicted case, connected to some exceptional specificities of Greece. The mainstream explanations of the Greek crisis stressed a common pattern of reproach for Greece's deficit, where supposedly "everyone", rich and poor, politicians and common people, were equally responsible for the country's insolvency. Greece was presented as a failed state existing at the margins of Europe. Such economic crisis explanations were highly problematic, because they only emphasised the structural problems of Greece alone, as if the country was cut off from the broader global and European historical and politico-economic framework. Such explanations also placed the blame on the lower social classes and their allegedly poor housekeeping practices and profligate consumption habits (Glynos & Voutyras, 2016). The standard crisis narrative, as uttered by Papandreou Jr. and other neoliberal politicians from both the left and the right in Europe and elsewhere, downplayed possible public queries over the flaws of finance that associated the Eurozone crisis with the US credit crunch of 2007–2008 and the responsibilities of the banking sector for the growing of public and private debt (Lapavitsas, 2012: ix), the centre-periphery relations in the EU (Amin, 2014), the problematic edifice of the Euro currency itself (Streeck, 2016) and, most of all, the objectives and limitations of the capitalist economic system itself (Harvey, 2014).

The failure of austerity to produce economic growth through foreign capital investment in Greece, which was meant to reduce the debt, the shrinking of Greece's (minimal) welfare, wages and pensions, the compromising of environmental and labour protection laws, and the reduction of public services

TABLE 1   The Greek sovereign debt before and after the bailout programs

geo	time	2000	2001	2002	2003	2004	2005	2006	2007
EU (28 countries)		60.1	59.3	58.8	60.3	60.9	61.5	60.1	57.5
EU (27 countries)		60.1	59.4	58.9	60.4	61.0	61.6	60.2	57.6
Euro area (19 countries)		68.2	67.1	67.0	68.2	68.5	69.3	67.4	65.0
Euro area (18 countries)		68.2	67.2	67.1	68.3	68.6	69.4	67.5	65.2
Belgium		108.8	107.6	104.7	101.1	96.5	94.7	91.1	87.0
Bulgaria		71.2	65.0	51.4	43.7	36.0	26.8	21.0	16.3
Czechia		17.0	22.8	25.9	28.3	28.5	27.9	27.7	27.5
Denmark		52.4	48.5	49.1	46.2	44.2	37.4	31.5	27.3
Germany		58.9	57.7	59.4	63.1	64.8	67.0	66.5	63.7
Estonia		5.1	4.8	5.7	5.6	5.1	4.5	4.4	3.7
Ireland		36.1	33.2	30.6	29.9	28.2	26.1	23.6	23.9
Greece		104.9	107.1	104.9	101.5	102.9	107.4	103.6	103.1
Spain		58.0	54.2	51.3	47.6	45.3	42.3	38.9	35.6
France		58.9	58.3	60.3	64.4	65.9	67.4	64.6	64.5
Croatia		35.5	36.5	36.6	38.1	40.3	41.2	38.6	37.2
Italy		105.1	104.7	101.9	100.5	100.1	101.9	102.6	99.8
Cyprus		55.7	57.3	60.5	63.8	64.8	63.4	59.3	54.0
Latvia		12.1	13.8	13.0	13.7	14.0	11.4	9.6	8.0
Lithuania		23.5	22.9	22.1	20.4	18.7	17.6	17.2	15.9
Luxembourg		7.2	7.3	7.0	6.9	7.3	7.4	7.8	7.7
Hungary		55.3	51.9	55.3	57.9	58.7	60.5	64.5	65.5
Malta		60.9	65.2	63.2	69.0	71.9	70.0	64.5	62.3
Netherlands		52.1	49.5	48.8	50.0	50.3	49.8	45.2	43.0
Austria		66.1	66.7	66.7	65.9	65.2	68.6	67.3	65.0
Poland		36.5	37.3	41.8	46.6	45.0	46.4	46.9	44.2
Portugal		50.3	53.4	56.2	58.7	62.0	67.4	69.2	68.4
Romania		22.4	25.7	24.8	21.3	18.6	15.7	12.3	11.9
Slovenia		25.9	26.1	27.3	26.7	26.8	26.3	26.0	22.8
Slovakia		49.6	48.3	42.9	41.6	40.6	34.1	31.0	30.1
Finland		42.5	41.0	40.2	42.8	42.7	40.0	38.2	34.0
Sweden		50.7	52.2	50.2	49.7	48.9	49.1	43.9	39.2
United Kingdom		37.0	34.3	34.4	35.6	38.6	39.8	40.7	41.7
Iceland		:	:	:	:	:	:	:	:
Norway		:	:	:	:	:	:	:	:
Switzerland		:	:	:	:	:	:	:	:

Eurostat (2018) General Government Gross Debt. Available (consulted 23 August 2018) at: http://ec.europa.eu/eurostat/tgm/table.do?tab=table&plugin=1&language=en&pcode=sdg_17_40.

2008	2009	2010	2011	2012	2013	2014	2015	2016	2017
60.7	73.3	78.8	81.4	83.8	85.7	86.4	84.4	83.3	81.6
60.8	73.4	78.9	81.5	83.8	85.7	86.4	84.4	83.3	81.7
68.7	79.2	84.6	86.6	89.7	91.6	91.8	89.9	89.1	86.8
68.9	79.4	84.7	86.8	89.8	91.7	92.0	90.0	89.2	87.0
92.5	99.5	99.7	102.6	104.3	105.5	107.6	106.5	106.1	103.4
13.0	13.7	15.3	15.2	16.7	17.1	27.1	26.2	29.6	25.6
28.3	33.6	37.4	39.8	44.5	44.9	42.2	40.0	36.8	34.7
33.3	40.2	42.6	46.1	44.9	44.0	44.3	39.9	37.9	36.1
65.2	72.6	81.0	78.6	79.9	77.4	74.5	70.8	67.9	63.9
4.5	7.0	6.6	6.1	9.7	10.2	10.5	9.9	9.2	8.7
42.4	61.5	86.0	110.9	119.9	119.7	104.1	76.8	73.4	68.4
109.4	126.7	146.2	172.1	159.6	177.4	178.9	175.9	178.5	176.1
39.5	52.8	60.1	69.5	85.7	95.5	100.4	99.3	99.0	98.1
68.8	83.0	85.3	87.8	90.6	93.4	94.9	95.6	98.2	98.5
39.0	48.3	57.3	63.8	69.4	80.4	84.0	83.7	80.2	77.5
102.4	112.5	115.4	116.5	123.4	129.0	131.8	131.6	131.4	131.2
45.6	54.3	56.8	66.2	80.1	103.1	108.0	108.0	105.5	96.1
18.2	35.8	46.8	42.7	41.2	39.0	40.9	36.8	40.3	40.0
14.6	28.0	36.2	37.2	39.8	38.8	40.5	42.6	39.9	39.4
14.9	15.7	19.8	18.7	22.0	23.7	22.7	22.2	20.7	23.0
71.6	77.8	80.2	80.5	78.4	77.1	76.6	76.6	75.9	73.3
62.6	67.6	67.5	70.1	67.7	68.4	63.7	58.6	56.3	50.9
54.7	56.8	59.3	61.7	66.2	67.7	67.9	64.6	61.9	57.0
68.7	79.9	82.7	82.4	81.9	81.3	84.0	84.8	83.0	78.3
46.3	49.4	53.1	54.1	53.7	55.7	50.4	51.3	54.2	50.6
71.7	83.6	96.2	111.4	126.2	129.0	130.6	128.8	129.2	124.8
12.4	22.1	29.7	34.0	36.9	37.6	39.2	37.8	37.3	35.1
21.8	34.6	38.4	46.6	53.8	70.4	80.4	82.6	78.7	74.1
28.5	36.3	41.2	43.7	52.2	54.7	53.5	52.2	51.8	50.9
32.7	41.7	47.1	48.5	53.9	56.5	60.2	63.6	63.0	61.3
37.7	41.3	38.6	37.8	38.1	40.7	45.5	44.2	42.4	40.8
49.7	63.7	75.2	80.8	84.1	85.2	87.0	87.9	87.9	87.4
:	:	:	:	:	:	:	:	:	:
:	:	:	:	:	:	:	:	:	:
:	:	:	:	:	:	:	:	:	:

alongside the sacking of public workers, is nowadays acknowledged by different parties, political, technocratic and academic, both progressive and conservative (Varoufakis, 2017). In their evaluation of Greece's first so-called "bailout program", Theodoropoulou and Watt (2015: 71) note:

> The success of these programs in achieving their stated aims has been very questionable. Public debt/GDP ratios increased everywhere by far more than originally foreseen, the health of the financial sectors remains fragile, while both the implementation of structural reforms has been delayed and their promised effectiveness in stimulating growth and correcting structural weaknesses has yet to be seen [...] The first Greek program, however, stands out as the only one to have been declared an outright failure, as it had to be discontinued and replaced by a second one in March 2012, following a haircut on the Greek public debt held by the private sector, a development which the original program had sought to avert.

Despite this critical assessment of the first Greek bailout program, accounts like the one by Theodoropoulou and Watt (2015: 75) follow a rather "conventional" take on the Greek crisis. They emphasise the local weaknesses of the Greek economy and its insufficient integration in the European and the global system. Conventional scholarship places at the core of Greece's deficiencies issues related to economic protectionism and "bureaucracy", the country's inefficient tax system, corruption, political clientelism, an unmodern and dysfunctional state apparatus and Greece's supposed excessive public expenditures on wages and pensions. Such scholars further mention Greece's loss of credibility among its European "partners", when its false statistics were publicly revealed (Papadimitriou & Zartaloudis, 2015: 38). Often, they stress European and global factors of the crisis, the "incompleteness" of the Euro and the failure of the austerity program due to technical faults and poor planning (Theodoropoulou & Watt, 2015: 73). In this sense, conventional assessments of the austerity reforms' failure do not emphasise the interests and political strategies that dictated the development of such a program in the first place:

> The EU-IMF bailouts, in the IMF's own words, "served as a holding operation" for European banks to reduce their exposure to Greek debt before an inevitable future debt restructuring. As it turns out, even Greece's official lenders ended up making significant gains from this creditor-friendly approach to crisis management [...] a parliamentary inquiry by the Green Party revealed that the German government made 2.9 billion Euros ($3.3bn) in profits from its holdings of Greek bonds. Even if Germany eventually returns these profits, as it has pledged to do under the new

> debt deal, a separate study by the Halle Institute for Economic Research has found that the country still "benefited substantially from the Greek crisis", saving over 100 billion Euros ($116.5bn) – or three percent of GDP – on lower interest payments between 2010 and 2015, with most of this reduction attributable to investor flight from Greece and other peripheral Eurozone countries.
>
> ROOS, 2018

Roos (2019: 270) further states that the IMF earned 3.5bn euros in interest payments and fees (which amount to 37% of the Fund's total net income between 2010–2015), while the ECB made from Greek bonds 7.8bn euros between 2012–2016. Mainstream economics does not address the contradictions of the crisis and austerity. These may probe towards an understanding of austerity as a political, other than a mere "technical" doctrine. Beyond the high abstraction of the technical and seemingly neutral vocabulary that economists and politicians use, austerity is quite strategic in advancing particular patterns of thought and political interventions that work best for the monopolies of particular states, usually those of the European core and the US (Varoufakis, 2017). Reforms in the Greek bureaucracy thus primarily mean abolishing labour and environmental protection laws, because these prove "dysfunctional" for capitalist accumulation goals and prevent a deeper penetration of various Western corporations in the country.

The German critical sociologist Wolfgang Streeck (2014) notes that the EU's economic integration created policies that liberated cross-border market activity at the expense of local laws, democratic procedures and popular sovereignty. The Euro currency itself emerged as a tool to compromise the democratic control of the economy while intensifying competition within an unequal transnational terrain. The peripheral EU states' main benefit from their entry into the Eurozone has been the possibility to borrow funds at low interest rates to support their shrinking national budgets (Roos, 2019: 227). Low-interest credit was to make up for the loss of the peripheral states' capacities to compete, after abolishing their own currency and losing along with it the possibility of national currency devaluation and the autonomy to develop protectionist policies from more advanced and aggressive economies of Europe's capitalist centre.

As far as Greece is concerned, Streeck (2014: 141) notes that it was unlikely that the EU officials did not know that the Greek economy was not strong enough to enter the Eurozone system. It also seems hard to believe that the EU was actually unaware of the concealment of Greece's actual sovereign debt – which was done with the lavishly paid aid of Goldman Sachs economists. EU officials like Mario Monti and Lucas Papademos – both appointed as unelected Prime Ministers for Italy and Greece respectively during the early Eurozone crisis years – were employed by Goldman Sachs before assuming key positions at the European Central Bank (Basu, 2018: 146). Therefore, it is hardly the case that the EU did not have any information about Greece's actual financial data through its highly networked global financial community.

In late June of 2018, the Greek government began proclaiming the coming of the end of the period when Greece's economic policy-making was dictated by the MoUs, which dictated the "structural adjustment reforms" to be implemented in Greece. The actual end date was 20 August 2018 when the MoU signed by the Syriza-led government was due to finish. From that point, Greece would be allowed to "return to the markets" in order to acquire credit and would not require "help" from loans provided by the Troika mechanism. In simple terms, investors would now be able to buy Greek bonds without fearing the country's insolvency. An agreement signed on 21 June 2018 between Greece and the EU, which was proclaimed as a form of "debt relief", set the goals that the Greek economy should aim for in the post-MoU times, so that in the future the country would not be placed under direct supervision and control by the EU. The EU officials congratulated Greece through various statements and propagandistic material[1] that stressed the "help of Greece's EU partners" (sic) and praised the "sacrifices of the Greek people" (sic) while defending the policies of devaluation that they imposed upon Greece and sustaining the EU's hegemonic crisis and austerity narrative. Nevertheless, the actual prospects of the crisis' end and the country's recovery remain grim. The political economist Mark Blyth (2018) stressed that Greece "returns to the markets" with an economy shrunk by 25% by austerity. Regarding the 21 June 2018 agreement, Blyth stated this:

> Consider the following. The ESM lent 86 Billion Euro to Greece between August 2015 and July 2018. The final tranche of these loans will not be paid back until 2060, with payments beginning in 2034. This ten-year deferral of payments along with an interest rate reduction to an average of 1.62% across issues is the much-heralded debt relief agreement of June 21st, 2018.

In his Al Jazeera article with the title "Why the debt deal with the EU is bad for Greece", the political economist Jerome Roos (2018) explains that

---

1 Like for example, a rather preposterous video posted at the European Commission's Facebook page on 22/06/2018, under the fancy title "New chapter for Greece": https://www.facebook.com/EuropeanCommission/videos/1818106688236803/ (accessed 23/06/2018).

The creditors' rejection of a formal debt write-down means that Greece's total debt load remains stuck at a staggering 180 percent of GDP, with the agreed extension of loan maturities merely pushing the problem further down the road. As a result, rather than ending the crisis once and for all by canceling part of the debt and thereby sharing the burden of adjustment equitably with European creditors, this deal simply shifts the burden of adjustment onto future generations of Greek workers and taxpayers [...] ordinary Greeks are unlikely to experience any improvement in their living standards in the short term. Nor are these fiscal pressures likely to ease in the long run. In fact, the terms of the latest agreement require the Greek government to continue running a primary budget surplus of 3.5 percent until 2022, followed by an average of 2.2 percent until 2060, effectively committing the country to 42 more years of austerity. To be clear, no sovereign state has ever managed to run uninterrupted primary surpluses for that long.

A country of the EU's periphery (Amin, 2014: 90) Greece remains tied to an economic model that is subjected to the monopolies of the European core, since for historical reasons it was not able to constitute the kind of national monopolies that emerged in the countries of the capitalist centre in Europe and elsewhere (Poulantzas, 1979). The Greek economy today is primarily based on services, on the extraction and export of raw materials, and on an incongruously growing tourist industry.[2] In principle, Greece's possible economic growth is based on export-driven endeavours, following the economic policy currents and ideological dictates of European and global capitalism and the neoliberal austerity reforms instituted there. An export-driven, "competitive" economic model, though, is highly volatile and cannot address the needs of the majority of the people living there.

Despite Greece's positioning as an exceptional and singular case that requires an equally exceptional "remedy" (such as the one that the Troika's

---

2 Tourism is generally seen as Greece's major industry. Its tourist development is based upon a model of economic development that sidesteps concerns related to tourism's environmental, labour, and cultural impact. In an export-driven economy, the demand of tourist services becomes the main vehicle of economic development, at the expense of other productive sectors that can benefit a given society. Throughout 2018, it was estimated that more than 32 million tourists would visit Greece (*Efsyn*, 01/06/2018), a country of 11 million inhabitants, occupying a limited geographical space. Many questions can be raised with regards to how sustainable such a perpetual form of growth actually is, and who benefits from it overall, particularly as not all parts of Greece are touristic destinations.

"reforms" represent), at the expense of established democratic, social and human rights, the construction of Greece as a paradigm has important European and global dimensions. The policies followed there are also implemented in varying degrees of intensity in Europe and in other parts of the world. In what follows, I develop a critical approach to the crisis with the use of the relevant literature. My intention is to demonstrate the systemic, global and historical character of the Eurozone crisis, understanding it as a geopolitical symptom of a crisis of global neoliberal capitalism. The account I develop below aims to critique capitalism and bourgeois liberal democracy along with it, rather than focus solely on the critique of capitalism's neoliberal branch, which is common in Keynesian accounts of the crisis. I depart from an understanding that Keynesianism was a phase of capitalism which functioned well for capital interests, in so far as it stimulated adequate capital growth and in so far as it constrained the radicalisation of the working class from a potential turn to communism and to revolution (Baca, 2017). I then approach the austerity regimes imposed in Greece and the European periphery as processes of accumulation through dispossession (Harvey, 2010), meant to produce new regimes of capital growth through a harsh and rapid socio-political and economic restructuring.

2.2 A Crisis of Capitalism and Capitalist Crises: A Brief Excursion into Marxian Analyses

Political economists and scholars working in the critical tradition of Marx's thought (Harvey, 2010, 2014; Streeck, 2016; Feldner & Vighi, 2015), explained the latest global economic crisis in systemic terms. In this light, the Greek and the Eurozone crises are symptoms of a broader phenomenon with structural and historical roots. Indeed, critical scholars have argued that the 2007–8 US credit crunch and the 2009–2010 insolvency of the Eurozone's periphery were further connected to the 1970s (so-called) "global oil crisis", which constituted a major crisis of growth in the global development of capitalism. This crisis, as such scholars have argued, has never been fully resolved.

The Danish critical theorist Mikkel Bolt (2015: 2) has also argued that the crisis that societies across the world are faced with today is multiple: there is a financial crisis, an economic crisis, a political crisis, an energy crisis and a climate crisis among others. Fundamentally, though, capitalism is the main systemic factor generating these crises. The global scope of capitalism and its penetration presumably into all aspects of life amount to the "creation of the world according to capitalism's own image", as Marx and Engels (2010) once stated.

While focusing on the ongoing environmental crisis, Jason Moore stresses that

> Capitalism and its driving relations have indeed directed horrific violence towards human and extra-human life. I would go so far as to say that an unusual combination of productive and necrotic violence defines capitalism. The Capitalocene,[3] as McBrien reminds us, is also a Necrocene – a system that not only accumulates capital but drives extinction (2016; also Dawson 2016). At stake is how we think through the relations of Capitalocene and Necrocene – between the creativity of capitalist development and its deep exterminism. That exterminism is not anthropogenic but capitalogenic.
>
> MOORE, 2017: 597

Accumulation is a central characteristic of the capitalist economy. At the same time, the seeking of profit is what objectively mobilises capitalism (Harvey, 2014: 232). Capitalist accumulation is the process of propriatisation and incorporation in the system's logic of anything that is deemed necessary for capital's viability and expansion. "Capitalism is expansive, imperialist and colonizing. It tries to subsume everything under the commodity form and to destroy realms of life that do not adhere to the commodity logic" (Fuchs, 2015: 25). The different limits and breakdowns met in this process are to be resolved so that the system will be reproduced.

The key nodes that shape the dynamics of capitalism and structure its social relations are a) the principle of growth, and b) the logic of acceleration (Dörre, Lessenich & Rosa, 2015: 76). Growth concerns the augmentation of the productive and circulating capacities of the economy, connected to the increase of profit rates. Growth often appears as a "neutral" prerequisite for social prosperity, an idea that is nowadays equally shared by conservatives, liberals and social-democrats. The critical sociologists Dörre, Lessenich and Rosa (2015), describe this approach as "one-sided growth totalitarianism" that would be inconceivable in pre-capitalist social formations. Growth appears as a process with no end, proclaimed to be limitless, despite the material finitude of our planet and the massive strains that the demand of growth put upon societies and individuals. At the same time, acceleration is a process that advances

---

3   Instead of the rather problematic concept of the "Anthropocene", which bears bourgeois and Malthusian connotations (Moore, 2017: 599) the author speaks about the "capitalocene". This way he places capitalism as the key variant behind the advancing ecological crisis of our times.

parallel to growth and concerns the hastening of capitalist accumulation and the revolutionising of its reproduction processes in order to advance growth in a perpetually faster pace. Acceleration is about the intensification of productivity, innovation and organisation of the overall capitalist accumulation process. According to the principles of growth and acceleration, "late modernity appears as a 'total mobilisation' process" (Dörre, Lessenich & Rosa, 2015: 78). Acceleration and growth are driven by competition, which is "the mechanism of capitalism's basic laws of motion" (Wood, 1999). Competition forces capitalists to constantly innovate their production modes, to grow their ventures and to accelerate the production process so that they will be able to sustain their position in the market.

Capitalism advances through the constant investment of a part of the surplus value extracted by the value production process (in other words, the capitalist's profits that remain after selling the end product and covering the expenses of labour, resources and machinery) for the expansion of the business itself. This implies a perpetual movement of capital expansion, which also requires the taming and adjusting of the various "moments" of the capitalist process. Harvey (2010: 138) points out that, as a system and as an economic process, capitalism is characterised by the dialectic relationship between particular defining moments; these moments include the organisational forms and issues of productive activities and the technologies involved in them in addition to the institutional and administrative dimensions that the economy is susceptible to in national and international settings. Capitalism is also governed by the laws and norms that define the social relations of labour, the consumption of products, the management and the uses of the natural resources and the natural environment, the various prevailing and competing mental concepts and values of a given society, and the general reproduction dimensions that are entailed in daily life for humans and other lifeforms on the planet as well.

Harvey (2010: 130) estimates the minimum degree of growth needed annually is 3%. A lower percentage of growth means crisis since it translates into lower profits. A stoppage of growth results in a withholding of financial capital from being invested in the economy because the conditions do not guarantee prosperous opportunities. Acceleration in this context means the pushing of boundaries further to resume higher levels of growth. Neoliberalism, deregulation, financialisation and economic globalisation, came in response to a crisis of economic growth in the 1970s and provided unprecedented capacities for profiteering, particularly by investing in credit, which nevertheless reached a new limit during the major economic crisis of 2008 in the USA (Harvey, 2010). This was a crisis of (hyper) accumulation, escalating to the eventual eruption of the "financial bubbles" that had developed, which were connected to predatory economic activity in the futile effort of pursuing perpetual growth through finance. It is at least questionable whether perpetual growth can literally be endless in a finite planet (Harvey, 2014: 235). Moreover, global deregulated finance allowed for the development of compound growth schemes. In reality, such mathematical formulas only work in the paper. Compounding has disastrous effects on societies, localities and economies, as the enormous expansionist outcomes it unleashes are likewise untenable in the long run. The advance of perpetual compound growth economic strategies means a deepening degree of commodification and monetisation of all aspects of the lifeworld, the broadening of enclosures for common or public entities (the privatisations of public assets is a good example of this aspect), the putting of mass strains on society and the physical world and the decisive colonisation of the future, which is succumbing to the weight of debt and property entitlements.

Ellen Meksins Wood (1999) emphasises the unprecedented centrality of the market in the capitalist system and its difference from pre-capitalist market models. Unlike in pre-capitalist markets, capitalist markets form the central mechanism in which all individuals are forced to enter to gain access to their reproduction means (Wood, 2017: 83). This kind of market is governed by the logics of competition, profit, accumulation and productivity. For Wood (2017), the market is the underlining principle that makes an economy, a society and a polity, capitalist. Although wealth accumulation, exploitation, commerce and markets existed in pre-capitalist formations, the market in capitalism is constituted as the defining apparatus that subsumes all aspects of life. Changing from a direct, physical and limited space under communal control, in the capitalist era, the market became a mystified process that is supposedly self-regulating and subordinates a variety of social practices (often non-economic ones) through competition and through scarcities imposed by the price mechanism (Wood, 2017: 69; Slobodian, 2018).[4] To that respect, Michel Foucault (2008: 31), too, has noted the rather metaphysical character of the market in the neoliberal era, in which the market "becomes a space of truth".[5]

---

4 As Wood (2017) demonstrates, the rise of the market into an economic, social and political central mechanism occurred due to historical reasons (Wood locates the rise of competition-driven capitalist markets in the pre-industrial, rural Britain), as well as through political decisions and, often enough, through military interventions.

5 The Eurozone crisis makes a good example of the ways that the financial markets play a decisive and direct political role, dictating policy-making and intervening in national elections. After the May 2018 national elections of Italy, the EU budget commissioner, Gunther Oettinger – obviously unhappy with the electoral results of a sovereign state – stated that, "the markets will teach Italy to vote for the right thing". Streeck's (2016: 186) quoting of

In a "free market" society anyone is supposedly a potential capitalist, striving to sell his/her product for the most beneficial terms. According to conventional economics, competition is a natural behaviour of individuals pursuing their best interests. The market appears as a perennial system, guided by "natural" laws. Despite the proclaimed neutrality of the market space, in reality, the market is highly asymmetrical, as those engaged in it hardly ever depart from the same economic or social backgrounds. Instead of a space of opportunity, the market in capitalism is a space of compulsion (Wood, 2017: 53), in which producers are required to function as capitalists, constantly improving production and developing and reinvesting surpluses to be competitive. Guided by a profit maximisation quest, the improvement of production concerns the intensification of labour and its productivity. In principle, this concerns the time required to produce a given commodity, because the exchange (market) value of the commodity is a quantity of "congealed labour time" (Marx, 1990: 130). The reduction of production time in capitalism due to the technological optimisation of work results not in the lessening of the total working hours for the worker, but in the intensification of productive labour resulting to the production of more commodities in a shorter time (Caffentzis, 2013: 144). In effect, this reduces the worker's income, which is roughly connected to the time required to produce a given product along with the expenses of the constant capital (machinery) owned by the capitalist. The intensification of production is connected to the periodical restructuring of the production process, through the introduction of new technologies, or through the establishment of new state regulations, which often reduce the labour force (variable capital) and deskill workers. As result, unemployment increases and competition among workers rises to the benefit of the capitalist, who can exploit the labour scarcity to minimise wages, the so-called "labour costs".

In any system, labour is the key source producing value. In capitalism, however, labour takes a substantially different form than in previous economic systems. According to Marx (1990: 250), a general formula of economic reproduction can be summarised in the scheme of C-M-C, where a given commodity (C) is produced, sold to the market for money (M) and this money is then used for the purchasing of other commodities. Capitalism is characterised by the inverted scheme of M-C-M, where money (M) is invested in the production of commodities (C), to be sold for money, which is reinvested and used to produce more commodities, so as to sell them for more money. This process aims at perpetually expanding the production and expansion process of any given

---

Merkel's understanding of the EU's polity as a "market-abiding democracy" is indicative of the centrality of the market in today's global capitalism.

FIGURE 1　Voucher used instead of money to pay productivity bonuses
SOURCE: PHOTO BY AUTHOR

capitalist venture. The surplus value (the profit extracted by the capitalist from the unpaid labour hours – in the sense that the commodity produced is sold at a higher price than that paid to the worker producing it) is usually invested for the further expansion of a given business (if conditions are evaluated as profitable for an investment), and part of it is consumed by the capitalist in a bourgeois society.

An important dimension that is raised by the analysis of the Endnotes group (2010) concerns what its study frames as "the constant crisis of capitalist reproduction". This fundamental crisis concerns the problems of reproducing the labour force itself and the social relations of production. The main stake is the making and sustaining of the necessary social relations required to create the disciplined and productive labour that characterises capitalism. Neoliberal austerity in this context emerges as a labour devaluation process to intensify productivity and, subsequently, exploitation, and to increase surplus value extraction (Figure 1).[6] In this regard, Greece's average wage was slashed by 19.5%

---

6 The image in Figure 1 shows vouchers which are given instead of money to substitute the productivity bonuses of low-paid workers in Greece, employed by the Deutsche Telekom owned Cosmote through subcontracted work agreements. The vouchers can be spent only at specific stores and have an expiration date. This practice has become widespread in recent years among low-paid workers in various service sectors throughout Greece. Besides the devaluation of labour that such substitutes of payment bring about, the work itself also colonises the free time and possibilities of the worker by setting a more direct control over his/her needs and "consumer choices".

during the crisis (from 863 euros a month at the pre-crisis levels to 684 in 2018) (INE-GSEE, 2018) and reports suggest that the average Greek became poorer by 40% during the crisis years due to wage cuts, the rise of unemployment, cuts in welfare services and increased taxation (Rodgers & Stylianou, 2015, Roos, 2019: 271). Furthermore, from the beginning of the crisis, investors, economists and politicians have called for the establishment of "special economic zones" across Greece, offering "special tax and administrative features", that also offer significantly low wages and minimal worker rights, to attract investment and to "create jobs" and "economic growth" (*Reuters*, 2012).

The term "crisis" refers to the limits that capitalism reaches, which need to be overcome so that it can effectively reproduce itself and expand its scope of activity. Capitalist accumulation is hardly smooth or non-contradictory. Its defining moments, in Harvey's sense (2010: 116), pose various barriers and are subjected to different sorts of challenges that capitalism needs to overcome. A periodic destruction (termed as a "creative destruction" by mainstream economists) of existing institutions, social relations, norms and physical entities (such as the natural and the built environment, or the fixed, variable and monetary capital [Harman, 2011]) is occasionally necessary in the times of crisis and growth stagnation, so as to have an effective reinvention of the whole process of capitalist reproduction (Harvey, 2014: 234). The cultural theorist of Modernity, Marshall Berman (2010: 100), explains that destruction is intrinsic to capitalism:

> If we look behind the sober scenes that the members of our bourgeoisie create and see the way they really work and act, we see that these solid citizens would tear down the world if it paid. Even as they frighten everyone with fantasies of proletarian rapacity and revenge, they themselves, through their inexhaustible dealing and developing, hurtle masses of men, materials, and money up and down the earth, and erode or explode the foundations of everyone's lives as they go. Their secret – a secret they have managed to keep even from themselves – is that, behind their facades, they are the most violently destructive ruling class in history.

In theory, crises tend to work in a "self-correcting" way to pave the way for the radical reconfiguration and restructuring of the capitalist mode of production (Harvey, 2010: 35). Crises thus concern the limits of capitalism itself and relate to the confines of economic growth in capital's terms. All crises of the capitalist economy are primarily crises of growth (Dörre, Lessenich & Rosa, 2015: 76), and the contradictions arising from the constant efforts to achieve capital growth (Dimitriou, 2016: 11). Capitalist restructuring is connected to political interventions on state and supra-state levels that primarily aim to intensify labour productivity, further the expansion of markets, and achieve an ideological consensus about the objectivity and necessity of such interventions.

2.3 Crisis and Restructuring: Neoliberalism, Globalisation, Financialisation

Critical scholars (Trenkle, 2010: 14; Fuchs et al., 2010: 194) argue that capitalism reached its historically highest moment of growth in the early 1970s, and has been in a constant crisis ever since. David Harvey (2014: 238) notes that the levels of growth reached in the last 250 years of human history are an exception, which cannot continue or last for too long, due to natural as well as social constraints. The constant pursuit of higher levels of growth and profits, however, is intrinsic to capitalism, since zero growth means the end of it.

The post Second World War social democratic model of growth, also known as welfare capitalism, entailed policies of economic regulation and social redistribution. This model achieved high levels of growth in the post-war reconstruction context, while also responding to some demands of social equality. It generally lasted until the late 1960s. The slowing down of economic growth that marked the early 1970s economic crisis was followed by the rise of inflation (Streeck, 2016: 78). This occurred because states attempted to keep both labour and capital content through the printing of extra money and by abolishing the metal (gold) standard that defined the value of money. Streeck explains that, although inflation was not a problem for labour (at least it was not in the 1970s when labour unions and similar organisations did not hold financial shares), it did nevertheless pose a threat to capitalism and the interests of creditors and shareholders. According to mainstream economists, inflation created distortions in prices, incomes and "incentives" (Streeck, 2016: 79). Soon, a policy of fiscal discipline was charted at the expense of labour wages and welfare rights, followed by mass unemployment and deindustrialisation.

In principle, economic stagnation causes various disturbances and tensions that cut across all social fields. Such tensions are usually resolved by state interventions. History has demonstrated that in the liberal democratic historical context, state interventions generally tend to work mostly in capitalism's favour. In this way, the decisive political answer to the 1970s crisis was connected to the ideas and practices of neoliberal economics. In brief, the neoliberal ideological framework publicly proclaimed that if capitalists profit, then society will also profit because the capital will eventually be invested back in society.

This largely fictitious idea, named "the trickle-down effect", in reality meant the compromise of welfare regulations, the shortening of workers' demands and the lifting of state protectionist policies from the economy. Such measures enabled the effective globalisation of capitalism, organised under a tight transnational framework of institutions and agreements that protect this economic formation (Slobodian, 2018).

Dardot and Laval (2013: 216) discuss (as did Foucault [2008]) an American and a European variation of neoliberalism. As far as the American "branch" of neoliberalism is concerned, Kotz (2009: 307) emphasised in his analysis its main characteristics, namely, the development of policies of economic "deregulation" on a local and global scale, the launching of privatisations of public property, the rise of a discretionary fiscal policy, the advance of reductions in social spending accompanied by a simultaneous decrease in the taxation of the wealthy, the legislation of flexible labour conditions and the escalation of aggressive competition traits.

The European branch of neoliberalism, which is connected to the aspect of the global economic crisis studied in this book, is based on the German ordoliberal thought. The main premises of European ordoliberalism are the following: a) the flexibility of wages and commodity prices, b) the reform of the welfare and pension systems by promoting individualised austerity, c) the general highlighting of enterprise and the entrepreneurial spirit, and d) the defence of "freedom" as opposed to "nihilism", a demeaning name to call socialism (Dardot & Laval, 2013: 196). While ordoliberalism advances a negative idea of freedom (e.g. freedom from state protectionism), it is not a doctrine that is against state interventions. On the contrary, ordoliberalism is in favour of state interventions, as long as they function in a way that will protect and advance "market freedom". The self-reliant individual emerges as a more important agent than collective interests (Amable, 2010: 6). In this context, public policy interventions are only to preserve the "fairness" of competition, with competition emerging as a key socio-political value in the ordoliberal doctrine (Amable, 2010: 5).

Quinn Slobodian (2018: 151) demonstrates that in the development of a global neoliberal framework of governance, aspects of both currents meet. Global neoliberalism (what Slobodian describes as "ordoglobalism") emerged through the active and uncompromising work of specific intellectuals, particularly those who comprised the "Geneva School". These intellectuals, starting in the 1930s, saw their work as a project to renovate liberalism and as an effort to defend the West and civilisational progress in a broader sense. Decolonisation, along with the rise of variations of Keynesianism in Western Europe and the US, and the spreading of Soviet Communism, were central events in the development of neoliberalism as a model of global governance (Slobodian, 2018: 5). Slobodian concludes that the neoliberals did not believe in self-regulating markets nor that democracy and capitalism were synonymous. They also did not believe in the possibility of fully understanding and controlling the economy; for them, the economy obtained a somewhat sublime form "beyond representation and quantification" (Slobodian, 2018: 18). The Geneva School's prime concern was to establish a set of rules and regulations that would protect the capitalist market on a global scale: "not knowing the totality while knowing the rules needed to maintain it is the Geneva School's neoliberalism" (Slobodian, 2018: 270). The Geneva School intellectuals thus sought alliances with Western politicians and business circles and took advantage of different historical events and opportunities. In this way, they managed to establish regulations, institutions, constitutional settings and norms that would develop the market at a global level and would work pre-emptively as well as proactively to insulate the economy (or encase it in Slobodian's terms) from democratic interventions, national sovereignty, wealth redistribution aspirations and trade tariffs. The securing of the global character of capitalism by democracy is, according to Slobodian (2018: 272), an important aspect of the neoliberal project. Furthermore, the transnational character of the institutional constraints developed would "prevent nation-states from transgressing their commitments to the world economy" (Slobodian, 2018: 15). Global neoliberalism thus obtained a rather totalistic form, as it aspired to contain the whole globe and aimed to institute itself as the only legitimate and possible option for the organisation of social affairs under economic premises.

Global neoliberalism advanced through emerging Western-based, "international" economic institutions like the World Trade Organisation and the realignment of older ones, such as the World Bank and the IMF, which assumed a new role in "integrating" peripheral states into global capitalism through the provision of loans to peripheral states in exchange for neoliberal reforms (Wallerstein, 2006: 86). Although growth was conditionally restored in the late 1970's, neoliberalism augmented inequality and developed a speculative financial sector, which was prone to fluctuation. The kind of reforms demanded by organisations such as the IMF, which provide loans to states so as to push for neoliberal reforms in return, resulted in the further loss of peripheral states' sovereignty and, along with it, any competitive economic advantages that their economies might have. Overall, finance has been a key tool in the spreading of neoliberal capitalism on a global scale. Pro-market regulations of the kind adopted from the 1970s onward sought to integrate the whole world into the "free market" and opened the way for financial capital to seek the most profitable undertakings possible across the world. Roos (2019: 64) notices three main developments that characterize the rise of financialization: a) the increasing influence of financial institutions in policy making b) the increasing official intervention (of states and central banks) in financial markets as moneylenders c) the dependence of the state on private credit. In effect, finance is central in the securing the interests of the affluent social classes (Dumenil & Levy, 2013: 13). Financialisation is thus a systemic phenomenon

> linked to different processes such as, the liberalization of finance, the internationalization and increased sophistication of financial markets, the growth of indebtedness among firms, households and states; the tendency towards the privatization of social security systems and the nature; the fragmentation of the workers' movement; the proliferation of financial crises".
> DURAND, 2017: 3

The "liberalisation" of finance occurred through national policy shifts, economic globalisation, technological innovation and organisational changes (Durand, 2017: 19). For one thing, the financialisation of the economy secured revenues. Moreover, the "liberation" of capital from national boundaries resulted to the minimisation of the socio-political power of organised labour and the subsequent deterioration of the living standards of the working classes. This situation produced further crises as unemployment and the stagnation of wages meant to intensify productivity caused the downfall of a cumulative demand for the consumer goods produced. Harvey (2014: 240) points out that one space for new investments was the lending of over-accumulated, financial capital to the national governments of second and third world countries, augmenting their national debt. In addition, loaning was also expanded to the general public of the West to make up for income loss and the wage value decrease (Kotz, 2009: 312); Durand (2017: 14) speaks about the rise of the NINJA (no income, no job, no assets) loans, which gave high revenues to bankers and brokers, deriving from the securing of such risky loans. Private loaning was also provided in order to boost consumption, particularly as wages begun to stagnate and inflation to rise.

The pressures for exponential (compound) expansion in the 1970s resulted in, among other things, the deregulation of finance and the abolishment of the gold standard that limited the production of currency, resulting in an unlimited possibility to produce credit: "with the suspension of the Bretton Wood system, the whole monetary system now rests on bank money" (Durand, 2017: 60). The decades that followed the 1970s saw the progressive "financialization of everything" (Harvey, 2005: 33). Simultaneously, the deregulation of the market system with the lifting of trade tariffs and state protectionist policies resulted in the worldwide expansion of the "free market" system. Financial mechanisms expanded not only in space but in time as well, forcing productive capital to succumb to the planned revenues of stakeholders. Such developments resulted in the creation and eventual bursting of financial bubbles, such as the mortgage loan crisis in the USA, which marked the initial phase of the 2007–2008 crisis.

The disconnection of money from its commodity value form allowed for the creation of an overflow of fictitious financial capital, invested in a variety of potentially profiteering endeavours. The loosening of financial regulations opened the path towards the development of financial innovations, such as the investment of financial capital in financial activities, because this provided higher and safer revenues. A common activity has been the purchasing of future derivatives, which reduce the shareholders' risk in the case of stock market failures. Derivatives are securities of real assets anticipating future price increases (Durand, 2017: 20). Derivatives involve a low financial commitment and the expectancy of high financial returns, and it is common that financial investors buy only derivatives and market options for stocks instead of stocks and actual assets (Varoufakis, 2011: 113). Durand (2017: 28) explains that the rise of prices increases the demand of derivatives, while indebtedness increases prices; security derivatives allow for the taking of loans in order to buy derivatives and create more profit out of them. Varoufakis notes that this process, called leveraging, resulted in the 2008 credit crunch in the USA. This increased risk-taking practice was enabled by policy-makers, to ensure that the central bank would prevent systemic risks. State policies limited financial loses and enabled the developing of risky investments for what seemed to be a self-regulating financial sector (Durand, 2017: 37).

Disconnected from the productive economic sectors, the so-called real economy, and the assets' fundamental value, highly profitable and secure speculation practices resulted in the appearance of what is often described as fictitious capital. Fictitious capital emerges through what is labelled as capitalisation. Fictitious capital "produces debts or securities whose value results from the capitalisation of the anticipated revenues" (Durand, 2017: 50). Marx indicates three forms of fictitious capital: credit money (e.g. bank loans in exchange for interest), government bonds and shares (Durand, 2017: 51). Fictitious capital concerns the generation of ex nihilo financial capital that is not based on previous savings. It is not connected to the process of valorisation through production, and only represents a claim on future real valorisation processes (Durand, 2017: 55); essentially its power rests on political decisions and institutional establishments. Debt creates credit money, which is based on the expected interests drawn by the process of debt repayment. Bonds have no connection to capital accumulation and the valorisation process, representing only "advances on tax receipts" and interest flows, while shares also stand for ownership titles to the surplus value that is anticipated (Durand, 2017: 53). In this way, state bonds sold by private banks to state banks, "under repurchase agreements, provide the raw materials to private banks to create credit money" (Durand, 2017: 52).

An asymmetry then lies between the actual produced value from productive processes, and the anticipated value to emerge from future valorisation processes. The profits of fictitious capital are real, though. They emerge as transfers of income from the productive economic processes related to labour, goods and services (Durand, 2017: 83). Finance directs the real economy towards projects that may generate more profits, generally not connected to social needs and use values. Consequently, finance operates upon the logic of innovation, parasitism and dispossession (Durand, 2017: 103), and not strictly on that of labour exploitation. The power of fictitious capital has dire consequences for policymaking and it is connected to the structural power that finance bears upon the state and the economy today overall (Roos, 2019: 51). Finance forces governments to guarantee the expected profits of the shareholders since the whole economy is subordinated to the acts of finance. To this respect, a lengthy quote from a relevant study on austerity regimes in the UK is particularly clarifying for the power that "self-regulated" finance achieved:

> The Federal Reserve, which oversees the US banking system, allowed Lehman Brothers a prominent New York bank to default. Economists use the phrase "moral hazard" to explain the reason for this decision. The Fed wanted to send a signal to financial markets that they – not the American taxpayer – would have to bear the consequences of their own ill-judged speculative activities and pay a price for their reckless behavior. The subsequent reaction of financial markets showed that this was a mistake since, to the Fed's surprise; the decision triggered a panic which threatened to engulf the whole of Wall Street. In the event, the Fed had to organize a rescue package of its own, although this did not include the hapless Lehman Brothers. Taxpayers ended up on the hook, after all. The financial panic caused a credit squeeze which severely disrupted economic activity as banks and other financial institutions stopped lending to businesses, to consumers and to each other. This rapidly affected

confidence and subsequently worked its way through into the real economy of jobs and growth.

CLARKE et al., 2016: 30

2.4 The Greek Crisis as a Symptom: Centre (Core) and Periphery Divisions

In most underdeveloped countries, capitalism has had a peculiarly twisted career. Having lived through all the pains and frustrations of childhood, it never experienced the vigor and exuberance of youth and begun displaying at an early age all the grievous features of senility and decadence. To the dead end stagnation of pre-industrial society, was added the entire restrictive impact of monopoly capitalism.

BERGER & MOHR, 2010: 40

Writing in the late 1970s, Mouzelis (1979) noted that what he framed as Greece's underdevelopment had its origins in the imperialist interventions of the capitalist centre. In this sense, underdevelopment is an outcome of the centre's strategic interpolations on the periphery, in which it served as a pool of cheap resources and raw materials and as a market for commodities produced by the centre. Likewise, the Greek crisis nowadays can be better understood in the framework of the centre-periphery analysis, as a peripheral Eurozone country and as a semi-peripheral country in the global capitalist economy (Amin, 2014; Fuchs, 2015; Stubbs, 2017), symptomatic of the uneven geopolitical, economic and socio-culturally diverse context of the EU. In other words, Greece's "peculiarities" are symptomatic of the uneven geopolitical and economic context of the EU and the centre-oriented construction of the Eurozone. An analysis based on the centre-periphery thesis that also takes imperialism into account – as a historical process of politico-economic pressure and domination, besides its purely militaristic form – can provide more adequate explanations (than those based on local culture and morals) to understand Greece's diachronic weak position in the European/Western politico-economic order, and its dependency on the capitalist centre.

To understand the meaning of center (core) and periphery, we can also follow Wallerstein's analysis of global systems where he highlights the centrality of the capitalist production in the center-periphery division:

Core-periphery is a relational concept. What we mean by core-periphery is the degree of profitability of the production processes. Since profitability is directly related to the degree of monopolization, what we essentially

> mean by core-like production processes is those that are controlled by quasi-monopolies. Peripheral processes are then those that are truly competitive. When an exchange occurs, competitive products are in a weak position and quasi-monopolized products are in a strong position. As a result, there is a constant flow of surplus-value from the producers of peripheral products to the producers of core-like products. This has been called unequal exchange.
> WALLERSTEIN, 2006: 28

Wallerstein later goes on to define the relations characterizing the core and the periphery, underlined by the strategic tasks of the core

> The strong states, which contain a disproportionate share of core-like processes, tend to emphasize their role of protecting the quasi-monopolies of the core-like processes. The very weak states, which contain a disproportionate share of peripheral production processes, are usually unable to do very much to affect the axial division of labour, and in effect are largely forced to accept the lot that has been given them.
> WALLERSTEIN, 2006: 29

Hence, innovation and the production of high quality and cutting-edge products is maintained by the core, and the periphery is assigned to the production of "secondary" goods with prices effectively controlled by the core, which dominates the "free market" framework. "Peripheral zones usually are lower-price, lower-amenity zones and the wages of cadres are accordingly below the norm of core zones" (Wallerstein, 2006: 78). The threats of competition, intensified in a global and vast changing socio-political space, are resolved through the establishment of oligopolies on the one hand, and on the other, through the possibilities that the periphery allows capitalists to move the production to places with low labour costs as well as places where various resources can be extracted at a minimal price. To this respect, as Fredric Jameson (2016: 13) argues, "postmodern politics is about land grabs on a local and global scale". In the course of time, the divisions between the centre and the periphery deepen due to socio-political and legal establishments that maintain reputable power privileges. The history of colonialism itself demonstrates the sophistication and ruthlessness of governing techniques of the periphery, and its links to submission, dependency and underdevelopment through biopolitics (for instance, by interpellating the colonised subject's subjectivity [Said, 2003]), and, as history has shown, even via thanatopolitical means, such as artificially introduced famine through "economic restructuring" policies (Davis, 2017).

The centre is the crucially important locus of power and decision-making. The periphery consists of a broad entity of differentiated parts unevenly connected to the centre. Although underestimated, the periphery is necessary for the existence of the centre as a privileged locus. Drawing on the work of Galtung (1971) on imperialism, Sepos argues that the periphery has limited interaction with the centre. The centre is characterised by a solid and advanced military, administrative and economic structure, while the periphery is characterised by "distance, difference and dependence" (Sepos, 2016: 38). The affluent classes of the periphery are tied to the interests and decision-making processes of the centre and assist the periphery's governance by the centre. As further observed, the centre-periphery conditions currently exist in the centre as well, with islands of deprivation growing in the prosperous, so-called first world. Hence, both the centre and the periphery have their own centres and peripheries as well.

As far as the EU is concerned, the center-periphery analytical framework addresses

> The division between the big, "strong", "founder" member states and the smaller, weaker, newer member states: the former seeks to form core, pioneer, avant-garde or directoire groups often at the exclusion of the latter. Such divisions entail a spatial recognition that not one but many Europes exist, with an identifiable center consisting of "Franco-German", "Benelux" and "Nordic" Europe versus a peripheral "Mediterranean", "Central" and "Baltic" (and "wider") Europe. In the context of the Euro crisis, this center-periphery divide has been defined or framed in terms of: rich (center) vs poor (periphery), hard-working vs lazy, responsible/disciplined vs irresponsible/profligate, debtors vs creditors, surplus vs deficit, lenders vs borrowers, growth vs austerity, regulatory vs redistributive and market-opening vs market-regulating [...] within the EU Empire, the center arguably consists of the Northern European countries (i.e. Germany, France, the UK, the Netherlands, Belgium, Sweden, Finland, Denmark, Austria), and the periphery consists of the Southern countries (i.e. Portugal, Italy, Ireland, Greece, Cyprus, Spain) and the Central and Eastern European countries. The EU Empire also has a periphery outside its sovereign borders; this periphery is arguably the Middle East and North Africa, the Southern Caucasus and the Eurasia region.
>
> SEPOS, 2016: 38–39

Samir Amir (2014: 89) argues that, as part of a generalised capitalist monopoly system, European capitalism is organised into three main levels. This first one comprises the national-based monopolies of the core North-western

European states, which as far as the EU is concerned include the UK, France, the Netherlands, Germany, the Scandinavian countries, Belgium and Austria. The second level includes Spain, Italy and Portugal, which developed their national capitalist monopolies after the Second World War. For historical reasons, these countries cannot effectively become equal to the first group of the EU core. The third group includes Greece and the former Soviet bloc countries that are now members of the EU. Such countries did not develop their own national monopolies and, for this reason, are ruled by the capitalist monopolies of the EU's core states and not by their own possible nation-based ones.

The Eurozone crisis demonstrated the existing divisions between the centre (core) and the periphery between the North vs. South and the rich vs. poor in the EU states (Sepos, 2016: 35). Becker (in Mihaljević, 2017) notes that there are two kinds of peripheries in the EU; the Visegrád countries and Transylvania, which are tied to the German export-industrial complex, and the Southern European countries, whose economic growth is based in tourism, real estate and construction, as well as on financial capital provided by the core EU countries' banking system. Critics agree (Streeck, 2016; Lapavitsas et al., 2010; Mihaljević, 2017) that financialisation in the EU (as elsewhere) and the advance of the European common currency policies along with the development of the Euro had detrimental effects on the economies of the European periphery, but benefited those of the core.

On the one hand, Greece is a peripheral country in the Eurozone, with the Eurozone being constructed according to the interests of Europe's economic centre. As Streeck (2016: 173; also: Lapavitsas et al., 2010: 321) argues, the Greek dimension of the Eurozone crisis (as well as the crisis of other peripheral Eurozone members), has to do with the poor integration of peripheral countries with the Euro, which is a currency connected to the realities of the core EU economies of the North, and Germany in particular. On the other hand, within a global economic framework and given the EU's position as a part of the North-western core, Greece emerges as a semi-peripheral country. Wallerstein (2006: 28) defines the semi-periphery as an entity that is based on its productive capacities to yield a mixture of core and peripheral products while performing specific political functions for the system's structure. At the same time, in its official politico-economic form, the semi-periphery tries to become part of the core, complying and participating in imperialist interventions, military, economically and politically. In this way, Greece participated with its military in different NATO-led expeditions and expanded economically into the Balkan regions during the 1990s and the 2000s, exploiting the restructuring process there during the so-called transition period after the demise of socialism and the restoration of capitalism.

The critical use of the centre-periphery analytical framework relates to an increased understanding of the EU through the metaphor of the empire

(Mikelis & Stroikos, 2017: 129). This metaphor addresses both the organisational structure of the EU as well as the internal hierarchies that the EU contains. Therefore, the culturalist crisis narrative coined to address the crisis as an inherent problem of the periphery bears notable similarities to the discourse developed by empires to address their governed lands, particularly in the colonial times. The bailout program of Greece itself has ties to Europe's colonial past since it was designed and developed from equivalent programs that were historically used to "ensure the timely servicing of foreign debts" (Martin, 2015) in non-Western countries. In this respect, the "restructuring of the European South" envisioned by the European North as well as the framing of the European periphery through the demeaning "PIIGS" acronym, coined by technocrats to refer to the EU states in crisis, notably Portugal, Ireland, Italy, Greece and Spain, suggest a neo-colonial attitude and practice within the EU (Mikelis, 2016). This implies specific "civilisational standards" presumably mastered by the EU's core countries that entitle them to evaluate the EU's periphery and to dictate the direction they need to follow, economically, politically, socially and culturally. In this respect, the EU has also been assessed as an "ordoliberal iron cage" (Cafruny & Ryner, 2016: 10), with regards to the advent of market-driven politics and technologies of governance.

2.5 The EU, the Euro, and Austerity

> Those responsible for the bankruptcy of the European project are not its victims – the fragile countries of the European periphery – but, to the contrary, the countries (which is to say, the ruling classes of those countries), foremost among them Germany, that have been the beneficiaries of the system. This makes the insults against the Greek people even more odious. A lazy people? Tax cheats? Mme Lagarde forgets that the cheaters in question are the shipowners protected by (IMF-supported) globalization's freedoms.
>
> AMIN, 2014: 99

Emerging in 1951 as the European Coal and Steel Community (ECSC), the EU has primarily been an economic establishment. Although it is true that Europe is marked by different intellectual and political traditions, at its core, the EU is based on Christian democracy and ordoliberalism. Although the EU is maintaining core social welfare regulations, they are continuously subjected to cuts and neoliberal restructuring. Economic competition has been a key priority protected through the emergence of the ECSC (Dardot & Laval, 2013: 194). Issues related to a "European integration" in political and cultural terms so as to avoid future wars and the misery that the working classes suffered during the Great Recession of the 1920s and 1930s, were secondary matters that gained ground in the capitalist advanced states during the "Golden Years" of social democracy, the 1950s and the 1960s. In the emerging European Community, Germany was a country burdened with some of the most horrific crimes against humanity perpetrated by the Nazi regime, which was decisively crushed by the Soviet Union (that paid by far the heaviest casualties toll and bared the most sacrifices in the anti-fascist struggle), the other Allied forces and the anti-fascist Resistance movements across the Axis-occupied lands. Germany was soon to rise with the USA's political and economic backing to a leading position as a front against the danger posed by the Soviet Union and its allies (Anderson, 2009: 15; Bauman, 2004b).

Wolfgang Streeck (2014) notes that during the 1970s, the EU curbed the South European states potential for turning to Eurocommunism after the collapse of their dictatorial regimes. This was achieved through the provision of subsidies of EU structural funds and the introduction of institutional reforms based on core EU state models. The possibility of the development of a social-democratic Eurocapitalism was abolished after the collapse of the socialist bloc and the EU's continuous broadening of its periphery. Instead, neoliberalism became the key doctrine of Europeanisation, constituting itself as a no-alternative policy framework. What emerged then was an ongoing de-democratisation, in which "democracy is tamed by markets instead of markets by democracy" (Streeck, 2014: 130). Streeck argues that the continuation of this process results in a Hayekian sort of social dictatorship, in which capitalist markets are protected by "democratic" interventions. The development of the common Euro currency across the EU signified a substantial decline in productivity for the EU's peripheral states that joined the European Monetary Union (EMU). History showed that the periphery could neither compete nor protect itself from the competition launched in accelerated pace by the core Eurozone countries (Varoufakis, 2017).

The 2007–2008 economic crisis intensified competition and fortified the financial markets' political power. Being the Eurozone's weakest links due to their heavy debt loads, the peripheral Eurozone countries would now have to perpetually increase their competitiveness to match the Eurozone core countries' standards, primarily in order not to undermine the financial market's trust in the Euro as a stable and resilient currency, something that could lead to the Euro's devaluation. Therefore, the Euro was deemed to function as a neoliberal apparatus to "reform" the economies of its member states according to the interests of the core Eurozone members. Streeck (2016: 180) states, "the donor nations behave as imperialists, interfering in the internal affairs of others and undermining their democracies". Simultaneously, Germany arose as "the de facto governor of the European Monetary Union (EMU)" (Streeck, 2016: 131), due to the structure of the Euro currency itself. Indeed:

> Germany, with its strong export-oriented specialist manufacturing and high corporate profits, is the powerhouse of the EU. Political dominance within the EU is assured not just by its economic prowess, but by the decline of French, Spanish and Italian economic power, as well as the isolationist path pursued by British Conservatives, which ultimately led to Brexit. The German perception that it foots the bills and assumes the burdens of leadership is true, to a certain extent. Yet to take this a step further, and claim Germany is a benevolent force within the EU, is to enter the distorted world of the ordoliberals.
> FEKETE, 2016: 8

There is a prevailing moralisation of the EU in the mainstream that stresses a benign dimension in the various policies that attempted the "integration" of the EU's poorer regions. This integration was done through the influx of EU-based funds into Greece and other countries in the periphery of the EU, in exchange for reforms that would achieve integration. Such policies have been presented in paternalistic terms as a form of aid that was abused by an irresponsible party, a case that supposedly proves the particularistic character of the crisis:

> Within this typical idealist line of thinking, capitalism did not rely on the antagonistic logic of continuous profitability (amid ever-decreasing rates of profit), but would rather be universally beneficial. Material progress was, at the very end, ignited by enlightened acts of dominant parties and relied on the further upholding of relations of mutual goodwill and trust on behalf of the dominated. In this sense, the construction of EU funds in terms of European aid addressed a liberal idealist epistemology, both as its result and as an argument for its validity.
> GKINTIDIS, 2018: 147

For Samir Amin (2014: 98), it is clear that the funds allocated to the EU's periphery by the centre, were principally directed towards the development of specific types of infrastructure that would allow the deeper penetration of monopolies, thus augmenting "the tendency to unequal development through a greater opening of the economies involved". Moreover, the construction of the Euro itself is connected to the ordoliberal principles that place the protection of the "market freedom" as their key objective (Streeck, 2016: 161). This objective comes at the expense of political strategies to protect national economies, as well as national institutions concerned with social and labour laws and rights. The increasing political power of the EMU meant that the EU's main focus of policymaking is the effective governance of national economies' finances, so as to be compatible with supranational fiscal policies (Streeck, 2016: 113). In that sense, the Euro currency emerged in relation to what Streeck (2016: 69) has described as the rise of the "debt state" and later the consolidation, or austerity state, which succeeded the "tax state" (also: Roos, 2019: 65). To this end, common fiscal policies for all EMU member states are now established, emphasising the importance of maintaining a state deficit below 3% and a public debt that does not exceed the 60% of the national GDP (Streeck, 2016: 130). The ECB and the European Commission (EC) safeguard the EMU's monetary policy and protect the "single market" from distortions that could be caused by the member states' nonalignment with the EU's decisions.

The Eurozone was designed in order to integrate the different national capitalisms existing in the EU under a common ordoliberal framework. This framework, however, was connected to the interests of the EU's core capitalist states, creating serious problems for the peripheral ones and threatening the existence of the EU itself (Fekete, 2016: 9). Streeck (2016: 173) argues that Southern Europe produced a kind of capitalism that was driven by domestic demand and occasionally supported by inflation, while the North European economies were export based and hostile to inflation and debt. The common currency abolished the possibility of devaluation, and the common economic policy penalized inflation, thus weakening the politico-economic position of the South. The crisis intensified the power of the core capitalist states in the ways that define the character and the function of the Eurozone, since they provided the major part of the so-called bailout loans to the South (Lapavitsas, 2012: xiii). The Euro is thus not just a currency. Instead, it is a policy instrument, benefiting the core capitalist states of Europe, and a cultural feature, since it also seems to formulate a central feature of the European identity.

The solutions proposed to alleviate the Greek and the Eurozone crisis were connected to reforms that stressed the radical slashing of public expenses connected to welfare. At the same time, cuts were introduced through a continuous increase in taxation that weighed particularly heavily on the lower and the middle incomes. Indefinite austerity regimes (Streeck, 2016: 136; Varoufakis, 2017), became the cannon and the only solution out of the crisis and were invested with moralistic appeals for individual and national redemption and salvation. The leading political forces of the EU, in their "liberal", "conservative" or "social democratic" variants, developed an apolitical public explanation for the crisis, which was further used to legitimise the policy-making decisions that followed regarding austerity reforms.

As the analysis will show in the coming chapters, an aggressive narrative stressing the ordinary Greek people's supposed moral and cultural deficiencies and liabilities was publicly launched by the European bourgeois establishment, pundits and mainstream media across the globe and was particularly harsh during the first years of the crisis. While emphasising the Greek people's cultural and moral shortcomings, the specific narrative also pursued a consensus for the necessity of instigating cuts in welfare and wages, pursuing privatisations of public property and tax "reliefs" for capital and introducing new taxes and increasing those that primarily affected the lower incomes. Austerity served as the condition for loaning strategies to Greece and other Eurozone countries that were most exposed to the crisis. These loans were to support these countries' national debt and prevent them from declaring bankruptcy, something that would have a serious impact on the Euro currency's ratings. Default would jeopardise the debt revenues for the banks that owned the debt of these countries (Roos, 2019: 261). Furthermore, economic collapse would also curb capital accumulation and the restructuring strategies through privatisations and the development of "market-friendly" policies to invest in lands with compromised labour, social and environmental protectionist legislation, quarantined by austerity. Austerity in that sense, meant a broader "destructive creation" process (Büscher & Fletcher, 2017) that resulted – like anywhere else where austerity "reforms" were implemented – in pauperisation, mass unemployment, depression, death, the loss of future prospects for the new generations and an unprecedented political crisis. Simultaneously, the economic recession continued to deepen and the debt to grow, despite draconian austerity. What is also important to note here is that the massive "emergency", or even "solidarity" loans – as they were euphemistically called by the EU's political establishment – given to countries like Greece only meant the transformation of a debt owed to private banks into a debt owed to other countries. This way, austerity could gain support from citizenries outside of the countries in crisis, since austerity would supposedly guarantee the national taxpayers' money.

The political economist Mark Blyth (2013) argues that austerity appeared as an objective logic taken out of (neoliberal) economy manuals. As a policy framework, austerity is generally associated with a reductionist approach to society and the world, where the economy marks the centre of all human affairs. With this perspective, the knowledge of the rules guiding the individual parts of the system – the micro-economical scale – is enough to allow their effective application to master the external reality, perceived and manipulated in economic terms. Likewise, according to neoliberal thinking, austerity is to mobilise national economies and individuals in more competitive directions. Competition, in neoliberal terms, is crucial for capital growth and also is a determining feature of human nature. Under such simplistic notions of individual and social living, the (capitalist) economy also becomes naturalised, as it supposedly comes out of "natural instincts". To be sure, contrary to neoliberal mantras, social reality is far more complicated. David Harvey (2014: xi) emphasises the politico-economic interests connected to austerity. In this sense, crisis and austerity are prone to generate optimal terms for capitalist reproduction and accumulation. Debt, in this context, is crucial in a political sense, because, if unchallenged, it imposes the creditors' will. The accumulation of Greece's debt, along with austerity, opens up the possibilities of what Harvey, drawing on Marx's idea of primitive (or primary) accumulation, named as "accumulation through dispossession".

2.6 Debt, Austerity and Primary Accumulation

Even though debt is integral to capitalism and connected to financial investment possibilities, national (as well as private) debt took on a burgeoning form during the advent of neoliberalism. The possibility of issuing and loaning cheap credit without restrictions, made national debt expand at unprecedented levels across the world. As discussed in the previous section, in the beginning of the crisis in the 1970s, states attempted to make two ends meet: on the one hand, to respond to capital's demands for less taxation and more "freedom" at the expense of labour demands and, on the other hand, to maintain their welfare structures (Streeck, 2016: 116). Harvey (2010: 31) brings to attention the equivalent rise of private indebtment in the post-1970s crisis era and argues that the partial economic recovery after the 1970s had to do with the substitution of wage losses with consumer loans, connected to the augmentation of private debt as well, in line with the national debt. National debt offered the pretext to suppress wages and successfully proletarianise the working force of a given state, particularly at capitalism's periphery. In the following years, private debt was to be rhetorically used to blame citizens for the national debt as well (Basu, 2018: 146).

From the late 20th century onwards, the burgeoning debt of nation-states was served through loans provided by financial organisations such as the IMF. Such loans were accompanied by policies of economic restructuring, which effectively opened new regimes of capitalist accumulation into the indebted lands. Relevant data demonstrate that all countries are nowadays indebted (Roos, 2019: 3). This debt accumulation has occurred due to a significant loss of taxation, following the neoliberal doctrines of trade "liberalisation". Schäfer and Streeck (2013: 4) stress the possibility of a permanent state of austerity in indebted countries in order to compensate for the losses caused by the reduction of taxation for the wealthier. As they explain:

> Permanent austerity [...] results when the ability to generate revenues is limited while at the same time spending needs to increase. In the 1990s, three causes came together that were not present in the decades immediately following the Second World War: diminished growth rates, the maturation of welfare states and an aging population.
> SCHÄFER and STREECK, 2013: 1

The loss of taxation revenues gave way to the rise of national indebtment, which later served as a tool of the public (and private) dispropriation through successive austerity waves. Streeck (2016: 120) argues that these developments caused to what he describes as the "debt" state, which was later transformed into the consolidation state, a case that characterises the EU's current policy framework. In the neoliberal era, in which financial activity is unconstrained by welfare regulations, debt is not a problem for capital; the main challenge is the ability of states (and other indebted agents) to serve the debt. When the debt is too large, then states have difficulties persuading the banks to provide them with credit under low interest rates.

Streeck's (2016: 122) "consolidation state" describes the transformation of a state's priorities. Under the consolidation era, one of the state's prime focus is the creation and the sustaining of confidence towards the given nation-state by international financial institutions, such as financial rating agencies and international banks. A primary goal is to attract financial investment. Investments are supposed to produce growth and sustain market confidence so that a given state is not threatened by insolvency. Insolvency is a main risk factor for the global financial system. Therefore, all political interventions are designed to avoid this possibility. The debt is thus placed under a political form of control that is organised under the seemingly "neutral" guidance of "experts", notably, neoliberal technocrats. This makes the debt into a device for political restructuring and capital accumulation, as the centrality that the serving of debt plays in fiscal policies secures financial activities (Vasudevan, 2009: 291) and the expected revenues.

With regards to the Greek crisis, it became increasingly more difficult to continue borrowing credit after the end of 2009, when the Greek public debt was estimated to be higher than expected; "the accumulation of debt by the countries of the periphery eventually led to a major sovereign debt crisis in late 2009, starting with Greek public debt. Escalating public deficits and manipulation of statistical data in Greece led to downgrades by ratings agencies, rising spreads and eventually loss of access to financial markets by the Greek state" (Lapavitsas et al., 2012: 99). Until the late 2009, the high credibility ratings of the Euro currency allowed the Greek state to effectively borrow at low interest, as the financial markets generally thought that no EMU state could go bankrupt (Lapavitsas et al., 2012: 91).

In his own account of the Greek crisis, Costas Douzinas (2013: 23) talks about a desire of debt, by "the elites" in Greece and elsewhere:

> as deficit, public and private debt grew, the political and economic elites turned a blind eye and continued drawing cheap loans. The evidence is not hard to find. Excessive borrowing and debt increased after entry to the Euro [...] The spiraling loans and mounting debt were used by the ruling elites to oil the wheels of state patronage and party clientelism. In an unprecedented first, the incoming government challenged the statistics of their outgoing predecessors twice and had the deficit and debt revised upwards. In 2004, the New Democracy government claimed that its Pasok [the "Panhellenic Social Movement" Party] predecessor had lied. The Papandreou government repeated the tactic in 2010, claiming that New Democracy too had lied. It upgraded the deficit to 15.4% triggering the European intervention. To cap it all, every set of measures adopted increased the debt.

Marx (1990: 919) associated national indebtment with the process he described as primary or primitive accumulation. Primary accumulation is the process of expropriation that is necessary to organise the norms and social relations required for the establishment of the capitalist mode of production. Primary accumulation separates the producer from possessing his/her end product, and divides the populace from its means of survival through the imposition of artificial scarcities. This workforce then relies solely on its labour capacity and its possibility to compete with others pushed into the labour market so as to obtain the means of survival. In effect, this is a process of proletarianisation, something that historically all "modern" countries went through, by massive grabbing of common lands and by the general passing of state laws in favour of the bourgeois class.

> This era of primitive accumulation gave rise not only to the "accumulation of capital" and the "accumulation of men" (Foucault, 1977: 221), but also a new world-praxis: Cheap Nature. This praxis was one of accumulating and organizing not only human bodies, but of assigning their value through the Humanity/Nature binary. That so many humans could be reassigned to the domain of the non-human (or not-quite-human) allowed capitals and empires to treat them cheaply – even as this cheapening was fiercely resisted.
> MOORE, 2017: 600

De Angelis (2004) among others (Davis, 2007; Harvey, 2010) show that primary accumulation is a continuous process, which is necessary so that capitalism will reproduce its social relations of production. This occurs through the violent imposture of new sets of enclosures of what was previously thought to be common, not commodified, and existing outside the market framework. This is the way for the market to enlarge and for capital to constantly develop, while constituting the work force by "liberating" it from any alternatives of reproducing itself outside the waged labour context. In particular

> characteristic cases of new enclosures are: human trafficking and gendered oppression, informational accumulation, land-grabbing and land dispossession, Structural Adjustment Programs of the International Monetary Fund (IMF) and World Bank (WB) in Latin America, Africa and recently in Europe, wars for raw materials, the debt crisis, environmental pollution and climate change, the fall of the Eastern bloc and the decline of the postwar welfare state of Western European countries.
> TSAVDAROGLOU et al., 2017: 5–6

In the Greek case, public debt has been deployed as a vehicle for the neoliberal restructuring of society. The Troika's structural adjustment reforms there "tend to restructure surplus value extraction by changing capital-labour relations and access to nature, accelerating the commodification of natural resources, while also transferring assets that were previously under communal or state control to foreign and domestic private capital, via both privatization and concessions" (Konstantinidis & Vlachou, 2016b: 1).

In debt-ridden Greece, primary accumulation takes various forms. The explosion of unemployment to unprecedented levels (about 20% of the total workforce) and the rapid impoverishment of broad segments of the population mark the most standard cases of proletarianisation. Capitalists can take advantage of such material conditions to deploy cheap labour and intervene in policymaking as "job creators" to demand an effective lifting of labour rights and welfare.

The process of primary accumulation can be viewed in the context of privatisations of public property in order to finance the debt (Hadjimichalis, 2011). For instance, the German state-owned companies of Deutsche Telekom bought the majority of shares of Greece's former National Telecommunications Organisation (OTE) and Cosmote, the country's largest mobile network operator; the Chinese Cosco bought two out of three platforms in Piraeus' port, which is the biggest port of the Balkan Peninsula; Fraport, another German state-owned company that is based in Frankfurt, bought fourteen airports across Greece, with plans to expand to other peripheral airports in the country, too. State-owned Italian Railways bought the Greek Railways (OSE). There have been constant pressures to privatise major public water companies in Athens and in Thessaloniki (EYATH [EYAΘ] and OYTH [OYΘ]). Furthermore, different funds have been interested in expropriating indebted households and further opening the real estate market in Greece; this includes the mass buy-outs of apartments across Greece to convert them into Airbnb facilities, a case which increases the value of housing while seriously affecting the urban fabric and socio-cultural character of towns and cities and converting them into tourist resorts (Dalakoglou & Poulimenakos, 2018). To this end, various funds have bought private mortgage loans owed to banks by ordinary civilians and then pursued legal reforms to allow the eviction of the indebted inhabitants from their homes. Such legal reforms have already occurred, but to a certain degree, they are not fully implemented due to the resistance of civilians against evictions.

Primitive accumulation examples also include the process of land grabbing for minerals and precious metals extraction, such as the case of the Skouries forest in Chalkidiki, a region of Northern Greece, which was subjugated by the Canadian-based, multinational mining company named "El Dorado Gold". Under the so-called "Fast Track" law (3894/2010) aiming at advancing strategic investments in the crisis context of Greece – following the mainstream explanation of Greece's recession that is attributed to a cumbersome regulatory framework (Konstantinidis & Vlachou, 2016b) – the company was allowed to operate in the region despite the detrimental effects to the natural environment. The company harmed the ancient forests of the region and the underwater reserves of the area and the surrounding coastline, which undermined the quality of life and the local economy of the communities living in the specific region and threatened the health of the people living in the neighbouring areas (Figure 2). Fast Track laws seriously compromise environmental and public health protection laws, while also circumventing protests so as to not

FIGURE 2   "Extraction brings illness and death" – Social Dispensary of Thessaloniki. Posters against the Canadian "Eldorado Gold" mining activities at Chalkidiki
SOURCE: PHOTO BY AUTHOR, THESSALONIKI, APRIL 2018

disturb business activities. As Konstantinidis & Vlachou, 2016b: 3) write, the Fast Track policy framework introduced by the Greek government "explicitly socialize the costs of private investment by providing significant support to private investors".

As far as the case of "El Dorado Gold" is concerned and its use of the fast-track legislation, the process described as extractivism by critical geographers, concerns intense, export-based mining activities. Kallis (2013: xx) sees extractivism as the key denominator commendably describing the transformation of Greece by austerity, where

> A regression from a developed to an extractivist state [occurs], similar to the process many Latin American countries underwent in the 1980s. [...] extractivism is a state whose sole function is to provide the global economy with cheap raw materials, often at the cost of its own people and its own development.
> TSAVDAROGLOU et al., 2017: 11

Other similar cases concern the process described as "green grabbing", where land and resources are appropriated under a Green capitalist ideological and policy-making imperative that advances "new accumulation avenues for capitalist expansion" (Siamanta, 2017: 260). Examples of this process concern the developing "Green energy" production regimes through the proliferation of photovoltaic and wind energy projects in common and private lands across Greece.

Lastly, the process of primitive accumulation also includes the sustained and increasing migrant flow from Greece to Europe's capitalist centre. In a detailed study, Labrianidis and Pratsinakis (2017) show that migration has been a constant characteristic of modern Greece throughout the 20th century and following the Second World War in particular, due to Greece's peripheral character. Since 2010, there has been an increase in the number of Greeks migrating. These authors estimate the total number of Greeks migrating to the West and North from 2010–2015 to range between 240,000 and 300,000 out of a total population of about eleven million (Labrianidis and Pratsinakis, 2017: 94). This number includes a large percentage of the country's most educated workforce (the so-called brain drain phenomenon), for people who received their education and training in Greece by Greek public and private funds and then used them to work in countries that can offer work positions that fulfil their qualifications (and to offer them a middle-class living standard), without the host countries having spent anything for the production of this qualified workforce.

Essentially, the structural adjustment reforms imposed in Greece by the Troika are processes of primitive accumulation, because they indebt the Greek middle and working class through cuts in jobs, wages, welfare and pensions, through the addition of various forms of taxation, property tax in particular, and the increase of prices, or through the introduction of more precarious forms of labour (Lapavitsas, 2012: 180; Roos, 2019: 271). The backbone of the Greek economy (Lapavitsas, 2012: 224), consisting of small and medium-sized private businesses run by a relatively independent middle class, has been seriously damaged by austerity, because it caused the closing of thousands of small business across the country from 2010 onward (Figure 3), with this gap in

FIGURE 3 Small businesses closed during the crisis years
SOURCE: PHOTO BY THE AUTHOR, CENTRAL THESSALONIKI, APRIL 2018

the marketplace usually filled by transnational oligopolies that can hardly be competed with.

2.7 Concluding Remarks: Understanding Capitalism as Religion

The chapter developed a synthesis of different theoretical concepts from critical political economy studies, to analyse the nature of the Greek crisis. The Greek crisis is a symptom of a global capitalist crisis and its magnitude concerns Greece's position as the Eurozone's weaker link. To that respect, the center-periphery theoretical framework is crucial to understand the Greek crisis, and the Greek specificities accordingly. The center-periphery analysis of the global capitalist system can adequately explain Greece's internal structural problems (such corruption, or, the existence of a shadow economy), which relate to the inability of the periphery to effectively compete with the center, the periphery's dependency upon the center, which effectively imposes its interests and meanings on the periphery. Furthermore, the broader, global institutional structure of neoliberalism, and the power of finance are central to understand Greece's indebtment and the country's inability to default its debt. Roos (2019: 75) explains that factors such as the contemporary states' dependency on credit, the political unity and concentration of the creditors, the possibility of the creditors to control credit flows and to provide credit conditionally, along with the alignment and support of local elites to the creditors, are central enforcing mechanisms of debt repayment. The sustaining of ideological hegemony and public legitimacy over crisis and austerity policies is important to this end. Simultaneously, debt is a mechanism of accumulation through dispossession, in an era where capital profits are low and perpetual and even compound growth is unattainable. The economic crisis' politics serve to advance processes of "creative destruction", or, to put it in a more critical sense, the destructive creation (Büscher & Fletcher, 2017: 659) necessary for capitalism in crisis to reinvent its process of accumulation. Critics understand neoliberalism as an upper-class hegemony restoration process (Dumenil & Levy, 2013: 7), or as a project of redistribution from the bottom to the top (Harvey, 2005: 12). In his own analysis of neoliberalism, Harvey (2005: 162) sketches four interrelated neoliberal strategies that include a) vast privatisation and commodification processes, b) the extended financialisation of the economy, c) the deployment of an economic crisis to develop political institutions that can further empower corporate power at the expense of labour power and welfare, and d) the public securing (through bail-out operations funded by state budgets) of major businesses when at risk of insolvency. The Greek crisis and the policies followed in response to it, entail all of these processes of expropriation that Harvey described.

In addition, the disregarding of the historical context and of the facts underlining the Greek context points towards not just the realpolitik dimension of the crisis politics to secure imperial interests; it also points towards the religious dimension of capitalism itself. In one of his lesser-known texts, Walter Benjamin argued that capitalism is a "cultic religion, without mercy or truce, leading humanity to the 'house of despair'" (Löwy, 2009: 60; also, Routhier & Bolt, 2015). Benjamin departs from Weber's thesis on the influence of the Protestant work ethic for the rise of capitalism to state that capitalism itself takes over the Christian faith and, from a parasite of Christianity, it becomes the religion itself. The cultic dimension of capitalism derives from its utilitarian practices (e.g. investment, speculation, selling and buying and stock exchange manipulations). Although not transcendental in essence, such practices also refer to objects of adoration, such as money and other commodities, and anything besides them has no meaning or value. Capitalism has its own moral codes and value system. It offers no possibility of redemption and salvation in life since the promise of happiness is to be forever deferred by the imperatives of continuous work, possessions and saving. The general idea of debt creates a permanent sense of duty and guilt. In that sense, the poor are guilty of failing to work enough and to save, and the rich need to attend to their possessions since it is their moral responsibility towards God himself, to whom the capitalist is only a devoted administrator (Löwy, 2009: 65). Indeed, the analysis later deployed will demonstrate how such religious beliefs are reflected in the Greek crisis mainstream thesis.

CHAPTER 3

The "Greek Crisis" in the Media: Hegemony, Spectacle and Propaganda

> I met this German guy that I know (in the US). I asked him what he thought of the Greek crisis; he said that it is their fault because they were very corrupt, did not reform in time and thus accumulated problems for too long that eventually burst; and now we (the Germans) have to pay for this. At that point, I asked him where he was getting his information from. Usually, people get defensive when they are asked this question. So he did, and said "from the Economist"; then I told him "aha, well that makes sense".
>
> PETER BEATTIE, 03/04/2017; conversation with the author

∴

3.1 Media Aspects

This chapter presents an account of the political role of the media. The discussion of media and politics begins with the notion of the public sphere and its critical conceptualisation as a field colonised by the strategic economic interests and ideological premises of capital and the upper classes (Dean, 2002, 2009, 2017; Negt & Kluge, 2016). In this regard, the concepts of hegemony and propaganda are important for making sense of the ways that the media work as strategic apparatuses and institutions to forge ahead the dominant interests through mass communication practices. While hegemony is achieved and maintained through the regular reproduction of dominant world-views and ways of thinking about various issues (such as what comes to pass as normal or "natural") on a daily basis, propaganda can be understood as a central method to strategically advance particular positions in the public sphere at critical moments, such as times of war or an economic crisis. As an important space of experience, the public sphere offers the pretext where hegemonic interventions unfold through the media in globalised, late capitalist societies. Simultaneously, the dimension of the spectacle is to be found in all aspects of mainstream media production and political communication today. The spectacle is part of the broader phantasmagorical experience of the world in the highly commodified social context of capitalist modernity. The phenomenon of phantasmagoria concerns the appearance of reality through technical manipulation that "floods" and simultaneously numbs the senses (Buck-Morss, 1992: 22). Walter Benjamin was one of the first scholars that tried to trace the rise of phantasmagorical forms in the modern public realm. Phantasmagorias have an "anaesthetic" effect as they direct the senses and attention to specific cognitive frames that are relevant to commodity culture at the expense of other social contexts (e.g. civic and political ones) that may generate different meanings and experiences (Buck-Morss, 1992: 25). Such a process occurs on a mass scale, and for this reason, the phenomenon may assume objective characteristics. As this chapter will demonstrate, the spectacle may both anesthetise and activate, according to the ideological leanings and strategic premises of the media content production process.

3.2 Political Communication and the Public Sphere

The media are key institutions for the conduct of politics. In particular, the media – as "bearers of political communication beyond face-to-face settings" (Dahlgren, 2009: 2) – are crucial in the dissemination and reproduction of prevailing ideas for people to make sense of the world. Likewise, the media may also potentially enable the destabilisation of dominant social meanings. In this regard, media scholarship has placed great emphasis on the democratic potential of digital media in particular, for developing, sustaining and deepening democratic culture (Carpentier, 2011: 17). In principle, this process may occur through the increase of participatory and inclusive media forms and structures, with content and practices that enhance civic values and identities, informing and educating, fostering dialogue and participation, engaging people in common affairs and triggering interest, reasons, and passions in socio-political issues.

The role of the media as a facilitator of the public sphere is connected to the seminal work of Jurgen Habermas (1992). Habermas studied the ways that modernity, and the changes it brought with the rise of new political institutions, new modes of economic production, and new social relations and identities, among others, allowed the development of a distinct societal sphere located between the state and the market that could enable civil society to become informed about common affairs and to debate and to reflect upon societal issues (McGuigan, 1996). The rise of the public sphere opened the possibility for civil society to form informed publics able to address questions that could make political authority accountable for its decisions and policies. In a historical sense, the emergence of the public sphere enabled the bourgeois class to challenge feudal power politically.

Publicity, in particular, has been a crucial component in such a democratising process. Publicity can create transparency, which in turn can enable critique, leading to the challenging and potential constraining of political power. Habermas saw in the public sphere the potential in "the unfinished project of modernity" to advance the universal democratisation of society (Calhoun, 1996: 40). The political position of Habermas is a liberal progressive one, abstaining from questions that concern the radical transformation of society and the abolishing of capitalism. This is due to what he saw as the flawed historical experience of socialist movements in struggles for radical and revolutionary social change. Furthermore, it also concerns the advanced complexity of contemporary (late) modern societies, making their change a highly complicated task (Stolze, 2000: 149). In a normative sense, the Habermasian idea of the public sphere is characterised by transparency and communicative rationality (as opposed to instrumental rationality that is connected to strategic communication and commercial logics), which are meant to foster an empowered citizen's engagement with common affairs. Communicative rationality may allow the possibility of dialogue by enabling the development of mutual understandings and the possible reaching of consensus between agents holding different opinions and agendas. In this way, a democratic culture can (in theory) progress.

Habermas' conceptualisation of the public sphere has been criticised by various scholars (Fraser, 1996; Fuchs, 2017: 220). The moderate and realist theoretical endeavour of Habermas has been seen to be restricted in the confines of the nation state, liberalism and capitalism (Stolze, 2000). Critics have emphasised issues of class, gender, ethnicity and race as under-theorised in Habermas' notion of the public sphere. As a bourgeois institution, the public sphere has been a socially exclusive space where only those who hold economic and cultural capital could enter. The access to information itself – distributed and deliberated in the public sphere – is to a great extent determined by the unequal material conditions characterising industrial societies (Golding, 2017: 4307). Political theorists like Chantal Mouffe (2000) have criticised Habermas' emphasis on reason and communicative rationality, with regards to the restrictions they pose towards expression and debate. Mouffe stressed the importance of passions in politics, something undermined in Habermas' account as potentially dangerous for politics (Dahlgren, 2013: 21; Sindorf, 2013). Enzo Traverso (2016), too, noted that political action is grounded both in strategic planning and reason and in passions (such as indignation, sadness, melancholy, anger), which provide the foundations of engagement and praxis.

In a comprehensive work, the German Marxist scholars Negt and Kluge (2916: 11) critically approached the public sphere in capitalist society as a bourgeois institution (something that Habermas himself has also acknowledged). In its dominant and mainstream form, the public sphere is an apparatus for the legitimation of the bourgeois society's structure, divisions and hierarchy. In bourgeois society, the public sphere is a broad but divided entity, located in the realms of the mass media systems, the lifeworld, and the various sociopolitical institutions (e.g. the parliament, the military, the education system), which, despite their differences, tend to run parallel, overdetermined by the organised interests located in the field of economic production. Maintaining that the public sphere is an indispensable realm for the overall human experience, its bourgeois character sustains the advantageous politico-economic and social positions. Thus, although acknowledging the socialisation opportunities offered and the possibilities for developing shared norms and meanings, Negt and Kluge see the actual public sphere to be overdetermined by the capitalist mode of production and the norms and values of the bourgeois society and democracy. This overdetermination has detrimental and alienating effects on the consciousness and the self-experience of the working class in particular. The bourgeois public sphere either incorporates or effectively excludes voices, social relations, identities and subjectivities that are located externally – or are opposed – to the capitalist reproduction processes (Negt and Kluge, 2016: 14). Simultaneously, the divisions between the different spheres of life and practice in bourgeois society (e.g. between politics and economy, the private and the public, education and entertainment, among others), make the expression and meaningful organisation of the general proletarian experience in critical terms a very difficult task. Its success is connected to the degree of the development of class struggle overall (Negt & Kluge, 2016: 94).

Bourgeois society tends to downplay and negate the realities of inequality, exploitation and exclusion while naturalising the established social hierarchies, the capitalist mode of production and its divisions. Even though the public sphere is potentially a space of reflection, knowledge and deliberation, its bourgeois character plays its own part in the social reproduction of not only upper-class interests, but also the culture, the values, the aspirations and the lifestyles of the bourgeois. In a thorough reading of Walter Benjamin's *Arcades Project*, Susan Buck-Morss (1991) notes that bourgeois culture encourages mass myths that sustain and reproduce capitalist modernity while diverting the utopic potentials of modernity and transforming them into commodity fetishes. Through this process, it suppresses people's creativity, their spontaneity, their potential to play and experiment, beginning in childhood. In this way, the potential for appropriating and developing meaning in more autonomous terms that reflect more authentic contexts of subjective experience is also negated. Instead, bourgeois culture leads to people "parroting back the correct answer, looking without touching, solving problems in the head, sitting passively, and learning to do without optical cues" (Buck-Morss, 1991: 265).

In a critical assessment of the public sphere idea in the context of late (or communicative) capitalism and the prevalence of commercial media, Jodi Dean (2009: 23) argues that in today's digital media framework

> The expanded and intensified communicativity neither enhances opportunities for linking together political struggles nor enlivens radical democratic practices-although it has exacerbated left fragmentation, amplified the voices of right-wing extremists, and delivered ever more eyeballs to corporate advertisers. Instead of leading to more equitable distributions of wealth and influence, instead of enabling the emergence of a richer variety in modes of living and practices of freedom, the deluge of screens and spectacles coincides with extreme corporatization, financialization, and privatization across the globe.

In Dean's (2002) account, the idea of the public sphere seems to be largely outdated in today's fragmented social contexts, dominated by digital media networks. The condition of individualisation that characterises capitalism corrodes the sense of community, its uniting bonds and the shared understanding of decisive common interests. Individualisation prevents the emergence of a common normative belief system, a common system of meanings, and even a common vocabulary, for individuals to be able to debate and communicate with each other in a constructive way. As Habermas also acknowledges, the corporate character of the media and its emphasis on entertaining content undermines the possibility of developing an interest in politics and the advance of critical forms of consciousness. Instead of the development of a democratic public sphere, the media create a commercially driven publicity that reproduces the "fantasy of a unified field of deliberative processes" (Dean, 2017: 198). This makes the public sphere itself to be more of an ideological construction (Dean, 2002: 42).

Consequently, the public is currently a fragmented entity, consisting of groups and individuals that, as far as the West in particular is concerned, inhabit a society that is supposedly democratic, and yet it is dominated by social relations that reproduce and naturalise capitalism, and institutions that delegitimise critique and political praxis. This fragmentation is intensified in the digital media environment and their market-driven goals. Communication, knowledge and information are mediated by market-driven ideas and fantasies as well as by structures of expertise, which cannot be challenged by rational dialogue alone: "the law of publicity doesn't transform the public-supposed-to-believe into the public-supposed-to-know. Instead, it affirms the split within the public, giving some the certainty of knowledge necessary for judgment while positing others who believe in them" (Dean, 2002: 19).

3.3 Understanding Hegemony

The polity of today's liberal, representative democratic states is based on civic consensus. According to the liberal philosophy, civic consensus itself is founded on an informed public that can be called to legitimise processes of policymaking, developed by the political representatives voted into government by the citizens of a given state. It is the dominant class, however, that poses the issues deemed as important for a given society (Ellul, 2011). Liberal-capitalist societies are deeply unequal societies. Nevertheless, they present themselves through their institutions as homogeneous ones. Dominant societal groups create and maintain power through a) the use and threat of violence against those challenging their interests and b) the creation of legitimacy for their preferred social relations and arrangements that establish and maintain their dominant position. We can also add here the achieving of hegemony through the structural power of finance and the effective control and subjugation of a state through its economy in the global capitalist market (Roos, 2019: 10). While all these practices are at play, the soft power of legitimacy-building through consensus-making in the public sphere has more enduring effects (Carah & Louw, 2015: 22).

In this regard, the concept of ideology is useful for interpreting how people concede to such an unequal and unjust form of social order. Ideology addresses the dimensions exceeding the realities of material coercion, imposed by unequal power relations and structures, as well as by artificial scarcities produced by capitalist accumulation. Ideology is concerned with the rationalisation of such processes as logical, normal, necessary and even natural. The concept of ideology advanced here is not a one-dimensional one, used to distinguish the alienated from the non-alienated beliefs and identities. Instead, the idea of ideology is more complex and overwhelming (Vincent, 2010). Other than a limited system that implies a biased way of thinking outside the realm of the normal, ideology is a key term referring to the various belief systems that people have, allowing them to develop their ways of understanding the world and reality and to structure their identity. "Ideology functions by offering symbolic resources to make social reality functional and possible" for people identifying with it (Carah and Louw, 2015: 25). "The 'raw materials' of ideology are meaning systems, social imaginaries and lived experience" (Sum & Jessop, 2013: 479).

Ideology is also not a singular entity; many (and conflicting) ideologies exist in a given society, all partially defined by socio-cultural and historical specificities. Ideologies "are not any kind of socially shared beliefs, such as socio-cultural knowledge or social attitudes, but more fundamental and axiomatic. They control and organize other socially shared beliefs" (Van Dijk, 2006: 116). Societies are founded on specific shared cultural traits such as values, ideas and identities that are naturalised over time and seldom questioned. Ideologies are collective, axiomatic (or fundamental, according to Van Dijk) belief systems organising broader forms of existing knowledge and belief systems.

The notion of hegemony, then, is crucial for understanding how specific ideologies and meanings become more plausible than others and are accepted as common sense by society (Carah & Louw, 2015: 16). Hegemony is the process of naturalising specific ways of understanding the world and social affairs. Hegemonic interventions produce the shared meanings and symbolic features that a given society generally identifies with and accepts as real and normal. "Hegemony is the capacity of dominant groups to establish and maintain political, intellectual and moral leadership, and secure the 'broad-based consent' of allied and subordinate groups to prevailing relations of economic and political domination" (Sum & Jessop, 2013: 201). In the sense developed by the Italian Marxist Antonio Gramsci, hegemony is both a discursive and a material process, connected to reputable societal structures and hierarchies. For instance, Gramsci's analysis showed "how hegemony in American Fordism was deeply rooted in the factory, the labour market and the reordering of domestic life, as well as in a broader array of social practices and institutions" (Sum & Jessop, 2013: 79). Established societal institutions such as the media and the education system play an important role in creating and in sustaining hegemony. Remaining on the symbolic and mass communicated dimension of a hegemonic intervention, we can conclude that professional communicators (e.g. politicians, journalists, pundits) build and withstand the hegemony of specific social groups and organised interests by a) naturalising and rationalising "the leadership, ideas and moral codes of powerful groups", b) constructing alliances and compromises among various societal groups and c) enacting symbolic forms of violence and implying threats of violence (Carah & Louw, 2015: 23).

3.3.1   The "Greek Crisis" in the Media: A Critical Overview

Critical media studies (Fairclough & Fairclough, 2012; Pleios, 2013; Mercille, 2013; Doudaki, 2015; Jacobsson, 2016; Vossole, 2016; Arrese & Vara-Miguel, 2016; Chun, 2017; Harjuniemi, 2018; Basu, 2018) have found that the mainstream media coverage of the global economic crisis (in the EU, the US and elsewhere) relied on elite understandings of the crisis and downplayed more complex explanations that would cast light on the systemic dimensions of the phenomenon. For instance, in his study of various mainstream newspapers across the EU concerning the ways that the Eurozone/Greek crisis was covered during its early years (2010–2011), Papathanassopoulos noted that the crisis was covered through a narrow, economic frame without addressing the global and systemic substance of the crisis. In a recently published study on the matter, Laura Basu (2018: 2) argues that, in general, the economic crisis' media coverage was characterised by (a) a lack of historical explanations, (b) the privileging of elite views and (c) a lack of global perspectives.

The account of Varoufakis (2017) about his attempt during the first half of 2015 to negotiate with his Eurozone "partners", to abolish austerity and to regain Greece's sovereignty is rather indicative of the ways that the media's overall position on the Greek crisis. By ridiculing Varoufakis and alienating his message from the European citizenry so that even the fairly moderate, Keynesian and Europeanist positions like those that he represented would appear as extreme, the media ensured that austerity would remain the only available option.

The media generally adopted a Eurozone-centered approach (Michailidou, 2017), emphasizing the problems that Greece causes to it and the threats to the Eurozone stability that Greece represents. Nikolopoulou and Cantera (2016: 4) point that

> factors such as the financial aid that was given to the private banking institutions, that is, the socialization of the losses they suffered due to their private management choices, were never conceptualized as a cause of the "debt crisis", although the country had to borrow money for their recapitalization; instead, they were represented as necessary and natural moves, directed at saving the country itself.

Consequently

> Merkel's prevalence in the Eurozone crisis media coverage suggests that the German Government has been at least partly successful in spreading its message and building public legitimation for austerity across the Eurozone.
> OJALA & HARJUNIEMI, 2016: 416

Jacobsson (2016b) and others (Graham & Silke, 2017) view such phenomena to be part of a broader tendency of today's media to depoliticise politics. This process occurs through a journalistic emphasis that places more attention on business and market perspectives than on civil society and class ones, which are downplayed and usually excluded from publicity (Jacobsson & Ekström, 2016). Thus, the talk about competition, efficiency, privatisations and economic growth, along with the reproduction of market-related views and objectives, appear in the media as topics of general agreement and concern. Chakravartty and Shiller (2010: 675) note the increasing importance that economic journalism and financial reporting began to obtain towards the end of the 20th century. Such media focus corresponds to broader structural changes that the media underwent due to deregulation and marketisation. In this context, economists emerged as highly credible public intellectuals (Chun, 2017).

As stated before, cultural stereotypes were widely used by the media to explain the Eurozone crisis (Ervedosa, 2017). The crisis received a highly sensualistic depiction in the European public spheres, providing a narrow, apolitical, nationalist and conformist discursive framework for citizens to understand the crisis (Kouki, 2014; Gintidis, 2016; Aitaki, 2017; Basu, 2017). This framework included the shaming of people, countries and cultures that were portrayed as the crisis' perpetrators, along with narratives of guilt and resentment (Stavrakakis, 2013; Sommer, 2014; Bozatzis, 2016; Free & Scully, 2016; Gumpert, 2017). The Southerners and Greece, in particular, were at the forefront of such media attacks and were blamed for causing an unprecedented crisis.

Cultural stereotypes were advanced by the German government and the German media in particular, but, as earlier explained, their roots lay in broader colonial legacies of the West and the way it sees and produces the periphery. Therefore, the crisis was made to look as if it were caused by the coercive, corrupt, reckless behaviours and cunning deeds of specific people, deemed as radically different from the normal West/modern/secular canon. Such a rationale was publicly launched in spectacular terms, deploying popular, exotic stereotypes of people and localities. To be sure, the strategic interests of core Eurozone countries had an important role to play in the proliferation of such stereotypes and their instrumental usage to divert the public discussion from any critical understanding of the crisis. Furthermore, the cultural-moralistic dimension of the crisis explanations is crucial for the advance of neoliberal reforms, targeting the "minds and souls" of individuals.

A small and rather peripheral country, Greece had – until 2010 – been receiving little coverage by international media. Exceptions to this case were spectacles that gathered the wide attention of international audiences like the 2004 Olympic Games, which took place in Greece and were celebrated as "returning to home" (sic). In such cases, Greek-related issues received a lot of – mostly positive – media attention. The eruption of the Eurozone crisis in early

2010 put Greece again at the forefront of the global media's attention, creating negative publicity for the country and its people (Papathanassopoulos, 2015: 107). In both cases (in 2004 and in 2010), common stereotypes about Greece, related to antique history and touristic folklore, predominated. Nevertheless, in 2004, these stereotypes of Greece had a positive slant, whereas from 2010 onwards, they obtained a highly negative one.

In his study of the crisis' virus-metaphors, Matthew Gumpert (2017: 31) talked about the development of specific Greek-oriented metaphors that he describes as "Hellenotropes", which "constitute important weapons or antidotes for conceptualizing and, by the same token, quarantining Greece as a form of economic, political and cultural ruin metastasizing within the European body politic". The medical language of the crisis bared important political effects (Maesse, 2018). On the one hand, the extensive use of virus metaphors implied an expert-driven approach to the crisis, as an issue that ordinary citizens could not understand and resolve. On the other hand, the virus metaphors reified the countries in crisis and their people as contaminated ones that required urgent treatment.

The discursive construction of the "Greek crisis" was based on falsehoods, half-truths, and misconceptions. In fact, the Greek crisis pseudo-knowledge, with its culturalist myths and "gut feelings", emotions and Orientalist/racial stereotypes, can be seen as a "post-truth" construction. A post-truth communicational approach is becoming crucial in today's public legitimation practices of neoliberalism, as neoliberal rationales become increasingly more unconvincing to the general public (Brevini, 2017). To use the words of a German critic:

> It is much easier to justify the massive seizure of everything Greek citizens may have gained during the three decades of democracy if they feel that they are morally responsible for the national debt of Greece as a whole. The public discourse has thus created various narratives that put the blame for the debt crisis on the side of the ordinary citizen. Tax evasion and profligacy are some of the stigmas that have been routinely used to make the Greek working and middle-classes responsible for the crisis. This diagnosis serves the cure. It forces those who have supposedly abused the goodwill of "democratic integration" to accept the adjustment programs deemed necessary to reestablish "credibility" and "honor".
>
> PFEIFER, 2016

The countries and peoples deemed as the crisis' perpetrators were effectively silenced by the crisis' publicity. Shaming practices intimidate and bully (Derber & Magrass, 2016) those that they target. Bullying blocks subjectivity and reduces one's confidence and ability to articulate and voice his/her position. Instead, when successful, bullying creates an introverted and melancholic state of being, seeking scapegoats and targeting those situated in an even weaker position. Shaming and the kind of resentment it brings to the shamed ones are noted to block the process of mourning that a trauma (such a as that caused by a crisis event) generates (Voutyras and Glynos, 2016). This process of blocked mourning through shaming and the subsequent feeling of resentment it causes, bears ideological functions, as it does not allow the crisis' trauma to be resolved through the development of critical public narratives. The "self-bashing" practice that developed in Greece during the first years of the crisis, in particular, may be indicative of what Voutyras and Glynos referred to as "blocked mourning". Here, the hegemonic crisis narratives were to a great extent internalised and domesticated, producing a self-blaming and a self-Orientalising narrative among many Greeks. This process further fuelled a vicious publicity within Greece that targeted specific ethnic, vocational and political groups and identities, such as migrants, civil servants and leftists, who were disparaged by mainstream media and politicians (Glynos & Voutyras, 2016: 121). By framing and constantly reproducing the Eurozone crisis as an unprecedented and somehow vital threat to European societies, mainstream media repeatedly manifested the "necessity" of austerity. By attributing the crisis to cultural and moral issues, connected to problematic or unmodern people and cultures, a mode of public discipline was advanced towards the kind of solutions coined by the dominant social groups.

Despite its destructive effects, neoliberal austerity has been the dominant policy followed across Europe during the Eurozone crisis (Dymski, 2013). As a policy without an alternative, neoliberal austerity gained broad consensus even among the working class and the poor, despite the fact that they were the ones who bore the negative effects of austerity policies (Bramall, 2013; Nikolopoulou & Cantera, 2016). This way, neoliberal austerity assumed a commonsense character (Pentaraki, 2018: 2). Ojala & Harjuniemi (2016) argue that the Eurozone crisis presented a good chance for the public legitimation of neoliberal austerity worldwide. This process occurred through the mass media's regular coverage of the crisis through the lens of the EU, along with the promotion of key pro-austerity politicians like Angela Merkel, as Europe's moral leadership (Ojala & Harjuniemi, 2016: 416). In effect, the pro-austerity media coverage achieved the hegemony of Germany's dominant class interests by establishing the policies and rationales that Merkel's government pursued.

3.3.2 *Hegemony, Propaganda and Biopolitics*

A fairly distressing, Orwellian, "newspeak" language, apparent in the hegemonic public reasoning over the Greek/Eurozone crisis and the policies addressing it (austerity), has been widely deployed by experts and the media (Tracy, 2012: 515). Austerity has been generally represented as a "painful", but just and vital "solution" for Greece's "recovery". Likewise, the loans provided to the Greek government to continue serving its debt – while blocking Greece's possibility of default (Roos, 2019: 29) – were presented as "helpful" and as acts of solidarity (Badiou, 2012). It cannot be stressed enough that austerity and the EU's crisis management augmented Greece's public debt, increased Greece's unemployment, and seriously undermined Greece's economy, democratic polity and social bonds. The loans provided by the Troika through the public funds of the Eurozone state members only transformed Greece's debt from one that was owed to private banks to one owed to states. The Troika's loans thus saved the big European and US banks, and not Greece. The loans only sunk Greece deeper into debt and dependency. The absurd and misleading framing of austerity as something noble and essential not only confuses citizens, but also produces enmity and spite, since the loans given to recapitalise banks were provided by state budgets in times of insecurity and constraint.

Although often appearing as a somewhat "dated" concept, the idea of propaganda is still relevant to understand the ways in which politics work through hegemonic interventions to achieve societal support and consensus, particularly during critical historical moments. Hegemonic interventions advance through more organic processes, situated in daily contexts and developed through seemingly calm and reasonable communicative practices. Nevertheless, the success of hegemony is based on different propagandistic communicative practices that may vary in context and circumstance. Essentially, propaganda consists of an array of practices for the development of hegemonic interventions. Often, propaganda relates to more intense and issue-focused practices of mass communication. Propaganda forms may also appear as rather polarising, or, depended on context, as a process that is supposedly unifying, through exclusions rather than through confrontations. In that sense, more "direct" forms of propaganda can materialise in times of uncertainty during ruptures of hegemony when hegemony is threatened and social tensions escalate.

Propaganda is thus usually connected with exceptional events, like different crises and conflicts. Moreover, propaganda is frequently understood as an exceptional strategy related to "totalitarian", or non-democratic regimes, which appear as the opposite of liberal democracies and their pluralistic systems that are founded on the idea of the freedom of speech. As already discussed, critics have detected an autocratic turn of liberal capitalist democracies, especially in their fundamentalist defence of the so-called free market system (Dean, 2009: 49; McChesney, 2009: 285). In this context, scholars have also addressed the propaganda practices of corporations and dominant politico-economic forces in capitalist democracies. Here, propaganda is inscribed in the development of a hegemonic communicational strategy, in which the dominant ideology is carved in forms of common-sense knowledge and reproduced in formal and informal everyday practices:

> Democracy is risky for capitalists, because voters are, theoretically, consulted about future planning. Capitalist propaganda is thus an effort to convince voters and governments that economic planning is best left to experts, who know how markets operate and how to make profits for everyone's benefit. In "Taking the Risk out of Democracy", Australian scholar Alex Carey says that corporate propaganda took a remarkably consistent approach to celebrate capitalism and condemning socialism [...] (In particular, the highly influential) US corporate propaganda constructs a stark dichotomy, where capitalism is identified with efficiency, freedom, opportunity, and patriotism, while communism is inefficient, controlling, demoralizing and subversive.
> SOULES, 2015: 179

The analytical categories developed by Herman and Chomsky (1988: 2) to identify propaganda in the news media concern questions of both ideology and structure in media production. These categories include (a) the size, concentrated ownership, owner wealth and profit orientation of the specific media, (b) the reliance on advertisements as primary source of income, (c) the media reliance on political, business and other experts connected to sources of power, (d) the development of slandering tactics and flak to discredit adversaries and (e) the advance of anti-communist discourse. These interrelated categories to classify particular media practices as propagandistic are evident in the mainstream news constructions of the Greek crisis and they also are apparent in all media studied in this book.

In effect, propaganda is part of the work of the daily mass media, with the hegemonic frames of mind to constantly reproduce and affirm themselves through an effective politico-economic control of informational and educational institutions (like the media). One can make a distinction between soft and hard modes of propaganda, which are all part of the broader technologies of developing and sustaining hegemony in the course of time. Ellul (1973) explained that propaganda often works more effectively when it appears smoothly, by using soft language and an entertaining and light media content, with the "message" or the "ideology" appearing in a generalised form. In this way, ideology is concealed under the pretext of what passes as normal or natural. Furthermore, educated people, such as the Northern European middle classes, are prone to being persuaded by modern media (and the kind of propaganda strategies described by Ellul), because of their belief in "facts" and the confidence they have in their supposed ability in recognising truth from lies (Soules, 2015: 33).

What is most important for contemporary propaganda according to Ellul is the cultivation of a mythical belief. A mythical belief is connected to a broad set of dispositions and practices that often exist in sedimented forms. Propaganda mobilises them by articulating them in specific discursive constructions during given circumstances. In the Greek crisis setting, consumer culture myths were mobilised to stereotype the Greek people as responsible for their crisis. Such myths are associated with ideas cultivated by tourism and popular culture, and also through enduring Occidentalist topics. Various Greek crisis "facts" were arbitrarily put together and constantly iterated by mainstream media. These facts were meant to produce the Greek crisis as an exceptional and self-inflicted case. According to Jonathan Potter (2011: 112), "fact construction is a process attempting to reify descriptions as solid and literal". The clinging to the manifested facts suggesting a Greek exceptionality during the Greek crisis sustained the rather narcissistic myths of the rational, informed, secular and democratic publics of the Western liberal states. In turn, such knowledge regimes legitimise (along with the power of the creditor) the middle class' sense of entitlement (Skeggs, 2003) to a symbolic "Greek-bashing", while mobilising public demand for the implementation of austerity in Greece.

A shocking case was made with regards to Greece's potential bankruptcy that created widespread anxiety. Experts expressed high concerns and worries over the future of the Euro and Europe's economy. As Chapter 6 will show, the crisis was constructed in eschatological terms, as a coming Armageddon that required exigent action. These arguments were amplified by the media. Various official voices and discourses discussed austerity as something urgently needed. This message was blended with the various Greek crisis tropes and stereotypes about Greece to make the case for austerity more plausible and practical:

> Greek bankruptcy: fear for our money! Are the bankrupt Greeks tearing down all of Europe? Greek government bonds are regarded as trash from yesterday.
> *Bild*, 27/04/2010

> Crisis summit; is Greece a bottomless pit? Wolfgang Schäuble sees Europe's financial stability at risk by the bankruptcy of Greece. Merkel even warns against a world-wide crisis.
> *Bild*, 28/04/2010

Likewise, the massive anti-austerity demonstrations of 2011 in Greece, during the time of the "Indignant citizens' movement", were largely represented across the world in negative terms:

> Greek protestors clueless in Athens: One of the most bizarre aspects of the Greek mess is how completely out of touch with reality the Greeks protesting the reductions in government spending are. They simply do not have a choice. [...] The strikes and protests themselves only increase the need for cuts because they weaken the economy and reduce tax revenues. The Greek union strikes are therefore as stupid as expressing dissatisfaction with the fact that you freeze by reducing heating further or taking off your shirt.
> *Uriaposten*, 2011a

As reproduced by a Danish far-right website (Askanius & Mylonas, 2015: 63), the anti-austerity demonstrations are viewed in bewilderment by observers that assume the position of the informed Westerner, abiding by the hegemonic crisis narrative, in which austerity cuts are the only available option. As public activities with high symbolic meaning, the demonstrations and protests are nullified and their counter-hegemonic messages blocked. Instead, the specific framing of the protests intensifies cultural dichotomies, with the anti-austerity demonstrations to verify the discursive construction of a failed and infantilised people, who are part of a "Greek mess" and who do not follow "common sense".

In another example of how the crisis' hegemonic positions were reproduced by experts, politicians and the media, and then were diffused into the Greek public sphere, Dominique Strauss Kahn, the IMF representative for Troika in Greece, gave the following reasons in support of Greece's entry into what became a prolonged and indefinite period of austerity during a joint statement with the Greek Prime Minister, the "socialist" George A. Papandreou:

> So I understand that there may be demonstrations against IMF, people saying the very well-known "IMF go home". I won't say I'm happy with that. But really you are better off with us here than with us home. And the sooner we will be able to go home, the sooner you will be able to fly alone, the better it is. The only hope of the IMF is to have its membership – in this case, one of our members, Greece – to overcome the different problems the country is facing. So don't fight against the doctor. Sometimes the doctor gives you medicine you don't like, but even if you don't like the medicine the doctor is there to try to help you. And I think that we both are on the good track.
> Prime Minister Press Office, 2010

Strauss Kahn presented an expert-based construction (coming from the supposedly neutral and technical IMF) of the economic crisis as an urgent threat. His claims were legitimised through medical references (the doctor, the patient and the medicine), which in principle produced an undebatable scientific authority (Maesse, 2018: 14). In this way, the iron neoliberal certainties of what the crisis and its threats are and what the remedy should be were explained and legitimised through the rhetorical authority of medical metaphors, in which the IMF appeared as a doctor and Greece as a patient. A rigid – yet dogmatic – image of the crisis was publicly launched for pursuing the establishment of austerity regimes in Greece, manifested through a language of urgency and underlined by eschatological narratives of "national salvation" and technocratic reason.

At the time, the mainstream media of Greece responded to claims such as Strauss Kahn's above, in the following way:

> If resorting to the support mechanism involving the IMF is bad, there is even worse: not to seek refuge there, as many irresponsibly argue for. [...] The whole mythology of the Greek left is based upon the diabolic capitalism, whose priests are international organizations such as the World Bank and the IMF. [...] The IMF is neither destruction nor blessing. For some countries, it is necessary. For Greece, it is a supplement to the financial assistance of the EU, an assistance mechanism introduced so that the Germans would feel better. [...] For 35 years we have moved forward tied to unreflected aphorisms. Now that these aphorisms brought us to the brink of bankruptcy, we need to change. Most of all, we need to start thinking.
>
> "Excommunications and the IMF" by Paschos Mandravelis, *Kathimerini*, 24/04/2010

On an intertextual level (Fairclough, 2003: 17), one can notice the way that the hegemonic ideology of the crisis is "domesticated" and its main arguments stressed by the local pundits and circulated in the Greek public sphere by an established liberal-conservative newspaper, *Kathimerini*. The article's author reproduces the key themes mentioned by the IMF's representatives: that the IMF is necessary for Greece and that it is a mere technical institution aiming to assist a country, while political debate and resistance to it are futile. In line with Herman and Chomsky's (1988) analysis of propaganda, anti-leftism emerges as a key crisis explanation, where the left appears as the one producing the crisis, despite the fact that Greece was always part of the Western geopolitical and economic framework. Simultaneously, the corporate structure of the Greek mass media, belonging to vast oligopolistic conglomerates and their commercial essence, makes them prone to propagandistic functions, in Chomsky and Herman's sense. Reports from investigative journalists suggested that during the crisis' initial phase, the Troika lobbied the mass media of Greece in order to influence the Greek public with positive coverage of austerity (*info-war.gr*, 2015). Roos (2019: 252) also mentions that from 2010, "local elites began to use their connection to the political class and their control over the media to champion the need for austerity, market liberalisation and privatisation of state assets".

Kathimerini's representation of the IMF as an impartial, technocratic institution was also done through the publication of articles by former IMF personnel, such as a Greek woman named Miranda Xafa, who served as a member of the IMF's executive board from 2004 until 2009. In one of her 2010 articles entitled "Austerity, debt and the IMF" (*Kathimerini* (25/4/2010), Xafa (who in 2018 is a fellow of the "Center for International Governance Innovation", a "think tank on global governance", and a "finance consultant" based in Athens) presented the IMF as a chance for Greece to "gain time" so as to "return to the financial markets" with its "irrationalities" resolved, and having developed a rather "open" and competitive economy. Such supposedly informed articles function in an affirmative way to the pro-austerity agenda. Simultaneously, by reproducing the IMF's agenda in merely technical terms, they conceal the IMF's highly political role in securing debt repayment and in opening new markets, which in most cases result in the periphery's underdevelopment and its social, political and environmental degradation (Amin, 2014: 115). In fact, the crisis management conducted by the IMF in its various interventions across the globe "amounted to the greatest transfer of assets from domestic to foreign owners in the past fifty years" (Dörre, Lessenich & Rosa, 2015: 52). Nevertheless, in a 22 April 2010 article entitled "The demonisation of the Fund", *Kathimerini's* US-based columnist Athanasios Ellis dismissed all public concerns against the IMF as "prejudiced", attributing it to Greece's "uninformed" public.[1]

From the late July 2017, one sees the iteration of the no-alternative to austerity dogma of neoliberalism, reproduced by the leader of Greece's (and to a large extent, the EU's) main counter-hegemonic political current, Alexis Tsipras, head of the left-wing Syriza party and Greek PM, who was voted in January 2015 to form government in Greece, under an anti-austerity agenda:

---

[1] Either way, the certainties, predictions and policy doctrines of the IMF were proven to be stunning failures in Greece, something also admitted by the IMF itself (Elliot, 2016), which in every case has left a deep mark of misery, death and destruction in all the countries in which it has intervened to implement its so-called "structural adjustment reforms" (Pentaraki, 2018; Matza, 2018).

> A compromise was the only option, says Tsipras, likening the measures that came with it to a ghastly medicine endured when life is at stake. "You hold your nose, you take it [...] You know that there is no other way [...] because you have tried everything else to survive, to stay alive". Despite the firestorm of criticism he now endures, non-Greek observers say the once-firebrand leader has also shown courage in implementing policies he evidently loathes. Tsipras has managed to persuade many of those in his own party opposed to austerity to swallow the bitter pill that has kept Greece in the family of nations it has long identified with.
>
> *The Guardian*, 24/07/2017

In that sense, one can see how the crisis and austerity propaganda advanced, sustaining the hegemony of the liberal-capitalist West and North and its financial, economic and social policies. The political stabilisation of austerity meant its effective hegemonisation across society, with the gradual use of its political logics even by its adversaries (Roos, 2019: 280). Despite strategic defeats, such as the one represented by Syriza's counter-hegemonic effort and its eventual caving into the Troika's demands for austerity, hegemony is not permanent or absolute (Carpentier, 2011: 142). In addition, regardless of the media's power to set the agenda and to legitimise hegemonic discourses, the general public may also develop more critical understandings questioning the media content offered to them and the elitist meanings inscribed in it. In that sense, while I do not imply that the crisis' media discourses are fully accepted by the public, I uphold that the hegemonic crisis-constructions are generally shared particularly by the vast majorities of German and other Northern European peoples.

Propaganda aims to mobilising citizens. In our case, it means encouraging their participation in the policing of the austerity reforms' implementation. On a further level, this mobilisation also focuses on the citizens' identification with the individualised requirements of neoliberalism, regarding the making of mobile, competitive and flexible individuals living in increasingly precarious conditions. Hence, the biopolitical dimension of austerity is advanced through the mainstream media's propagandistic content, which spreads the hegemonic narratives confirming the preferred socio-political relations and identities of late capitalism. This process is specifically linked with the neoliberal transformations of the welfare state (Dörre, Lessenich & Rosa, 2015). To this end, the activation and "responsibilisation" of citizens is an important task of policies reforming welfare. The increasing economisation of virtually all aspects of social life has been accompanied by what Dörre, Lessenich and Rosa (2015: 130) described as the "subjectification of the social". Here, welfare is transformed from a public into a privatised entity and a private matter of individuals that are to be responsible for themselves and for the community as a whole. Responsibility is also primarily translated into economic terms. Individuals are to act pre-emptively and responsibly (Dardot & Laval, 2013: 166). Connected to a broader, neoliberal austere political logic (Bal & Dóci, 2018: 4) valorising competitiveness and entrepreneurship, "irresponsible" (which here means not being active) personal conduct is imagined as "immoral" and as an indication of insufficiency and failure. Such "politics" concern the kind of politics advanced by neoliberalism, which relate to the "politics of the self" placed within an economically defined social terrain. Following the earlier depiction of class hegemony in Chapter 1, the values of the upper-middle class emerge as constitutive of this hegemonic political logic.

The "activated self" appears after political interventions and the development of public knowledge regimes that presuppose and sustain the specific narrative. These constitute the areas of social activity that one should be active (e.g. the economic), and those that one should not be active (e.g. the political):

> The political governance of the active society represents an act of, as it were, governing in the realm of possibility: the primary objective is not to actually make the subject be active at all times and in all places, but rather to make them think of and develop knowledge of themselves as potentially active.
> DÖRRE, LESSENICH & ROSA, 2015: 133

Hegemonic knowledge regimes lie in the development of the form of consciousness that will mobilise individuals to participate in the specific transformation of society into a "self-activated" realm, reflexively controlled by the state and also by the individualised subjects themselves, according to economic imperatives. These knowledge regimes are reproduced and redistributed in the public realm through uncountable ways, amplified through the media's omnipresence.

3.4 Spectacular Dimensions of the "Greek Crisis"

> During the past decades, the culture industries have multiplied media spectacles in novel spaces and sites, and spectacle itself is becoming one of the organizing principles of the economy, polity, society, and everyday life.
> KELLNER, 2003: 1

Intrinsic to the way that the media function today, the spectacle is connected to the increasing commodification and mediatisation of the world. The media's omnipresence creates what Abercrombie and Longhurst (1998: 68) call "diffused audiences", where "everyone becomes an audience all the time". For Abercrombie and Longhurst, "the world as commodity demands attention and performs" (1998: 82). Furthermore "the world and everything in it is increasingly treated as something to be attended to. [...] The world is constituted as an event, as a performance; the objects, the events and the people constituting it are made to perform for those watching or gazing" (1998: 78). Therefore, the spectacle produces reality in aestheticised ways that can be performed, represented, gazed, consumed, possessed and controlled (Abercrombie & Longhurst, 1998: 83). The spectacle develops identities and performances, which respond to preferred ways of understanding the world (Skeggs & Wood, 2012).

With phantasmagoria being intrinsic to the experience of modern life in the capitalist world, hegemonic strategies function through the utilisation of public spectacles, exploiting the spectacle's potential to indoctrinate mass audiences (Soules, 2015: 52). The spectacle intensifies hegemonic messages and diverts attention from counter-hegemonic narratives and cognitive frames. Nevertheless, "media spectacles can backfire and are subject to dialectical reversal as positive images give way to negative ones. Spectacles [...] are difficult to control and manage, and can be subject to different framings and interpretations" (Kellner, 2004: 336).

The concept of the spectacle developed as a critical idea to address consumerism and alienation in modern societies (Debord, 1985; Lefebvre, 2014: 198). Debord's analysis draws on Marx's work on commodity fetishism, as well as on Lukacs' concept of reification (Kaplan, 2012: 460). The integration of the working class' free time into the objectives of capitalist production and growth through the production of leisure commodities, such as those fashioned by the cultural industries and the experience economy, give to the spectacle an omnipresent position in social life. The all-pervading essence of the spectacle becomes entrenched in all social relations. The form of the spectacle is that of images, narratives and fantasies that become mass collective topoi of reference. Rather than an external entity, found in the media world, the spectacle is internalised through the proliferation of images and fantasies daily reproduced, to the point where any aspect of social life gets mediated by it. Anything, ranging from material commodities to spaces, people, cultures, intimate relations or historical events, can be transformed into a spectacle to be gazed, fetishised and performed by what Abercrombie & Longhurst (1998: 77) describe as diffused audiences. In this way, people build their identities, desires and social relations along the lines found in commodity culture.

The spectacularisation of the Greek crisis has been crucial in reaffirming the cultural Greek crisis' myths: according to these, the crisis was caused by the problematic culture of the Greeks and other Southern Europeans. The reproduction of the Eurozone/Greek crisis by the media is two-fold, with both dimensions being interconnected. Firstly, it is related to the construction of the Greek crisis as an unprecedented, emergency event. Such events

> Disrupt the ordinary and habitual flows of information and become popular stories which capture the attention of the media and the public, and circulate through broadcasting networks, the Internet, social networking, smartphones, and other new media and communication technologies. In a globally networked society, media spectacles proliferate instantaneously, become virtual and viral, and in some cases become tools of sociopolitical transformation, while other media spectacles become mere moments of media hype and tabloidized sensationalism.[2]
> KELLNER, 2016: 3

Secondly, the Greek crisis is caught in the more permanent and omnipresent dimension of the spectacle. This viewpoint reduces the Greek crisis into an already "known" banality, fabricated through the use of pre-existing Orientalist prejudices, which correspond to widely believed myths. The making of the "Greek crisis" into a banal, common-sense tautology comes from popular cultural

---

2 In his work, the media scholar Douglas Kellner deploys the concept of the spectacle to analyze the contemporary media culture and its political implications. Kellner's analysis of the US cultural industries brings forth the political economy of media production showing that "the cultural industries have multiplied media spectacles in novel spaces and sites and that the spectacle itself has become one of the organizing principles of the economy, polity, society and everyday life". This way, Kellner also perceives the US politics as fully spectacularized, with the US elections being highly spectacular processes performed by media experts (Kellner notes the case of Ronald Reagan who used his acting capabilities in all his public performances as the US president in the 1980's). So are many other events of political importance in the US, from the 9/11/2001 terrorist attacks, to the Occupy Wall Street movement in 2011, and of course the 2016 Trump electoral victory. With the advance of the internet and social media as well as personal information and communication technologies (ICTs), Kellner saw the multiplication of the spectacle and its resonant diffusion in the lifeworld.
   Among the media events analysed from the spectacle's point of view, Kellner (2005: 31) argues that the "war on terror" was constructed as a public spectacle through its regular appearance in different media genres like news bulletins, films, documentaries, books, and television series among others. Kellner (2005: 22) also notes the spectacular launching of the Euro currency through mass-mediated events celebrating it across the Eurozone member states during 2001–2002. The celebration of the Euro as a common currency did not address the political power of finance and the asymmetries involved in the making of a currency that was to be shared between the EU's core and peripheral countries. This way, the spectacle played the propagandistic role manufacturing public consensus for the creation of the EMU, undermining critical positions towards the Eurozone's architecture, eroding the potentials of developing a substantial public discussion of the matter.

spectacles, taken from the realms of mainstream cinema, reality television and tourism. For example, the exotic image of Greece and the Greeks that was produced during the 20th and the early 21st centuries by touristic spectacles, popular travelogues, and Orientalist films (e.g. the blockbuster "My Big Fat Greek Wedding" [Kosma, 2015]), can be as a "species and genus" topos (Wodak & Boukala, 2015: 94) in the Greek crisis mainstream culturalist discourse. Mass-media, like *Bild* – Europe's most widely sold newspaper – and *Focus*, both from Germany, expressed both aforementioned tendencies. Such news media amplified the German/EU establishment's "Greek-crisis" emergency discourse and simultaneously sustained a regular reporting of the matter, draped by popular cultural stereotypes of Greece.

The British *Channel Four's* 2011 weekly reality television show entitled "Go Greek for a Week" makes another interesting example of the Greek crisis' spectacle. There, the producers attempted to simulate the causes of the "Greek crisis" by following some personal stories to allow "British people and families to experience the patterns of tax evasion, corruption and mismanagement that have helped to sink the Greek economy" (Channel Four, 2011). It is important to know that reality media programs emerged after the media's deregulation policies during the dawn of neoliberalism and are connected to the general trend of media commercialisation. This involves the blending of media genres, the tabloidisation of journalism and the rise of infotaining and personalised modes of content production (Hill, 2005: 23). Therefore, such a "docu-soap" series aimed at establishing some sort of factual truth for its viewers through the cheap production of easy explanations that could trigger audience attention. Infotaining programs supposedly allow "viewers to see for themselves and potentially learn from experience" (Hill, 2005: 82). Nevertheless, this is a deeply flawed idea, as content and modes of learning are overdetermined by prevailing ideas, practices and narratives. Relevant research has also shown that the spectacle in reality TV genres is amplified through affectivity and shaming (Johanssen, 2017: 197). In their extensive study of reality TV shows in Britain, Skeggs and Wood (2012: 67) show that reality TV "underpins the normative stands of gender, race, and class as they are spectacularly performed. It enables us to see ourselves as part of a wider sociality, where other people are subject to similar 'proper performance standards'". In this sense, the biopolitical dimension of the spectacle emerges in such programs, since it is the neoliberal reflexive self who forms the vantage point to assess the misdoings of the Other, while (in the case of "Go Greek for a Week") educating the "British people and their families" on the neoliberal subjectivity proper.

After inquiring on the sources behind the show's rationales, *Channel Four* viewer inquiries section replied by email on 10 November 2011 as follows:

The three case studies used in this current affairs film, were based on what was common practice in Greece in recent years, and were used to translate, for the viewing public, the big picture behind the economic crises into real human experience by providing an insight into the country's tax, pensions and work practices which have contributed to the country's financial problems. As well as these case studies, commentary was garnered via expert interviews from a range of respected financial analysts; Faisal Islam (Economic Editor, Channel 4 News), economist Vicky Price (Former Head of Government Economic Service) and Platon Tinious (Dept. Statistic & Insurance University of Piraeus) who established the patterns of tax evasion, corruption and mismanagement.

The rationale of *Channel Four's* reality TV show on the Greek crisis was based upon the kind of knowledge on the case that was offered by mainstream economists. Therefore, the ideological hegemony of neoliberalism comes forth through the interdiscursive (Fairclough, 2003: 35) link that the economists establish with popular culture, which amplifies and exemplifies their views.

In another study, Fouseki and Dragouni (2017) use the concept of the spectacle to address the political function of the media representation of the Amphipolis archaeological excavation in Northern Greece during the Greek crisis years. In August 2014, this excavation received an unprecedented amount of attention in the Greek public sphere. Politicians, pundits and the mass media of the country elevated the discovery of an ancient tomb into a matter of national importance. As the authors of the article argue (along with Hamilakis, 2016), "the spectacularisation of [the] Amphipolis excavations constituted a powerful, political medium for disorientating the wider Greek public from issues related to the severe economic crisis of the country" (Fouseki & Dragouni, 2017: 1). The heritage spectacle that advanced during the Amphipolis excavation diverted the public's attention from the structural issues of the crisis and the grim realities and future prospects that the majority of the Greek population was faced with. Instead, a nationalist-oriented escapist vision was produced through the spectacular publicity of the excavation, which presumably promised the revelation of a true, glorious Greek identity, connected to the classical Greek one, to alleviate the identity trauma caused by the crisis and austerity. Simultaneously, the spectacle of the excavation offered the pragmatic potential for economic growth based on the prospects of the region's tourist development due to its unprecedented archaeological findings. Applying Kaplan's (2012) analytical categories on Debord's theory of the spectacle, the authors concluded that the Amphipolis spectacle a) created a banal fantasy about the importance and the prospects of the possible findings of the excavation site, b) presented the divided Greek society as a united whole under a supposed classless nationalistic perspective and c) symbolically eradicated from the public sphere the deepening inequalities developing from austerity politics.

Last, but not least, it is also important to see how the spectacle colonises presumably critical spaces as well, such as artistic and intellectual practices (Kompatsiaris, 2017b). For instance, it was decided that the 14th edition of the Kassel-based art exhibition "Documenta" would take place in both Athens and Kassel in 2017. Documenta 14 was funded by the City of Kassel, the State of Hessen, the German Federal Cultural Foundation and the Federal Foreign Office of Germany. The publicity of Documenta in Greece and abroad can be seen as an exercise of the soft power of Germany, and (re)affirming its strategic role as the supposed helper of Greece, while preying upon the Greek crisis' creative and cultural potential and exploiting Athens in crisis (Fokianaki & Varoufakis, 2017). Last but not least, German cultural institutions have also financed different films produced by Greek directors who have problems finding funds to pursue their work. Such films have reproduced the hegemonic crisis narrative, given that directors need to apply to the German sensibilities in order to get access to funding (Pfeifer, 2016).

3.5 Concluding Remarks: Interpellating and Disciplining the Working Class

This chapter approached the persistent glitches of media culture and politics, departing from a critical assessment of the concept of the public sphere, which is understood as a key space of human experience overdetermined by the dominant logics of capitalist society (Negt & Kluge, 2016). Specific critical concepts, such as hegemony, propaganda and the spectacle were also discussed to further explain the deeply ideological role of the media. The hegemonic economic crisis narratives are immersed in the dominant socio-political and ideological paradigm. This emerged in the early 1990s, after the collapse of the so-called "socialist" bloc by proclaiming an "end of history" thesis, which supposedly marked the end of politico-ideological struggles and the universal (and perennial) predominance of capitalism and liberal democracy. As Fredric Jameson (2016) argues while referring to Stuart Hall, one of the fundamental strategies at work in the victory of neoliberal capitalism concerns the delegitimation of the language of its adversaries in public spheres across the world, allowing the "free market" rhetoric to becoming omnipresent, qualifying the system it represents as "natural", "perennial" and even "actually existing" to the minds of the people. The media's anaesthetic effect (Buch-Morss, 1992) may thus be apparent here through the oblivion and the negation that the capitalist society advances against its rivals.

Hegemony is a process that creates consensus and normalises highly politicised realities (Phelan, 2014: 4). Propaganda is an intrinsic dimension of hegemonic communicative practices that can function in intense and explicit as well as in subtle ways. The Greek crisis coverage has been rather propagandistic (Doxiadis, 2016). It was particularly intensified during the crisis' most crucial moments when the imposition and stabilisation of austerity regimes were at stake. The purpose of this propaganda has been multifold. Certainly, it depoliticised capitalism and sustained the "free market" ideology, associating capitalist markets and capitalist activities with "nature" and "common-sense reason", a quite paradoxical association (to say the least) as it is seldom that nature and reason coincide.

The hegemonic interventions to normalise austerity have also had an important biopolitical aspect, which is best exemplified by the spectacularisation of the crisis through a variety of infotaining media programs (Couldry, 2010; Giroux, 2009). The disciplinary dimension of the spectacle in the Greek crisis context is two-fold (Johanssen, 2017: 206): while looking at the spectacularisation of the Greek crisis in the media, we can observe that, on one hand, the shamed "Greek scroungers" are called to accept the accusations made about them and to succumb to austerity regimes. On the other hand, the audience addressed by the media, which claim to speak on its behalf, is positioned as affirmative to hegemony and invited to further shame the Greek people by consuming the spectacle that the media made out of the Greek crisis, and by taking sides on the matter, since their own well-being is presented to be at stake due to the Greeks' supposed wrongdoings.

Activation, a key process of capitalist restructuring, as identified by Dörre, Lessenich and Rosa (2015) is central to the media representations of the Greek crisis. Activation has different forms. It aims to involve the Greek people in austerity reforms; activation also aims to mobilise the European public in effectively surveilling the Greek crisis and the reforms' processes, given that their wellbeing is propagated to be tied to the implementation of austerity regimes in Greece. As Dörre, Lessenich and Rosa note (2015: 236), in today's capitalism, the immobility of one group (in our case, the Greeks) is the precondition for the mobility of the other. Samir Amir (2014) writes that the neoliberal crisis pushes the working classes of the North to compete with those of the South, something that places great pressures on the former. In this sense, the hegemonic discourse of the crisis and austerity intensifies the norms of neoliberal society connected to competition, entrepreneurialism and risk-taking through the vilifying, blaming and shaming of the economic crisis' scapegoats.

Hegemony requires political agency and tries to form a public consensus. Biopolitics, though, relates to more faceless processes connected to the societal integration and diffusion of governing logics and their effective reproduction on individualised levels. Hegemony and governmentality relate to different theoretical traditions and a critical synthesis of both theoretical approaches may speak of a "subjectless hegemony" (Dörre, Lessenich & Rosa, 2015: 207) of neoliberalism coming into effect through discourses as well as through institutionalised norms and practices that engage individuals in specific modes of thinking and conduct.

CHAPTER 4

A Cultural Failure: Reification, Orientalism, Nationalism

In November 1943, I went out on the highway so as to find a car and come to Thessaloniki. And so, I got into a German truck. The driver was a sergeant and he needed company, so he took me on board. After some kilometers, we got into a village. He stopped in front of a yard full of people. He got off and started talking to them. They could not understand. He hit a man. I got off too and showed him that I spoke German. I told the villagers that he wanted a rooster to eat. The German got the rooster, tied his legs up, put him in the truck and we left. On the way, he started singing Opera and asked me if I knew the tune. I said no. Ah, he said, you Greeks are uncivilised. Later on, he started singing another one. He asked me again if I knew that one. I said that I didn't. You Greeks are uncivilised, retarded, he repeated. At that point, I could not hold it any longer and so I told him: we may not know much about opera, but we do not steal chicken. I got scared but I reckoned I'd tell him: we do not steal chicken, but you do. We carried on. He shut his mouth. When we reached a village outside Thessaloniki, he took the rooster, untied him and let him loose. I liked that.

APOSTOLOS VENETIS, Resistance fighter; in WEBER, 1996: 18

∙∙∙

Fass mich nicht an, du dreckiger Grieche, don't touch me, you filthy Greek.[1]

PETER RAMSAUER, German Transportations Minister, 2016

∙∙
∙

---

1 These words were uttered by the (nowadays former) German Transportations minister, Peter Ramsauer, to a Greek reporter, after an unintentional physical contact, on 30 June 2016, during an official visit to the Greek Prime Minister. More information on this incident can be found here: https://en.wikipedia.org/wiki/Peter_Ramsauer#Alleged_Racist_Attack (accessed 17/09/2018).

4.1 Introduction: (I)liberal Uses of Culture

In this chapter, I draw on the critical theories of race and racism, discussed in Chapter 1, that problematise the uses of the concept of culture today in the West. Culture is often deployed to explain issues like poverty and civic disempowerment as well as economic crisis, state bankruptcy and corruption, in a rather depoliticised way (Lentin & Titley, 2011: 61). Therefore, the uses of culture to explain systemic flaws only depoliticise social problems, diverting public attention from the structures of power and privilege that undeline such problems, while blaming those oppressed by the politico-economic system the most.

The analysis of the culturalisation of the Greek crisis in the media is primarily based on Ernesto Laclau's (1996; Laclau & Mouffe, 1985) discourse theory and its advances in the study of media texts (Carpentier & De Cleen, 2007; Carpentier, 2011; Schou, 2016; Mylonas, 2009, 2012b, 2014, 2018b). In particular, discourse theory is deployed to emphasise the crisis' hegemonic identity constructions depicting "us" (the Western/European self) and "them" (the Greek/Oriental Other). In that respect, an essentialist notion of identity and culture forms the vantage point of the hegemonic take on the crisis. Accordingly, the socio-political conflict emerging on the crisis and austerity is displaced and all counter-hegemonic arguments are invalidated. Nevertheless, the identity constructions deriving from culturalist allegations are utterly political. They rely on an effort to stabilise neoliberalism's hegemony, given that the crisis' dislocation effects bared serious repercussions in the social consensus over the naturalised, late capitalist, "post-historical" social order (Dahlberg, 2014: 259).

The inquiry that follows also deploys different analytical tools from CDA. These help to view how the media reproduce the hegemonic culturalist crisis and austerity notions and stakes in their respective public spheres. Relevant CDA concepts demonstrate how politics and class interests are effectively abstracted and displaced from the discussion, and become effectively neutralised into issues of culture. CDA also shows how culture becomes essentialised, objectified and naturalised as a legitimate explanation for the crisis and austerity in Greece. The key issues examined through CDA are precisely the ways that semantic abstraction occurs and the ways that semantic legitimacy is established. The analytical categories of nominalisations and the use of generalisations and stereotypes, along with the development of metaphorical schemes and the use of passive voice, allow the semantic disembedding of politics and class issues from the hegemonic crisis narrative. Culturalist explanations are then legitimised through the use of authoritative and common-sense topoi that warrant the claims made, developing a mythopoetic construction of the Greek crisis.

4.2 Hegemonic Constructions of the (Occidental) Self and the (Oriental) Other

The analysis of the media texts disclosed specific themes that are coded in the tables below. Table 2 demonstrates the ways that the German and the Danish media construct the identity of Greece in their culturalist constructions of the Greek crisis. Along with it, Table 2 also shows how these media's self-image (that of the Northern and Western Europe) emerges. Greece appears as Oriental and comprises all the negative features that affirm Europe's positivity and supremacy. The identity of the European Self thus appears through the making of its opposite, as situated in the Greek crisis context. Table 3 shows the ways that the Greek media construct the identity of a "European Greece", as opposed to the "Oriental Greece". Even though departing from the same hegemonic crisis' discourse, the German and Danish media advance a "Greek-bashing" representational mode, while the Greek media develop a "self-bashing" representational mode.

Tables 2 and 3 demonstrate what Laclau and Mouffe (1985: 144) describe as hegemonic logics of equivalence, or as "chains of equivalence", regarding the construction of a common (or equivalent) identity structure between different groups of people, while being opposed to a negative identity formation (Carpentier, 2017: 23). The notion of "chains of equivalence" is used analytically, to show how hegemony produces the "Greek crisis". This is something that primarily occurs through a language of exceptionality. Identity here emerges as an important analytical concept, because cultural explanations are central in the hegemonic framing of the Greek crisis. Furthermore, as Laclau and Mouffe (1985: 96) stress, the establishing of common meanings for people to identify with is a precondition for achieving hegemony in the social realm.

Discursive constructions (such as a given identity formation) are composed of specific semantic elements that are articulated as discursive moments organised in reference to central signifiers (e.g. "the Greeks"), the nodal points of a discourse (Laclau & Mouffe, 1985: 106). Laclau and Mouffe named these elements as floating signifiers, whose meaning (and their transformation into discursive moments) is contingent upon the process of discursive articulation. Discursive articulations are not always situated in an antagonistic political framework (Carpentier, 2017: 22). In moments of crisis where common-sense,

TABLE 2   Constructions of Europe and Greece in the German and the Danish liberal press

Europe	Greece
Modern, secular, integrated	Unmodern, traditional, fragmented
Democratic – vibrant civil society, transparency	Authoritarian, weak civil society, opaqueness
Foreword thinking, future orientated, progressive	Back-warded, segmented in the past, conservative
Industrious, entrepreneurial, innovative	Non-ambitious, reserved, stagnant
Paying taxes	Not paying taxes
Protestant, Catholic	Orthodox (Byzantine, Ottoman)
Cold	Warm
Western/Northern	Oriental/Eastern/Southern
Fast	Slow
Flexible	Bureaucratic
Productive	Unproductive
Functional	Dysfunctional
Active	Fatalistic
Honest	Corrupt
Rich	Poor/bankrupt
Fair	Unreliable
Generous – helping Greece	Sly –exploiting the EU
Hard-working	Idle
Mature	Infantile
Responsible	Irresponsible
Meritocratic	Nepotistic
Incarnating the true spirit of classical antiquity	Cannot live up to the ancient Greek legacy
Competitive	Non-competitive
Prudent, realist, cautious, living within its abilities	Careless, illusionary, extravagant, living above its abilities
Normal	Exotic/not-normal
Male	Female
Juvenile	Hoary/ Worn out
Cosmopolitan, open	Provincial, closed
Strong	Weak
Reflexive, confident	Complaining, blaming others
Deserving, entitled	Undeserving

Europe	Greece
Guided by Science/technocracy	Guided by Ideology
Mobile	Stagnant
Moral	Immoral
Professional	Amateur
Ordered	Chaotic, dangerous
Far-sighted	Short-sighted
Rightful	Erroneous
Dynamic, active, mobile, extrovert	Passive, inert, stagnant, unconfident

TABLE 3   Constructions of "European Greece" and "Oriental Greece" in the Greek liberal media

Codes denoting the European Greece	Codes denoting the Oriental Greece
Modernity, evolution, secularity, progress, future	Non-modern, backwards, traditional, past-orientated
West, Europe, European bourgeois history and culture, core (West/North) EU states	Orient/ Byzantine/ Ottoman habitus-culture, "Greek Sovietia", resembling "non-secular" societies (Islamic countries, Russia), "Third world" countries (African countries, Latin American countries led by Left-populist governments)
The EU institutions/The Eurocurrency	The 1974 polity change (Metapolitefsi) and the "ideological hegemony of the Left"
Common-sense, dialogical, education, openness, civility	Partisan, dogmatism, fundamentalism (political and religious), closure, lack of education
Digital technologies and the Internet/ information society	Sterile negativity, phobia towards novelty
Free market, globalization	Socialism, statism, "North Korea", "Cuba", "Venezuela"
Innovation, mobility, competition, entrepreneurship	Passivity, parasitism, dependency (on welfare, state funds...)

TABLE 3 Constructions of "European Greece" and "Oriental Greece" in the Greek liberal media (*cont.*)

Codes denoting the European Greece	Codes denoting the Oriental Greece
Civil society, expert driven governance, efficiency	Party system, dysfunctional institutions and laws, nepotism, clientalism
Success (in business, politics, academia…)	Failure (individuals, business, academia, politics/economy…)
Liberal cosmopolitanism	Provincialism, nationalism
The (productive) private sector	The ("unproductive") public sector, civil servants
One part of Greek society: affluent, successful, pro EU/ Euro/ "reforms"	Leftists, National currency supporters ("Drachmists", 'Drachma lobby", "underdog culture")
Meritocracy	Mediocracy
Technocracy/positivist science	Populism, ideology, "conspiracy theories"
Reign of law	Lawless state
"New" ideas, novelty, progress	Past, old, stagnation, decay
Affluence	Scarcity/poverty
Transparency	Cleptocracy/Nepotism, corruption
Democracy (the EU, the Troika, the structural adjustment reforms' program, EU governments and politicians, EU citizens)	Totalitarianism: anticapitalist Left, / Terrorism/Extremism (Syriza, Communist party, Anarchist groups, student leftist groups, labour unions, protestors, Occupy movement, Indignados, Golden Dawn)Religious power (Orthodox Church), Mob/Ochlocracy
Economically dynamic/ independent, middle/upper class, mature, honest, responsible citizens	Failed citizens: poor, uneducated, infantilized, corrupt, without ambitions, traditionalist, oppressive, unmannered, relying on welfare and on family support
Stability	Chaos
Enlightened	Unenlightened
Rational/correct	Irrational/erroneous
Reforming	Unreformable
True bourgeoisie, old-established bourgeois	Fake bourgeoisie, nouveau riche

Codes denoting the European Greece	Codes denoting the Oriental Greece
Normal	Not normal
Reasoning/calm	Fanatic
Unbiased, beyond Left/Right	Biased, totalitarian (Left and Right)
Business friendly, pro private sector	Anti-business, pro public sector

hegemonic patterns erupt and new, counter-hegemonic possibilities surface, signification and meaning-making form key loci of contestation.

Although the signifiers used by the media to denote and objectify the identity of the Greece are multiple, the positive terms that make up the identity of Europe are usually implied in the media. The identity of Europe is thus connected to an established Occidental/bourgeois hegemonic ideology, which is accepted as common sense. The identity of Greece is produced through various ideological myths that are recontextualised, coined and mobilised so as to suture the rupture that the crisis produced in the hegemonic order and its prevailing meanings, values and subject positions. As mentioned in Chapter 1, any sense of objectivity is political and discursive in Laclau's post-structuralist sense (Carpentier, 2011: 177), connected to an established social imaginary, founded by successful hegemonic interventions.

The struggle between different political logics, demands and identities in the Greek public realm intensified during the crisis years. Often, it took a directly antagonistic and even conflictual form. This way, the discursive constructions of "us" vs. "them" time and again take a rather dichotomous and confrontational mode. The Danish and German media function in a more stable politico-economic and social space, which is less affected by the crisis and where hegemony is less threatened by politico-economic contingencies and counter-hegemonic interventions. Hence, the encountering of Greece and the politico-economic threat it represents assumes a more confident (and patronising) rhetorical style in which the basic hegemonic themes are reproduced and sustained for the preferred audiences addressed, which presumably incarnate the specific "Europeanist" identity traits. In times when austerity is highly contested in Greece (during strikes, demonstrations, elections and a referendum), the liberal hegemony represented by the Northern and Western states is more threatened because the policies that it stands for (the neoliberal asterity regimes) are contested. On such occasions, we have a much more antagonistic hegemonic articulation, where more rigid and competing identity constructions emerge between "us" (as Westerners) and "them" (as Greeks). Both Tables 2 and 3 include class and political signifiers in the formation of the rival identities. These will be explained in Chapters 5 and 6. In fact, a language of culture, morality and politico-economic technocracy aims to overdetermine notions of class and politics. This constitutes an important dimension of the liberal hegemony's effort in naturalising its order by concealing the class and political interests that compose it.

The following sections proceed with a thematic analysis of the three main constructions of cultural explanations found in the media. These make the leading subthemes under the broader culturalisation of the crisis umbrella heme that this chapter unpacks. Textual examples are used and scrutinised through CDA tools. Social and cultural theory is also deployed to comment upon the specific themes and to disclose their deeply problematic sense.

4.3 Greece as a non/quasi-European Other

The articles from the German and the Danish media often describe Greece and its people in demeaning terms, as a pseudo-European, pre-European or para-European Other (Gumpert, 2017: 35). The construction of Greece as Western or Northern Europe's Other is done through the utilisation of common-sense Orientalist stereotypes against Greece and the periphery. These stereotypes are never questioned, but instead are deployed as affirmative logical topoi. On the antipode of that lies a stereotypical self-image of Europe, articulated in reference to neoliberal capitalist and Occidentalist signifiers. Thus, while "Greece" is immoral, profligate, corrupt and bankrupt, "Europe" is moral, austere, honest and affluent.

The Greek press follows a complimentary course affirming the hegemonic Orientalist framing of Greece. Unlike the German and Danish media that speak about a different country from their own, the liberal Greek media self-Orientalise their own country, while perceiving its population within a European vs. non-European conceptual framework. In this way, the Greek media produce an extra division through the same hegemonic culturalist frame.

This chapter's analysis will present three interconnected constructions of the Self and the Other: the first concerns the making of the culturalised Other, the second has to do with the commodified dimension of the Other and its uses, and the third concerns the nationalist making of the Self, which constitutes a benchmark for the Other in order to reform him/herself accordingly. The analysis will show how the Greek Other (as Europe's pariah) is produced through a culturalist explanation and framing, how s/he is produced through a fetishistic fantasy related to consumer culture and tourism especially, and how the (Western) Self is equally produced in this process. Political and class repercussions are hindered in the construction of Greece as Europe's Oriental Other; they will be elucidated in the following pages.

4.3.1 The Culturalisation of Greece and its Crisis
Post by Wagner, Poor Greeks

> When your ancestors did not know what to do anymore, they went to the oracle of Delphi to have their future foretold. At the entrance of the temple where the seer Pythia sat there were two inscriptions. I write them in Latin letters: "Gnothi seauton – know thyself" and "meden agan – nothing in excess". Your survival principle is the Fakelaki. Simply translated "fakelaki" means "little envelope". This envelope contains bribes. [This way] whoever wanted to issue a driving license in Athens put the envelope before the examiner. Patients gave the envelope to the chief physician before surgery. Everyone, from policemen, to customs officers, or, to administrative officers, was handed over the envelope. Greece is broke; you Greeks have gone broke with your shadow economy. What would the oracle at Delphi say today? It would say: Greeks, you should cheat no longer! Greeks, you should recognize yourself! Sincerely Yours FJ Wagner.
>
> *Bild*, 28/04/2010

A didactic tale is presented in this infotaining post coined by a "chief columnist" of Axel Springer named Franz Josef Wagner. This unfolds through a reference to the ancient Greek culture and its wisdom. A contemptuous (German, middle-class) gaze is cast upon the "poor Greeks", assuming (as the collocational scheme of "poor Greeks" suggests [Fairclough, 2003: 213]) a habitual knowledge about the object (the Greeks), which, apparently, the object itself does not seem to possess. Nominalisations ("the Greeks", "your ancestors", "patients", "everyone", etc.) are heavily deployed to produce a flat and devalued image of the Other (Fairclough 2003: 13). Put in a generalised manner, the identity of "all" Greeks is constituted by corruption, cheating, poverty and ignorance.

On a preliminary interdiscursive level, the author reproduces the standard neoliberal Greek crisis trope of petty corruption, blaming all Greeks for the eventual bankruptcy of the national state budget. This subtly negates society's uneven class structure, something that could allow for the development of a more sociological understanding of the crisis and corruption itself. In fact, sociological studies have shown that petty corruption and anomic practices are frequently defensive tactics against power, privilege and injustice (Dimitriou, 2016). As critical anthropology (Matza, 2018: 228) has also pointed out, informal social practices that often go beyond the law can also be viewed as practices of a moral economy that functions informally due to the broader restrictions that the structure poses. Such practices also allow more space for negotiation and resistance towards systemic subjugation and inequalities.

What is also problematic is the solution proposed: "recognise yourself". Intertextually (Fairclough, 2003: 47), this proposal is in line with the "self-help" popular book genre, with numerous related editions that are circulating across the world. On an interdiscursive level, we can also see how a fragment of an ancient Greek text (gnothi seauton -know thyself) is recontextualised in a hegemonic discursive construction, which instrumentalises it to launch particular ideological claims. The yellow press' call for "self-awareness" forms another sign of the neoliberal social imaginary, with its prevailing individualist discourse and its psychologising of social problems (Matza, 2018: 220). This occurs in an era marked by the eclipse of democratic politics, the decline of communities, and the diminishing of "safe havens" such as welfare institutions, the family and stable relations. In a time of diminished upward social mobility, with commodities being substituted for achievement, self-knowledge constitutes an unattainable entity (Lasch, 1991: 59). As the self is not a fixed unit, the kind of self-knowledge called by this contributor is a deceiving euphemism meant to intimidate the Other by enforcing the image that the bully has coined. Of course, the reference to oracles (and even the performing of an Oracle, as the specific yellow press contributor does) to legitimise an argument implies fatalism and escapism to mythical reason. Indeed, a mythopoetic reason (Van Leeuwen, 2009: 106) legitimises such claims, which supposedly expose the Greeks' wrongdoings, while establishing causality between the claim for generalised petty corruption and a national bankruptcy. By reserving the oracle's role for himself – as the ultimate holder of truth – *Bild's* "chief columnist" assumes a divine role. To a more attentive reader, this exposes the author's own reactionary inertia (and along with it, *Bild's*, too), in an expression of authoritarian irrationalism (Adorno, 2002) that is concealed in the seemingly "friendly" or "intimate" – but patronising – generic construction of the text (pretentiously signed with the dedication "Sincerely Yours…").

The manifested radical difference between Greece and Europe is often stressed with the mobilisation of historical and cultural arguments. These reconstruct the politico-economic perspectives of the crisis through a fundamental claim of "Greek exceptionalism". In another example, this time taken from the "serious" *Der Spiegel*, a certain Dietmar Pieper wrote in its "Cultural History" section an article entitled "What separates Greece from Europe" (18/05/2012), claiming, among other things, the following:

> The chain of dark centuries with foreign powers ruling the Greeks has left deep scars. [...] The former greatness exists only in museums. Politics and economics are oligarchical in modern Greece; power is almost inherited by dynasties like those of Papandreou or Karamanlis; personal relationships are often more important than election results or formal rules. Everything is pretty Byzantine. [...] The Oriental Schism of 1054 [...] has torn a deep trench in Europe. Such ancient antagonisms do not disappear without a trace.

Here, a "pop-science" narrative emerges, related to a more specialised article genre ("cultural history"). In such articles, Greece is presented as exceptional to the European norm from a historical determinist point of view. An unredeemable event (the Church Schism of 1054 – which *Der Spiegel's* author describes as the "Oriental Schism") is selected to form the constitutive basis of Greece's radical difference from Europe. Because of that, Greece somehow remained stagnant in an "eternal" form, tied to an unresolvable pre-modern/Oriental condition. Nominalizations ("Everything is pretty Byzantine") rationalise the article's claims by unfolding common-sense knowledge patterns. Generalisations without context ("power is almost inherited"; "personal relations are often more important than election results or formal rules") reinforce the established dichotomies of the Greek crisis myths, between the Western, secular, rational, rule abiding society and the Eastern one, which is traditional, emotional and unruly. The narrative developed produces in dramatic terms a myth of "a self-reinforcing, and self-containing character of a closed system in which objects are what they are because they are what they are, for once, for all time, for ontological reasons that no empirical material can either dislodge or alter" (Said, 2003: 70). This way, the "dark centuries" of "foreign rule" are made to have left "deep scars" on Greece. An eternal form is reproduced as the essential characteristic of Greece, making it the quintessence of all aspects of Greek life. Politics and the economy are constituted by unchallengeable relations of patronage, kinship ("dynasties") and inherited privileges, unlike the (supposed) sovereign, meritocratic and liberal essence of Western political and economic realities. This historical narrative, though, mainly marks the temporalities of hegemony, with an understanding of historical time shaped by political priorities (Stubbs, 2017). The hegemonic crisis' account highlights particular preferred historical moments that can legitimise its claims while downplaying others that may jeopardise and subvert its reasoning.

An attentive reader, may juxtapose to the Papandreou and Karamanlis families of Greek politicians the Clinton or the Bush families in the US – "the West's beacon". Liberal authors often tend to associate democracy and social transformation with individual politicians. According to the excerpt above, a regular change in politicians is a sign of democratic health. The belief in the making of social change through a mere renewing of individuals in the political arena, often leaves the socio-economic structure of the modern political power untouched. Established interests delimit the potentials of individual politicians to excersise independent politics. Under a critical reading the liberal modern state "constitutes the political unity of the dominant classes" (Poulantzas, 2000: 127).

In that sense, one can also go further by noting the enduring presense of the various German corporate monopolies that have survived (and thrived) through the modern German history, despite the various changes in government that Germany had. Corporations such as ThyssenKrupp, Siemens, Bayer (as part of I.G. Farben) among plenty of others, were proven to be more resilient than any politician and political party that ruled modern Germany, as they survived and prospered through the history of German capitalism from the 19th century onwards. The influence of German capital in Germany's political life is notable (like in all capitalist states) – one can additionally think of the support that Hitler received by German industrialists like Krupp so that the Communist movement would be effectively repressed. One can also think of the usage of slave labour by the German industries during the Nazi reign. Fuchs (2015: 129) notes that at least 2500 German corporations used slave labour from the Nazi concentration camps, with many of them still active today. In this sense, the main differences between Germany/Northern Europe and Greece/Southern Europe are in reality more connected to the centre-periphery positioning of these countries in the European and global capitalist constellation.

Liberal authors do not tackle questions related to the dynamics and asymmetries of global capitalism. Such questions could also emphasise the ways that the German capital (and German politics, as its extension) supports established power hierarchies in Greece, provoking high corruption scandals, which have so far amounted to the loss of some billions of Euros for the Greek state, such as the bribing scandal of Greek officials by Siemens that resulted in estimated losses of two billion Euros for the Greek state (Mavraka & Papatheodorou, 2012; Varoufakis, 2017), or the sale of defunct submarines by ThyssenKrupp Marine Systems to the Greek armed forces (Watt, 2014). Liberal authors often seem to forget that corruption, as Basu (2018: 146) notes, has two sides: on the one hand, it is the public sector accepting brides and, on the other hand, it is the private sector that provides the bribes. Nevertheless, the highlighting of the private sector and the defaming of the public sector is a common strategic choice among liberal pundits so as to praise the private economy.

Of further interest is the specific date chosen to mark the essence of Greece's radical difference with Europe. Out of all possible dates during the nearly thousand years that have passed since, 1054 is picked precisely because it denotes a fundamental religious break between Orthodox Greece and Catholic/Protestant Europe. The stressing of religion as the main factor of the (non-Western) Other's problems is a principal argumentative topos in cultural racist discourses (Salem & Thompson, 2016). Simultaneously, important dates for Germany and Europe, such as 1933 or 1945, which are much closer to the present than 1054 and concern Germany's own historical burdens and unresolved legacies, disgraces and defeats, related to its colonial, imperialist and Nazi trajectories, denoting the potential failure of modernity itself (Bauman, 1998), are left out of the Greek crisis discussions provided by liberal media. The German public today is largely unaware of the atrocities conducted by the German occupation forces in Greece and the circle of violence that followed Greece's liberation, escalating into a civil war that was initially fuelled by the Germans, while mobilising Greek reactionaries and the lumpenproletariat, who were wretched from the conditions of the occupation, to fight against the Resistance movement (and to save "German blood" (sic) [Kostopoulos, 2005]). Greek fascists and local Nazi collaborators were later rearmed by Britain and the USA in their military, economic and political interventions to secure imperial interests in the region and to suppress the Greek Communist movement. The Cold War context allowed Germany's rapid rebirth from its utter defeat (including the 1953 indefinite deferring of its war reparations debt to Greece) while escalating an anti-communist frenzy in Greece targeting the Resistance members (Voglis, 2002; Kousouris, 2014). This even allowed notorious Nazi criminals, such as Max Merten, a Nazi responsible for the persecution and the eventual annihilation of Thessaloniki's populous Jewish community and for the looting of Jewish properties (Fleischer, 2008), to return to Greece as tourists or as businessmen shortly after the occupation's end (Buck-Morss, 1987: 206), without being held accountable for their crimes. The German Federal government of the time threatened Greece with economic sanctions in the event of it pursuing the persecuting of Nazi criminals like Max Merten and, along with that, war reparations for the crimes committed by Nazi Germany on Greek soil.

The social anthropologist Theodora Vetta (2014: 3) notes that "Greece is one of the countries with the highest casualties during the Second World War. There are various estimations of human losses, ranging between 5.5% and 7.6% of the population, which counted around 7,344 million residents in the pre-war period". In this sense,

> The Greek demand for the payment of war reparations from Germany is fully justified, since Greece was the only non-Slavic occupied country by Nazi Germany, which (after Poland, Yugoslavia, and the Soviet Union) had the greatest loss of human lives and suffered the greatest material damages, says the Austrian historian and professor of Modern History at the University of Athens, Hagen Fleischer, in an interview with the Austrian newspaper *Der Standard*. Enumerating these losses, he notes that, beyond the 60,000 Greek Jews who were murdered, tens of thousands of other Greeks were also executed; furthermore, at least 100,000 died of hunger; one in three Greeks suffered from epidemic diseases after the German withdrawal; many were left homeless after the destruction of 100,000 houses; the whole economy and the country's infrastructure was destroyed during the German occupation, and Greece has never recovered since then. [...] In the Cold War context and under the US pressure, the question of reparations was practically "choked" to make Germany a front against the eastern countries.
>
> To Vima, 18/09/2012

Thus, a reference to the years of the German occupation of Greece that took place between 1941–1944 would provide more plausible hints in understanding modern Greece's peripheral state and its particularities. After all, if thousand-year-old events are to leave "deep scars" in a country, what should be the impact of seventy-five-year-old events of total war, including mass and indiscriminate murder based on Nazi Germany's racist ideology, a policy of scorched earth (e.g. Figure 4) and a generalised endeavour of looting and pillaging perpetrated by the German army in Greece? Either way, the stressing of Germany's own problematic dimensions would expose the contradictions and the partiality of the culturalist crisis explanations. As Gumpert (2017: 31) explains "what finally underlies Europe's resentment of Greece is [...] the fear that Greece is either not enough or too much like Europe".

Instead, designated historical instances (like the church Schism of 1054) are utilised to avow the liberal fables of progress and secularism.

> Reason itself has become the mere instrument of the all-inclusive economic apparatus. It serves as a general tool, useful for the manufacture of all other tools, firmly directed toward its end, as fateful as the precisely calculated movement of material production, whose result for mankind is beyond all calculation.
>
> ADORNO & HORKHEIMER, 1989: 30

A CULTURAL FAILURE

FIGURE 4 The monument of the destruction of the Cretan village Kandanos by the Wehrmacht[2]
SOURCE: PHOTO BY THE AUTHOR

Historical references highlighting Germany's Nazi past and the crimes it perpetrated in Greece are strongly confronted by the liberal press in Germany, Denmark and elsewhere. Such a rather recent past (particularly in comparison to the medieval references above) and its horrors are denied legitimacy as relevant arguments for debate. This shows the crisis politics' double standards, as only Greece is to honour its debts. An example of this case can be seen in the following example taken from the Danish media environment, where references to the German Occupation of Greece are dismissed as "old" and contextualised in an overall dubious strategies pursued by the Greek authorities so as

---

2 The monument shown in the figure 4 presents copies of the inscriptions left by the Wehrmacht on the destroyed village. The inscription on the reader's left writes (in German and Greek) the following: "Here stood Kandanos. It was destroyed to avenge the murder (sic) of 25 German soldiers". Kandanos was destroyed on 03/06/1941 by the Wehrmacht, in retaliation for the citizens' Resistance against it. It is important to note that Kandanos is only one out of hundreds of villages destroyed by the Germans in Greece during the Nazi Occupation of the country between 1941–1944.

to halt the "reforms". As stated in a 04/03/2015 article with the emphatic title "The Greek crisis is self-inflicted", appearing in the readers' letters section of the liberal-left Danish newspaper *Information*[3]

> The Greek authorities' position and strategy in the EU have so far been reminiscent of Strepsiades from Aristophanes' "Clouds" comedy. Here, the debt-stricken Strepsiades sends his son to be educated with Socrates for the sole purpose of the son becoming eloquent enough to have Strepsiades talked out of his debt. But eventually, the son turns against his father. In Greece, debt has risen to an unmanageable level. There must be a solution, but unlike the case of the Strepsiades myth, it must be clear to the Greeks that this solution is not to be found in bad apologies and more or less subtle references to a German occupation of Greece that happened more than 70 years ago. The Greek economy is a self-inflicted tragedy. The economy has been treated with patience and the necessary reforms have been overridden for too long.
>
> *Information*, 04/03/2015

This piece demonstrates again the instrumental usage of references to classical Greece (such as the specific comedy of Aristophanes), fetishistically deployed as authority topoi to make claims about modern Greece. The common use of the myths and theatrical plays of the Ancient Greeks relate to the "Greek drama" crisis trope. The use of the Greek drama idea is rather fatalistic since it implies an already known and didactic story with a bitter end. In this sense, the authors deploying such themes as interpretative frameworks of Greece imply the mastery of knowledge unknown to the Greeks, who are caught within the drama. In this way, these authors and their readers appear as spectators of the (eternal) Greek drama. The contemporary spectator, of course, is a narcissist in Christopher Lasch (1979) sense, because s/he cannot grasp his/her own state of being in an elusive society such as the late modern one. Therefore, such references reinforce the hegemonic crisis and austerity rationales, by depicting the devious character of the Greek authorities that offer "bad apologies" and make "subtle" use of past events such as "a German occupation that happened more than 70 years ago", by affirming the "Greek economy" as a "self-inflicted tragedy", by stressing the benevolence of the EU that is addressed in absentia through the use of the passive voice ("the economy *has been treated*

---

3 *Information* started as a clandestine publication of the Danish Resistance during the German Occupation of Denmark, 1940–1945. As a country deemed "Aryan" by the Nazis, and due to the effective capitualtion and collaboration of the Danish government with Germany, Denmark (like other Western and Northern European countries occupied by Nazi Germany), was spared from the oppresion and the war of annihilation conducted in the East and the Balkans (Fleischer, 2008).

by patience"), and by referring to austerity as "necessary reforms" through the neutral jargon of technocracy. The implied dialogism of a "free indirect reporting" (Fairclough, 2003: 49) of the leftist Greek government at the time trivialises its counter-austerity arguments and downplays the overall Greek context. The excerpt's author objectifies the neoliberal repertoire by deploying it as the anchorage point to rationalise his public reaction towards counter-hegemonic possibilities.

As the article in *Information* showed, the Danish press Orientalises Greece through common-sense themes, equivalent to those found in the German press. Two more examples are as follows:

> On the edge of Europe: Greece's crisis is not only economic but also existential. In love with Western Europe but still anchored in its Oriental cultural inheritance, the country has struggled during many centuries to find its place in Europe. A Greek exit from the European community will have fatal political consequences.
> *Berlingske*, 28/06/2015

> There is not and there has never been a special binding between Greece and West Europe. [...] You cannot just exchange five bottles of olive oil with the European project, as the Greeks are different from the Europeans in many important aspects. The Greeks have another religion, even the alphabet is different. Culturally, they are much closer to Serbia and Russia, with whom they have the same religion, rather than Western Europe.
> *Jyllands Posten*, 14/07/2015

It is often stated in the relevant literature (Balibar & Wallerstein, 1991: 18), that racists nowadays (particularly in the "politically correct" Northern and Western Europe) abstain from mentioning biological differences, and resort to cultural differences to make supremacist claims. *Jyllands Posten's* excerpt is indicative of this case because cultural differences such as religion and written language ("even the alphabet is different") are used to demarcate supposed inconsistencies between (Western and Northern Europe and Greece. The essence of Greece is also emptied of its substance through the utilitarian substitution with known, locally produced commodities ("five bottles of olive oil"). The development of this metaphor is meant to stress the incompatibility of Greece to that of the "European project". Likewise, in the presumably more modest piece in the *Berlingske*, Greece is "anchored in its Oriental cultural heritage" that causes an "existential crisis". In that sense above all, the "Greek crisis" is an existential crisis, because the country "struggled during many centuries to find a place in Europe". A process of semantic disembedding occurs here as the economic crisis is displaced and substituted by a crisis of culture and psychology (Fairclough, 2003: 68), abstracting the Greek counter-austerity case through a display of generalizations. The struggle against austerity is really about being European or not, something that can only be achieved through austerity. In both excerpts, nominalisations ranging from words ("Greeks", "the country", "Western Europe", "Serbia", "Russia"), to grammatical metaphors ("a Greek exit", "on the edge of Europe", "in love with Western Europe") make a cultural comparative topos that establishes the cultural hierarchy claimed by Western Europe and its Others. Western Europe appears positively, as an entity of adoration and a direction for Greece, while Eastern Europe (notably, Serbia and Russia) is transformed into a symbol of entropy.

"Europe" is an empty signifier that assumes in the liberal press a sublime form as a "universal" entity deemed "beyond discussion". Laclau (1996: 59) has shown that universality provides a symbolic centre to sustain a given hegemonic project. The public exclusion of Greece from the "European identity" was the Western/liberal hegemony's response to the antagonistic politics launched by the left-led government of Greece. In line with the understanding of Orientalism as a continuously changing and broadening discriminatory process (Buchowski, 2006), the use of the European discursive construction above can be associated with what the Danish anthropologist Lasse Lindekilde (2014: 364) calls the rise of liberal intolerance in Denmark. Migrants and foreigners are mostly discriminated on civilisational claims on the basis of liberal arguments related to the migrants' supposed cultural incompatibility with the West because of issues related to gender equality, social cohesion, civility and individual autonomy, among others.

The standard Orientalist topoi, according to which the Oriental subject is infantile, female, passionate and fatalistic (Said, 2003), as opposed to the Occidental one, who is mature, active, calm and male, are likewise found in the studied media. The examples below lucidly demonstrate the developing of such metaphorical schemes as crisis-explanations:

> Euro-future debate: Should we let Greece go broke? Greece is the biggest problem child in Europe. Now, the over-indebted state could finally face the financial end. But is a bankruptcy of the country the best solution? Top politicians and top economists answer the most important question of the Euro crisis.
>
> *Der Spiegel*, 15/09/2011

> For years, the relationship between Greece and the EU has resembled the marriages where the woman threatens, charms and murmurs, while the man is getting worse with his corrective stubbornness. The EU has acted equally structurally and pedantically, as Greece has acted anarchically and fatalistically. However, it is usually the case that the man in the end

just gives up. Afraid of losing her; because according to his rules, one cannot be divorced. ... The EU began to behave Greek. [...] For the first time, the husband was out of control.

Berlingske, 16/07/2015

Nominalisations (e.g. Greece, Europe, "we") and grammatical metaphors ("the biggest problem child in Europe", "the EU has begun to behave Greek") constitute the infantilised and effeminised Other. The *Berlingske* article further reproduces gendered stereotypes through the sketching of a supposed "average" and common-sense pattern of marital life. Metaphors that point towards patterns of traditional gender roles (where the woman is irrational and the man rational) are developed to simplify geopolitics. Greece is thus an angry and sly woman, neurotic, anarchic and fatalistic, and the EU is a prudent (petty bourgeois) husband, putting up with her only because he is too afraid of losing her. The rather stereotypical construction of gender relations in such an excerpt demonstrates Denmark's own conservative turn. A country that still takes pride in its gender egalitarian values and lifestyle seems to be using them only as markers of white middle-class distinction, denoting nationalist narcissism and laying out the culturalist basis for excluding foreigners over their supposed incompatibility with the "Danish ways", self-proclaimed as secular, egalitarian and tolerant (Wren, 2001; Lentin & Titley, 2011; Lindekilde, 2014; Yilmaz, 2016).

Sexist lifestyle topoi are also arrayed by the crisis' spectacle:

> Beautiful Greek ex-super model weeps for her broke country. She is beautiful and she is Greek! Supermodel and businesswoman Vicky Koulianou (41) explains why the Greeks actually do not want to be helped.
>
> *Bild*, 10/10/2011

This excerpt from *Bild* develops a diffused frame of exoticisation here by arraying a "beautiful Greek" woman, who was successful in the Greek modelling business, to explain "why the Greeks do not want to be helped". The utterance "she is beautiful and she is Greek" seems to present viewers with a paradox or with an exception of someone being "beautiful and Greek" at the same time. The racialised Other is additionally represented as "ugly" and "failed". With beauty and success (she is presented to the German readers as a supermodel and businesswoman) being characteristics of the ideal (Western/bourgeois) self, the specific woman acquires the authoritative legitimacy to speak, as she is potentially standing out of the (reified and flattened) realm of the failed Other. An exoticised woman is called to explain an exotic people deemed as incomprehensible for the German readership of *Bild*. To be sure, the text is not about explaining, but about sustaining a specific fantasy of the incomprehensible Other, reified and commodified by the crisis-spectacle.

The Greek liberal media assert the above-mentioned Orientalist framing mode by deploying "Western values" as universal standards for the successful politico-economic management of a country, and by establishing the correct normative rules for ideal individual conduct. The Greek liberals are in an ambivalent position, identifying with the hegemonic neoliberal/Occidentalist notion of "Europe", while at the same time "being Greek". Therefore, they develop an equivalent (if not harsher) Greek-bashing strategy, in a redeeming/apologetic stance for "Greece's misdoings". The Greek liberals self-Orientalise Greece and its people from within, acknowledging, reproducing and amplifying the hegemonic cultural and moral blaming of Greece for its disadvantaged position.

Stelios Ramfos, a neoliberal, pop-philosopher, has expressed his support for both progressive and conservative neoliberal political parties in the recent years (ranging from "To Potami" to "Nea Dimokratia"). In a TV interview in 2010 for Greek national television, Ramfos, who became very popular in Greece during the crisis, argued that the "Greek psyche" is the root cause of the Greek debt crisis:

> We [sic] are not interested in self-awareness. […] The crucial thing to see is that this is the point where pathogenesis is born. As soon as we understand this the yield spreads [the difference in percentage between the credit quality of Greece and Germany] will go down. The yield spreads are right to be where they are because they know that we are not capable of managing ourselves. Despite all the speculative games, this is the deepest truth. We have an unmanageable self.
> MYLONAS & KOMPATSIARIS, 2013

Likewise, in his articles, the popular liberal author and journalist Nikos Dimou draws similar conclusions. For example, in "Nevertheless, Huntington was right!" (*Protagon*, 28/10/2014), Dimou deploys Huntington's "clash of civilisation" neoconservative thesis to sketch a cultural dichotomy between Europe and Greece, with the latter belonging to what Huntington termed as the "Eastern Orthodox" bloc. Occasionally, Dimou has also been interviewed by the German media on similar matters:

> "We like to live beyond our means". In a Spiegel interview, the Greek writer Nikos Dimou analyses the state of his country's psyche, describing the "deep fears that torment the Greek soul". He blames Greek politicians for the current crisis but insists the EU and Germany only have themselves to blame for the resentment that many Greeks feel.
> *Der Spiegel*, 07/06/2012

The culturalisation of the Greek crisis is sustained through a constant circuit of exchange of Orientalist topoi developed in Europe and the West and also in Greece. *Der Spiegel* uses the words of a Greek liberal while sustaining its Orientalist construction of Greece. The studied media seldom draw upon the voices of critical Greek intellectuals. Their preferred self-Orientalising Greek authors create an aura of authenticity as, along with experts, natives also express and verify the pathologies "tormenting the Greek soul" (sic). In another case, drawn from a 01/04/2015 *AthensVoice* article entitled "Lessons of political aesthetics", one reads the following:

> Humor fought and won because the German state television is a democratic institution. [...] Yes, the German state television has the courage to witness reality and accept the historical responsibility for Germany's past. This is required by the Enlightenment, Humanism, and Democracy. Here, in the country of the Balkan Peron and Evita [...] all appear satisfied due to the devaluation of the common-sense. The tragedy lies in the fact that everyone [the author mentions Syriza government ministers] was elected by the citizens' vote, in full conscience.

In this excerpt, a contributor named Nikos Georgiadis discusses an episode of *Die Anstalt*, a satirical German TV show. The particular episode addressed the massacres committed by the Wehrmacht in Greece, as well as the forced loan imposed on Greece by the German occupying forces, which, along with the war reparations, remains unpaid due to Germany's strategy of political manoeuvring, public diplomacy and the use of historically favourable conditions (its position in the Cold War) to avoid paying its debts (Fleischer, 2008). Georgiadis' claim is produced through a comparative approach. Germany is positively defined through highly abstract nominalisations that denote the essence of liberal universality such as "Humanism", "Enlightenment", and "Democracy". Greece, on the other hand, is represented with negative nominalisations and grammatic metaphors, such as "the country of the Balkan Peron and Evita", where "all" seem satisfied by a "devaluation of the 'common sense'". Although he praises the German Democracy, he resents the voting choices of the Greek citizens. The author uses *Die Anstalt's* program to prove and to celebrate the German democracy, since in his view, such shows demonstrate that the "German state TV is a democratic institution", even though the particular show exposed to the German public the double standards of neoliberal austerity's morale, where only Greece is to "honour" its debts. This way, Georgiadis abstracts and displaces the actual content of the particular TV program, recontextualising it as a "floating signifier" in his own argument, which aligns with the hegemonic Greek crisis repertoire. Along with the specific author, other Greek liberals often dismiss the demands for war reparations as "nationalist", mere proofs of Greece's constriction to a long-gone past. In this way, they fail to acknowledge the topical relevance of historical demands for justice and recognition (Fraser & Honneth, 2003) and their connections, indeed, to the mores of "the Enlightenment, Humanism and Democracy" (Mylonas, 2017: 204).

4.3.2 Greece as a Commodity: Media Rituals to Sustain Ideological Myths

In her work on the encountering and the making of strangers, Sara Ahmed (2000: 114) demarcates the fetishism of the stranger in the context of consumer culture: "consumer culture involves the production of the stranger as a commodity fetish, through representations of difference". Consumer culture allows the encountering of strangers through the material and symbolic consumption of commodities associated with the (commodified) image and form of the Other. The fetishistic relation with the Other concerns "the transformation of fantasies into figures that take a life of their own, cut from the historical and material relations that over-determine their existence" (Ahmed, 2000: 5).

The exotic, reified construction of an Eternal Greece, which, on the one hand, appears in a pure and idealised form of classical antiquity (as the West's cradle of civilisation), and on the other, as an example of underdevelopment (of a country and a people failing to live up to their antique ancestors), produces a fetishised encounter with Greece and its people. Western mainstream media actively reproduce this fetishistic construction of Greece, connected to the regular iteration of specific tropes (related to the topoi of antique glory and contemporary underdevelopment) that form manifestations of a general common-sense view that Westerners carry. This gives a specific form to Greece that takes a life of its own, disconnected from the social and material and symbolic contexts determining the life of the Greek people.

Most crucially, the "Greek crisis" and its tropes are commodified by media culture to boost sales and publicity. *Bild's* "infotaining" approach is indicative of this regard, as the Othering of Greece is a condition of Greece's spectacularisation. Popular stereotypes are constantly iterated by *Bild* to demonstrate "how Greece is":

> Bankrupt Greeks are sinking in the debt whirl. By Zeus, where does this end? The debt hole of the bankrupt Greeks is much bigger than expected. Do we have to help out with 18,000,000,000 euros? (22/04/2010).

Bankrupt Greeks; they celebrate their financial injection. They are demonstrating against their prime minister, they are mad at Germany and the EU – they just want to keep going like they always have! The day after the bankruptcy shock in Athens – the Greeks should actually know how serious the situation is for them now (25/04/2010).

Why do we pay the Greeks their luxury pensions? Pensioners in Greece are doing so well. German billions in help for the Greeks is only a matter of days away, says Chancellor Angela Merkel. But for experts, Greece is a bottomless pit. And many are asking themselves, why should we pay, for example, for the lavish pensions and the pension system of the Greeks? (27/04/2010).

Daily fresh shock-news from Athens: Panic on the Titanic? You must be joking! The Greeks celebrate! It is the biggest bankruptcy party in Athens! (11/06/2010).

The government in Athens now wants to save a lot – but what if that's not enough? Sell your islands, you bankrupt Greeks [...] and the Acropolis right away! Now the Greeks are serious about saving their country from bankruptcy without relying on EU aid! (27/10/2010).

In *Bild*, the Orientalisation of Greece primarily occurs through the mobilisation of widely shared, common-sense, pseudo-knowledge of the country obtained by consumer culture. Stereotypes are seldom questioned and are taken for granted instead. Greece and the Greeks are represented in homogenous terms as a solid, reified and known object. Banal historical mentions of the "Greek antiquity" (e.g. the allusion to Zeus above) along with references to holiday resorts and commodities of tourist consumption (e.g. "Papandreou at Kastelorizo: debt call for help against an idyllic background. Greece on the brink of bankruptcy – and the head of government is pacing on nearly deserted, far-off islands!" [*Bild*, 27/04/2010]), portray the essence of Greece and its people.

In the threatening economic crisis context (which is "contagious") the fetishistic image of Greece as a reified, exotic commodity is reversed to its negative form. The celebration of Merkel's "toughness" on Greece by *Bild* shows the tabloid's alignment to her government's ideology, strategies and objectives. Greece is made to appear as incomprehensible, standing for everything that the German/European is not. Through various falsehoods, Greece is represented in a totalistic form as idle, carefree, hot, irrational, bankrupt, corrupt and backward. Greece is also composed of specific antique monuments and ruins (e.g. the Acropolis) and represented by references to nominalisations about the tourist experience of the country (e.g. islands, luxury, celebration, party, holidays, vacation), which concentrate the tourist attention and, on a further level, are cherished by financial investors for their potential economic value.

In its post-Fordist phase, the tourist industry is known to trigger narratives of uniqueness (Urry, 2002: 132). Tourism is a highly individualised activity, sustained by the fantasy of distinctive experiences and authenticity related to extraordinary encounters with locations, events, material objects, and especially with local people. Besides their fragmented and ephemeral character, the events connected to such aspirations are often staged in order to sustain and fulfil tourist expectations. The tourist gaze seeks and withstands difference, while the activity of tourism itself and its political economy do not allow adequate space for different encounters with the local people and their culture, which might potentially enable the development of common identities, experiences and solidarities, focusing instead on activities that do not escape the boundaries of consumption.

The Occidental gaze projects the tourist experience into the native population's genuine state of being. The fetishised image of Greece only reflects the indolent doings of the petty bourgeois tourist, who remains detached from the subsisted realities of the host country. Occidentalist knowledge regimes and consumerist desires of Greece overidentify the country and its people. They come to form constitutive foundations of a shared local reality, concealing the closely guarded hierarchies of power that they represent. Such hierarchies are further connected to colonial and imperial legacies, with tourism being a peaceful form of invasion, which nevertheless uses forms of knowledge and organisation common to military expeditions (Buck-Morss, 1987: 204). The experience of the tourist is turned into a topos of authority verifying the knowledge of the Other, despite the self-referentiality of this case. Accordingly, *Bild* represents the "Greeks" living like tourists in their own country, deceiving the (honest) EU and abusing its funds that are supplied by the hard-working Northern/Western European taxpayers. In this way, the division between the tourist and the native persists and takes on a confrontational form in the crisis context.

Beyond their pejorative use, exotic stereotypes are also sometimes arrayed in a way so as to bring forth supposed "positive" sides of (the fetishised) Greece and the persisting allure of this country to the West. This positive image, though, is contained so as not to disrupt the hegemonic symbolic divisions as expressed through culture, avow the manifested as the superior identity of the North/West, and assert the presumed correctness of the policies it imposes on the South. Indicatively, the following article from the Danish press seems to do just that:

> After having randomly wandered a bit around the city's myriad streets – past tourists, beggars, and street performers – I came past a glass elevator with bright red flashing lights that would lead me straight up to paradise. Upon the sixth floor of a rooftop high above Athens I soon entered a cocktail bar called "A for Athens". The bar did not only offer an outstanding view of an illuminated Acropolis but was also filled with beautiful, well-dressed guys with a scoring gaze and Greek goddesses in silk dresses, designer handbags and colorful cocktails in hand. [...] Perhaps the Germans and all of us Northerners, who seek the sun most of the summer since the winter torments us through the long dark days of snow and rain, are just envious; envious for not having the Greek sun, cocktail parties on open-air roof terraces, sandy beaches, beach bars, relaxed life, Ouzo, retsina, feta, the juicy sun-ripened tomatoes, the ingratiating Greek captain and the seductive Aphrodite. And therefore, it is now the hour of vengeance. So now they must learn the Northern lesson: that it is crucial for one to live within his means, that duties come before pleasure, and that, after a party, there is always a bill to be paid [...] [Perhaps we are envious indeed] but sanity quickly returned.
> "At least they have the sun", *Berlingske*, 19/07/2015

Published in the *Berlingske's* "globetrotter", a tourist oriented column, the text evokes the "conclusions" of the crisis and Greferendum story. The contributor of this text, the author and investigative journalist Michael Bjerre, narrates his experience in Athens in July 2015 after the Greferendum and the Greek government's subsequent capitulation to the EU, while addressing a Northern/Western audience. He describes his retreat from the baffling and vile Athenian public space to the private and exclusive realm of a roof bar, exposing an enhanced and beautified image of Athens (offering a sight of its antique monuments), and being surrounded by middle/upper class Greeks that he can relate to and who can affirm his own sense of normalcy. His point of view is sustained through the accounting of bits of information obtained by his random encounters at the bar, deployed as proofs to reinforce his self-referential statements. Thus, the hegemonic account of the "self-inflicted" Greek crisis is sustained, where "all Greeks" lived beyond their abilities, having "partied" through borrowed funds in an eternal holiday setting. References to the weather are deployed to explain in a depoliticised and irrational, "naturalistic" manner, labour. Instead of a historically contingent process, labour comes to assume

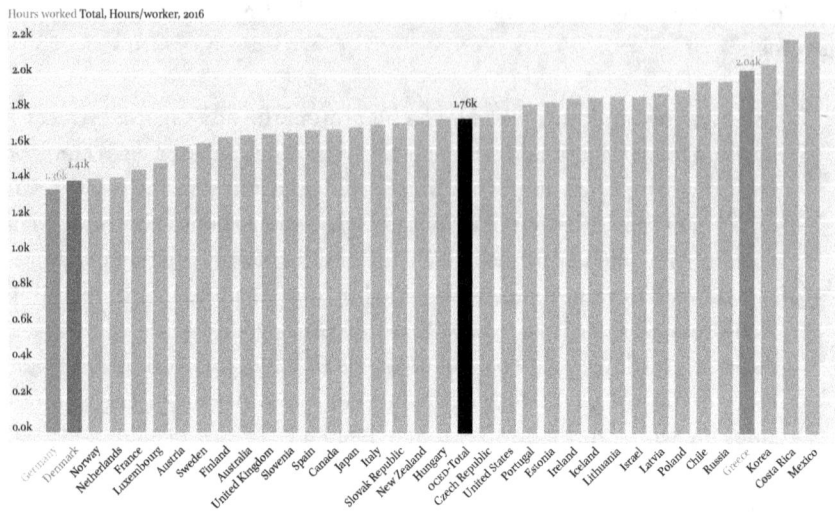

FIGURE 5   The crisis falsehoods: OECD (2017) charts on average annual work hours

a naturalised context, defined by the climate only. Nevertheless, as Figure 5 shows, despite the warm sun, the Greek workers are actually working longer hours on an annual basis than the Germans and the Danes do, while being paid considerably less and while being entitled to fewer benefits or welfare than their counterparts in the capitalist centre states are. As was the case with most media texts examined in this study, this penurious journalistic demeanour fails to consider facts that may challenge his ideology.

The specific author also implies a Northern/Western gesture of "reprisal" to "Greece", narrated in the form of a morality/narcissistic tale (Van Leeuwen, 2008: 119) of the good, hard-working Northerners, who set the standards of how the rest should live. This is an expression of sadism, enunciated with the repetition of hegemony's rationales, that make austerity and the suffering that it causes to be non-negotiable, necessary and just. In this sense, the journalist has the position of the instructor who, by standing on the side of high power, calmly presents the logics of authority without negotiating them. For Deleuze (2006: 18), this language is violent and forms a constitutive act of the "punishment" imposed.

Nevertheless, this is done while admitting a certain degree of envy to the lifestyle in the idyllic image of Greece that he is exposed to. To draw an analytical analogy, Jeffries (2016) notes that for the Frankfurt School scholars, the Jew was loathed in the interwar times and during the Nazi reign, because s/he came to symbolise a lifestyle that the repressed and impoverished working and middle classes could not have. This Dane is quick to dismiss his envy through a masochistic reversion to the North's severe ways while applauding the sadistic punishing of those defying them, legitimised through the authoritative use of the term "sanity" that he claims to be resorting to. Sanity, a signifier that constitutes a nodal point of an Occidentalist-bourgeois supremacy discourse, warrants this Danish author to make his claims appear as common sense to his Nordic readership. "Sanity" in this sense also emerges as a self-disciplinary technology.

The constant iteration of commonplace features of supposed Greekness, familiar to the petty bourgeois tourists of the North, reproduces a rather ritualistic construction of what Hamilakis (2016: 237) described as an "eternal Greece". In a similar article with the title "Thanks for the feta", published in the same Danish newspaper, we read the following:

> Greece is not only about the Euro crisis and a debt of billions. The country has contributed to the world history, democracy, and philosophy, and it has given to the Danish people the taste of feta, calamari, olive oil and retsina.
> *Berlingske*, 12/07/2015

This ritualistic representation of Greece in the Danish and Western/ Northern European public spheres is stereotypical, as it iterates a few popular aspects of antique history (such as images of ruins and references to drama, "philosophy", "democracy"), mixed with gastronomic references (calamari, ouzo, feta cheese, retsina wine and olives), and along with them, mentions of sexualised exotic fantasies, as in the Bjerre piece above (regarding the existence of "captains" and "Aphrodites" in Greece and the appeal that their potential encounter and experience triggers for tourists). All these reifications summarise the "package" of consumption promises that the tourist industry makes for the Western middle class for Greece, which are surely sexist and racist. Indeed, Greece in the Western consumerist fantasy appears as an assemblage of commodities (Mylonas & Noutsou, 2018: 61). Either way, rituals constitute a symbolic centre of normality (Carah & Louw, 2015: 32). In the case of a global crisis, were the periphery attempts to challenge the exploitative status quo of global and European capitalism, refusing to accept the burdens of capitalist recovery, the ritualistic stressing of Orientalist stereotypes sustains ideological stability within capitalism's core, by diminishing the possibilities of identification and solidarity between the oppressed people and classes.

Indeed, the countries of North-western Europe and Scandinavia in particular, are often propagated to be the happiest countries of the world. Denmark, for instance, was declared by the United Nations' "world happiness" report as the happiest country in 2016. This distinction was optimised by Danish national institutions and corporations to brand the nation and its products: to attract socio-cultural capital – in line with Richard Florida's "creative cities" model – tourism, economic investments, and to further promote Danish-based products across the world. The idea of happiness itself, however, needs to be problematised as a trait highly connected to a bourgeois form of subjectivity, which is exclusivist and competitive. The state of a supposed permanent sense of happiness amounts to an unreflective mode characteristic of stupidity and, in postmodern times, happiness becomes an order, a command (Žižek, 2011). The objectivised construction of happiness according to the UN's criteria above boosts expressions of nationalist narcissism, developing in a highly insecure, competitive and exclusionary world:

> Pleasure always means not to think about anything, to forget suffering even where it is shown. Basically, it is helplessness. It is flight; not, as is asserted, flight from a wretched reality, but from the last remaining thought of resistance.
> ADORNO & HORKHEIMER, 1997: 144

Indeed, on the antipode of the Danish high rank in happiness lies the steady rising of Denmark as one of the world's most racist countries (Wren, 2001: 141).

4.3.3 Nationalism, Narcissism, Anxiety: Europe as a Panopticon and a Benchmark

The negative and inferior construction of the Other organises the positivity of "us". Hence, the Other sets the frontiers of what "we" are not. Therefore, "Europe" incarnates all the qualities that the Oriental/poor Greek does not. As Tables 2 and 3 showed, the Greek is irresponsible, idle, irrational, living above his/her abilities and deceitful, among other things; on the antipode, the "European" is responsible, hard-working, rational, prudent (living within his/her abilities), honest, entrepreneurial, etc. The positive construction of the self is overall represented in national terms and celebrated as such.

An excerpt from *Bild* can demonstrate the kind of jingoism and social conformity advanced by Germany's most widely sold newspaper. Before one of the Greek Prime Minster Giorgos Papandreou's visits to Germany in 2010, *Bild* circulated an open letter to him:

Dear prime minister,

> If you're reading this, you've entered a country different from yours. You're in Germany. Here, people work until they are 67 and there is no

14th-month salary for civil servants. Here, nobody needs to pay a €1,000 bribe to get a hospital bed in time. Our petrol stations have cash registers, taxi drivers give receipts and farmers don't swindle EU subsidies with millions of non-existent olive trees. Germany also has high debts but we can settle them. That's because we get up early and work all day. We want to be friends with the Greeks. That's why since joining the Euro, Germany has given your country €50bn.[4]

National excellence is here verified through the accounting of daily life banalities connected to automatised processes of commodity exchange (cash registers in petrol stations), and stereotypes generalising petty corruption cases (e.g. farmers deceiving the EU for subsidies, patients bribing hospital staff). The celebration of work in particular, through a Calvinist life/duty morality, incarnated and applied by a people that is "getting up early" to "work all day", possibly performed in a mood of collective joy, according to *Bild*, signifies the celebration of the essence of the German nation, as constructed by *Bild*. The "exposition" of the Other's constitutive failure is made-up by the systematic allocation of moments that prove this very failure, as s/he cannot live up to the German/universal standards of excellence (summarised by automatisation, mass conformity, and the sanctification of "hard work"). Of course, the Organisation for Economic Cooperation and Development (OECD) statistics on the average annual work hours per country falsify *Bild's* fictitious claims. According to Adorno and Horkheimer (1989: 126), for the cultural industry "the whole inevitably bears no relation to the details – just like the career of a successful man to which everything is made to fit as an illustration or a proof, whereas it is nothing more than the sum of all those idiotic events".

Likewise, in *Bild*, the idea of "national success" is fabricated through the narration of selected ideas and trite facts, made to look as if they are *naturally* guided by a kind of a Divine Prudence siding with the German nation (which is possibly further aided by the "invisible hand" of the market ideology). Everyday banalities come to symbolise the narcissistic pleasures of the nation. Their overemphasis symbolises the nation's distinction. The nation also appears as practically without problems, given that the national citizens' inherent qualities of dedicated hard work (in a seemingly Stakhanovite mode) provide the solution to all social and individual problems.

The Greek crisis is also represented as a national conflict that occurs between Greece and Germany, with Germany being on the defensive. In this way,

---

4 This excerpt is retrieved from https://www.theguardian.com/business/2010/mar/05/bild-open-letter-greece-papandreou (accessed 09/11/2018).

international class affinities are blocked, while the nationally defined people are called to celebrate the advance of German capitalist interests as "national interests". The daily news headlines of *Bild* during the first years of the crisis are telling:

> Greek press hate-speech against our Chancellor. You get money from us. A lot of money! And what do the bankrupt Greeks do: they swear against our Chancellor. There are even Stasi-Nazi comparisons!
> *Bild*, 04/05/2010

> 25 billion for the Greeks. And what about us? Germany lends the highly indebted Greece about 25 billion Euros. What if the Greeks go bankrupt? And we just have to support this.
> *Bild*, 01/05/2010

> The good godmother of Europe, Merkel was able to reject any offer. At EU summits, the one who holds out the longest wins, along with the one who in the end makes the "offer" that one cannot refuse.
> *Bild*, 27/10/2011

> Greek drama; Mrs. Merkel, we want to vote! PRESENT IT TO US NOW! We provide hundreds of billions of Euros to save the bankrupt Greeks – this should be affirmed with a referendum.
> *Bild*, 03/11/2011

Bild victimises Germany by representing it as the "helper" of Greece (which is aided by the German taxpayers' funds) while depicting Greece as an ungrateful and irresponsible freeloader. The German people are likewise represented as a homogenous nation assaulted by irresponsible Others. Chancellor Merkel is presented as a German/European symbolic centre (with Merkel being the "good godmother" of Europe) unifying the nation despite its manifested European challenges. In another way, Merkel is perhaps also associated with the symbolic figure of the Mafioso, through the intertextual connotation of the "godmother" to Martin Scorcese's famous "Godfather" film. To that respect, the social anthropologist David Graeber (2011: 163) has pointed out the theoretical affinities between the creditor and the Mafioso, using the power of debt to make compulsory demands to debtors as well as "offers that people cannot refuse". The calls for a popular "referendum" so that the German people will decide where the "help" will be allocated to, are mere cries that sustain the illusion of popular sovereignty and boost nationalist narcissism, nourishing the myth of the rich and powerful nation that is mistreated.

The general, potentially worldwide, consensus on Germany's ordoliberal policy framework (Ojala & Harjuniemi, 2016), as realistic, responsible, just and even "altruistic" (which "helps" Greece), effectually serves as a national branding process, establishing Germany's geopolitical might and boosting its economic competitiveness. As William Davis (2014: 134) argues, within global neoliberalism, a specific kind of nationalism emerges that is meant to establish the competitive features of one nation against others in order to score high in competitive rankings, such as those produced by the World Economic Forum (Schwab & Sala-i-Martín, 2016).

> Immigrants from southern Europe: at the economic miracle! Germany is not sexy – but it is rich. Many young southern Europeans want to escape the crisis in their homeland and set a future in the Federal Republic. But the hurdles are high: the only ones welcome are those complying with the German ideals.
> *Der Spiegel*, 09/08/2011

Germany in such excerpts is celebrated for "being rich" and an "economic miracle". The understanding of richness in national terms hides the class structure of society. Although the German working class may experience better conditions than the working class of the periphery, Germany is still a class-structured society of established inequality. Furthermore, the mythic representation of the "rich country" as an "economic miracle" conceals the labour put in by the native and the migrant working force to create such a "miracle", as well as the ways that the dynamics and contradictions of global capitalism and crisis benefit the core at the expense of the periphery. The imposition of austerity in the South benefits the German economy in different ways: by enjoying the best national bond ratings that allow credit to be given even on negative interest rates, and through the multiple possibilities of expropriation offered to German oligopolies in indebted countries (Dörre, Lessich & Rosa, 2015: 27).

Similarly, the brain drain caused by the crisis in Southern Europe to Germany's (and other EU core countries) benefit is applauded by *Der Spiegel*. Particular attention seems to be paid to the migrants' challenge to successfully integrate into German society. The empty signifier "German ideals" form the benchmark of inclusion, implying not only the need for labouring skills, but for the effective engineering of the soul as well, and the achieving of the Southerners' conformity to ordoliberal Germany.

Der Spiegel confronts the negativity towards Germany with a positive victimisation of the national German self. Thus, in the texts studied, both a negative victimisation of the Other and a positive victimisation of the Self emerge. While the Other-as-victim is addressed as a failure, the self-as-victim is moralised in nationalist and also in "Europeanist" (and consequently, "universalist") terms. Jan Fleischhauer, a conservative German journalist and author (susceptible for racist remarks after comparing all Italians to the captain of the shipwrecked cruise ship Costa Concordia in 2012 in *Der Spiegel*),[5] in one of his articles in *Der Spiegel* column s.p.o.n. – *Der Schwarze Kanal*, entitled, "We, the new world-villains", approached this acclaimed negativity from a German nationalist perspective:

> The German parliament is set to approve a new multi-billion Euro-bailout package for Greece on Monday, but instead of thanks, southern Europeans are expressing their dislike of us. The Germans will have to get used to their new role: We have become the Americans of Europe. Sentiment towards the Germans isn't very good in the region right now. Hardly a day goes by without Chancellor Angela Merkel being depicted in a Nazi uniform somewhere.
>
> *Der Spiegel*, 27/02/2012

Nominalisations construct national homogeneity: "we", "us" and "the Germans" address the national community of the German people. "Greece" and "the South of Europe" are signifiers addressing the Other, while "the Americans" and "the Chancellor" are signifiers forming the identity of "us". Moral legitimacy is, again, provided to "us" due to "our" graciousness and responsibility, working as Europe's "rescuers". As the above article continues:

> If the calculations of the experts are right, we are long past the point of guarantees. We will never see again a good deal of the 130 billion euros of aid decided by the Bundestag today. But if what is done is interpreted according to the main opinions of the crisis-regions, for which the money is destined, then we only want to accomplish what our grandfathers 70 years ago failed to do.

A theoretical rationalisation legitimises Fleischhauer's indignation towards the opposition to austerity policies, based on analogies he draws from a selective

---

5 More information on this issue can be found here: https://en.wikipedia.org/wiki/Jan_Fleischhauer (accessed 09/11/2018).

interpretation of history and geopolitics. In this way, the author explains Germany's current position in the EU and the source of the Southern European negativity towards Germany in ways that are favourable to the positive construction of the national German Self. Furthermore, a German "graciousness" is presupposed that is justified by the risky bailout loans decided on by the German government. These loans are, however, addressed as "aid". The nominal entity of "aid", along with the sum of money it concerns (130 billion euros), authorise the expression of "our" resentment towards the Other. Affective descriptions like "we will never see it again" make a conceptual metaphor of the implied common "hard-working German taxpayer", who is aiding ungrateful people living "beyond their abilities".

As is the case with *Bild*, *Der Spiegel* also responds to the public critique of Germany and its politics on the South with expressions of nationalist indignation. Such a response focuses on the crudest public displays of resentment expressed towards Germany, so as to effectively displace and dismiss critique and to present Germany as the crisis' main victim, despite its benevolence. The same article continues as follows:

> The treacherous feeling of inferiority
> Before we complain about so much ingratitude, we should remember that ... as long as America was the world-villain, the Germans were happy to feel part of the party. [...] The function of the United States as the world's policeman was secretly allowed by all, just as our neighbours leave it now to the Germans to save the Euro. Unfortunately, the feeling of inferiority is at least as dangerous as that of superiority. Of course, you can try to make yourself smaller than you are. We will see how far this self-denial takes ... in the end, the hegemon can never conceal his size permanently.
> "We, the new world villains", *Der Spiegel*, 27/02/2012

Fleischhauer's article here advances a nationalist moral tale while developing analogies between the tasks and the problems faced by the world's leading countries (in the author's view), Germany and the USA. A series of abstract nominalisations ("world policeman", "America", "all", "save the euro") are deployed to produce a robust argument manifesting positivity over the role of "the West" in the world. The passive voice ("allowed by all") reduces agency while justifying the consent of "all" for America to act as "world policeman". A rather psychological explanation is constructed to explain political antagonisms. Fleischhauer suggests that the Germans feel "inferior" due to the shadow of Germany's atrocious Nazi past and implies that this past is unfairly used by today's critics of his country. On an interdiscursive level, the author reproduces the US neo-conservative ideological claims that justified the various US administrations' imperial strategies and military expeditions, moralising them, and deeming them "necessary" for the "world safety". Such nominalisations are hardly explained. "World safety" is taken for granted as a universal entity consented by "all", and so is the idea of the US playing a role of a "world policeman". Later he recontextualises the neoconservative discourse in the German/EU context to loosely dismiss (in a colloquial way) the German left for aligning with the critics of US imperialism ("as long as America was the world-villain, the Germans were happy to feel part of the party"), and to legitimise Germany's neo-colonial role in EU politics on an emergency discourse of "salvation" (regarding the rescuing of the Euro). The author thus implies that the Germans need to feel nationally proud and unashamed, because, sooner or later they need to come to terms with Germany's leading position that the euro crisis opened to it ("We will see how far this self-denial takes [...] in the end, the hegemon can never conceal his size permanently"). This call for national conformity is based on a "realist" premise, positioned outside questions of justice, equality and democratic legitimacy, implying a Hobbesian understanding of society and global politics, in which imperialism is naturalised.

The textual uses of the crude labelling of today's Germany as Nazi by a variety of voices in Southern Europe, in particular, is rather intriguing. They show how the German right recontextualises the memory and the meanings of Germany's Nazi past in contemporary contexts so as to advance a German geopolitical hegemony (Anderson, 2017). One's acknowledgment of one's wrongdoings can become an authoritative topos to claim superiority. Unlike "us" (here, "Germans"), the Other is unable to accept responsibility and repent in the ways that "we" did: "we admit our past wrongdoing and stress the successful process of 'coming to terms' with it in order to present us as morally superior vis-a-vis an external other" (Forchtner, 2014: 411).

In an extended study of the politics of public history in Europe, Hagen Fleischer (2008) noted the German political right's constant effort to constitute Germany as the main victim of the Second World War and its aftermaths. Eventually, this was also extended into the German mainstream. The victimisation of Germany meant the relativisation and reduction of the crimes committed by Nazi Germany and along with them, the responsibility of the German nation for them. Such a responsibility also involves the younger generations. In his study of the Frankfurt School scholars, Jeffries (2016: 265) also highlights that the crimes and the Nazi period were quickly forgotten in Germany right after the war and life continued without a general reflection on complicity in the crimes committed and Germany's overall responsibility for the war and crimes against humanity.

In his first speech as chancellor Adenauer did not refer to German responsibility for the murder of Jews – underlining how the new republic was to refuse to acknowledge Germany's shame during the Second World War. Worse yet, the West German government hired many individuals who had served as civil servants and lawyers under the Nazis; responsibility for the country's economy was taken over by those whom Marcuse and his team at the OSS (Office of Strategic Services) had called economic war criminals.

Upon their return to Germany, the Frankfurt School members found the country to be in a state of mass denial. This is something stressed by many German-born critics, such as the German psychoanalyst Titus Milech (2013). In a detailed study, Heer, Manoschek, Pollak and Wodak (2008) also show that the Wehrmacht soldiers' heavy participation in the Nazi crimes commited in the East especially, is generally denied, both in Austria and in Germany. While reflecting on the Holocaust and its remainders in Germany, Milech notices that obliviousness, the emphasising of "our" post-war suffering, the placing of responsibility on a few individuals (like Hitler himself and a few other top Nazi masterminds and criminals), along with the stressing of Germany's supremacy, are common in his native Germany. These features effectively block a true recognition of the Nazi crimes as a thing that concerns all Germans across all generations.[6] To be sure, such an oblivion and a relativisation of responsibility of horrendous crimes has deep structural roots, related to modernity's discontents, as further noted by Adorno and Horkheimer (1989) among others (e.g. Arendt, 1994; Bauman, 1998). Of further interest, as noted by Jeffries (2016), is that the German capitalists that supported the Nazis also escaped persecution in the Nuremberg trials, although German critical scholars like Marcuse and Neumann, who worked for the US government during the war so as to provide insight on the root causes and the political culture of Nazism, established the association between capitalism in crisis and fascism.

According to Habermas, there is a need to engage in a constant critical dialogue with the past and particularly with perpetrated crimes, so as to advance a more democratic potential for the present and the future. The past always

---

6 The memory of the Hollocaust and the war of annihilation in the East and the Balkans, among other Nazi crimes, are not something that only the German people should be concerned with; all humanity needs to constantly reflect upon and to remember the murderous historical experience of fascism and Nazism, particularly today, given the rise of nationalism and the far right in the West. Nevertheless, it is Germany that is burdened with the actual crimes of the Nazis, perpetrated in her name, while still owing war reparations to countries like Greece for the crimes perpetrated by its troops there. These should also not be forgotten, especially when faced with the rise of German nationalism and its neoracism, as the Greek crisis case vividly demonstrates.

resides in the present and attempts to impose regimes of forgetting are connected with ideas, identities and politics that require obliviousness. As Jeffries (2016) indicates, on the side of the so-called "historians' debate" over the origins and the legacies of the Holocaust in Germany, Habermas had already noted the rise of nationalism there from the 1980s onwards, something that has possibly intensified during the reign of Angela Merkel.

The visual exhibition of Greece in the media (e.g. through a constant recycling of pictures of despair, chaos, poverty and along them, images of holiday sceneries as well) provides factual evidence that make Greece Europe's Other. The upper-class, Occidentalist gaze surfaces in the production of the cultural/racial other. Mirzoeff (2011: 2) notes that "the ability to assemble a visualisation manifests the authority of the visualizer. The authorizing of authority requests permanent renewal in order to win consent as the normal or every day, because [this authority] is already contested". Indeed, contradictions place hegemony's narrative at constant risk. The counter-hegemonic crisis politics, in particular, jeopardise not just the claims and the ideology of the crisis, but also the policies designated to alleviate the crisis as well. Therefore, besides turning Greece into Europe's pariah, the ritualistic iteration of the features reifying Greece into a stable entity, which is controlled (and even owned through debt) by North-western Europe, organise the regime of stability that is necessary for politico-economic power to reproduce the social relations characterising it.

The (Occidental bourgeois) gaze makes an important disciplinary apparatus that captures and enables an effective control of the object. This gaze is also performed by the object itself. The gaze works best when it is internalised by the object. In his article "The hour of truth" (*Kathimerini*, 01/07/2011), Angelos Terzis notes "Europe's anxious gaze" cast upon the Greek parliament regarding the passing of the "necessary" austerity reforms. This gaze was cast while massive protests, which were violently crushed by the police, were taking place outside the parliament (while "Europe" was gazing):

> The same political system proclaiming change and the "end of Metapolitefsi" seems essentially trapped in what it learned to do best for all these years. Although it tries to manage change, itself remains unchanged. It does not listen to the voices – not just the inarticulate cries of the "indignant" citizens – but also to the agony of the vast, silent majority. *Whilst all of Europe was anxiously looking at the Greek Parliament,* Syntagma Square was burning. Although the media was talking about the "most critical vote of all time", our politicians operated as they did in the previous decades, focusing on their own political survival and succession.

"Europe" in this excerpt appears as an (internalised) panopticon, observing "us" (the Greeks) from a distance and being wise enough to make accurate evaluations. This elevation of Europe into a figure of supreme knowledge and judgment makes the Greek liberal crisis-discourse a highly biopolitical one, deemed to play a disciplinary role, in order to reform the Greek people from within. Here the gaze, the agonies and most importantly the expectations of "Europe" from "us" are to be internalised. "We" need to believe and to implement austerity for Europe to accept us as equals, in order to become "true Europeans". This seems to be the crisis' central stake according to the Greek liberal voices. Surely, a neoliberal form of Europeanness is set forth by *Kathimerini*, related to the technocratic and economic understanding of society, the "Greek crisis" and modernity itself.

Likewise, in a quotation from the Danish press, a Greek professor designates a surveilling role to "Europe" over Greece, so that it can develop what it presumably lacks:

> Corruption has not been removed, it is too rooted – or as Stavros Katsios, a Greek professor of economic crime, said: "The core of the problem is that we do not have a civil society culture. In Greece, complying with the rules is a matter of dishonor. You will be declared stupid if you follow the rules. This is precisely what Europe will ensure – a compliance with the rules so that the Greek state will secure tax collection, reforms and the fighting of corruption, before paying more for loans to Greece".
> *Berlingske*, 12/07/2015

According to liberals such as the professor quoted in this Danish article, Greece lacks a "civil society culture". This claim is warranted through the use of a colloquial story full of flattening generalisations, according to which "in Greece complying with the rules is a matter of dishonour". The "problem" is not defined, nor are "the rules" that are supposedly not being followed by the Greek people. Passive voice ("you will be declared stupid") (Fairclough, 2003: 146) abstracts agency and difuses it to the general Greek society, which lies at "the core of the problem". For the Greek liberals, the economic crisis makes an opportunity to reform Greece so that it becomes "European". "Europe" is the nodal signifier of the professor's overall claim, because it supposedly provides the solution to "the problem". A rationalised and overall positive construction of Europe is advanced in a chain of discursive equivalence that articulates signifiers such as "civil society culture", "reforms", "tax collection" and "compliance with the rules". A civil society culture is denoted by conformity to neoliberal technocratic imperatives and not by political engagement, civil associations, critique and democratic participation. The essentialisation of "Europe" as a rigid haven of "civil society", "democracy" and "compliance with the rules", among other things, hides the general democratic deficit characterising Europe, something that the citizens voting for far-right parties in governments across the EU powerfully shows.

Such a technocratic notion of Europe and the West forms the normative stance to address Greece as a problematic entity. It provides a horizon of "realism" and "truth" for Greece to follow in order to redeem and to come to terms with its own "true" self, which is also "the cradle of the West". The advanced capitalist, liberal West/North is a benchmark orienting the outcome of the austerity reforms deemed to be necessary for Greece's European course. However, it is quite unlikely that austerity will bring such results. Austerity weakens the periphery, exposing her to the centre's competition, and secures the debt repayment to the creditors (Roos, 2019: 231). Given that austerity also bears an important ideological role, aiming at inscribing the "free market" values to the citizens (Dörre, Lessich & Rosa, 2015: 46), the ideology of the liberal, modern and secular Europe forms the imaginary horizon that presumably lies at the end of all hardships (often described as "sacrifices") caused by neoliberal austerity, playing the role of a "carrot" for citizens to conform to austerity. In this respect, a quotation from Adorno and Horkheimer (1989: 133–134) captures the repercussions of such discursive constructions, seen through the prism of uneven power relations:

> Capitalist production so confines them, body and soul, that they fall helpless victims to what is offered them. As naturally as the ruled always took the morality imposed upon them more seriously than did the rulers themselves, the deceived masses are today captivated by the myth of success even more than the successful are. Immovably, they insist on the very ideology which enslaves them.

4.4 Concluding Remarks: The Occident, the Orient and the Liberal Meritocracy Cult

> An.Gil. One of the biggest problems in Greece, the biggest impediment to progress is the absence of meritocracy. Greece is a classist and nepotistic society. Only those with family contacts succeed. There is no motivation to succeed – much less excel – because (1) It won't get you anywhere and (2) because you'll be hated for your excellence. (I know this from personal experience). On the contrary, rewarding excellence is the PRIMARY weapon against classism.

Ak.Gav. Who will judge and "reward" "excellence"? Who else but a set of persons – or rules, this doesn't change anything- who are already superior. So, a ruling class.

An.Gil. So you think there is no such thing as objective criteria? Yes, there are biases, yes other humans in power positions create some criteria. But there are indeed such things as facts. And science. And skills. But you do judge an engineer on whether their bridge will stand. I'm afraid this is simply Greek fatalism – or inertia. So a ruling class, so we just take pot luck and things go on in their slipshod fashion.

Ak.Gav. I don't "think". I know there is no such thing as objective criteria. I also know there is no such thing as "Greek fatalism". But there certainly is a thing called orientalism and national essentialism.

The specific discussion that occurred at a Facebook post during the Fall of 2017 is quite indicative of mainstream understandings of Greece. Often enough, such understandings are presented under pseudo-scientific arguments that can oscillate between sociology, anthropology, moral philosophy and engineering, as the excerpt above demonstrates. The Facebook commentator above seems to highlight meritocracy as being the essence of "a true modern" subjectivity and a modern society. Greece, in her view, is "classist", "nepotistic", and not meritocratic. The author implies that traditionalist and classist stagnancy blocks the rise of meritocracy in Greece. If we take her words for granted, it turns out that social classes and traditional social relations and institutions exist only in backward countries like Greece, causing a vicious circle of stagnation there. In effect, fatalism and inertia assume the status of a national characteristic. Therefore, we have a rather totalistic explanatory scheme, with meritocracy being the vantage point of analysis and the solution to this "Greek fatalism and inertia" that the commentator suggests. The Greeks thus need to understand their problematic culture and to transcend it in order to "achieve excellence" and general societal "progress". In the absence of empirical support to such claims, the argument is self-referential, drawing upon pseudo-scientific views and racial prejudices. Critical concepts like "Orientalism" and a critical understanding of society, politics and culture as systems built and reproduced by uneven power relations, can effectively challenge such delimited, poor and conservative understandings of the periphery and its problems, exposing the cultural and class entitlement of such popular claims, while questioning the alleged supremacy of the Occident to judge and to set the objectives to reform the problematised peripheral Other.

The cult of meritocracy is an enduring theme reproduced by the liberal establishment of Greece, formed by ardent public supporters of neoliberal austerity reforms, the "free market" and the EU. Kyriakos Mitsotakis, the current (2018) leader of the conservative Nea Dimokratia party, set meritocracy to be an important political objective in his campaign against "populism" in order to modernise Greece: "Meritocracy everywhere, evaluation everywhere; the best ones will advance according to their work and according to their abilities. This is what the Greek society needs" (*Naftemboriki*, 06/05/2017).

It is rather paradoxical that the son of a former prime minister and a descendant of a highly influential political family of Greece, Kyriakos Mitsotakis (who emerged as the head of the Party that his father had also headed a couple of decades earlier), also speaks about meritocracy. In a detailed study, Littler (2017) demonstrates that meritocracy has been a historically persistent upper-class myth that has become hegemonic because it has progressively been adopted by parties of both the right and the left. In the contemporary, neoliberal context, this term has been used to sustain privilege and to legitimise social mobility and competition as the only resources available to presumably escape the general decline of living standards for the majority of people across the globe.

The cultural construction of the Eurozone/Greek crisis and the culturalisation of Greece's problems serve a) to block systemic critique and the politicisation of the crisis and austerity; instead the culturalisation of the Greek crisis aims to naturalise both the "self-inflicted" crisis thesis and austerity reforms; b) to dismiss political opposition by presenting it as another cultural exception of a modern/Western norm, symptomatic of the broader pathology of a failed country and people; and c) to sustain nationalist narcissism through the making of the secular, hard-working, Western subject, entitled to abuse and to exploit the peripheral Other. Either way, the lack of political thought further asserts the common-sense versions of the world, where things are taken for "what they are" (Lukacs, 2001).

Thus, the culturalisation of the crisis and austerity is part of an upper-middle-class ideological framework, crucial for sustaining its hegemony. Identified with the Occident and its assumed essence, meritocracy appears as a promise and a benchmark to interpellate the peripheral subject into consent to the misery of neoliberal austerity and the degradation of his/her living circumstances. Culturalisation is the flip side of a meritocratic discourse to advance a continuous inert, self-bashing process upon the periphery's working class. In times of low upward social mobility, the discourse of meritocracy and cultural flaws aims to stabilise unequal power relations by pushing competition to the bottom.

CHAPTER 5

Under a Middle-Class Gaze

5.1 Governing Inequality

> Capitalism harms human beings through neglect, rather than through terror. Compared to the personal will of the dictator, the structural violence of the market "forces" appears benign. Those individuals or groups excluded from capitalism's dreamworlds appear themselves to blame. The fate of the poor is social ostracism. Their gulag is the ghetto.
> BUCK-MORSS, 2002: 188

> An important aspect of the neoliberal transformation of society is the recruitment of civil society to serve its objectives. Foucault has pointed to the central role of the new homo oeconomicus in this, a figure thought of in terms of the individual as an "entrepreneur of oneself", maximizing himself or herself as "human capital" in competition with all other individuals [...] this process not only adds to the general insecuritization which the neoliberal government of conduct promotes, but it is also destructive of social bonds and the conditions for social cohesion. This poses a severe problem for the neoliberal state, which it attempts to resolve by reconstituting racism and through war.
> LAZZARATO, 2009: 111

These two citations above disclose different structures and dimensions of inequality, exclusion, coercion, and exploitation met in capitalist states. Susan Buck-Morss' citation demonstrates the limits of the kind of "freedom" associated with capitalism and the regimes of exclusion it creates, particularly in the absence of welfare institutions. Exclusion occurs organically, and its violence is much more abstract than the one potentially exercised by a dictator. For this reason, it can be normalised easier. In Lazzarato's text, one reads about the possible trajectory when the norm described by Buck-Morss is ruptured. Given that the capitalist society is in a process of constant flux, crisis and restricting, racism and war can emerge as viable options for the system's conservation in critical moments. Within the generalised social mobilization context of the neoliberal society, competition between all creates an extensive state of insecurity with detrimental effects on social cohesion. Apparent in state policies and institutions, racism is further triggered during historical moments of high insecurity especially in the absence of a counter-hegemonic political horizon. War then becomes the ultimate frontier, when racism fails to produce the desired systemic effects.

5.2   The Middle-Class Gaze and the Media

Skeggs (2003: 99; 1997) demonstrates that there is a long history of representing the lower/working classes through the idea of excess: as being wasteful, tasteless, self-damaging, deceitful, infantilised and irrational. The lower/working classes are generally constructed as regressive and senseless by the middle/upper classes (Skeggs, 2003: 111). Opposed to such excesses, the upper/middle classes are liberal, rational, self-constrained, mannered, smart, austere and motivated.

Departing from Bourdieu's (2010) seminal text *Distinction*, scholars (Bennett, 2013; Eriksson, 2015) argue that mass media organise their representational frames on social affairs under a middle-class gaze, which suggests to audiences the preferred ways of looking at things. The media's middle-class positioning affirms core bourgeois values shared and aspired to by the middle-class. The middle-class forms the ideal social position, setting a "middle-class normative" (Skeggs & Wood, 2012: 52) that is reproduced by the media through the ways that representations are framed. In this context, the working class and the poor often lapse into the position of the "underclass" (Jones, 2015), associated with different forms of social and individual problems and pathologies, and charged with violence, ignorance and despair. Skeggs (1997) noted that the weight of upper-middle-class values, lifestyles and aspirations establishes a general disidentification with the working class position. The hegemony of the middle class makes a deeply ideological process, connected to the rise of neoliberalism and the efforts of Margaret Thatcher in the UK during the 1980s, to "eradicate class as a social category (and not as a social distinction)" (Skeggs, 1997: 78) and, along with it, to destroy the power of the labour unions and parties, as well as the working class culture, values, social relations and lifestyles associated with it; "No doubt Thatcherism has informed this slippage from working to underclass and has influenced the construction of distinctions within the working class" (Skeggs, 1997: 76).

The working class does not have "access to the legal, aesthetic or moral authority which gives legitimacy to social positions (Lamont, 1992) which could generate positive valuing" (Skeggs, 1997: 76). Political economy studies demonstrate that the media are capitalist businesses reproducing bourgeois ideology (Fuchs, 2016), blocking the working-class experience from emerging into the mainstream public sphere (Negt & Kluge, 2016). In principle, the institutions of capitalist democracy are dominated by the upper-class logic and values. Holders of politico-economic and socio-cultural capital, the upper classes bear sufficient access to social institutions and the media to establish their own agendas and viewpoints (Van Dijk, 1991: 49). Thus, the upper/middle class yields the identity of the working class, along with its hitches, in the public sphere.

The upper/middle-class gaze organising the media's representations of Greece is based upon a sense of ownership and entitlement (Skeggs, 2003: 158). These features are crucial for understanding the culture of class difference and hierarchy. As Skeggs demonstrated in her research on class (dis)identifications, the upper/middle classes assume a sense of entitlement, with their members bearing a right to whatever they do, something that the lower classes are not allowed. In elaborating on such points, Skeggs (1997: 92) quotes her respondents:

> When I first went to work as a nanny I couldn't stand it. They really think they're something else. They treat you like shit. What I've noticed is they never look at you. Well they do at first they look you all over and make you feel like a door rag, but then they just tell you what to do. One of them once asked me if I had any other clothes. Some of them want you to know you're shit in comparison to them. I jacked it in shit money, being made to feel like shit. Even the kids. They learn really early that you're not worth the ground they walk on. They're bastards.
> CYNTHIA, 1992

> They always assume they have a right to anything and everything. It's like whatever they are doing that's their right. They just think the world is made for them.
> ANGELA, 1989

> When we were at school we used to beat them all up. We'd wait for them coming down our way going home from school. They frighten dead easy. But it's like now they're the ones getting their own back. They have money and cars and we're still hanging around here.
> THERESE, 1989

As discussed earlier, ownership is material but also symbolic. On the one hand, it is connected to economic affluence. On the other hand, it is associated with the knowledge regimes that the upper classes develop and accumulate. "Property-thought, or, thought-proper, regulates the distribution of resources and also our ideas of self, knowledge, belonging, law and language" (Skeggs, 2003:

174). Additionally, property defines entitlements exclusive to the owner. Class entitlement defines both the exclusion from and access to, different entities, ranging from objects to people and practices. In the Greek crisis case, the bailout narrative about the "German and European taxpayer's money", constructs a particular claim to address the Other in crisis, as s/he is jeopardising "our" (middle-class) wellbeing. Bourgeois culture presupposes a knowledge of the (working-class/peripheral) Other his/her problems and their solutions. The medical metaphors of the crisis that we saw in the second chapter provide evidence for this thesis. Again, tourist/popular culture and colonial stereotypes affirm such knowledge regimes. Hence, the upper/middle class sense of entitlement emerges from this influx of material and symbolic regimes of ownership, further legitimised by the political and media talk in the public.

Relevant research shows that there are variations and divisions within the middle class, reflecting differences in background, work, education or consumption patterns (Bennett et al., 2009: 179). The varying middle-class gazes evident in the media may also denote regimes of distinction existing within the middle-class world. To use an example from the present study of the German press, both *Bild* and *Der Spiegel* show middle-class dispositions in their making of the Greek crisis. Nevertheless, *Bild* deploys a much more spectacular way of constructing the Greek crisis, while *Der Spiegel* assumes a rather "austere" mode of representation. The analysis of Chapter 4 shows the different rhetorics deployed by these media while covering the Greek crisis. This difference can be explained by the audiences addressed by such publications. *Bild* is a popular yellow press largely consumed by conservative, lower-middle-class Germans, while *Der Spiegel* is consumed by an ostensibly more informed, upper middle-class, liberal audience, distancing itself from the aesthetics and the rhetoric of *Bild*. Nevertheless, as is the case with all the media studied, both these publications abstain from issues of class conflict, investing in the making of their case in national terms, victimising Europe/Germany as a benefactor, and blaming Greece.

5.3   "The Loser" as a Master Class Frame

According to the American sociologist Richard Sennett and his significant work "The corrosion of character: the personal consequences of work in the New Capitalism"

> Failure is no longer the normal prospect facing only the very poor or disadvantaged; it has become more familiar as a regular event in the lives

of the middle-classes. The shrinking size of the elite makes achievement more elusive. The winner-take-all market is a competitive structure which disposes of large numbers of educated people to fail.
SENNETT, 1998: 118

A central class frame in late capitalism, the "loser" is an idea connected to the process that Sennett (2006: 94) describes as the "the broadening spectre of uselessness". Uselessness, Sennett argues, has become a modern threat due to "the global labour supply, automation, and the management of aging" (Sennett, 2006: 86). This development puts great pressures on both the lower and middle classes due to the tendency towards the deskilling and redundancy of both blue- and white-collar workers, forcing people to become more competitive in order to remain active in the labour market and "employable".

Embedded in the generalised logics of competition, the idea of "winners" and "losers" constitute an enduring ideological theme of the entrepreneurial culture, coupled to the fear of becoming economically redundant. In this research, the "loser" is a general category implied to discredit the whole of Greek society for not occupying a place next to the "winners" of neoliberal globalisation. As the flip side of the "loser", the "winner" defines the preferred identity manifested in the media studied. The winner/loser dichotomy can also be seen as a disciplinary technology, aiming to reproduce the unequal social status quo. As Derber and Magrass (2016: 48) note

> The ideology of winners and losers [is] conveyed in a particularly bullying discourse [...] Thus, the rich deserve all their wealth and blessings, whereas the poor deserve their low station and misery. Since the market is seen as a Darwinian selection process, it is only natural and good that the rich – those who have proved their worth – assume control over the society as a whole [...] The system will not function unless the poor learn that they deserve their fate; workers must be bullied until they embrace this Darwinian view that they are inferior and deserve their fate.

The concept of "the loser" is a subject position emerging from the ideology, the rationalisation, the practices, and the social relations of competition. The precariousness of work, the decline of welfare, the loss of trade union power, globalisation and the eclipse of an anti-capitalist political horizon and mass movement – all of these things intensify social exclusion, pauperisation and anxiety. Neoliberalism individualised the systemic pressures posed on the workforce. In this way, failure to meet the pressures and requirements of work came to be seen as individual shortcomings, related to the morals, incentives and determination of particular people. The dismantling of welfare was also publicly legitimised as an institution that was too costly for taxpayers to be sustained and a burden to the most innovative and ambitious workers: "the ideology of social parasitism is a powerful disciplinary tool in the workplace; the worker wants to show he or she is not feeding off the labours of others" (Sennett, 1998: 140). Furthermore, the eclipse of socialist politics and a communist horizon, along with a political vocabulary addressing the systemic character of the exclusionary and exploitative processes of late capitalism, have also been significant in the advance of such individualistic narratives of work. In short, the depoliticised construction of the working class as a social formation of "losers" has advanced alongside the defeats of working-class struggles (Skeggs, 2003: 47).

5.4 The Greek Crisis and the Construction of "Losers"

Let us now deploy the theory above analytically. A moral and seemingly depoliticised argument frames the Orientalised subject in equivalent class terms. The "winner/loser" comparative topos helps make evaluative claims about the Self and the Other. Competition, wealth, property and success form the criteria to judge one as a winner or a loser. As explained earlier, these are part of a bourgeois value system that is material and symbolic. Moreover, the authoritative voices of the Western liberal establishment warrant the specific decrees. As a loser, the cultural/class Other is spectacularised to produce entertaining and affective media content made to be consumed by the middle class, real or imaginary.

A thematic analysis is developed in the sections that follow, where various class signifiers are organised according to the central analytical theme of "the loser" that denotes the failed Other in class terms. The construction of the "loser" produces the problematic social identity of individuals and groups (or nations) that cannot compete, lag behind, or cannot adjust to the "reality" of capitalism. This analytical point is connected to neoliberalism's demands for "turning of oneself into a marketable and competitive product" (Skeggs, 2003: 73). As a broader cognitive frame, "the loser" makes an analytical master theme comprised of various other subthemes signifying subject positions deemed as "non-bourgeois", economically unproductive and generally incompatible to the neoliberal restructuring demands. These subthemes include the "immoral", "irresponsible", "irrational", "angry", "immature/infantile", "confused", "ignorant/uneducated", "uncivil", "lazy", "bankrupt", "poor", "unemployed", "afraid", "victimised", "unmotivated", "ungrateful", "scrounger", "populist", "communist", "complaining", "protesting", "intolerant" and "threatening" Other. It is important to note that the tactic of displacement that was diagnosed in the previous chapter is at full play here as well. Many of these themes are meant to downgrade, to shame and to slander the Other (e.g. the "lazy" Greek allegation is simply not true) so that s/he may identify with hegemony's logic.

The discursive construction of the loser is meant to affirm the dominant and entitled position of the winner, while the loser needs to accept his/her subordinate position and his/her subsequent "undeserving" status. The construction of the social loser, associated with cultural traits, relate to what Wallerstein (Balibar & Wallerstein, 1991: 33) described as the ethnicisation of the work force. In the media, this incites an expression of nationalist narcissism, inviting a racially/nationally-defined working class to identify with the upper classes through the celebration of the nation and its success in the European/global market. The Northern/Western reader is called to rejoice for his/her national belonging, or (in the case of peripheral subjects) to identify with the model that the rich and competitive nations project, in the hope of dissociating him/herself from the disturbing and embarrassing position of the "loser".

The middle-class gaze cast upon the Greeks' somewhat poor deeds makes the Greek people uncivil, as their actions and "character" come into sharp opposition with those of the "Europeans". In this way, the European self versus the Greek/non-European Other is reproduced in class terms as well, through the establishment of civility standards. The regular depiction of images and reports of unrest, urban decay, violence, poverty and misery, estrange the Greek space and its inhabitants from the European norms and civility standards. Giroux (2016) associates discourses of incivility with conservative ideology, which shrinks political practices into mere performances and appearances. In this process, the motivated, prudent and constrained bourgeois subject surfaces as the vantage point to observe and assess the malfunctioning Other. A seemingly objective and often ironic gaze is cast down especially towards those resisting austerity.

The "loser" frame is contingent on various events and circumstances. Its varying attributes and characteristics are further connected to different representational modes. Depending on context, the "loser" is pitied, ridiculed and loathed. Developed from theory, these categories express specific affects relevant to middle-class modalities (Mylonas, 2018d). According to Fairclough (2003), modality is about the politico-ideological dispositions of a discursive edifice. Affect has to do with the impact of the emotions triggered by specific objects. As objects are also discursively constructed, meaning regimes are central to the development of affects. To understand affect, I return to the work of Sara Ahmed (2004: 28), who develops a rather performative understanding of emotions. This understanding concerns the sway of an object: "affect does not reside in an object or sign, but is an effect of the circulation between objects and signs" (Ahmed, 2004: 45). In our context, the object is mediated and produced by hegemonic discourses, and widely communicated through spectacular mass media publicity. This process overdetermines the object, reducing its subjectivity and blocking its voice. During circumstances of civic unrest against austerity in Greece, the research shows that spite emerges as the leading affective modality producing the Greek other. Spiteful publicity is targeted against a dangerous underclass of scoundrels that (supposedly) threaten "our" well-being (Skeggs, 2003: 85). At the same time, while expressions of spite are more clearly elaborated in the nationalist and the yellow press, a contemptuous form of pity appears to be the key expression of resentment in the progressivist liberal publications like *Der Spiegel*. In this regard, the post-structuralist conceptualisation of discursive logic (Glynos & Howarth, 2007) is analytically deployed to demonstrate the fantasy of retaliation that emerges in the hegemonic discourses of the crisis and austerity.

The analysis that follows develops the main subcategories of the "loser" theme: these are a) the irrational, b) the immoral and c) the threatening. Concurrently, the analysis of the specific subcategories advances through the depiction of the main affective modalities identified in the texts studied. The main categories of affective modalities identified are a) ridicule, b) pity and c) loathing/spite. These affects appear in all three thematic subcategories of the "loser" construction. Yet, the specific kind of loser represented is often connected to a particular kind of affective modality as well. The construction of the loser as threatening is accompanied with prevailing expressions of spite and loathing and, to a lesser degree, with ridicule. The irrational and immoral notions of the loser are enhanced by the affects of pity/contempt and ridicule, which often work in a complementary fashion. The sections that follow will establish these relations in a more elaborate mode, through the use of concrete textual examples.

5.4.1 *The Irrational: Ignorant, Irresponsible, and Frustrated*

Reason and objectivity have a central place position in the liberal-bourgeois world because, based on positivist science, they constitute the foundational blocks of the Western subjectivity and worldview. Capitalism's ideal subjective form, the homo economicus, aims at establishing objective knowledge regimes to claim universality and to avoid inclinations to more subjective contexts (Feldner & Vighi, 2015: 55). In principle, Western positivist science and economics, in particular, provided the authoritative legitimacy to frame capitalism as an objective system. Over time, these became sedimented forms of common-sense knowledge regimes dictating the imperatives of individual and societal conduct.

The idea of "irrationality" constantly emerges in the media as an explanation for the Greek crisis and the failure of austerity. Irrationality is pivotal in explaining the "self-inflicted" character of the Greek crisis, an idea connected to the causalistic crisis explanations within which the Greek people "lived beyond their abilities". It also underscores the representation of various practices of resistance to austerity regimes, ranging from protesting and striking to voting. In that sense, austerity's failure to achieve its proclaimed goals is attributed to phenomena deemed "irrational".

Media constructions of "irrationality" can be seen in the excerpts below:

> Mass strikes: did the Greeks lose their dreamland? The mass uprising against the shock-saving program of the government threatens to destroy the self-image of the Greeks. Are they now striking their destroyed country?
> *Bild*, 12/03/2010

> The left has a huge share of responsibility for the bankruptcy system [...] with its outrageous and stubborn negativity, it verified its full inability to make any serious proposals while staying trapped in violent populist politics.
> *AthensVoice*, 19/5/2010

> Debt crisis: Greeks complain about the ugly Germans. The Greeks fight against the state bankruptcy and their financial descent. Many are foaming with rage. They make external enemies responsible for the crisis: the EU, the Monetary Fund, but above all, the Germans. Why?
> *Der Spiegel*, 09/09/2011

> Frustration over saving-plans in Greece: a nation of protest voters.
> *Der Spiegel*, 04/05/2012

> Greek left-wing politician Tsipras: The Euro-horror: His furious performances – combined with a good dose of patriotism – are appealing to many Greeks in the confusing times of crisis.
> *Der Spiegel*, 26/5/2014

> Europe's most erratic leader: Prime Minister Alexis Tsipras has refused to follow the normal rules and pushed Greece completely into the economic abyss, but the Greeks still love him.
> *Jyllands Posten*, 05/07/2015

"Irresponsible Greeks": The Greek government and the Greek people have succeeded in drawing a picture of them as victims of great injustices from the creditors. But the fact is that Greece and the Greeks have lived beyond their means for many, many years. You have used 10 per cent more than you have earned. If we exceeded our budget by 10 per cent year by year, our banks would soon close our loan options ... It is, of course, the responsibility of the individual Greek voters. One's voice has weight and one's choices have consequences.

Jyllands Posten, 08/07/2015

In Greece, there is an abuse of the word solidarity [...] [solidarity] means that the strong give up some of the privileges in order to help the weak and not to reward irresponsibility [....] They (the Greeks) want help by voting a government that does not have any political will to reform the Greek society in a way, that can guarantee growth and a responsible management of the billions that other countries have risked in order to help this nation in crisis. It is a weird form of solidarity that they demand from the others.

Berlingske, 07/07/2015

All excerpts above relate to different events. Yet, they are underlined by the prevailing idea of "irrationality", common to the media representations of all three countries studied. The idea of irrationality emerges as a conceptual metaphor, through the use of "framing devices" such as the following signifiers and utterances: "frustration", "foaming with rage", "irresponsible Greeks", "did the Greeks lose their dreamland?", "confusing times", "In Greece, there is an abuse of the word solidarity", "refused to follow the normal rules", "complain", "outrageous and stubborn negativity".

The reduction of collective civic practices and legitimate democratic processes to "irrational" actions implies a conformist form of the authorisation of the dominant, "common sense" crisis and austerity meanings (Van Leeuwen, 2008: 109). Conformist authorisation means the turning of specific logics and practices into normal or common-sense solutions, on the basis that "everybody" does or accepts things "as they are". This way, Syriza's rise to power appears to be an abnormal incident that can be attributed to confusion, as stated above by *Der Spiegel* in 2014. In addition, instead of being self-reflexive, the Greeks tend to blame others; they construct external enemies and scapegoats, particularly in the form of the Germans. For this reason, they are frustrated because, if they acted rationally, they would not vote for populists like Syriza, but for "normal" (conservative-liberal) parties for whom the majority of "Europeans" usually vote. By voting for Syriza, they acted irrationally, remained alienated from reality and reproduced the "same mistakes" that bankrupted their country in the first place. Likewise, what solidarity is and how it is (supposedly) abused by "not complying with the rules" (of the austerity dictates) and by voting for Syriza in Greece is explained to the Danish readership of *Berlingske* in terms of equivalent causalistic themes. Either way, a common ideological belief that underpins the irrationality frame, is the Greeks' denial of the self-inflicted character of the Greek crisis, and the necessity and rationality of austerity reforms. In such discursive edifices, class structure and class conflict are negated (Block, 2018).

Nevertheless, middle-class meanings are argumentatively legitimised as common-sense by the expert authority of neoliberal pundits, such as economists, politicians and business people, and also through the like-minded representatives of the Greek upper classes. In the few cases where working-class Greeks are given a voice, the media's contributors and journalists confront them with the hegemonic crisis arguments. In this way, they succeed in blocking the voice of the Greek working class, constituting its members as examples and actual proof of the "Greek irrationality" ideological thesis. In a *Jyllands Posten* (29/06/2015) article entitled "In the Greek Hellerup" (Hellerup is a well-heeled Copenhagen quarter), one reads interviews with Greek upper-class persons where, among other things, one explains that with regard to the Greek referendum:

> It is wrong that the government wants us to vote: we have not been part of the negotiations so we are not able to know what to vote [...] People that want the Drachma do not have anything to lose, but they have to think about the future of the country.

The "future of the country" here appears as a nominal entity, presented as something that is supposedly above class interests. Therefore, "everyone" needs to identify with the "national interests". The class bias, however, is evident, as the person interviewed represents the class of rich Greeks and discusses the position of those that "do not have anything to lose". Here, he represents national interests according to his upper-class position, which dictates that he is in favour of the Euro and sustaining the country's regime of austerity. Likewise, in a *Berlingske* article bearing the rather ironic title "Maybe they expect us to die", a disabled pensioner is interviewed about austerity reforms and the early days of the Syriza-led government in 2015. During the process, she is regularly confronted by the Danish journalist:

> "Syriza is better than the previous government; not everything they do is just wise, but they at least try to defend us against our enemies". "Enemies?" [asks the journalist] "Yes, the Europeans, and of course, the Germans; I do not know what they want us to. We cannot continue with austerity when we have almost nothing. Maybe they just want us all to die". "Maybe they just want their money back" [the journalist replies] "Maybe, but it's not very smart, because you cannot get money out of a person that owns nothing, or, has died".
>
> Berlingske, 01/07/2015

Challenged by questions suggesting that no one actually hates or wishes anyone to die, the working-class voice is reduced to a mere expression of exaggeration and frustration. The seemingly "naïve" (even "shocked") rhetorical style of the questions, and the ironic mood of the article's title quoting the interviewee ("Maybe they expect us to die"), legitimises the hegemonic crisis and austerity discourse through the authority of conformity to a common sense over the Greek crisis that is confirmed by authority figures such as mainstream politicians, economists and upper-class voices. The journalist's questions reproduce the ideological assumptions of austerity, where the EU is supposed to "help" Greece with bailout loans. By probing the word "enemies" (as uttered by the interviewee) in seeming bewilderment, the journalist also evokes a post-political understanding of society, where, along with the class, political enemies and adversaries are also made to appear as anachronisms of a bygone era that surely have no place in the EU "partnership".

5.4.2 The Immoral: Lazy, Profligate, Deceitful and Bankrupt

The "lazy Greek" idea has been one of the most central and enduring themes in the publicity of the Greek crisis. Despite its fictitious essence, this recurrent theme gained notable popularity to the point of becoming a general common-sense framework, not just in Northern Europe, but across the world. To summarise the specific stereotype, the Greek Other is poor and bankrupt because s/he spent his/her time in idleness (which supposedly comes "naturally" in warm climates) and also "lived beyond his/her abilities" by taking advantage of the wealth that was created in the prudent West and North of Europe. Instead of saving and of taking care of the property trusted to him/her, the Greeks (and other Southerners) were proven to be pathetic spenders, who enjoyed a lavish, hyper-consumerist lifestyle.

The "lazy Greek" stereotype was regularly repeated during the first years of the crisis in particular. It was blended with other equivalent ideas that imply passivity, profligacy and fraud. The following news reports headlines and summaries demonstrate this point:

Athens pays pensions for dead pensioners; millions for dead pensioners! No wonder why the Greeks are broke: millions of pensioners, already dead, have been being paid for years! That's what a study revealed.
   Bild, 27/08/2010

Merkel increases pressure: The Greeks should have fewer holidays. The pressure on Europe's debtor is growing: Chancellor Merkel wants people in the debt-states to work longer and to take less vacation.
   Bild, 19/05/2011

Greece's poor rich pensioners: "Actually, we would all have to concede" [*Der Spiegel* here quotes a Greek pensioner it interviews]. Early retirees and employees of state enterprises have become a symbol of mismanagement in Greece. Polyvios Tsirkas is both. He receives quite a generous pension, has a cottage by the sea – and sees himself as a victim of the system.
   Der Spiegel, 20/06/2011

Oppressed Greeks: "I want my life back" [*Der Spiegel* here quotes a person that it interviews]. They lived their dream as highly paid train drivers of the Greek railway, but then came the crisis. Now many officials have to toil in Athens hospitals. The story of a state-organized decline.
   Der Spiegel, 28/06/2011

The "lazy Greek" stereotype is a classist stereotype as it seldom (if at all) refers to upper-class Greeks. The Greek working class in the excerpts above is represented in homogenous terms through various nominalisations like "they", "we", "the Greeks", "oppressed Greeks" (Fairclough, 2003:146). In such texts, the Greek workers appear as privileged ("being highly paid", having a "generous pension" and a "cottage by the sea"), mindless and profligate (having "lived their dream"), self-victimising ("sees himself as a victim of the system"), wasteful (with some receiving "money for dead pensioners") and excessive ("millions of pensioners", "employees of state enterprises" and "early retirees", who "should have less holidays"). Sloth emerges through the connotations triggered by the touristic experience of Greece (common to the readers of the German and the Danish media), as a holiday place with warm weather and as a place to live one's (petty-bourgeois) dream. Sloth also emerges through the acts of deceit, which were done so that one could avoid working. The construction of the Greek workers as unable to grasp their condition further shows their indolent state, as the lack of willingness to work is also the cause of one's infantilisation. Hence, the irrational Greek working class cannot understand its own condition and cannot self-reflect. On the contrary, it resorts to escapism, dreaming of a return to an unrealistic place, a dreamworld. In this way, the Greek working class becomes chiefly responsible for Greece's economic crisis and is positioned as a symbol of the Greek state's alleged dysfunctionality and corruption. Here, the individual emerges as the one that bears the prime responsibility for his/her debilitated state, and not the system. This view summarises a central ideological thesis of neoliberal capitalism, serving the naturalisation of capitalism and the symbolic elimination of class conflict and class hierarchy (Block, 2018).

Irony organises the rhetorical mode of ridiculisation advanced through publicly shaming the Greek working class. Often enough, irony makes poverty seem fictitious. The examples shown above make the voice of the oppressed to appear as exaggerated and untrue, and its political demands as false. Most importantly, in such representations, the pauperisation that is caused by austerity seems "self-inflicted", "natural", and deserved. Scholars (Skeggs, 2003) note that the pathetic, non-motivated image of individuals and groups is usually attributed by the upper to the lower classes, calling them to blame themselves for their own unprivileged condition. In this way, the dominant classes can potentially make the poor responsible by making them concede to the diagnosis reckoned for them. Overall, the working classes are represented in demeaning ways in the mass media, as irresponsible, tasteless and lacking agency and culture; in contrast to that, the middle and the upper classes are represented at the forefront of the modern, as the beacon of national identity and as a cultural reserve (Skeggs, 2003: 104).

The voice of the working class and poor Greeks is undermined through the journalists' ironic expression (Potter, 2011: 112), making the working-class people come out as both naïve and devious. The irony is organised through a factual assemblage that depicts the Greek working class as affluent. The making and use of a colloquiality scheme composed of two antithetical adjectives (poor rich) to describe the state of Greece's pensioners by *Der Spiegel* demonstrates the sharp contrast that presumably rests between the actual reality and the working class' own self-image (as being a victim or poor). Accordingly, Greece is made to appear as a poor country inhabited by somehow rich (yet devious) people. A conceptual metaphor is implied here (Wodak & Boukala, 2015: 95), suggesting a general "Greek deficiency", with regards to why the country is poor and bankrupt. The revelation of fraud and corruption cases from below makes expressions of journalistic irony emerge naturally, through the very acts of the Other.

> So corrupt are the bankrupt Greeks [...] Anyone in need of a driver's license or a clinic place, must pay a bribe. [Bribes amount to] 1300 Euro per year (per person)!
> *Bild*, 02/03/2010

> 600 blind on an island: Greek authorities check social fraud. An apparent mass blindness is causing problems for the Greek authorities: more than 600 residents of a Greek island receive state support for alleged disability. It would not be the first case of social fraud in the crisis-state.
>
> *Der Spiegel*, 02/08/2011

As laziness is, in essence, corrupt, the poor and insolvent are also deceitful. Therefore, along with an economic one, insolvency has an important moral dimension, because the Greeks are (supposedly) guilty for not working, not saving and not being reserved.

> The downfall of the Fakelaki state. The Greeks have far from stopped using the "fakelaki" envelopes with bribery, which is a decisive cause of Greece's economic moral collapse [økonomiske morads]. Money under the doctor's table is believed to have risen by billions.
>
> *Berlingske*, 12/07/2015

Morality is central to making classed selves (Skeggs, 2003: 23). In this respect, capitalism is seen as, not just a rational, but also a moral system by its supporters (Feldner & Vighi, 2015: 36). Morality is an overarching theme of the self-inflicted Greek crisis narrative. As the above Danish article mentions, the economic collapse of Greece is moral in essence and concerns "all of Greece" that is flattened by the metonymy "fakelaki state" coined by the preceding Danish journalist, Michael Bjerre. (Petty) Corruption is one among equivalent "sins" regularly reprimanded in the bourgeois press. Along with idleness and profligacy, they form the root causes of the Greek crisis, which comes out as moral in essence. Indolence lies on the antipode of work. Work, let us recall, has been an enduring theme that legitimises bourgeois property and sense of entitlement. Historically, the notion of work has also been deployed to legitimise colonial conquests. In classical liberal theory, work is the measure of honesty and integrity. Moreover, work is supposed to produce wealth and to improve the natural and the social world as well (Wood, 2017: 157). "Hard work" provides authoritative legitimacy for lay explanations of the Greek crisis, bearing a moral force upon subjects in the bourgeois world. The state of "not working", as defined by the capitalist mode of production, means failure and decadence. In that sense, insolvency and indebtment are attributed to a failed work ethos, accompanied by an insufficient sense of responsibility. Together, these features legitimise the claiming of the assets and the property of the failed and bankrupt, so as to supposedly improve them and to fulfil the meaning of progress that capitalist modernity proclaims to be standing for. Along with the symbolic and material power of debt to dispropriate, one of the most iconic media statements of the "Greek crisis" that best captures all these characteristics, is possibly the following one, entitled "Sell your islands, you bankrupt Greeks! And sell the Acropolis too!" published in *Bild* in 27/10/2010 and reproduced in other media across the world. As it reads:

> Although it might sound crazy: If we still have to help the Greeks with billions of Euros, they should also give something back, for example, some of their beautiful islands. Motto: You get coal. We get Corfu. In fact, it is the largest treasure of the Greeks: 3054 islands, with only 87 of them being inhabited. And there is a market for that! For example, in the Hamburg brokerage firm Vladi Private Islands, an uninhabited Greek island has the negotiable price of 45 million Euros. CDU [Christian Democrats Party] senior member Josef Schlarmann: "Those in insolvency have to sell everything they have to pay their creditors. Greece owns buildings, companies and uninhabited islands, which could all be used for debt redemption". The coalition partner FDP's [Free Democrats Party] financial expert Frank Schäffler said to *Bild*: "… The Greek government has to take radical steps to sell its property – for example, its uninhabited islands".

The possibilities of capitalist expansion and accumulation offered by the Greek debt crisis are celebrated by *Bild*. The authoritarian voices of the politicians interviewed legitimise the possibility of a "crazy" idea. The relevant markets for such "commodities" and the related business normalise the particular claims through the evoking of common-sense themes. The imperative of the debt is what lies at the core of such an expropriating process, offering a moral evaluation principle that requires no further justification (Van Leeuwen, 2008: 109).

At the same time, besides fiction, social impoverishment is also presented as a fact, particularly during the later years of the study's timespan:

> Economic crisis: Greece threatens mass poverty. Greece saves – and the number of people living in abject poverty is growing dramatically. By the thousands, hungry people are looking for food and searching for something useful in the garbage. Apart from the financial bankruptcy, the country is now threatened with social bankruptcy.
> *Der Spiegel*, 16/07/2011

The coverage of Greece's humanitarian and social catastrophe, striking the lower classes in particular, often emerges in the overall Greek crisis publicity, predominantly evident in the accounts of *Der Spiegel*, such as the above. In principle, however, such representations are underpinned by sensualising and depoliticising notions of poverty.

> Now Greece compares with Somalia, Sudan and Zimbabwe.
> *Jyllands Posten*, 01/07/2015

> Greek pensioners gather en masse and desperately push each other to get money. Greece's banks are running out of money.
> *Berlingske*, 01/07/2015

> Penniless Greeks create uncertainty and discord in the Eurozone. Tsipras desperately needs money to avoid a Greek collapse, but he comes to the summit without any proposal for the way forward.
> *Jyllands Posten*, 07/07/2015

Images and stereotypes of misery and poverty (e.g. the reference to African countries in the Danish press above deployed as metaphors of wretchedness) are being reproduced, especially in the most politically critical moments of the crisis, when the continuation of austerity regimes was being challenged by elections or protests. Such representations alienate Greece from Europe, which appears to stand on Europe's antipode. Pity in this sense is more associated with contempt over the pathetic state of the peripheral Other in crisis. Boltanski (2004: 5) has explained that the publicity of human suffering "does not necessarily lead to a politics of pity", which could develop a sense of indignation. Instead, it is the mode of representation that largely defines the identification or not with the sufferer and accordingly, the development of solidarity, and the possibility of political action.

The construction of the Other in pathetic terms, as poor, infantile and helpless also has a spectacular dimension:

> Greeks' boycott call against German products. That was enough for the bankrupt Greeks: they do not want to be called by the Germans as Euro fraudsters any longer.
> *Bild*, 26/02/2010

> Greece begs the EU for help! Greece's Debt Crisis: In the Greatest Crisis, Prime Minister Giorgos Papandreou Seeks Help from the EU!
> *Bild*, 03/03/2010

> Greek financial misery: Athens begs Berlin for political help. The Greek Prime Minister Papandreou advocates during his visit to Berlin for German

support in the debt crisis. The federal government should help this country to receive better credit rates in the financial markets. The CSU and SPD make it clear: Athens cannot expect direct payments unconditionally.

Der Spiegel, 05/03/2010

Predicative nouns and adjectives denoting helplessness are used to construct the doleful status of Greece, its people and its politics in passive and fatalistic terms. This kind of crisis publicity also nurtures nationalism in the readers of the German and Danish media, whose countries are framed through equivalent nominalisations denoting authority and centralisation ("Berlin"), enhanced in power to decide upon the fate of a failed Other.

Overall, such moralistic accounts see the economic crisis, neoliberal austerity and the suffering caused by it, as a form of theodicy. This has been a recurrent theme appearing in the Western and Northern media of capitalist advanced states. It marks the metaphysical essence of capitalism, which in addition to being a system is also "a religious phenomenon through and through", demanding unconditional and absolute dedication without offering chances of redemption, and with "self-destruction being the only path to salvation" (Feldner & Vighi, 2015:1).

5.4.3 *The Threatening Other: Resentment, Spite, and Loath*

The religious faith in capitalism is most explicitly expressed in upper-class accounts, often by developing some theoretical arguments and imperative statements that are meant to be followed by "all". The lower classes may express a more subtle kind of conformity and consensus towards capitalism. Nevertheless, in moments of material pressure, this can take a form of resentment towards those that the capitalist ideology deems as scapegoats.

The emotion of resentment has been noted by scholars (Demertzis, 2006; Giroux, 2016) as a key expression of class dissatisfaction, connected to the feeling of an "undeserved advantage" (Barbalet, 2004: 63) that is experienced by specific social groups at the expense of other ones. Scholars highlight the sociological dimension of this emotion, to distinguish it from the mere individual-psychological aspect of spite and resentment. Though class-related and bearing the aforementioned characteristics of indignation due to advantage, this kind of resentment expressed in the media is based upon a politically regressive logic (Glynos & Howarth, 2007: 141; Hirschman, 1991). This is because resentment targets the poor and the working-class of the EU's periphery instead of the capitalist class, which, in the midst of the crisis, sustains and expands its privileges. At the core of this political logic, lay the depoliticisation of the economy, inequality, and the lack of a working-class identity.

A key identity construction here is formed around the nodal point of the "hardworking European/German taxpayer", advanced by all media studied, though in a different tone and in a different language:

> Germany is to pay 18 billion Euros! Greece is for the German taxpayer a financial nightmare! 18 billion euros from Germany to the bankrupt Greeks.
> *Bild*, 21/04/2010

> Greeks in Euro-crash make our bread more expensive! The Greeks weaken the Euro. That we can already see today: the prices are rising. Even the bread is more expensive. The recovery is in danger!
> *Bild*, 04/05/2010

> Greece is broke, Germany is debating: Should we pay billions for the ailing country on the Aegean, this bottomless pit? Should the European Union finally become a transfer union? It's finally time for clear words, says Stefan Kuzmany.
> *Der Spiegel*, 15/09/2011

> Bankruptcy: What would a Greek bankruptcy cost to every German Citizen? The Eurozone's finance ministers are not satisfied with the Athenian reforms' plan, while the always open debate on national bankruptcy continues. How much would a Greek bankruptcy cost to each individual German?
> *Der Spiegel*, 10/02/2012

> Finance Meeting: Europe's citizens have to pay for Greece. The IMF and the ECB demand a radical haircut for Greece. But who should bear the costs? Most creditors are already protected against potential losses, which, the citizens of the Eurozone will end up paying.
> *Der Spiegel*, 26/11/2012

The different kind of language that the media use to express the same thing, notably the costs of the crisis and the bailouts to Greece for the "German taxpayer", unfolds hierarchies of middle-class positions. Lower middle-class sensibilities are expressed by *Bild*, mainly organised around populist-nationalist social logics, and middle-class ones for *Der Spiegel*. Such social logics make the common-sense framework underlining the discursive construction of the bailout politics. A right-wing tabloid, *Bild* addresses the German working-class in victimised and nationalist terms, while representing Germany as a homogenous whole. *Der Spiegel's* audience is a bit different because it is generally read by middle/upper-class liberal, educated German citizens. *Bild* instead, is generally consumed by the lower/middle-classes of "patriotic" Germany. Therefore, *Der Spiegel* deploys a more subtle, somber and politically correct language, speaking to a liberal and upper/middle-class audience. In the case of *Der Spiegel*, in particular, liberal civic identity and the regimes of taste and knowledge of the upper middle-class legitimise the sense of entitlement to scrutinise the Other. While loath is more directly expressed in *Bild*, in *Der Spiegel*, it surfaces in the expressions of ridicule and contempt.

The myth of the "Greek scrounger" legitimises the compromise of the Greek peoples' political, social and even human rights, which are reduced by austerity regimes, in the name of the hard-working European/German/Danish taxpayer. To this respect, Stuart Hall (2011) argued that the idea of the "hard-working taxpayer" is fundamental in the public communication of neoliberal policies and reforms. In the neoliberal context, the identity construction of the "taxpayer" is the flip side of that of the "consumer", which constitutes a key dimension of neoliberal civic subjectivity. Just like the consumer, the taxpayer pays his lot and is entitled to specific claims and services. Simultaneously, the taxpayer is the opposite of the "welfare scrounger" who lives off hard-working people's labour. The hegemonic construction of the taxpayer also reflects the broader biopolitical changes in welfare policy across the EU, where social rights are increasingly being understood as exclusive services to those entitled (Lorey, 2015: 42). Inequality here is governed (and publicly normalised) by the neoliberal policymaking in the EU through the Othering of the Greeks, who, by not conforming to the requirements of capitalist reproduction, are precarised (Lorey, 2015: 37). To be sure, the taxpayer is not solicited on the use of his/her taxes, nor is s/he informed on how the public funds are managed. For instance, the bailing out of bankrupt banks after the 2008 credit crunch worldwide (Harvey, 2014: 132), or, the transmuting of Greece's national debt from a debt owed to banks, to a debt owed to nation states, through Greece's excessive lending, are good examples of the taxpayer's disempowered civic position.

In times of high uncertainty, the media's constant blaming of specific groups of people and individuals (such as migrants and the working-class) as supposedly threatening, produces affective representations that can potentially trigger regressive socio-political tendencies (Fuchs, 2017b). Portrayed as a potential threat to "our" (European/German/Danish) well-being due to his/her deceitful acts (and his/her hate towards "us"), the Greek Other emerges as a primarily national antagonist (Carpentier, 2017: 349). The media produce a simplistic comparative topos between "good" and "bad" nations. The depiction of the Greek people to be living at the expense of (hardworking) others evokes the conceptual metaphor of the (undeserving) parasite. As the Greeks deceived the hardworking Germans, they should now pay the price of their wrongdoings through harsh austerity reforms. Hence, austerity in Greece is imposed in the name of the German/European taxpayer. Due to his/her hard work, the German/European taxpayer is entitled to call for austerity in Greece, in order to secure the return of his/her money. Moreover, the German/European taxpayer is invited to police the developing of austerity in Greece through the crisis' publicity. This way, the disciplining of "the Greeks" (through the imposition of austerity regimes) can only signal "good news" for "our" national community. Besides the material side of austerity's support, as it is manifested to be the only possibility of guaranteeing payback, the cult of capitalism offers no possibility of redemption but destruction. The moralistic dimension of debt along with the sense of guilt it entails ostracizes from the realm of right-bearers those that fell into insolvency.

Austerity regimes and among them, the dispossession processes that they unleash are supported and occasionally celebrated:

> The government wants, by all means, to make the Greeks dismiss the riotous and non-tax paying living, with extraordinary savings methods.
> *Bild*, 25/02/2010

> The EU increases pressure: the Acropolis on the sales list. Does Greece have to sell the Acropolis? The EU is increasing the pressure! Bankruptcy candidate Greece is supposed to sell the silver of its state property in order to finally get some money into the coffers, as Brussels demands.
> *Bild*, 17/05/2011

> The hand that feeds you [...] That's going to be hard! Not only for the Greeks. For the whole of Europe! That's why Papandreou, like an ancient hero, relentlessly fights for saving up [public funds].
> *Bild*, 16/06/2011

> Every second survey in Germany wants the Greeks to go bankrupt. A majority of Germans agree that we should let Greece go bust. Only 43 percent, according to a recent survey are in favor of more financial aid.
> *Bild*, 10/09/2011

150 000 officials kicked out. The Greeks will be bankrupt in October – if they do not save at last! Athens wants to take drastic measures.

Bild, 20/09/2011

New savings plan must now bleed the Greeks properly. The Greek government is serious and slashes even more public sector jobs than previously planned.

Bild, 21/09/2011

In such excerpts, resentment and spite emerge through demeaning nominalisations ("bankruptcy candidate Greece"), the declarative grammatical mood ("A majority of Germans agree that we should let Greece go bust") and grammatic metaphors ("the hand that feeds you", "Papandreou, like an ancient hero, relentlessly fights for saving up") that signify positivity for austerity. The idea of sadism is surely relevant here too, as this declarative mood expresses commands and wishes ("every second survey in Germany wants the Greeks to go bankrupt in October"), as well as conditions ("the Greeks will be bankrupt if they do not save at last!") that make the events described to appear as symbols of victories achieved against the threatening Other. The "extraordinary saving methods", the sacking of "150.000" civil servants, the making of the Greeks "to bleed", the selling of the state's "silver" are transformed in necessary means for a "relentless fight for saving up", which seems like an objective goal. As the crisis' myths attribute the crisis to Greece and its people, the media fetishize austerity as a method of both reparation and retaliation.

The conceptual framework of discursive logics (Glynos and Howarth, 2007) can help us here to see how the mainstream austerity discourse functions. As a social logic, austerity is reduced to a common-sense, "saving" pattern connected to a prudent bourgeois mode of life-conduct. The political logic of austerity is realist and concerns the ensuring of the bail-out loans pay-back. The fantasmatic logic of austerity concerns the idea of retaliation, by evoking the fantasy of revenge and victory over the deceiving and threatening Other. Austerity here emerges as a deus-ex-machina apparatus, a form of a theodicy, to restore order. These reactionary logics abstract the primitive accumulation process released by austerity, and divert the possible understanding of the effects of such policies, which are not just destined for the punishing and the disciplining of the Greek working-class. The spiteful representations of Greece are caught within the general structural insecurity that is provoked by neoliberal globalisation and the demands for competition, mobility, and the demise of welfare institutions, in Europe and elsewhere. Again, this process emerges in line with the general absence of a popular socialist vision; instead of a discussion of class exploitation, socio-economic insecurity is laid out in common-sense nationalist and middle-class social logics by mainstream media.

The spiteful gaze also targets the political alternative and the popular resistance against austerity. These are seen as constituting radical threats to the established status quo of "Europe". To turn to the Danish media, in his *Berlingske* "The humiliated savior", the aforementioned Michael Bjerre appears to be wondering "what has Alexis Tsipras actually obtained for the Greek people?" to claim that

> The former Communist must suffer the humiliation [...] the humiliation is absolute for the man, who the Greeks saw as a savior upon taking office as prime minister in January, after his socialist-flamed rhetoric issued promises of reinstatement of thousands of public employees and a "cancelation" of the requirements of the loan agreements with the EU.

The specific Danish author attempts a "realist" account of Syriza's accomplishments, in retrospect, after the defeat of Syriza's anti-austerity strategy. Tsipras is ridiculed and loathed. What surfaces as important in the social logics underlining Bjerre's retrospective evaluation of Syriza's strategy, is what "works" and what "wins", and not the principles behind practices and the obstacles that these meet. This way, the "de-ideologised" neoliberal political logics of competition and the crude economistic logics of efficiency and cost-benefit analysis surface (Dardot & Laval, 2013: 254), along with the "no alternative" rationality of neoliberal policymaking.

The moderate left government of Syriza is generally presented as "extreme" by economists, right-wing politicians, and upper-class citizens. The antagonistic political underpinnings of the liberal press are well captured in another article from the Danish press too:

> Obviously, there is an overall ideological goal that is more important than preventing an economic collapse. Technically, Greece is already in a state of bankruptcy, and its banks are on the edge of insolvency. The EU must sharply confront the use of such a critical reality to promote fantasies to transform not only Greece but the rest of Europe into a Marxist-Anarchist experiment.
> *Jyllands Posten*, 05/07/2015 -lead article

A manifestation of bourgeois spite (Ross, 2008: 150) is apparent in such excerpts, triggered by anxieties over the possible loss of class privileges, threatened by the political activity of the oppressed. Additionally, a stereotypical demonisation of Communism is expressed while discussing Syriza, a party that is far from being communist, or even socialist. Historically, anti-communism has been a central propagandistic instrument in Western politics and ideology, "to mobilize the populace against anyone that may advocate policies that could challenge property interests or promote radicalism" (Herman and Chomsky, 1988: 29). Therefore, in the liberal press, the class experience of crisis and austerity and the subaltern/working-class political subjectivity is negated and dismantled.

5.4.4 Idealising the Bourgeois; the Enduring Myths of a Peripheral Upper Class

In a 5 July 2015 article from *Berlingske*, someone named Dimitrios Svolos (interviewed as "a member of the rich Greeks") stated,

> The country has always flirted with communism [after the fall of the dictatorship]. The socialist governments have adopted an extreme left mentality, where the entrepreneurs and businesses have been forced to be in the background while allowing the public sector to grow.

In principle, one notices a general alignment of the Greek liberal media studied to the claims and logic expressed by the German and the Danish media. Nevertheless, while the German and the Danish media reproduce a social imaginary of national homogeneity that is based upon the premises of wealth, hard work, and law-abidance, the Greek media, in line with the liberal European press, tend to blame the Greek people, their country and their state. From a Laclauian perspective, the Greek media reproduce the hegemonic crisis-myths and sustain the hegemonic Western/bourgeois social imaginary.

As the *Berlingske* excerpt above shows, the political left and social democracy are blamed for Greece apparently not being capitalist enough, even though Greece was always part of the Western geopolitical constellation. Centre-periphery theorists (Amin, 2014) see the matter in quite different terms though, arguing that the peripheral bourgeoisie is, in fact, tied to the interests and the strategic planning of the capitalist core because it has not developed its own, nation-based monopolies. In Poulantzas (1979: 71) terms, the peripheral bourgeoisie is not a national bourgeoisie[1] but a "comprador bourgeoisie", because

---

1 According to Poulantzas (1979: 71) definition "national bourgeoisie is that fraction of the indigenous bourgeoisie which, on the basis of a certain type and degree of contradictions with foreign imperialist capital, occupies a relatively autonomous place in the ideological and political structure, and exhibits in this way a characteristic unity".

it does not have its own base for capital accumulation and is forced to act as intermediary for imperialist capital. For such reasons, it is economically, political and ideologically subordinated to foreign capital. This connection may adequately explain the Greek upper-class resentment of the Greek working class and allow us to understand better the self-orientalisation practices it publicly unfolds.

A key idea of the Greek liberal media's discontent towards Greece here has to do with the alleged "bourgeois" shortcoming of Greece. In this sense, as the quote above suggests, the Greek liberals tend to attribute Greece's shortcomings to the country's supposed leftist governance and culture. These seem to have suppressed entrepreneurship and the private sector, while advancing a clientalist state with an enormous and dysfunctional public sector. Fundamentally though, the country also seems to face a lack of embourgeoisement. Thus, Greece's cultural shortcomings are also connected to a "true bourgeois" deficit. According to such a narrative, Greece did not develop a true bourgeoisie and for this reason, it did not become a true secular liberal state. Greece also did not develop a mass bourgeois culture, maintaining a rather provincial, non-secular and traditionalist habitus.

In "the provincialisation of the bourgeoisie" (*AthensVoice*, 09/12/2014), Haris Xirouhakis discusses the particularities of the Greek bourgeoisie:

> The loss of Greece's urban consciousness is now a fact that is accelerated by the economic crisis [...] not that the bourgeoisie ever had strong roots in Greece. [...] In due time, the bourgeoisie downplayed its criteria of social distinction by upgrading people not deserving of it. Celebrities and the nouveau riche, with their exhibitionism, shallow sensationalism and kitsch, became paradigmatic. [...] Along with their economic success, the bourgeois succumbed to fraud. [...] Many bourgeois did not avoid the easy enrichment through indecent methods. Eventually, the bourgeoisie lost its civility.

The bourgeois class is represented here according to the very bourgeois myths legitimising its existence: meritocracy, entrepreneurialism, civility and honesty are highlighted through their opposites in Xirouhakis' account of the Greek bourgeoisie. The hegemony of the bourgeois ideology remains affective across the globe, despite that late capitalism offers minimal possibilities for upward social mobility (Sennett 2006). Hobsbawm (1975) has convincingly demonstrated that the bourgeois myths were largely created by cynical opportunists, who used any available tool to enrich themselves. The bourgeois features, presented as perverse due to Greece's unenlightenment, are in fact the typical features of the bourgeois identity (Ellul, 2007).

In another article published in *Protagon* entitled "The Enlightenment that we did not live" (02/08/2014), Chrysanthos Stephanopoulos, an economist, argues that:

> If someone attempted to identify the real causes of the crisis, he should start from the period of Enlightenment that Greece never experienced (because of the Turkish rule). The system of landowners was never turned into a well-governed bourgeois system but simply transformed into a new oligarchic system, controlled by the state and their affiliations. One should not go that far back in time: The main causes of this crisis came during the post-junta period. Consumerist nirvana engulfing the years of prosperity blinded us from reality. Few exceptional politicians who tried to warn us in due time were summarily sent by us to historical oblivion while deifying populists and demagogues who gave away borrowed money.

Stephanopoulos' description summarises the two main causes of the liberal "Greek-deficit" narrative: the Ottoman rule of Greece and the post-junta period. The Ottoman rule ("Turkish") and the "post-junta period" are semantically fixed entities negatively assessed. The Ottoman rule is disregarded for "stalling of Greece's Westernisation". The author also seems to imply that the post-military-junta period was even worse than the military junta, although the post-junta period was marked by a general democratisation of society and the lifting of the general living standards of the country (Tsoukalas, 2012). Historical events and meanings are recontextualised (Fairclough, 2003: 139) in ways favourable to the author's ideological position, excluding consideration of the context and social difference. Likewise, Greece and its people (through the use of the pronoun "we") are nominalised as perennial and homogenous socio-cultural entities. Most importantly, this "Enlightenment deficit" deprived Greece of the "true" bourgeoisie, who would organise politics, the economy and civil life in harmonious ways, like those of the West. The clause a "well-governed bourgeois system" positively defines the noun "bourgeois" in a self-explanatory manner. Socio-historical accounts (Hobsbawm, 1975; Polanyi, 2007; Marx, 1977; Chibber, 2013) demonstrated that the development of bourgeois societies was neither smooth and uncontradictory, nor a complete process: on the contrary, the establishment of the bourgeois class domination and mode of production was confronted by revolutions and revolts, met by violent state interventions and processes of harsh land-grabbing and accompanied by a violent proletarianisation of the peasantry to create a class of "free labourers" to work in the inhumane conditions of the industries. As Harvey (2014: 135) notes, "monopoly power is inherent in private property forms"; the bourgeois class has never been fair or redistributive, but instead used its politico-economic power to create institutions to sustain its interests, becoming a new oligarchy that was reactionary to "progress". Similarly, Vibek Chibber (2013: 89) argues that popular rights enjoyed in Western countries were not granted by an enlightened bourgeoisie but claimed and fought for by the working classes. Finally, consumerism is an attribute of the contemporary world (Bauman, 2004), as economic growth is based on over-production of commodities which is connected to the increase of consumption and the opening of new markets. The kind of consumerism targeted by Stephanopoulos is the supposedly unearned one, related to the earlier mentioned bourgeois morals of entitlement and hard work. As the analysis has already showed, related privileges are not warranted to the Greek people.

5.5 Concluding Remarks: Reaction, Diversion, Division

> To that, I agree with Mr. Schäuble. Societies do not change that easily, dear. But I also have to say that those failing to adjust, die!
> ADONIS GEORGIADIS, Vice President [from 2016] of "New Democracy" (the Greek Conservative party). *Enikos*, 2012

> I have no illusions with regards to the impossibility of a society to exist without inequalities; this would be in contrast to human nature and those who have pursued it, eventually compromised democracy and the rights of the individual.
> KYRIAKOS MITSOTAKIS, President [from 2016] of "New Democracy" party. *The Press Project*, 2017

A discussion on class and inequality is important in order to expose and challenge the normalised neoliberal ideology, which, as Henry Giroux (2008: 88) has noted, aims to establish "a winner take all society where inequality and private power rather than justice and equality shape the larger social order". As the quotations above show, a Hobbesian-Malthusian, regressive view of the world is envisioned by prominent supporters of neoliberal reforms in Greece, and elsewhere. In the years after Syriza's succumbing to the Troika over the continuation of austerity, the conservative-neoliberal block in Greece – further encouraged by the general rise of conservative and far-right governments in the EU and in the Americas – emerged in much more uncompromised terms, aiming to achieve a reactionary ideological hegemony that goes beyond the mere establishment of consensus over the necessity of austerity. As the rise of far-right movements in Europe and the USA suggests, the Greek mainstream conservatives are not alone in publicly advancing such ideological assertions. Conservatives join hands with the neoliberals (Giroux, 2008: 7) in an effort to re-establish a "meritocratic" (or rather, aristocratic) order based on the laws of "nature" that seemed to have been overcome by the time of the French Revolution. Despite their appeal, such positions are deeply classist because they aim at constructing rigid social hierarchies and at abolishing egalitarian institutions and rights.

To this end, Hirschman's (1991) analysis of reactionary argumentation is useful. Hirschman argues that reactionary arguments are based upon three theses: the perversity, futility and jeopardy thesis. In brief, according to the perversity thesis, any effort to change a given socio-political system or condition brings worse results; according to the futility thesis, the attempts of social transformation are doomed to fail; finally, according to the jeopardy thesis, efforts for social change have too high dangers and costs for what already exists. The quotations of the right-wing politicians above seem to go beyond these points as they speak about introducing a form of a natural order of natural inequality and adjustment, beyond institutions and aspirations for equality and justice. The analysis of the Greek crisis mainstream media repertoire can indeed be read through Hirschman's points in so far as it negates the potentials of political opposition and resistance. To establish a class-based critique thus aims to advance an offense to the conservative-neoliberal counter-revolution, questioning and refuting their core-values, rather than positioning itself in an apologetic fashion to the questions that hegemony sets.

This chapter addressed the class dimension of austerity politics and their public construction. The subject in crisis is produced in primarily moral, cultural and psychological terms (Mentinis, 2013). An issue of character and discipline emerges in the exotic image of the Greek people, masking economic and political power inequalities and injustices while advancing the biopolitical dimension of neoliberal reforms. As the capitalist system is not to be criticised, and the Greek crisis is self-inflicted by "all", and as austerity reforms are not to be contested because there is no alternative to them, the Greek government needs to implement austerity and the (guilty) people need to accept, believe and support it instead of "blaming others" for what they themselves have caused. A post-political position is expressed, in which technocracy – as far as governance is concerned – and conformity – as far as citizens are concerned – are to resolve social problems "objectively". Such a position, however, masks wealth and other inequalities and advances the interests of the bourgeoisie. Austerity is a class assault, aiming to restructure the position of the working class to capital's post-crisis requirements and to reproduce the capitalist politico-economic order. Within that, the entrepreneurial, mobile, risk-taking, flexible, individualistic subject is central to the modelling of society by the enterprise (Dardot and Laval, 2013: 259). This implies the lack of a mainstream systemic analysis for the general state of insecurity caused by the political interventions pursuing this agenda, and the blaming of individuals and groups of people (usually the poor) for systemic problems, such as the construction of pauperisation as a "culture of dependency" (Skeggs, 2003: 87). Counter-austerity resistance and politics are also presented as either hopeless, or as dangerous, by providing an image of the chaos and misery caused by protests, instead of one of struggle and potential; these images have been reduced into mere reactions of confused, angry people bearing inferiority syndromes and lacking knowledge, strength and incentives.

In its different facets, racism has always been a constitutive part of bourgeois societies' disciplinary technologies that reproduce power relations and social hierarchies (Balibar & Wallerstein, 1991). In today's crisis context, this is further connected to what Isabelle Lorey (2015) describes as the development of governance through precariousness. Precariousness involves the rise of an individualist type of subjectivity that is risk-taking, competitive, entrepreneurial and hostile towards taxation and various forms of institutional solidarity, seeing human suffering in subjective terms (as something that individuals are responsible for). Those failing to adapt are vilified as parasitic "losers" through a Malthusian repertoire that individualises pauperisation, disempowerment and exclusion (Harkins & Lugo-Ocando, 2016: 79). The Orientalist framing of the "Greek crisis" is thus connected to the reproduction and intensification of established bourgeois values associated with the primacy of private property and hard work. Indeed, as Wendling (2012: 178) demonstrates, "the demoralisation, infantilisation, and alienation of the working class, as practiced by its domination by capital, serve the productive interests of capitalism as a whole". Thus, race and class constructions are intimately connected.

The vilification of different populations that fail to meet the market criteria of living, along with the stressing of enduring bourgeois aspirations for life more generally, destroys the potential of developing politics of international, class solidarity. International class identities would be based on the acknowledgement of equivalent contexts of exploitation and disempowerment. Instead, the shaming of the working class confirms the hegemony of the bourgeois and intensifies the working-class identification of the individualistic ethos of neoliberalism. The German finance minister Schäuble, for instance, responding to concerns over Germany's growing politico-economic power in the EU's decision-making processes, rejected the idea of a European Germany:

> It is not about creating a "German Europe". That's nonsense. [...] It is about creating a strong future for Europe on the global stage.
> *Deutche Welle*, 2015

Austerity is thus meant for all working-class people: Greeks, Germans and anyone holding an EU passport. The exceptionalisation of Greece, however, due to its alleged moral, cultural and political shortcomings, is about setting a negative example: that of the "bad" or maladjusted "European" needing to achieve class conformity in the EU and to create a scapegoat to channel the stress and the insecurity produced by austerity and its effects, including unemployment, poverty, competition, isolation and uncertainty.

CHAPTER 6

Exceptionalising the Crisis, Normalising Austerity

One of the most despised figures by Greeks after his country backed harsh austerity measures in return for bailouts, German Finance Minister Wolfgang Schäuble said he deserves credit for forcing reforms to be adopted. "One day, (the Greeks) will erect a monument in my honor" Schäuble was quoted by *Handelsblatt* newspaper as saying during an election rally in Germany.
     The National Herald, 26/08/2017

∴

Those that are poor are not mean, fools, or uneducated; they just make the wrong (voting) choices in critical moments.
     ANTIGONI LYMPERAKI, Parliamentary Representative of "To Potami" Party, 30/06/2015; *info-war.gr, 2015b*

∴

6.1   Technocratic Politics

Chapters 4 and 5 presented the cultural and moral construction of the Greek crisis in the European mainstream media. Both dimensions are interrelated and stem from authoritative political and economic institutions and establishments. The technocratic expertise of neoliberal economists in particular, outlines the economic crisis in a seemingly depoliticised manner. Acts of depoliticisation though are in themselves highly political as they aim at advancing particular political agendas (Dean, 2009b: 23). In our case, these agendas derive from the politics of the neoliberal right in the EU, associated with the overall neoliberal project of advancing and safeguarding capitalist globalization (Slobodian, 2018).

The cultural and the moral construction of the crisis (alleged) perpetrators, is connected to the hegemonic politics of the crisis. The mainstream media's sensualistic crisis representations intensify the specific politics. The mainstream public explanations of the economic crisis and austerity are meant to make public sense as objective, "realistic" and "reasonable" (Harjuniemi, 2018: 2). They are intended to function as obvious, natural, self-evident and plausible accounts of the economic crisis and emergency politics, and for this reason, they reproduce a depoliticised and causalistic reasoning that is based on selected facts, with regards to how the crisis happened and what should be done about it. As we already saw, the "Greek crisis" makes public sense as something caused by people who lived "beyond their abilities". In a similar fashion, austerity is supposedly the logical thing to do, because, when you are bankrupt, you need to start saving up and to cut down on your expenses so that you will be able to pay off your debt.

Although an objective event, the capitalist crisis is sublimated as something that only experts (e.g. technocrats) can decide upon. The rapid enforcement of neoliberal austerity aims at deploying the crisis as an opportunity for restructuring capitalism. The crisis itself, as the different constructions of the threatening Other showed, entails serious dangers that require quick resolutions. The threatening Other is threatening insofar as s/he blocks the crisis' (preferred) solutions, which concern the establishing of neoliberal austerity reforms. An objective of the hegemonic strategy of capitalist restructuring is to contain social antagonisms and to maintain social stability.

The analysis of this chapter aims at showing how the European dimension of the global economic crisis, seen through the lens of the Greek crisis, is constructed as an exceptionally threatening event that requires equally exceptional responses. Although political, this character is often denied and the politics of exception are represented as realist, rational, scientific, and procedural. The analysis here also wishes to show how the neoliberal hegemony discredits the various forms of oppositional politics that politicise austerity and how austerity is communicated as a no-alternative policy framework that requires urgent implementation. What is interesting to note is that, both the outcasting of political opposition and the no-alternative-to-austerity policy framework are framed as "democratic" practices. This particularly occurs in moments when counter-hegemonic and oppositional practices challenge the hegemonic politics of the economic crisis.

6.2   Establishing the Crisis and Austerity in Depoliticised Terms

The analysis of the media's crisis and austerity coverage is organised according to main themes that denote the ways that the crisis and austerity are publicly reproduced in seemingly depoliticised ways. These consist of three central and interrelated themes running across all the media studied. I deploy CDA tools to show how austerity is represented as the only policy available that is "painful but necessary" (and fair), advancing through a crisis' eschatological (Apocalyptic) mythic depiction. To that respect, I look at the argumentative topoi that ground austerity. Then, I focus on the legitimation strategies of austerity. These are threefold: they are mythopoetic, authoritative and conformist (Van Leeuwen, 2008).

The establishing of an exceptional policy regime – after communicating the economic crisis in Apocalyptic terms – austerity is legitimised through a mythopoetic reason stressing fear and insecurity, on pending worse catastrophes, if austerity is not to be rapidly implemented. In that sense, the argument is constructed in a dilemmatic way, where, it is either "austerity or catastrophe", with the "catastrophe" never being adequately explained (Doudaki, 2018: 148). Austerity and its catastrophological rationales (based on a crisis as Apocalypse myth) are publicly legitimised by the hegemonic neoliberal-nationalist discourse, by referring to both expert accounts and to lay, common-sense explanations of the economy and of the state of affairs of peripheral (and exotic) countries such as Greece; here popular stereotypes are effectively mobilised to sustain an exceptionalist construction of Greece and the alleged "self-inclined" character of its crisis. In Van Leeuwen's (2008) sense, the discursive legitimacy of austerity is established through authoritative reason (by referring to experts and to authority figures such as established politicians), as well as through the invocation of conformity and prevailing societal (common-sense) understandings of things "as they are". The analysis shows how the hegemonic narrative of austerity is sustained in time, despite the contingency it encounters and the negativity the latter entails, when reality contradicts austerity's aspirations and political action confronts its strategic plans.

6.2.1   *The Eurozone Crisis as an Apocalyptic Spectacle: The Mediatised States of Exception*

According to mainstream economics, the 2008 crisis and its European version were exceptional events that shocked experts and the dominant social power structures. In one of his final texts, the late German Marxist theorist Robert Kurz (2012) argued that the economic crisis of 2008 signified the implementation of emergency politics, such as austerity reforms, in the West for the first time after the Second World War, starting with Europe's periphery. Kurz maintains that up until 2008, this has been a practice implemented in the non-Western periphery, in order to sustain imperial spheres of influence as well as to respond to the shifting needs of capital accumulation and security for economic transactions. Nevertheless, as the political scientist Alexandros

Kioupkiolis notes, although peripheral, Greece was in fact fully integrated into the Western politico-economic and cultural system, with its liberal democracy, free market economy, and consumerist lifestyles. In that sense, the emergency crisis-politics implemented in Greece were also later to develop in core Western countries too, though in different intensity. To be sure:

> The violent oligarchic regime change which has been initiated with the first "bailout" package in 2010 marks an authoritarian turn which might augur similar trends in other western liberal democracies, using the Greek "weak link" as a guinea pig for a new mode of rule in crisis capitalism, at a time when the "historical logic of dependent relationships between the center and the periphery" moves inside the capitalist empire.
> KIOUPKIOLIS, 2014: 144

In her influential work, "The Shock Doctrine", Naomi Klein (2007) demonstrated that during the late 20th century across the world, different forms of crisis, from armed conflicts to economic and natural crises, are constantly instrumentalised by dominant politico-economic agents and their pundits to launch "free market" reforms (Ojala & Harjuniemi, 2016: 415). This concerns the development of free market laws and institutions, as well as the commodification of a variety of aspects belonging to the natural and the social realm that previously existed outside the range of market-driven activities. Besides Greece, equivalent exceptional policies were later applied in other EU states too, notably Ireland, Portugal, Spain, Italy, and Cyprus. The overcoming of capitalism's crisis required a change of rules, norms, policies, and institutions, and in that sense, Greece became a laboratory (Žižek, 2010; Badiou, 2012) testing the limits of neoliberalisation.

Greece's formal entry in the so-called rescue mechanism formed by the EU, the ECB and the IMF (what is commonly known as Troika), declared by Prime Minister George Papandreou junior on the 23rd of April 2010, formalised Greece's entry into a state of exception. Agamben (2000, 2005) among others (Diken, 2009: 584) maintain that the state of exception is the "nomos of modernity". With the duration of austerity regimes being indefinite, there is indeed a normalisation of austerity, despite its earlier emergency character.

> Shocked Greeks: "God, help us". The Greeks are in a collective state of shock. The savings plans have caused pure terror. Newspapers titles: "God, help us!".
> *Bild*, 04/03/2010

"It's about survival". With a dramatic speech, Prime Minister Papandreou has prepared the Greeks for a horror-saving package. EU and IMF aim to tinker with a shock [reforms'] list.
   Bild, 30/04/2010

Chaos Days in Greece; Hellas makes the whole world astray! Here are the heads of 20 major industrial countries from around the world who have enough problems already.
   Bild, 03/11/2011

Crisis in Greece: Papandreou speaks of a "war situation". On Wednesday, Greece's head of government Papandreou announces drastic austerity measures. Tax increases and salary cuts in the civil service are mentioned. With pithy words, he prepares his compatriots for it.
   Der Spiegel, 02/03/2010

Financial Crisis: Greece is making more debt than expected. The Greek financial disaster is even greater than expected: The budget deficit of the heavily indebted country in 2009 was 13.6 percent, as statisticians of the EU have calculated. It is already the third correction of the Athenian data within a year.
   Der Spiegel, 22/04/2010

On the edge of Europe: Greece's crisis is not only economic but also existential. In love with West Europe but still anchored in its oriental cultural inheritance, the country has struggled during many centuries to find its place in Europe. A Greek exit from the European community will have fatal political consequences.
   Berlingske, 28/06/2015

The examples above demonstrate the dramatic character in which the media represented the Eurozone/Greek crisis. These evoke the conceptual metaphor of a hampering ontological catastrophe, an Armageddon that the financial crisis carries. Terms such as chaos, war, disaster, shock, horror and survival are emotionally loaded, metaphorical expressions widely used to describe the crisis and its social impact in eschatological terms. Eschatology here concerns a state of an immanent and final risk, where "survival" is in peril. These public utterances intensify the manifested necessity of the development of emergency policies like austerity reforms, as, in *Bild*'s spectacular frames above, things are so bad (for Greece) that perhaps, only supernatural powers may resolve. Drawing on CDA (Fairclough, 2003: 99), we can argue that the prevailing legitimating mechanism of austerity regimes at the earlier stage of the crisis, was mythopoiesis. The crisis was communicated to the general publics of Europe and the global by mainstream media, politicians, and experts as a myth of catastrophe, as a coming financial Armageddon.

This way, the Eurozone/Greek crisis emerges as a moral panic, as its consequences are unpredictable and concern potentially everyone, not just the (already) "bankrupt Greeks". Continuous reports stressing uncertainty produce audience suspense over the prospect of an imminent total economic collapse, reifying the crisis as an objective reality and at the same time, mystifying it, as something ungraspable. The mystification of the crisis is also part of the commercial exploitation of the latter and its converting into a media spectacle as well.

> US intelligence file: a Greek bankruptcy would cost 2 trillion Euros; Banking meltdown, financial market turmoil, and trillions of costs: a secret CIA report estimates the cost of a possible Greek bankruptcy.
> *Bild*, 01/10/2011

The crisis is sublimated into an ungraspable entity, similar to unforeseen natural catastrophes. No-one (not even the financial experts) seems to know what will actually happen. Secret file revelations announced by the German tabloid press, bearing the authority of the CIA, disclose astonishing threats of economic ruin.

> Are the Greeks pulling us into the abyss? The drama is worsened day by day; Tuesday is the day of the decision: Are the Greeks pulling us into the Euro-abyss? Vote!
> *Bild*, 24/06/2011

The cultivation of public fear makes the crisis-spectacle more engaging while calling upon to German reader to respond to the pre-fixed agendas posed by the crisis-publicity. The reader is also asked to take a position upon the dilemmas constructed by the hegemonic crisis-discourse. The apocalyptic construction of the crisis is further discursively legitimised through the use of authority voices. Economists, media pundits, leading politicians are frequently being referred to, with their grim estimations being spectacularly highlighted. The evaluations of financial institutions and the signals given by the financial markets are central to the development of crisis policies and their public communication. As Durand (2017: 102) argues, "financial institutions and asset markets become the control room of economic development, by guiding capital flows to the most profitable sectors, and by forcing policy-makers to advance policies that may allow the increased profitability and shareholder value".

> The Euro bomb is ticking! The explosive mood in the financial markets! Before the EU summit, everyone is waiting for a signal to rescue the bankrupt Greeks. The Euro-exchange rate threatens to crash.
> *Bild*, 24/03/2010

> Minister warns: Greeks are broke in July! The Greeks are waiting for even more money from the EU! If the billions are not there by the end of July, Greece is bankrupt, according to the Minister of Finance Papakonstantinou.
> *Bild*, 24/05/2011

> Economists Warn Against Euro Crash. Europe is sinking into the debt crisis – with potentially dramatic consequences for the Euro. Managers and economists fear a rapid decline in the value of the common currency. In Germany, the fear of inflation is already rising.
> *Der Spiegel*, 09/05/2010

> Debt Crisis: Who bears the biggest Greek risks? What happens if Greece goes bankrupt? Experts warn of a second financial crisis – a chain reaction that will cause banks worldwide to collapse. Big risks could be in the USA.
> *Der Spiegel*, 26/06/2011

Metaphors of collapse, catastrophe and decay are frequently deployed, in order to draw historical parallels between events despite their contextual differences. For instance, the collapse of the German Democratic Republic (GDR) is detached from its historical context and recontextualised in the Greek crisis framework in order to demonstrate to the German public the danger of Greece's possible collapse.

> Does Greece threaten to collapse like GDR? The Euro is in free fall. The Greeks are guilty. Economists and politicians debate the consequences.
> *Bild*, 10/05/2011

The teleological crisis-narrative is universal, as the possible financial collapse of Greece may also lead to the collapse of other countries:

> Will the whole world soon go bankrupt? Greeks, Irish, Portuguese, Spaniards, Belgians, Italians – half of Europe is sinking in debt. In the US, the president warns of insolvency.
> *Bild*, 13/07/2011

> Billions in aid for debt state: Merkel sees recovery threatened by Greece crisis. The Chancellor warns of dramatic consequences, if Greece would go bankrupt: a national bankruptcy [of Greece] could endanger Germany's growth. Merkel believes that even a crash as in 2009 is possible. FDP Member Lindner sees even private cash deposits of citizens to be endangered.
> *Der Spiegel*, 11/06/2011

> Vote on austerity package: The world is shaking with Greece. In Athens, the decisive meeting on the government austerity package has begun, a small majority seems certain. But what happens if the program still fails? A Óxi, a No, could have devastating consequences for the indebted country and the rest of the world.
> *Der Spiegel*, 29/06/2011

> Chaos threatens Greece after "No". The Greeks have said a clear "No" to the reform requirements of other Euro-countries. This sends Greece into sharp economic uncertainty. The country may be on the way out of the Euro. A new emergency summit of the Eurozone countries on Tuesday evening; the next days will be crucial for both Greece and Europe.
> *Berlingske*, 05/07/2015

One notices a frequent use of modal verbs (as appearing in the translated versions of the articles originally published in German language) such as "will", "may", "would", "should" or "could". The possibility of the worst possible scenario is stressed by the use of modal verbs in excerpts such as the above, in the case that Greece refuses to comply with the creditors' policies, represented by the Troika and the memorandums' program of austerity reforms. Modality denotes what one commits oneself to, and so the use of modal verbs in crucial moments of political decision-making processes, signify the modal dispossitions of the media, that intensify the claims of European right-wing politicians (Fairclough, 2003: 166). Along with the emphasis on catastrophological senarios, the imperative of recapitalizing Greece's debt through public funds is also stressed through the depiction of the dire consequences that a potential Greek bankruptcy will have on Germany in particular.

As part of a political strategy of achieving social hegemony over austerity across the EU, the eschatological construction of the crisis aims at (1) organizing the public consensus of austerity policies by spreading of fear and insecurity, (2) legitimizing the provision of massive loans (drawn from the state budget of the Eurozone states) to serve the Greek public debt, (3) the securing of Greece's public debt and the avoiding of a possible cancelation of it d) the silencing of oppositional voices and politics towards crisis and austerity politics. The apocalyptic construction of the crisis forms a mythopoetic legitimation process of the neoliberal TINA (there is no alternative) doctrine, emphasizing a "cautionary tale" (Van Leeuwen, 2008: 118), of what might happen if the dominant crisis politics and logics do not pass. In effect, this blocks counter-hegemonic politics that would question austerity and the debt itself (Durand, 2017: 90).

6.2.2 Naturalising Austerity; the Only Solution (*Without an Alternative*)

In 2017, when asked to reflect on his decision to concede to the EU-led austerity program in Greece, George Papandreou Jr., the politician who signed Greece's first memorandum of austerity reforms with the Troika argued that a rejection of austerity would have had even harder effects on the Greek people (*Ta Nea*, 2017). The specific logic, that anything other than austerity would have had even worse consequences, has been a central and repeated theme, told by all the Greek governments, economists and EU officials that have been managing Greece's crisis from 2010 until now (2018). Underlined by the Apocalyptic myth of the crisis explained in the previous section, this enduring theme relates to Thatcher's earlier TINA (there is no alternative) thesis while dismantling welfare and developing neoliberal policies in the 1980's Britain.

> ECB warns against a debt restructuring in Greece. A clear message: The ECB warns about the consequences of debt restructuring in Greece. In the opinion of chief economist Stark, the fast-sinking state must fully repay the investors' money and pursue further reforms: "There is no painless way".
>
> *Der Spiegel*, 23/04/2011

Any other policy, such as one that would advocate a partial or a full debt cancelation, is severely prohibited by the side of the creditors, who "present a united front vis-à-vis the debtor" (Roos, 2019: 77). The idea that "there is no painless way" to overcome the economic crisis has been strongly and repeatedly emphasized by mainstream media and politicians across Europe and elsewhere. The securing of debt and its repaying, through its effective conversion, from a debt owned by private banks to debt owned by states, is crucial to the viability of the financial system. Austerity and the sustaining of indebtment (though the bailout loans) pave the way for future accumulation processes and profits (Durand, 2017: 55).

Neoliberal austerity is generally framed in technical terms and legitimitsed by experts, usually economists: "reforms" is the prevailing word used to describe the neoliberal austerity policies in seemingly neutral ways. These reforms are barely questioned. Instead, those questioning them, such as public intellectuals, civil society groups, political parties, and social movements, are confronted and delegitimised. For instance, the distinguished political philosopher Jurgen Habermas is disdained as an "Apocalyptic minded hysteric", along with the emerging – at the time (2011) – Occupy Wall Street movement:

> Under the Apocalypticists' view; Habermas belongs to the camp of the apocalyptic-minded hysterics. The philosopher Jürgen Habermas has turned to the euro debate: Europe is on its way to "post-democracy", with Angela Merkel being an agent of capital. Thus, the debt crisis has finally reached the stage of hysteria [...] there are currently two competing interpretations of what actually happened: an analysis of the economic laws that led to the crisis of confidence in Europe, and the outcry of the heart, which describes the current confrontation with the terms of an ideological contest.
> *Der Spiegel*, 07/11/2011

Here, Jan Fleischhauer again attempts to advance the supposed supremacy of the objectivist "analysis of economic laws" offered by neoliberals and economists, as opposed to the outdated "ideological" and "emotional" one developed by Habermas and the left. Key binaries themes, concerning politics vs. science, or rationality vs. emotion form central argumentative topoi that ground the logics of the article.

In another of his *Der Spiegel* articles, Fleischhauer further attempts to dismiss critical analyses of the crisis and neoliberalism, by reducing them into mere conspiracy theories.

> Paranoid thinking in critical circles: The Greece plot
>
> Everywhere it is said that the Greeks have attributed their own crash. But what if everything is different? If behind their decline in truth is a big

plan? Conspiracy theorists have found a new field of activity: the euro crisis. Take the official version of the euro crisis. For the inexperienced contemporary, the decline of Greece is the result of a policy of excessive debt rather than growth, for which, with some delay, the bill is now being presented. As the Chancellor explains, we also read it in the newspaper. But should we really believe that? What if there was a plan from a completely different angle behind it? If, in fact, the point is to play through the example of this small, peripheral euro-zone state, how to destabilize a country so much that it becomes a training ground for neo-liberal coercive measures. Isn't it necessary, on a closer reflection, to arrive at the conclusion that the Greeks were deliberately pulled through cheap loans, into a debt bondage so as to make them into a social laboratory?

This interpretation of the Greek bankruptcy is called "shock therapy". Anyone who thinks this is a joke circulating in the blogosphere at best has not heard WDR's lunchtime program for a long time, or, read Naomi Klein. Four years ago, the Canadian hero of globalization criticism uncovered the basic concept of the "shock doctrine" with which the capitalists attempt to establish the new order of the global economy. Everything comes together, the torture chambers in Chile, Milton Friedman, the CIA, the Pentagon and, of course, the lords of the Wall Street. It works like brainwashing: Capitalism needs the catastrophe to make people docile, as we learn from Klein; Where this does not happen by itself, the men in the background like to help a little.

Der Spiegel, 12/09/2011

Nominalisations ("everyone", "everywhere") that denote common-sense themes are used by Fleischhauer in order to ground his idea of the true version of what the economic crisis is. To be sure, this is related to what "the Chancellor" (Angela Merkel) has explained, which, the mainstream media also iterate: "as the consistently most visible decision-maker in the European press, Merkel has effectively personified the politics of the crisis and emerged as the face of Germany's 'intellectual and moral leadership' in the Eurozone" (Ojala & Harjuniemi, 2016: 416).

Without addressing the structural, political economy analysis of the crisis, which is what critical scholars do, mainstream public commentators like Fleischhauer reside to common-sense economic and political thinking, connected with the bourgeois morals of debt, and capitalism's axiomatic belief in endless economic growth and the naturality of the market (Wood, 2017). The defense of the hegemonic crisis' understanding is built on a distorted idea of critical thinking, caricatured as something absurd, associated with "paranoia", secret plans of world domination, and political manipulation. This way, Fleischhauer attempts to associate Klein's work with 9/11 related conspiracy theories that usually have right-wing origins. By failing to acknowledge the systemic dynamics of capitalism and imperialism, he downplays the historical facts mentioned by Klein (and also bu scholars like David Harvey [2005]), like the CIA-organised coup to overthrow the democratic government of Salvador Allende and the establishment of a military dictatorship under Augusto Pinochet in Chile which marked the birth of neoliberal governance. By taking "things as they are", this author overlooks the importance of critical concepts (like that of the "Shock Doctrine") and theories to criticise and explain a highly abstract and destructive system (like that of global financial capitalism). Most crucially, Fleischhauer appears to not fully understand the phenomenon of conspiracy theories as such. As Dean (2009: 148) argues, critique, revelation, and doubt have been crucial in the development of democracy and the advance of the public sphere, so as to question authority and its absolutism. On the contrary, conspiracy theories are non-credible, lacking scientific basis, and are based on convictions, emotions, and drives; other than questioning, they are meant to establish a specific form of reality. Today, their popularity needs to be attributed to the decline of civic culture, the civic disempowerment and uncertainty that market-based policies advance, as well as to the confusing informational surplus that corporate media generate (Taguieff, 2010).

Similarly

> ATTAC's criticism: Most of the billion-aid to Greece went to the banks. Who benefits from the Greek bailout? Certainly, not the citizens, say the critics of globalization, Attac. They have calculated that more than three-quarters of emergency loans went to banks and investors have flowed. But this is at best a half-truth.
>
> *Der Spiegel*, 17/6/2013

Der Spiegel here presents the critique of the so-called bailout program as exaggerated and mistaken. The same article continues in this way:

> It is known and logical that the emergency loans have flowed to those actors who have lent money to the Greek state. And these are just mainly banks and investors at home and abroad. In addition, if the Euro-rescuers had not helped Greece, the country would have been insolvent within a few weeks – with predictably devastating consequences for citizens. The federal government rejected the allegations of Attac. People in Greece have benefited from that of the government in Athens gives time for

reform and the banks had been saved from collapse, said, according to "SZ", the Ministry of Finance. From the so-called troika of the EU, the International Monetary Fund and European Central Bank stated that the billions for the banks would also benefit the citizens. An economy cannot function without reasonably equipped banks.

As was the case with the previous examples, what Van Leeuwen (2008: 109) describes as "custom authority" related to the authority of conformist views widespread in society, legitimise the hegemonic crisis' arguments grounded in common-sense ("it is known and logical") knowledge patterns. In all excerpts above, custom authority works parallel with expert authority, concerning the word of politicians and economists (e.g. "the Federal government" and "the Ministry of Finance"). A win-win situation is sketched in the excerpt above, because, the (supposedly) rightful bailing out of banks also benefits the general population of Greece, because "an economy cannot function without reasonably equipped banks". Simultaneously, the article sustains the aforementioned Apocalyptic myth of a coming, even greater catastrophe in the case that neoliberal austerity reforms are not implemented. Here too, the author attempts to establish an epistemic modality, regarding the hegemonic perspective on the crisis and austerity. Scientific rationality, connected to the article's references to various political and economic experts, legitimises the claims attempted against Attac's critique. Hence, the position of the German government and the Troika in defense of Greece's bailout program is emphasised. A positive national representation of Germany, framed with the metonymy of the "Eurorescuers" sustains the Orwellian language of austerity, where impoverishment and expropriation are branded as "help".

The "reforms program" is reproduced unquestioned – as something scientific, objective and correct. The media's attention then is placed on the implementation of these reforms. This is also what the Troika is mostly concerned with: the rapid implementation of austerity reforms in Greece. The media intensify this stress and exercise pressure by developing a case of a public demand for austerity, through the daily dramatisation of the crisis.

The media here follow the logics and the statements produced by leading politicians and economists on the matter. The so-called reforms and the reformers behind them are represented positively; so are the civil society groups, political parties, and politicians in favor of them.

> Fight against debt crisis: EU forces Greece to radical austerity. Brussels increases pressure on the government in Athens: EU Monetary Affairs Commissioner Rehn demands Greece to step up its austerity efforts.

> Finance Minister Papakonstantinou appears to be understanding – and announces tough cuts for the population.
> *Der Spiegel*, 01/03/2010

> Greece on the brink: clash of civilizations. The Greek government is resisting bankruptcy – but the real struggle is raging in the population: between property rights holders who cling to their privileges and those who are willing to sacrifice for the common good. A report from the everyday front.
> *Der Spiegel*, 05/03/2010

> Appeal: Greek economists urge their compatriots to reform. Privatizations, tax increases, regulations: In order to avert the state bankruptcy, Greek economists call for radical reforms in their homeland. Otherwise, Greece is threatened to "degrade into an impoverished third world state".
> *Der Spiegel*, 27/06/2011

Speed is a crucial element in developing austerity policies to supposedly avoid the worst of the crisis and the presumed Armageddon it carries. The stressing of time through the evocation of the conceptual metaphors of Apocalypse diverts the possibility of political debate on austerity, "because political debate slows down the speed of implementation" (Buck-Morss, 2002: 266). In a recent study, Stubbs (2017: 25) links the dimension of time to expert governance and austerity regimes: "Invocations of time, much as those of space, structure and restructure the power relations of austerity and debt, enabling specific forms of rule and limiting, or at least seeking to limit, alternative possibilities". Stubbs (2017: 27) speaks about hegemonic temporalities, associated with the prevailing temporalities dictating the "rules of the struggle" and setting the sociopolitical agendas and priorities. The use of time and the emphasis on speed (e.g. during the various political negotiation processes or by imposing difficult deadlines to implement the memoranda policies) have been crucial in advancing austerity regimes in Greece:

> Debt crisis: Risk premium for Greek bonds soaring to record highs. The Greek debt crisis is worsening: risk premiums for Athens government bonds have reached their highest level since the foundation of the euro. On top of that, the ash-chaos is delaying negotiations for a rescue package for the sluggish Hellenes.
> *Spiegel Online*, 19/04/2010

> New cash injection: IMF increases pressure on EU and Greece. The next injection of funds for Greece seemed assured, but now the International Monetary Fund questions the payout in July: the EU must first make tough decisions. Thus, there is pressure on the government in Athens to push for a strict austerity.
>
> *Der Spiegel*, 07/06/2011

> The IMF criticized the reforms' snail's pace. The reform process in Greece is stagnating. The government in Athens have changed the business practices of the country not fundamentally criticized the International Monetary Fund. In particular, there was little progress in the fight against tax evasion.
>
> *Der Spiegel*, 13/12/2011

> New study: OECD holds for Greece completely incapable of reform. Officials who did not speak to each other, spending plans at will, lack of databases – two years after the start of the Greek crisis certifies the OECD the government apparatus complete failure. According to the OECD lacks any form of control, the experts are now pushing a "big-bang reform".
>
> *Der Spiegel*, 08/12/2011

Along with the technocrats (related to experts of the IMF and the OECD in the quotes above), mainstream media stress too the "need" for a fast implementation of the reforms. Likewise, mass media regularly address austerity reforms enthusiastically, celebrating austerity through what I have described elsewhere as "the panegyric frame" (Mylonas, 2015: 262). While speaking to a national audience, austerity's positive representation is meant to trigger public enthusiasm for (harsh and anti-social) reforms that are to take place elsewhere. Austerity is stressed as a reasonable policy framework that primarily works for the best interests of (ordinary) Germans, but also for the malfunctioning Greeks, who, as Schäuble suggested in his earlier quote at the beginning of this chapter, will learn to appreciate in due time, possibly when they become "mature enough". To use some relevant examples:

> Austerity approved: Europe cheers, Greece revolts. The EU and IMF's relief is great: After the Greek Parliament passed the austerity program, the state bankruptcy is fading – but in Athens, the violence escalates. Ministry of Finance on fire, a luxury hotel was evacuated.
>
> *Der Spiegel*, 29/06/2011

> Privatization: Greece brings trust to the start. The Greeks advance with a privatizations' program. The debt country has established an authority to state ownership to make quick money. The conditions are good: One of the top sellers is an investment banker.
> *Der Spiegel*, 11/07/2011

> Greece: government parties decide for a billion austerity package. For weeks, was negotiated, the agreement is now here: The ruling coalition parties in Greece have the new 11.5 billion euro austerity program decided heavy. Apparently, Socialist Party leader Venizelos has waived a claim.
> *Der Spiegel*, 01/08/2012

> Austerity: OECD praises "spectacular turnaround" in Greece. Through hard cuts, Greece is heading for a budget surplus [...] Its president speaks of "the most impressive program that I have ever seen".
> *Der Spiegel*, 07/11/2013

Under a positive light, austerity's spectacular publicity makes two ends meet. On the one hand, the benevolent German/European efforts in (supposedly) "helping" the problematic Greeks are proclaimed to actually work, and on the other hand, these efforts are securing "our" hardworking German/European taxpayers' money, in line with the growth of "our" national/capital interests. Obviously, here too, the positive evaluation of austerity's success is warranted on references to expert assessments and statements (e.g. from the OECD, the EU, and the IMF) (Fairclough, 2003: 98).

Moreover, the privatisation of public assets, the cutting of wages and welfare, the shutting down of vital public sectors connected to health and education among others, the shacking of workers, or, the appointing of unelected, technocratic governments (as was the case of the banker Lucas Papademos, appointed as the Greek Prime Minister of a technocratic government in November 2011 in Greece), and the election of conservative governments (such as the election of the Conservative Antonis Samaras and the Nea Dimokratia party in June 2012), are represented as "hope" and as victories for Germany, the EU and the Eurozone, Greece, and the financial markets:

> After an extraordinary summit: the Greeks' Saviour builds a new Euro-Land. The decision appears to have succeeded. The markets calm down after the adoption of new aid program for Greece. Nevertheless, the

summit decisions are likely to profoundly change Europe. Especially rich countries such as Germany could, in future, be regularly asked to pay.

Der Spiegel, 22/07/2011

Greece's new government: A man shows edge. It took long agonizing days until the two major Greek parties agree on their interim Prime Minister Lucas Papademos. But the marathon of negotiations also shows the strength of his 64 years: He has managed to keep socialists and conservatives in their place.

Der Spiegel, 10/11/2011

Conservatives win in Greece: A little bit of hope. The Conservatives won the election in Greece – the country of permanent crisis gives only a brief respite. The nation is deeply divided, the coalition negotiations start in difficult conditions. New Chaos threatens as the Greeks finally pull themselves together.

Der Spiegel, 17/06/2012

To this regard, the analysis of the "new spirit of capitalism" (emerging from the 1970's and onwards) by Boltanski and Chiapello (2007: 164) is useful. Neoliberalism, they argue, is rhetorically displayed through a) inspiring themes on new developments of capitalism (such as deregulations, privatisations or the financialisation of the economy), b) the manifestation of such processes as secure ones, c) the underlining of the dimension of fairness entailed in such processes. These dimensions surface in the overwhelmingly positive representation of austerity examined: the (austerity) reforms are meant to be "good" for "all"; the reforms are deemed to work if they are to be correctly implemented; the reforms are also fair due to the material and moral demands posed by debt, "hard work" and (large) private property.

6.2.3   *The "Extreme Center" and Constructions of "Realism"*

The invisible hand continues to shovel money; Contrary to popular belief, capitalism continues to function brilliantly: the invisible hand continues to shovel money into the pockets of the most competitive, faster and faster, but it is no longer the pockets of the western industrialized nations. We are currently experiencing a gigantic redistribution to China, and that is only the beginning. India will follow, Latin America, and eventually Africa. Europe has to be united in order to be able to survive in

this new, emerging world order. And if this unity can only be achieved by Germany paying for it, then, firstly, this is money well spent. And secondly, this should not change. Should Germany be the paymaster of Europe? Yes, please. By conviction.
> Der Spiegel, 15/09/2011

We can't really apologize for the ability of our industries to compete internationally. But the accusations point out a problem that doubtless exists and can be damaging: the German trade deficit. It's a problem because, in the near future, all EU states will have to start reducing their debts. It will be the task of the century. At that point, it will be inevitable that our neighbors will buy less from us because they don't have the money. So it's also in our interest to create more balance in this relationship.
> THOMAS MEYER – Deutsche Bank, Der Spiegel, 25/03/2010

Often, *Der Spiegel* represents the realpolitik side of the so-called bailout programs. In this sense, the bailout loans are acknowledged to be mainly benefiting Germany, while taking into account the geopolitical and global economic dimensions of the crisis and the challenges of global capitalism. This way, the bailout programs need to be supported so that the German capital will continue to be at the forefront of European and global capitalism and in this way too, the German working-class can hope to benefit from the increase of German competitiveness and the development of value surpluses. This "realist" understanding of the crisis and its stakes comes before any considerations related to the ideology of the structural reforms' program and the politics that breed inequality and injustice. This sort of realism is linked to dominant interests, and presents itself as non-political and non-ideological, authorised from an expert-based, objectivist grasp of "truth".

The possibility of changing the crisis/austerity politics through elections or other political means is something feared by the EU's politico-economic establishment. Mainstream media align with this view: "On Monday, most stock markets in Europe reacted with relief at the outcome of elections in Greece" (*Der Spiegel*, 18/06/2012). In such excerpts, financial institutions, such as stock markets, are topoi of expert-authority that are more important and valid in determining policy-making and the future of a country, than popular voting. Elections are to be avoided because they "waste time" from reforms produce stress to the financial markets and are not only dangerous, but potentially useless too, because they can hardly change anything.

Opponents to the hegemonic policies and logics of the EU are derogatorily framed, as "populists", among other characterisations (Karavasilis, 2017;

Stavrakakis & Katsampekis, 2018; De Cleen, Glynos, Mondon, 2018). Populists are charged with demagogy, irresponsibility, fanaticism, irrationalism, nationalism, statism, along with a general lack of understanding of how "the economy" works. As opposed to the populists, the technocrats are meant to provide a rational and efficient form of governance, prioritizing economistic considerations.

> The biggest risk for the Euro (currency) is not the markets, but the protest parties. They grew not only in Greece but also in Spain, Italy or France. With a battle cry against "austerity", and populist attacks against Germany in particular, political newcomers win support among voters. In Berlin, it is generally agreed that the euro crisis in each country was self-inflicted and that the crisis can only be dealt with a mix of austerity and reform.
> *Der Spiegel*, 05/01/2015

Accordingly, the populists are loud and conflicting opportunists. "Berlin" on the other hand, appears as calm and reasonable, with a consented view on what the crisis is and how it should be resolved. Neoliberal austerity is here legitimised by reference to the "calm reason" of the German government. Simultaneously, nominalisations ("protest parties", "populist attacks", "political newcomers") reduce the political identities and characteristics of counter-hegemonic agents and activities. The term "austerity" itself (appearing in the article above in brackets) is also challenged as a politically biased one. As mentioned in the article, the political priority is the saving of the Euro currency. For this reason, there is an emphasis on the need for stability, so as to defend the Euro, which is EU's main economic policy tool (Streeck, 2016).

Likewise, Syriza's leader, Alexis Tsipras, prior to his election into Greece's Prime Minister in January 2015, and his capitulation to the dominant politico-economic establishment of Europe in July that year was represented according to what Reisigl and Wodak (2001: 73) termed as the "straw-man fallacy":

> Greek-left politicians Tsipras: The Euro-horror [Photo of Tsipras and note: Alexis Tsipras: he declared the Reforms required by the EU and the IMF as null and void]. Alexis Tsipras likes simple sentences. One goes like this: if the bank is owed £ 5000, it's your problem, but if you owe the bank £ 500,000, it is a problem of the bank, said the head of the Greek radical left (SYRIZA) to the British Guardian. This simple picture is to represent the situation in Europe – where the problem should fall on the creditor. Tsipras has one main theme: the impoverishment of the Greek society by austerity. His party alliance comes with a ten-point program promising

resistance to the labor market reforms [...] rejecting the conditions of the EU rescue package. His furious performances – combined with a good dose of patriotism – appeal to many Greeks during the confusing time of the crisis.

Der Spiegel, 26/05/2014

The democratic election of a left-led, Syriza-based, government in 2015 was viewed as scandalous by the EU's conservative/neoliberal establishment. So did the July 2015 Greek referendum and its outcome in rejecting austerity, despite the EU's calls for a positive vote to austerity. Mainstream media amplified these positions, expressing, fear, anxiety, indignation, contempt and ridicule towards such developments. This rejection of the counter-hegemonic developments in Greece has been based on expert-led opinions, and on the popular "Greek exceptionalism" myths.

By the same token, the Greferendum and its outcome were represented as illegitimate and disastrous:

> Europe's most erratic leader, Prime Minister Alexis Tsipras has refused to follow the normal rules and pushed Greece completely into the economic abyss, but the Greeks still love him.
>
> *Jyllands Posten*, 05/07/2015

> Irresponsible Greeks; with closed eyes, the Greeks have voted for the sister party of Enhedslisten, Syriza, which plays Russian roulette with Greece and therefore with the rest of the EU.
>
> *Jyllands Posten*, 08/07/2015

The leading Syriza politicians during the first period of Syriza's government (January-July, 2015), Tsipras and Varoufakis, were frequently sensualised, ridiculed and defamed, which, in Varoufakis case, reached the point of character assassination.

> Europe's most erratic leader [...] until he [Tsipras] met Peristera, "Betty" Batziana, his later partner and mother of his two sons, one of who is named "Ernesto" after Che Guevara.
>
> *Jyllands Posten*, 05/07/2015

> A gambler by profession: The now former Greek finance minister, Yanis Varoufakis, is known to be very informal and, for example, often arrived on motorcycles for ministerial meetings in the Greek government.

> Yesterday he resigned, after the Greeks on Sunday voted no by the referendum.
>
> *Berlingske*, 06/07/2015

> Greek new finance minister: from a leather jacket to corduroy [...] Varoufakis, who got worldwide attention with his leather jacket, motorbike, his raised middle finger and his airy quotes.
>
> *Berlingske*, 07/07/2015

The regular sensualistic depictions of such left-wing politicians meant to abnormalise them and to discredit them politically, despite their rather moderate stances, which were not even opposing the Euro-currency. This was advanced through the turning of the political reporting into a prosperous spectacle, with its obvious distortive effects on meaningful public deliberation (Mylonas & Noutsou, 2018). Thus, the liberal media paid a great deal of attention in the turning into scandals, the life-choices and preferences of the specific politicians (e.g. the name of Tsipras' son, or, the clothes of Varoufakis) that may differ from the rather gray standards of typical European bourgeois politicians.

Hence, the counter-hegemonic politics taking place in Greece are constantly undermined and delegitimised. The media associate the oppositional voices and movements of Greece against austerity to the culturalist-moralist flaws they attribute Greece. Counter-hegemonic politics are discredited because they allegedly derive from emotions, from inadequate information, and from ideological misconceptions, among other. These politics are equally represented as "not democratic" because they defy not only the European rationales and policies but also, the European "silent majority" that is supposedly paying for the "Greek flaws".

> The Greeks do not lose any opportunity to stress that democracy was born there. Nevertheless, the Greeks cannot be so proud of how this heritage has developed since. The referendum is not an exception to that [...] the referendum was announced only a week ago, and even its question is very complicated ... even diplomats and experts in the economy cannot agree on its content. The referendum looks like a farce, as, at the end of the day, is the government's effort to avoid taking responsibility and to drive attention away from the core of the problem: excessive public spending [...] *Even if a majority of Greeks vote "yes" today, it will change hardly anything, as long as Syriza is in power. The fundamental problem is that so many Greeks seem blind to reality.*
>
> *Jyllands Posten*, 05/07/2015

By referring to the Greferendum, the Danish press also objects the outcome of the Greek elections that brought the left-wing Syriza to power. This objection emerges from a conviction that is based on a fundamental notion of "reality", which, although comprehended by Europeans, it is something that the Greeks remain "blind to". The experts again, along with authority figures such as diplomats, are deemed as the most credible agents to assess election dilemmas and election decisions. The American political theorist Kristin Ross argued that, as was the case with the Irish 2008 vote against the EU constitution, elections defying capital interests are objected through various moralistic or legalistic urgings, favoring a supposed "silent" majority that is bigger in size than that of a dissident minority. Nonetheless, "the power of demos is neither the power of the population nor its majority but rather the power of anybody. Anybody is as entitled to govern as he or she is to be governed" (Ross, 2009: 86). The resentment towards electoral results from a "democratic" point of view, and the regular evoking of democracy to highlight the supposed undemocratic essense of the Greek counter-hegemonic politics, show the actual limits of what Nancy Fraser described as the actually existing democracy, to advance left-wing politics, as Dean (2009b: 20) has explained, in the sense that the political right and neoliberals dominate the representative liberal democratic system, and voice their "goals and aspirations in democratic terms".

Likewise, the Greek liberal press adheres to the hegemonic views seeing the Greek democracy as problematic. Here, "democracy" becomes a synonym to "Europe". A nodal signifier of a developmental agenda, Europe, is supposedly fundamentally democratic. In the Greek liberal discursive artiiculations, Europe obtains the mythical position of a realised liberal utopia that is well functioning, honest, secular, fair and democratic, as table 3 showed earlier. In that sense, Europe is to dictate the rules of democracy, and not the Greek voters. Europe is warranted the authority to discredit Greek politics on the premise of democracy, given that it safeguards its "true" spirit. This way, the (austerity) reforms become a stake of "democratisation" (from above) that is higher than the citizens' sovereign vote. Democracy is presented as something that can be practiced correctly only by the advanced countries of the capitalist center in the West. In these terms, democracy emerges as a rather elitist, but also dysfunctional and inefficient system (Streeck 2016: 110).

Despite the EU' establishment's public position (reproducing the aforementioned eschatological themes) in favor of a "yes" vote, followed by punitive measures targeting the Greek economy, such as the imposition of capital controls that reduced the cash flow ability of the Greek banks, the Greek citizens voted against the continuation of austerity, with a sweeping "no" vote. Dignity, damaged by slander and material degradation, was said to be the prevalent reason in the choice of voting (Varoufakis, 2017). Nevertheless, the Greek liberal commentators discredited the citizens' majoritarian vote against austerity as undemocratic:

> On Sunday, it was not fear that was defeated but it was the true fear that won. The fear of a people to change [...] because this nation never went through the Enlightenment [....] We [sic] were, again, afraid to change, we were afraid of the reforms, and we were afraid of democratic Europe.
> "The victory of the true fear", *Protagon*, 07/07/2015

The specific excerpt is full of generalisations (through the making use of nominalisations such as "we", "this nation", "the Enlightenment", "the reforms") and essentialist constructions ("the true fear", "this nation never went through the Enlightenment", "we were, again, afraid to change"). The Greferendum's result is contextualised in a discursive construction that discloses a genealogy of a Greek, pathologically stagnant condition. The fantasmatic logic of austerity for the Greek liberals emerges, as austerity is desired for its (supposed) potential in the making of Greece European. Austerity is thus not about its actual policies and their concrete outcomes, which impoverish the middle and the lower social strata, but about Europeanising Greece. The liberals' mythic view of Europe displaces austerity, by sublimating it in a discourse of development and modernisation. This way, the actual referendum result is discredited and sidestepped, as it is attributed to a fundamental democratic deficit that is historical and can only change by abiding to "the democratic Europe". The Orientalist myth of Greece surfaces here, on the antipode of the Occidentalist myth of Europe (Mitralexis, 2017: 128).

While studying the Greek liberal press, contributors there are usually meant to abstain from identifying to either the left or the right. These binaries are presented as outdated forms of politics, on the basis that they are ideological. Realist, common-sense, rational and future-orientated dispositions are expressed instead, connected to a linear understanding of the world that is presumably moving towards progress. Progress is here connected to technological innovation, expertise, entrepreneurialism, and secular/bourgeois values. A Fukuyama-based, "end of history" view can be observed here, confirming the supremacy of liberalism as the final and supreme universal political system. In this simplistic thinking, anything rival has a totalitarian predisposition, and/or is simply unmodern, and, "in transition". As Prozorov (2009: 8) maintains, however, history does not come to an end by itself. History does not follow a specific logic. It is rather brought to an end by dominant politico-ideological forces.

In his "what will the liberals become?" an Andreas Zamboukas predicts that

> The battle for dominance will be given by the two great conservative poles of the political system. The major trends of today's "updated" populism are apparent in both rival parties. One concerns the promise of a "generous" statism, defending past achievements from the era of "cleptocracy" (capital, work positions, salaries, and pensions). The other is based on right-wing phobias against the Left [...] Within this terrorizing backdrop, there are not many common-sense forces to enlighten the political system and the Greek society in general.
> *Protagon*, 27/12/2014

A (post)political horizon is decreed that is not understood through the premises of a "left/right" reading of politics and identities but in terms of common sense vs. ideology, "forward-backward", and populism/anti-populism. Both the left and the right opposing neoliberal agendas and reforms are discredited as "populist". The use of this term is derogatory as it describes manipulators and demagogues making irresponsible and non-realistic promises to the people (Stavrakakis & Katsampekis, 2014: 120). As only going "forward" is a valid and realistic option, anything framed as backward is eschewed from public debate. Forward is signified by endorsing all late capitalist developments, realities, and dictates, as facts beyond discussion (Fairclough 2003: 56). These constitute a post-democratic perspective because the space allowed for the opposition is shrunk. Yet, the left/right political distinction belongs to modernity's secular social imaginary and the understanding of the difference in ideas and in interests (Dyrberg 2005: 177). The left/right distinction offers a conceptual space to apprehend debates and contests in political means, social diversity and economic, national, cultural and class divisions.

Although liberal authors proclaim to be dismissing both the left and the right as anachronistic political distinctions that belong to the past, in their linear and progressivist understanding of history and its laws, it is the left that concentrates their fury. The left becomes a constitutive obstacle that prevents the accomplishment of the liberals' ideological vision of a "final" Greece, to emerge as European, secular, developed, efficient, competitive, industrious and "normal" (Galanopoulos, 2015). To refer to one of the most ardent liberal polemicists of the left in the press studied, we can read "On the left deficit", an article authored by the writer Soti Triantafyllou, the following:

> Apart from the Enlightenment and the Industrial Revolution, we [sic] also lost the 1960s, the emergence of alternative movements, the demands of individual freedom, the radicalization of the multiracial, multicultural

left. So our social movement is poor, dogmatic, and primitive; it lacks imagination, and is guided by perverse thinking: it translates the so-called "class hatred" into envy, jealousy and manifests itself with acts of ugliness and destruction [...] Are we still in the Dark Age before the Enlightenment? And why does nobody from the Left talk about these things? Why should we accept the nonsense and arbitrariness of a "movement" that is not interested in justice and goodness that forcibly interrupts theatrical plays, threatens with terrorist operations and reviles anyone disagreeing?.

AthensVoice, 22/07/2009

Triantafyllou's claims against the Greek left articulate the aforementioned linear and developmentalist understandings of Greece's exceptionalism, sketched in comparison to the Western normality. Further, they also seem to recount what has been conceived as the "artistic critique" (Boltanski & Chiapello, 2006: 169). Emerging from the left's defeat of May 1968 and the rise of neoliberalism and the turn to individualist solutions to systemic contradictions, the artistic critique became prevalent in the Western left in the late 20th century. As Boltanski and Chiapello show in their account, the artistic critique damaged social movements because it compromised socio-economic demands, allowing capital to assimilate many of the individual-freedom based demands (e.g. for non-alienating labour) in ways that turned out to be highly productive. This led to the biopolitical mode of production and consumption that operates today, connected to the neoliberal modes of subjugation and disaffection, exacerbated in the eclipse of critique and action that confronts the politico-economic and social conditions of late capitalism (Harvey, 2014: 267; Mylonas, 2017: 211).

Other than a center-periphery analysis, the Greek liberals in principle adopt a developmentalist idea based on binary dichotomies between modern vs. unmodern, or, "Enlightened" vs. "Unenlightened" people and countries. Such constructions are evident in various excerpts from the Greek media studied:

> Everyone agrees that Greece needs a new revolution [...] My own idea of the new Greek Revolution is described by Nikos Dimou in his book "talking with an indignant for new revolutions – technological and other" [...] we need a technological revolution [...] a new generation, not afraid of scientific novelty, that will put technology to good civil service. Besides bureaucratic and organizational matters, the way of thinking needs to change [...] the country went generally bankrupt because we lack rationality [...] because the Enlightenment never touched Greece. The scientific way of thinking and working will be a great revolution for

Greece. Who does not want more science, technology, and rationality in Greece? Only those burdened with dogmatism, stagnation, darkness, and charlatanism.

> "The revolution of 2021", *AthensVoice*, 16/06/2014

Basing his arguments on a book that he read by a known liberal writer and journalist (Nikos Dimou), the article's author, Spiros Kitsinelis, speaks about the prospects of a technocratic revolution for Greece. This revolution is supposed to be driven by science and technology, which will organise a rational and objective form of progress and development. "Revolution" is the nodal point of the discursive construction that appears in the text above. Although not explained, revolution is associated with a general notion of "progress". Kitsinelis claims that "everyone" supposedly agrees for the need of a revolution in Greece; this nominalization warrants him to describe his own envisioning of the revolution. Technology, science and rationality are signifiers that define the notion of progress and also probe towards the way to reach it. To be sure, major modern revolutions, like the French and the Russian, aspired to be scientific and objective, in order to shatter "dogmatism, stagnation, darkness, and charlatanism". The author though avoids considering the politics and the ideology driving technology and science. Technological progress is here "fetishistically equated with social progress" (Buck-Morss, 1991: 282). The notion of progress in Kitsinelis' text appears as a limitless process that, in the Greek case, it is only blocked by the ignorance of the masses. However, in a critical reading of the progress idea, it is the uneven social relations of production that compromise the modern potential of social progress (Buck-Morss, 1991: 87). To this regard, the perpetuation of the myth of an automatic historical progress is a crucial ideological trait to sustain class domination. Instead, as Susan Buck-Morss (1991: 95) writes

> A construction of history that looks backward, rather than forward, at the destruction of material nature as it has actually taken place, provides dialectical contrast to the futurist myth of historical progress (which can only be sustained by forgetting what has happened).

By claiming that "we" (a nominalisation meant to address "all Greeks") "lack rationality, because the Enlightenment never touched Greece" (sic), Kitsinelis in his *AthensVoice* article above, among others, also adheres to the hegemonic crisis-narrative and its local version that, as we already saw, is self-orientalizing Greece. The flattening idea of a unanimous whole is seemingly contradicting the individualistic ideology of liberalism. Yet, as liberalism happens somewhere else, in places that "went through the Enlightenment", the Greeks are reduced to a mob, which cannot be trusted to bring social change. The idea of the Enlightenment itself appears in essentialist terms, as a historical passage that was missed beyond reach (Mylonas, 2017: 196). The Enlightenment in such a context is, in Laclau's terms, a nodal signifier meant to articulate Greece's shortcomings and its "missing fullness", according to the Greek liberals' ideological vision. Other than a critical and contingent concept, the Enlightenment here is a reified discursive construction constituting an authoritative topos to legitimise claims of entitlement, to address Greece in demeaning terms and to defend "Europe" and the policies it represents in the midst of the economic crisis. Thus, the kind of technocratic revolution aspired is something that would occur from above, driven by experts. Therefore, class privilege is obscured and sustained. As Buck-Morss (1991: 285) notes "the bourgeoisie can never come to a fully enlightened consciousness of itself" as it would have to give up its privileges to allow the emancipatory potential of modernity to emerge for all.

This way, the internal divisions and inequalities of Greece are downplayed, and so do the regimes of responsibility for Greece's underdevelopment, economic crisis and subsequently, loss of sovereignty by the Troika. The Greek liberals advance a general sense of responsibility, by communicating their arguments in general national terms: it is "we" (meaning, all Greeks) that were corrupt, took advantage of the EU, borrowed excessively, and voted for wrong governments. "We all ate them together" has been a key phrase uttered by a leading figure of the neoliberal, "modernizing" social-democratic establishment that thrived during the 1990's and the early 2000's, Theodoros Pangalos, himself the grandson of one of Greece's military dictators who, in the 1920's developed a military coup drawing aspiration from Mussolini. Either way, Pangalos' ludicrous claim is a deeply classist construction of responsibility, as it creates a fictitious and vulgar sense of civic "equality", which only propagates an equal sense of responsibility towards a systemic crisis of a hierarchical and uneven society.

6.3 Concluding Remarks: Authoritarian Capitalism with Fascist Dispositions[1]

Professor Verbon of the University of Tilburg argued that "Greece needs a dictatorship, not elections, so as to come to terms with itself. EU member

---

1 Fuchs (2017b); Yurchenko (2018: 202).

states that receive financial assistance from the EU need to give up part of their democratic autonomy".

De Volkskrant, 26/08/2015

In an inflammatory article published in the Greek public sphere by *Kathimerini* on 16 September 2012 entitled "The Golden Dawn's opportunity for democracy", a certain Stefanos Kassimatis provocatively declared that:

> Those believing in the democracy owe a big "thanks" to the Golden Dawn – and I fully mean this. This derives from the opportunity it offered us [...] to fix mistakes of decades and to make a fresh start in political life. It is the opportunity given to law and order to finally deal with the quasi-legitimate violence of the left [...] which constitutes today the main obstacle of the country's transition from the era of "soviets with lobster-pasta" (the Greek model of socialism ...) to contemporary reality.

Beyond the mainstream liberal assumptions related to the reactionary, ahistorical equation of Communism with Nazism, deeming them to supposedly be equivalent "totalitarian extremes" (sic), Losurdo (2016: 33) notes that, among others, Gandhi too thought that Hitler resembles to Churchill, because, Hitler too sought to advance a colonisation of Eastern Europe and countries he deemed as inferior, disregarding the cost of life to accomplish that. In an excellent work, Mike Davis (2017) has also presented the murderous famines that Britain caused millions of victims in India and in other countries colonized by the British; to this regard, the spiteful racism of Churchill in such events is telling. Losurdo also shows how influential have the US racial segregation politics been for the Nazis. The colonial practices of the UK have also been equally influential for the Nazi's quest in colonizing Eastern territories and enslaving their populations.

The detrimental effects of neoliberal policies on democracy and on society are evident in all countries where the so-called structural adjustment reforms have been implemented. In her own study of the demise of the Soviet Union, Susan Buck-Morss (2002) notes that the "transition" from a state-controlled economy (state capitalism as often described by critics), to a "free market" economy, were implemented in a "shock" form by the IMF economists and local liberal politicians. Buck-Morss (2002: 256) noticed that in the post-socialist "transition" era, a compromised, controlled democracy emerged, so as to control the "risks" deriving from elections, which may threaten the economistic orthodoxies and imperatives of the "free market". The "reform" strategies implemented by the IMF and other Western neoliberal institutions to many of the former socialist countries and in other parts of the world, are similar to those implemented in Greece and have detrimental effects on society, ecology, and democratic polity. The so-called shock therapy policies are about the developing of fast reforms centered on the doctrines of currency stabilisation, anti-inflation, economic liberalization (concerning the development of an export-orientated, competitive economy) and privatisation, connected to deregulation and denationalisation processes (Buck-Morss, 2002: 266).

The failure of austerity measures, to meet their objective goals – related to the achieving of economic growth, competitiveness, debt reduction and unemployment decrease – as well as to attain the financial markets' confidence, along with the general misery of austerity and its destructive effects on society and democracy, is usually attributed to Greece's presumed dysfunctional particularities. In addition to that, popular resistance to austerity is also viewed to add up to the obstacles posed to the reforms and the reformers. The media articles cited and analysed in this chapter show the discontent of mainstream liberals with counter-hegemonic politics, putting forth the primacy of the market and the maintenance of "stability" at all costs. In the crisis context though, stability is concerned with the creation of a socio-political environment for neoliberal austerity to unfold, which will guarantee the continuation of debt repayment (Roos, 2019: 44). Moreover, stability also concerns the sustaining of class privilege.

As the analysis of this chapter showed, the opposition to austerity in Greece has been viciously confronted, publicly and politically. In this context, the rise of the Nazi party of the Golden Dawn, from a marginal group of Nazi thugs to an enduring parliamentary force in Greece, is associated with the defeat of social movements and left-wing parties, along with the broader class anxiety that stems from the crisis and austerity (Kompatsiaris & Mylonas, 2015). Anti-leftist rhetoric within Greece and elsewhere also played its own part in the legitimation of the fascists, as the Kassimatis excerpt above shows, which is not unique but indicative of the political thinking of what has been called "the extreme center". According to Tariq Ali (2015: 15) the extreme center relates to the historical emptying of differences between the main parliamentary parties in liberal democracies, and their "acting in unison to defend capitalism". The expressed desire for the Nazis in Greece to save democracy (sic) from the left, as read in Kassimatis' delirius text above, shows the logics of the distressed bourgeoisie, which in critical moments may support fascism to sustain its status. In times of crisis, fascism historically emerges as the safeguard of the status quo and of socio-economic divisions and hierarchies (Poulantzas, 1979b). The individualist, consumer-orientated, neoliberal society also cumulates fascist and nationalist dispositions, particularly due to the anxieties it breeds (Askanius & Mylonas, 2015: 57; Mylonas, 2017d). The exceptionalisation of Greece in cultural and in political terms, as well as its quarantining through austerity regimes, are anti-democratic acts, which were nevertheless often defended through a language of democracy. Likewise, the Greek people's sovereign vote was also confronted and disputed (as an allegedly "wrong" vote) by the EU's liberals and conservatives through references to democracy. The politico-economic hierarchy here comes to define the limits and the meaning of democracy. For Jodi Dean (2009, 2009b) the mere focus on democracy then is not sufficient to advance counter-hegemonic politics given that democracy is also part of the narrative of the adversary. Instead, Dean (2009: 17) argues that the left should politicise capitalism and defend a vision of equality and solidarity, other than remaining in the confines set by its adversaries. This implies the setting of socialism as the strategic goal of counter-hegemonic politics. After all, with its egalitarian premises, universal socialism constitutes the horizon and premise of a substantial, deep and inclusive realm of democracy.

CHAPTER 7

Conclusions: Context, Politics, Negativity

> I was met on the ground floor of the Federal Ministry of Finance by a junior minister. Before getting into the lift, he asked me playfully, but with enough of a hint of aggression to establish that he was not actually joking, "When am I getting my money back?" I was tempted to reply, "When you persuade Deutsche Bank to return it to you".
> VAROUFAKIS, 2017: 210

∴

> It feels like I committed a war crime.
> JEROEN DIJSSELBLOEM, *Politico.eu* 04/10/2017

∴

7.1   Reinventing Critique, Reinventing Politics

In "Capitalism and Schizophrenia: Anti-Oedipus", Deleuze and Guattari (1977) highlight the importance of dis-identifying with the values and the ideology of the dominant, exploitative politico-economic establishment. This implies the development of new identities, new narratives, different practices, and social relations, and in broader terms, new ways of understanding society and history, as well as and new desires that would deterritorialise the dominant structure and locality of power.

The reintroduction of a critical vocabulary that was made redundant by postmodernism and the subsequent hegemony of neoliberalism as a post-historical project can demonstrate the systemic and structural aspects of the crisis and among them, the values and the social relations naturalising capitalism. This way, critical theory can estrange and defamiliarise (Shklovsky, 2015: 163) what passes as common sense through the depiction of capitalist society's deep flaws. Under this view, the capitalist market emerges as an oppressive system other than as a somewhat prerequisite of "civilisation", "progress", "freedom" and "democracy". Instead of an essentialist feature of "human nature", competition also surfaces as a destructive force, beyond the simplistic and crude arguments attributed to it by a rather misanthropic and oversimplified ideological narrative aiming at naturalising capitalism. Moreover, the West and Europe may be understood not as smooth places that follow a linear historical course of civilisation progress, but as complex and contradictory entities. To this regard, the defining marks that capitalism, colonialism, imperialism, and fascism have left in the West should be accounted for, to deflate Western-centrism and to expose the processes that produce and subjugate whatever is deemed as the West's Other.

This study attempted a critical contextualisation of Modern Greece so as to speak about its particularities. The purpose was to dismantle Greece's overdetermination by western-centric and bourgeois narratives, something typical to all peripheral and semi-peripheral states. The destruction of meanings, and along with them, identities, subjectivities, and experiences, is a constitutive element of the neoliberal restructuring strategies, associated with the broader process of material expropriation advanced (Buck-Morss, 1987: 219). Besides through force and economic stagnation (Anderson, 2017; Fuchs, 2017b: 9), dominance is maintained ideologically, by coercing the Other to constantly question him/herself. After all, the dominant subject will hardly endorse a self-bashing process, something that the peripheral Other is often called upon, while deemed "guilty" for its own frail position.[1] To this regard, self-reflexivity is to be distinguished from self-bashing. While reflexivity can be connected to critical thinking leading to an inquiry of one's structural and social life circumstances, self-bashing is a deteriorating process overdetermined by powerful others. Self-bashing is induced by forms of shaming cast upon peripheral subjects and the working-class, strategically blamed for systemic problems and crises.

As Badiou (2001) and Toscano (2010) argue, the sustaining of memories circumvented by hegemony, the "anachronistic" belief in ideas and causes often

---

[1] To this regard, Fleischer (2008) noted how, in the aftermath of the Second World War, the West German state carefully observed foreign media and the ways that the public discussion on Germany was made in the countries that Nazi Germany had occupied. This was followed by public advice on how to behave and how to tackle so as to avoid the burden, and consequently the responsibility of the Nazi Germany crimes. Fleischer notes that behavior and talking suggestions were offered to the German diplomats, businessmen, and citizens, so as to overcome their historical flaws more adequately and with the least tensions until they are forgotten and become secondary matters. History showed that eventually this strategy paid off, as Germany was able to avoid much of the war reparations it owed to countries like Greece, with the Germans being able to return as tourists to the lands that Germany enslaved, raided and pillaged, only few years after the war had ended.

deemed as dated or irrelevant, are truth producing processes: "for whom is a truth absent? For the human animal as such, absorbed in the pursuit of his interests, there is no truth, only opinions, through which he is socialised" (Badiou, 2001: 61). Badiou notes that truth is produced through events, which are singular entities with a profound impact on subjects. Events may rupture the hegemonic order of things: "the power of a truth is that of a break, it is by violating established and circulating knowledges that a truth returns to the immediacy of the situation" (Badiou, 2001: 70). To that respect, Badiou provides four general categories as sources of events: politics, science, love, and art. Fidelity to the truth that events reveal constitutes a truth process. A truth process opposes what Badiou frames as "evil", which is a context characterised by betrayal, terror and total power, the opposites of truth and universality.

7.2   Debunking Hegemony's Crisis' Myths

All media studied share common liberal ideological leanings. They reproduce dominant economistic, (upper) class and cultural discourses. In doing that, they downplay specific facts, events, and discourses that contradict their claims. The general culturalisation, moralization and technocratisation of the so-called, Greek crisis, is in fact, a form of a semantic displacement from questions of politics and class.

The reason for studying mainstream news media has been because they represent hegemony. By studying them, we can trace the ways that hegemony endures. Besides the use of crude force and violence through state apparatuses, as well as the use of finance to impose policies from above while curbing political challenges, hegemony also works softly, through the achieving of public consensus and legitimacy. Communication-wise, hegemony is a process interconnected with the practice of propaganda, which in moments of social crisis, obtains a more direct, confrontational and agitating form of communication.

Scholars of propaganda demonstrate that propaganda works best when an organised myth acts as an anchoring belief, activating outlooks, moods, and memories (Soules, 2015: 4). Moreover, propaganda can function well in the context of advanced liberal-capitalist democratic states, due to the fact that citizens there believe to be invulnerable from propaganda while showing high conformist attitudes to their state and authorities. The organised myths of the Greek crisis included rather enduring tropes, related to central Occidentalist and middle-class values, entangled with popular culture stereotypes. Such myths were instrumentalised by leading EU politicians, but also by technocrats, economists and businesspeople, producing legitimacy for austerity regimes and emergency policy agendas, often on premises of reprisal and punishment.

Neoliberal austerity policies were presented as the only solutions for the Euro/Greek crisis without an alternative. The no-alternative thesis is central in the advance of neoliberalism, dating back to the early 1980's and the reign of Thatcher in the UK and Reagan in the USA. It is a deeply anti-democratic policy doctrine as it aims at blocking oppositional political imaginaries, ideas, and identities. For, as Harvey and Chomsky have noted, austerity is class warfare, launched against the working-class and the poor across the globe. As Colin Crouch (2013: 3) also notes, "existing, political neoliberalism, as opposed to the models of economics textbooks, is about enhancing the power of great corporations and wealthy individuals".

The protection of the creditors' claimed entitlements over the Greek people's human, social and civil rights may be of no surprise. As relevant historical research on the development of neoliberal institutions on a global scale, property rights, along with business and investors' rights were actively lobbied by neoliberal intellectuals, politicians and related stakeholders after the Second World War. This way, neoliberal political activism managed to achieve a global constitutional protection of capitalist markets, with capital rights emerging as superior to civic or human rights (Slobodian, 2018: 245).

The hegemonic crisis construction stressed cultural, moralist and technocratic claims which advanced a rather particularistic explanation of the economic crisis. The instrumentalisation of Orientalist prejudices portraying the periphery in blunt and fatalistic terms, as infantile, irrational and unmodern was crucial for the public legitimation of neoliberal austerity regimes. The symbolic "Greek-bashing" tactic that advanced particularly during the first years of the crisis served well a "divide and conquer" strategy. The crisis publicity created a false dichotomy between the victimised "hard-working and honest" north/west European taxpayer, who has to pay to supposedly "help" the irresponsible and idle Greek/South European. The EU citizen was called upon to participate at the imposition of harsh austerity regimes in the periphery. Here, the middle-class ideology surfaces, demonstrating its weight over the working class, and its conservative and regressive dispositions. For, the middle-class position is noted to support policies that may produce a sense of stability and the sustaining of privilege. In the stressful times of economic crisis, such conservative attitudes fuel xenophobic socio-political tendencies, evident everywhere in the present Western world. One should remember though that Greece was always a member of the Western politico-economic establishment and part of the US sphere of geopolitical influence, although in the periphery of capitalism. Orientalism is, therefore, a historically conditioned, ideological construction.

Blyth and Harvey (among other scholars) have noted that neoliberal reforms produce more recession. Nevertheless, the ultimate failure of austerity to reach its proclaimed goals (e.g. to make the economy competitive, to make the national sovereign debt "sustainable", to reduce unemployment and to bring growth) has been attributed to the countries subjected to it, as another symptom of their own cultural and moral deficiencies that require "reform". Here, the resistance of the working class, which is mostly affected by the crisis and austerity, has been attacked by the EU's hegemonic discourses and the mainstream media, attributing austerity's failure to protest events (such as strikes, demonstrations, expressions of public criticism of austerity), and to the voting of parties with opposing political programmes. In the moments of mass political mobilisation against austerity during 2011–2012, demeaning media representations defamed the acts of opposition as culture-specific, undemocratic and senseless, with no positive or pro-active basis. Economists, technocrats and media pundits reasoned over the necessity of austerity while downgrading critical readings of the crisis and its politics. The analysis of the Danish media performance in a moment when austerity was highly contested in Greece on an EU policy-making level is exemplary to this regard.

The tremendous and disastrous effects of austerity in Greek society have, to some extent, also been tolerated due to the Greek liberals' persistence in reinforcing and internalizing the neoorientalist Greek crisis discourse within the Greek public sphere. The Greek liberal press studied intensifies the key Greek crisis' hegemonic themes, under a developmentalist pretext, deploying "Europe" as a vantage point of departure, in a way that Europe becomes a benchmark and a panopticon to discipline the Greek people, particularly the working class and the poor. In this process, the Greek Other remains in his/her reduced position, as s/he is overdetermined by hegemonic narratives that sustain existing political, economic and cultural hierarchies.

The Greek crisis has also been produced as a media spectacle to be consumed by the Western, white middle-class audiences in particular. The spectacularisation of the Greek crisis served as both a propagandistic entertaining form (producing public consent to austerity regimes as necessary for Greece) and a disciplinary dispositif, shaping the subjectivities required by neoliberalism, to effectively reproduce capitalism. As Dörre, Lessenich and Rosa (2015) argued, acceleration and activation are key drivers of capitalism. In our context, the activation of citizens' participation in the establishing of austerity regimes occurs through the mobilisation of public support for the implementation of austerity policies in Greece and elsewhere.

The continuous iteration of culturalist stereotypes across all media during the timespan of the research (2010–2015) points towards a ritualistic function of the media (Curran, 2003: 155). The crisis publicity formed around the reified anthropological type of the exotic – but failed (and therefore guilty) – Greek in North/West public spheres can be seen as a strategic, ritualised form of communication. The constant restatement of economistic jargon that publicly neutralised austerity and sanitised it from its violent effects makes another form of ritualised communication that is necessary for the achieving of hegemony. Such media rituals reproduce the class order and the national identity and have a constitutive effect in the establishing of the "normal". Simultaneously, the ritualistic representation of the Greek crisis in stereotypical terms maintains the petty bourgeois promises of life gratification through the consumption of exotic spaces, experiences and reified Others, as touristic commodities and as media spectacles (Mylonas and Noutsou, 2018: 64). *Bild's* spiteful spectacularisation of the Greek crisis epitomises the combination of both the political and economic uses of the crisis by mainstream media.

The analysis aimed at demonstrating the impoverishment of the public dialogue over the crisis, along with the processes of civic disempowerment and conformity advanced by such media representations, probing publics to identify with the objectivised interests of powerful social groups. As a bourgeois sphere, the mainstream public sphere of the nation states studied is dominated by specific strategic interests of the political and economic establishment of capitalist democracies. Represented by the Troika, the creditors sustained a united front led by Germany. Propaganda tactics, police repression, and overall, the structural power of debt itself, managed to dissolve and delegitimise the opposition to austerity in Greece and elsewhere. Writing about the recent political crisis of Ukraine, Yurchenko (2018: 200) notes the characteristic double standards of the right-wing, neoliberal EU, where the Euromaidan protests in Ukraine were supported as "democratic", despite the strong presence and eventual predominance of reactionary, anti-communist, fascist and neo-nazi currents in that movement. For Samir Amin (2016), the support of fascists by the EU in Ukraine is a strategic choice to pursue imperialist interests in the European periphery, turning it into a form of Germany's Latin America. On the contrary, the suppression of the democratic anti-austerity politics and struggles within the EU's periphery was supported by the EU mechanism, because their suppression served the economic and geopolitical interests of the EU's core. Similarly, financial forms of punishment were also deployed in 2015 to force the left-leaning government of Greece to accept further austerity, despite the astonishing Greferendum results against it (Fuchs, 2017b). Therefore, economic and geopolitical interests seem to deem what will be framed as "democratic" in the mainstream.

7.3 The Making of Regimes of Entitlement: Class is at the Heart of the Matter

> French Tourists Deny to Pay Ticket at Greek Archaeological Site Because "France Offered Loans to Greece".
> *Greek Reporter*, 19/07/2015

> German Tourist in Crete to Taxi Driver: "I don't have to pay you because Greece owes Germany money".
> *Greek Reporter*, 20/08/2016

The culturalist construction of the "Greek crisis" has been rather evident across all media studied. As explained, racism is based on the historical Occidentalist gaze cast on Greece by Western imperialism and its remainders. The study also showed that all forms of racism entail classist elements. Race and class discrimination is historically connected to the development of capitalism and the bourgeois identity.

Along with its surviving Occidentalist legacies in today's "post-colonial" times, racism is also connected to neoliberal policy making. Although racism is prevalent in the thought of some prominent neoliberals (like Röpke), it is not a persisting issue in all aspects of neoliberal thought. Neoliberalism though is an Western-centric project (Slobodian, 2018: 181), prioritizing the West as the foundational block of civilisation and progress, which, in neoliberal thought is epitomised by the development of capitalist markets and their spreading across the globe. The West is thus to set the political and cultural example for the development of the world according to the principles of a globalised capitalism. The culturalist construction of the Eurozone crisis as a Greek crisis is also associated with neoliberalism's Occidentalist biases and its anti-democratic thinking, where non-market conformity is viewed as a sign of a somewhat cultural backwardness.

Either way, the constructions of cultural exception, their popularity, as well as the propagation of expert-led, "non-political" solutions to the crisis are mediated by (upper)class values and class politics. As austerity is a form of a class warfare, the politics of austerity aim at disciplining the working class to the post-crisis, "new norm". Mainstream liberal ideology though proclaims the category of the working class to be rather "dated". Class-based politics are also dismissed on similar grounds, even by the mainstream left. In a recent article, Vivek Chibber (2018) demonstrates that the working class is characterised by two interrelated characteristics: (a) the necessity of one to work, due to material scarcities (b) the loss of autonomy and freedom due to work, because in capitalism the worker, forced to work by scarcities, does not control his/her work conditions. In Chapter 2, I discussed how work emerges in capitalism and the social relations it entails. Thus, to talk about the working class makes good sense today because, to put simply, capitalism has far from ceased to exist. On the contrary, its ideology imposed a silence over issues of class, despite the escalating of inequalities across the world.

The cultural "deficiencies" attributed to the Greeks by politicians and mass media are based on bourgeois moral imperatives and on class-related entitlements to possessions and consumption. Entitlements are granted by the bourgeois values of hard work, saving, and property, which constitutes the quintessence of the bourgeois existence. As the Greeks are deemed "lazy", they do not have the right to property and to consumeristic lifestyles, because they did not work hard enough to sustain their possessions and to access consumer culture. Among them, the Greeks are also not entitled to welfare and to civil rights. Besides organizing regimes of primary accumulation, austerity is meant to punish and to discipline the Greek working class.

The dominance of capitalism occurs through the hegemony of the bourgeois and their culture, value systems, morals, lifestyles, social relations and tastes, as mediated by the middle-class. Europe itself, as represented by its capitalist core, manages to sustain a rather deceiving image of itself, as democratic, fair, tolerant, happy and successful, and to be popular and attractive to the global periphery. The allure of Europe to the people of the periphery is mediated by upper-middle-class fantasies, regularly reproduced by mainstream media, through narratives and images of success, comfort, beauty, and extravagance, staged in gentrified cities, which project promises of consumption, joy, and happiness. Such features, which in a capitalist social framework are exclusive, entitle the making of a Western and middle-class gaze, that observes, judges, and potentially shames the Other.

The annulment of the category of social class and class stratification, along with the downplaying of class inequality and the deepening exploitative class relations in social theory, even in some of its radical branches (that may prefer to talk about identity instead) today, in a global politico-economic system that is capitalist is highly problematic. For, it precisely shows the success of class hegemony, where the bourgeoisie manages to present itself as natural, fair and reasonable, dismissing class critique and along with it, the existence of a working class and its political possibilities. In this context, the working-class is associated to the old, the failed and the dangerous; and so, by disavowing it, one aligns him/herself to the "successful" ones, the dominant upper and middle-classes. The constitutional myths of the bourgeoisie, such as that of the narcissistic, privileged and entitled bourgeois, who may occasionally appear as "self-made", or as a charismatic and gifted individual that is deserving his/her material and manifested supremacy due to various reasons ranging from God's providence to supposed "genetic factors" (sic), should be tirelessly deconstructed and have their ludicrosity exposed publicly. Likewise, the notion of "success" in its bourgeois essence defined by tough competition and rewarded through consumeristic possibilities and superfluous ideas of eternal joy, or happiness, need also to be discredited as simply unsustainable. Political economy and cultural studies offer indispensable concepts and ideas to accomplish such as task of estranging from the "capitalist realist" (Fisher, 2009) commonsense.

7.4 Capitalism is Apocalyptic: Politicising the Crisis, Austerity, the "Free Market", and the (Capitalist) Economy

As the analysis showed, the economic crisis was constructed and represented by neoliberal politicians, pundits, economists and other related agents in eschatological terms, as a coming economic Armageddon. Eschatology, I argue, has been a central conceptual metaphor of the economic crisis as an impeding ontological threat, not just for Greece and the EU, but potentially for the world and the "global economy". The media amplified this construction as it allowed unprecedented opportunities to spectacularise the crisis and to develop an easy, infotaining content to be consumed by mass audiences. The spectacular representation of the Greek crisis in apocalyptic terms created a shock effect. The media created a moral panic around the crisis where countries (or continents) were faced with an imminent destruction unless harsh "economic reforms" were to be implemented. Such a dramatised media representation of the crisis organised the public legitimacy for exceptional policies to be implemented, bypassing democratic sovereign laws, norms and processes, as well as national labour, social, and human rights establishments. Politically this has been useful to block public critique and deliberation of the matter and to force austerity as the only available "remedy" to avoid an impending Armageddon. The no-alternative doctrine of austerity was thus publicly legitimised by authoritarian voices from the EU's politico-economic establishment, appearing as rational and neutral (thus a-political) experts that try to resolve an objective, exceptional event.

The Apocalyptic construction of the crisis is compatible with the neoliberal understanding of the economy which often arises in an agnostic and sublime form, beyond representation. The mystification of the (capitalist) economy has been part of the neoliberal understanding of the economy as a sublime that escapes full conceptualisation and representation (Slobodian, 2018: 87). Additionally, austerity policies were publicly represented with metaphors of prudent housekeeping and hard-work, as well as with metonymies drawn from the medical practitioners' vocabulary. In essence, the eschatological construction of the latest global capitalist economic crisis, besides its political function for the implementation of emergency policies of neoliberal restructuring, also encapsulated the religious dimension of capitalism, by expressing this system's core values and beliefs. This way, the apocalyptic construction of the crisis entailed a notion of Theodicy, which befell upon the guilty ones who disobeyed the rules and laws of the "economy". The essentalist notions of austerity presupposed a rather punitive role for it, that evoked the fantasy of retaliation in a sadistic sense, castigating the failed ones (those deemed as insolvent, profligate, idle and irrational), while simultaneously "delivering justice" to the obedient ones that follow the rules (the hard working, and prudent civilians, particularly of the capitalist core nations).

Alberto Toscano (2010: 60) notes that the use of millenarian terms to advance political agendas is a feature of the fanatic. The millenarian imaginary allows one to proceed and to struggle without compromise so as to fulfill his/her goals while remaining loyal to his/her ideas and value system. Research (Slobodian, 2018) has shown too that the globalisation of neoliberalism, through the construction of a global framework of laws, institutions, and norms that encase the capitalist economy and the capitalist market has been a form of a utopia that the neoliberals strove to realize relentlessly.

In his analysis of fanaticism – a term that generally holds highly negative meanings in the liberal context – Toscano (2010: 253) argues that fanaticism is born out of urgency and shock and emerges in conditions when things cannot be negotiated because power hierarchies and unequal social relations that sustain regimes of injustice and subjugation make deliberative change impossible. In this regard, liberal representative democracy has proven to obtain a rather functional use for neoliberals, insofar as it is useful to sustain stability and protect the economy from various socio-historical disruptions (Slobodian, 2018: 108).

The capitalist economy itself, however, is Apocalyptic. The ongoing climate and environmental catastrophe, the depletion of natural resources, the immiseration of vast numbers of people across the globe, and the degradation of life and democracy, are events and phenomena that make the Apocalypse metaphor useful to understand the destructive nature of capitalism, and to politicise it as the root cause of all major problems that humanity and the planet Earth are faced with today. Many accounts stress that humanity, civilisation, and life in the planet Earth itself are "confronted with an ontological break, or an apocalyptic zero point" (Feldner & Vighi, 2015: 7). In this sense, the millenarian thinking should be directed towards the horizon of a communist utopia.

Slobodian (2018: 124) also notes that, in their quest to protect capitalism, the neoliberals have been influenced by the militancy as well as the strategies of the left to set particular social agendas and to dominate the public discussion over a variety of topics. Simultaneously, the neoliberals also developed their own form of internationalism, which primarily concerned the freedom of capital and trade to move without state tariffs and restrictions across the globe. Along with a market-based democracy and a capitalist form of internationalism, the neoliberals also developed a "human rights" agenda that, again, focused mostly on the rights of investors and businessmen to be protected from nation-state laws and acts, in their transnational activities. Human rights were further used by neoliberals to undermine social and civil rights while emphasizing capitalist agendas and capitalist interpretations of what human rights should be. Slobodian (2018: 267) demonstrates the flexibility of the neoliberal project to incorporate a variety of concepts, demands, as well as tactics and strategies that were developed by progressive agendas, so as to reproduce, upgrade and further tighten the global capitalist market framework, deeming it invisible, permanent and unavoidable. To that respect, one also notices the mobilisation of citizen participation in the reproduction of neoliberalism, through the biopolitical advance of disciplinary technologies that progress on a societal and individual level. Furthemore, concepts related to leftist culture and political agendas, such as solidarity (let us recall that the so-called bailout loans in exchange for austerity in Greece were euphimistically branded as "European solidarity") evident in the EU's public communication of the Greek crisis, are also appropriated by the neoliberal governing assemblage. The analysis offered in this book aimed at exposing the contradictions behind such a resonating usage of progressive agendas to cover up policies that bring misery, humiliation and death, and to expose their propagandistic instrumentalisation.

7.5 Negativity and Utopia

> Many of us nursed a blind faith in Europe, in which the greatest European minds have never ceased to doubt.
>
> MATVEJEVIĆ, 2013: 256

> In comments reported by the Spanish press, Mr. Dijsselbloem told FAZ: "During the crisis of the Euro, the countries of the North have shown solidarity with the countries affected by the crisis. As a Social Democrat, I attribute exceptional importance to solidarity. [But] you also have obligations. You cannot spend all the money on drinks and women and then ask for help".
>
> The Financial Times, 21/03/2017

Jeroen Dijsselbloem, a neoliberal social democrat from Holland and former president of the Eurogroup said the particular words in early 2017 when the EU's crisis repertoire begun to change on a formal level. According to the analysis advanced in this study, his statement demonstrates the widespread existence of enduring prejudices (molded by former colonial superpowers like the Netherlands), as well as the general bankruptcy of third-way social democracy. What has been even more interesting in the specific example though, was the quick condemnation of Dijsselbloem's statement by various EU officials, which seemed to adopt a more politically correct wording. This way, EU officials scapegoated Djisselbloem. After all, Djisselbloem only repeated what has now become the Eurozone crisis commonsense in Europe and elsewhere, with regards to the profligate and promiscuous "Southerners" stereotypes. Furthermore, Djisselbloem only expressed what solidarity came to mean under its strategic colonisation by the EU's technocratic jargon. It was due to such a sudden eruption of political correctness from the EU that Dijsselbloem later stated (in a rather hyperbolic manner) that he felt as if he had committed a war crime. Indeed, although displaced, this latter statement of his makes sense, with regards to the kind of policies he advocated as a central EU bureaucrat. Nevertheless, in their current form, market-related policies are insulated from democracy and justice.

Either way, manifestations of political correctness such as the above, signify neoliberalism's strategic colonisation of progressive agendas, so as to encase the "free market" and to deem it above politics. Likewise, lately (during the summer of 2018 and after announcing that Greece will soon "return to the markets") various EU officials, who have been ardent supporters of austerity, made self-reflexive publicly appearances. For instance, the current "European Commissioner for Economic and Financial Affairs, Taxation and Customs", Pierre Moscovici, noted that the "Eurogroup should become more democratic" acknowledging the disregarding of the voting choices of the Greek people that took place from the beginning of the crisis in 2010 (*Efsyn*, 17/08/2018). The meaning of "democracy" evoked by figures like Moscovici is far from clear. For, it is hard to imagine how such predominantly economic institutions can ever

CONCLUSIONS: CONTEXT, POLITICS, NEGATIVITY 225

democratise. It is indeed hard to understand the meaning and the limits of democracy in governing institutions dominated by unelected technocrats and politicians of neoliberal convictions, with neoliberal austerity being presented to the general public as a no-alternative policy framework, with the national debt never being challenged as such, and with the capitalist market system being taken for granted as a natural entity. Nevertheless, claims such as Moscovici's should be seen as constitutive of hegemony's communicative strategy. Democracy here is a nodal signifier of the liberal-capitalist social imaginary that effectively marginalises the opposition to the realm of the "non-democratic", while sustaining the hegemonic, end of history, narrative of (Western) liberal democracy vs. totalitarianism.

As is generally known, the etymology of the term "crisis" (χρίση), points towards the existing of two distinct meanings: that of crisis as a rupture of the existing, and that of crisis as critique. In a Greek Public Television documentary series entitled "What does it mean to live?" and during an episode called "Crisis of Capitalism", Badiou deployed the Debordian notion of the spectacle as a critical concept to reflect upon the 2008 global economic crisis:

> Capitalism is spectacularized. Most people watch this current crisis as a spectacle. Most people are not financial economists, they are not merchants and they are not bankers. They can do nothing in reality so they observe the particular crisis with fear, worry, hope. In the end, it is a structural spectacle. We have to analyze and explain this spectacle; it is our prime duty to explain it as a crisis of capitalism and a collapse not only of the financial and monetary system but of a particular way of seeing the world. This task is in the scope of our powers and it will have consequences because according to the dominant propaganda of the last 20 years, this system is the best and no other system currently exists. But even if this system is the best, we still need to search for at least something else. Perhaps, we can enter into a new sequence of the process of truth in politics. But clarity is required [...] the particular spectacle, if anything, is educative. In a spectacular form, capitalism presents to us its own nullity.
> KERAMIDIOTIS, 2008

Badiou aligns with Debord's negative stance towards the capitalist society while foregrounding the possibility of a "strategy of negativity" that can have a constructive form towards systemic change. Benjamin Noys (2010: 149) argues that Badiou endorses Debord's analysis that sees the spectacle as something immersed in all aspects of social and individual life. In the Situationist fashion, Badiou calls for a "detournement" of the crisis publicity in order to expose the scornful essence of capitalism itself. Therefore, Badiou calls us to use the economic crisis in a critical way, so as to expose the "nullity" of capitalism.

Badiou's call implies a rather negative attitude towards what currently exists under global capitalism, which can be marked by a belief in a different world to emerge. The experiences, memories, and historicities of resistance may inspire a desire and a vision for another world. Further, the engagement with socialist ideas and politics can also enact a counter-hegemonic collective identity, along with the crafting of different forms of social, political and economic organisation, based on egalitarian, participatory, communal, decentralised and grassroots democracy forms. Here, a utopian imagination is implied that organizes hope under a political way of thinking. Utopian politics are largely discredited under the "no alternative to capitalism" thesis, which makes a rather intellectually and politically crippling case. For Fredrik Jameson (2007: xiii) utopian thinking can have a negative effect, by exposing the alienating effects of the current state of being; most importantly though, utopia can be both an impulse and a desire, as well and a program.

To return to the work of Deleuze and Guattari (2003), in their monograph on Franz Kafka, they address Kafka's oeuvre as a form of a "minor literature". With the term "minor" they foreground the subaltern and marginal character of Kafka's language and experience, and its importance for the broader historical community of his time and the challenges it faced by processes (such as bureaucracy and proletarianisation) that remained largely inarticulate by the general public, which seemed unable to grasp them in a critical manner. By deploying the idea of minor while referring to today's European and global counter-hegemonic politics, I wish to challenge both the progressivist and the regressive Euro and Western-centrism, and to highlight instead the critical narratives of groups and tendencies existing in different European countries and elsewhere, in their efforts to develop critical, working-class and internationalist cultures and organisations resisting neoliberal capitalism. Such minority groups were those that showed solidarity to the Greek people that took a political stance against austerity, along with other oppressed and exploited groups from across the world, without prioritizing Europe, and without seeing what they do as inherently "European". While policy is the process of governing and creating consent, politics, for Rancière (1992: 58) make a process of emancipation. Although engaging and encouraging, the minoritarian condition of such groups and practices is limited to its potentials in seriously challenging hegemony.

The mainstream left's embrace of neoliberalism (e.g. as in the third way social democracy) meant the marginalisation of critique and the impoverishing of political praxis and political thought to the confines of the establishment and its urges for "stability", so as to sustain itself. Therefore, at our current historical moment, the (anticapitalist) left finds itself in a very weak position, due to its low popular support and its effective marginalisation from the mainstream public sphere. This, of course, is something that could potentially change, as history suggests. Fidelity, courage, unity, organisation, and strategy, are indispensable elements for the reinvention of leftist politics. So is an internationalist and socialist vision for the society of the future. The development of theory, through a nuanced and reflexive reading and a creative synthesis of the ideas and the analyses of political writers such as Karl Marx, Piotr Kropotkin, or Henri Lefebvre, among many others, may advance the possibility of crafting new political desires, imaginaries, identities, institutions, organisational forms and strategies.

Bibliography

Abercombie, N. and Longhurst, B. (1998) *Audiences*. London: Sage.
Adorno, T. and Horkheimer, M. (1989) *The Dialectic of the Enlightenment*. New York: Continuum.
Adorno, T. (2001) *The Culture Industries*. London: Routledge.
Adorno, T. (2002) *The Stars Down to Earth and Other Essays on the Irrational in Culture*. London: Routledge.
Adorno, T. (2004) *Negative Dialectics*. London: Routledge.
Agamben, G. (2000) *Homo Sacer: Sovereign Power and Bare Life*. Stanford University Press: California.
Agamben, G. (2005) *State of Exception*. Chicago, Chicago University Press.
Ahmed, S. (2000) *Strange Encounters: Embodied Others in Post-Coloniality*. London: Roultedge.
Ahmed, S. (2004) *The Cultural Politics of Emotion*. Edinburgh: Edinburgh University Press.
Aitaki, G. (2017) Domesticating Pathogenies, Evaluating Change: the Eurozone Crisis as a "Hot Moment" in Greek Television Fiction. *Media, Culture & Society* 1–16 DOI: 10.1177/1464884917708870.
Ali, T. (2015) *The Extreme Center, a Warning*. London: Verso.
Amable, B. (2010) Morals and Politics in the Ideology of Neo-Liberalism. *Socio-Economic Review* 3(30): 3–30.
Amin, S. (2009) *Eurocentrism: Modernity, Religion, and Democracy, a Critique of Eurocentrism and Culturalism*. New York: Monthly Review Press.
Amin, S. (2014) *The Implosion of Capitalism*. London: Pluto Press.
Amin, S. (2016) *Russia and the Long Transition from Capitalism to Socialism*. New York: Monthly Review Press.
Anderson, P. (2009) *The New Old World*. London: Verso.
Anderson, P. (2017) *The "H" Word: the Peripeteia of Hegemony*. London: Verso.
Arendt, H. (1994) *Eichmann in Jerusalem, the Banality of Evil*. London: Penguin.
Arrese, Á. and Vara-Miguel, A. (2016) A Comparative Study of Metaphors in Press Reporting of the Euro Crisis. *Discourse & Society* 27(2): 133–155.
Askanius, T. and Mylonas, Y. (2015) The Economic Crisis of the EU in the Media Discourses of the Extreme Right: the Cases of Denmark and Sweden. *Javnost, the Public* 22(1): 55–72.
Baca, G. (2017) Neoliberal Narratives of Crisis: The Feeble Cries of a Vanishing "Class." *Dialect Anthropol* https://doi.org/10.1007/s10624-017-9474-5.
Back, L. and Solomos, J. (eds) (2000) *Theories of Race and Racism: A Reader*. London and New York: Routledge.
Badiou, A. (2001) *Ethics: an Essay on the Understanding of Evil*. London: Verso.

Badiou, A. (2012) Save the Greeks from Ther Saviours! Available (consulted 26 August 2018) at: http://www.crisismirror.org/library/articles/alain-badiou-save-the-greeks-from-their-saviors/.

Balhorn, L. (2016) Merkeling to the Right. Available (consulted 6 February 2017) at: https://www.jacobinmag.com/2016/12/merkel-burqa-ban-refugees-cdu-germany/.

Balibar, E. and Wallerstein, I. (1991) *Race, Nation, Class: Ambiguous Identities*. London: Verso.

Barbalet J.M. (2004) *Emotion, Social Theory, and Social Structure, a Macrosociological Approach*. Cambridge: Cambridge University Press.

Basu L. (2017) Living within Our Means: The UK News Construction of the Austerity Frame over Time. *Journalism* 1–18 DOI: 10.1177/1464884917708870.

Basu, L. (2018) *Media Amnesia: Rewriting the Economic Crisis*. London: Pluto Press.

Bauman, Z. (1998) *Modernity and the Holocaust*. Cambridge: Polity.

Bauman, Z. (2004) *Wasted Lives: Modernity and its Outcasts*. Cambridge: Polity.

Bauman, Z. (2004b) *Europe: An Unfinished Adventure*. Cambridge: Polity.

Bauman, Z. (2011) *Globalization: The Human Consequences*. Cambridge: Polity.

Bauman, Z. (2013) *Do the Riches of the Few Benefit Us All?* Cambridge: Polity.

B'béri, E. and Louw, Eric. P. (2011) Afropessimism: a Genealogy of Discourse. *Critical Arts: South-North Cultural and Media Studies* 25(3): 335–346.

Beck, U. (1999) *World Risk Society*. London: Polity Press.

Beetz J. and Schwab, V. (2018) Conditions and Relations of (re)production in Marxism and Discourse Studies, *Critical Discourse Studies* DOI: 10.1080/17405904.2018.1456946.

Benjamin, W. (1974) On the Concept of History. Available (consulted 7 November 2018) at: https://folk.uib.no/hlils/TBLR-B/Benjamin-History.pdf.

Bennett, T., Savage, M., Silva, E., Warde, A., Gayo-Cal, M. and Wright, D. (2009) *Culture, Class, Distinction*. London: Routledge.

Bennett, J. (2013) Moralising Class: A Discourse Analysis of the Mainstream Political Response to Occupy and the August 2011 British Riots. *Discourse & Society* 24(1): 27–45.

Berezin, M. (2013) The Normalization of the Right in Post-Security Europe. In: Schäfer, A. and Wolfgang Streeck, W. (eds.) *Politics in the Age of Austerity*. Cambridge, Polity Press, 239–261.

Berger, J. and Mohr, J. (2010) *A Seventh Man*. London: Verso.

Berger, J. (2015) *Portraits: John Berger on Artists*. London: Verso.

Berman, M. (2010) *All that is Solid Melts into Air: The Experience of Modernity*. New Edition. London: Verso.

Beveridge, R. (2017) The (Ontological) Politics in Depoliticisation Debates: Three Lenses on the Decline of the Political. *Political Studies Review* 15(4): 589–600.

Bickes, H. Otten, T. and Weyman, C.L. (2014) The Financial Crisis in the German and English Press: Metaphorical Structures in the Media Coverage on Greece, Spain and Italy. *Discourse & Society* 25(4): 424–445.

Block, D. (2018) Some Thoughts on CDS and its Marxist Political Economy Bases. *Critical Discourse Studies* DOI: 10.1080/17405904.2018.1456943.

Blyth, M. (2013) *Austerity, the History of a Dangerous Idea*. Oxford: Oxford University Press.

Blyth, M. (2018) Still the Land of Extend and Pretend? What Being Back in the Markets Actually Means for Greece Going Forward. Available (consulted 21 August 2018) at: https://www.thepressproject.gr/mnimonio/en/details.php?aid=133037.

Bolt, M. (2011) On the Turn towards Liberal State Racism in Denmark. Available (consulted 08 August 2018) at: https://conversations.e-flux.com/t/on-the-turn-towards-liberal-state-racism-in-denmark/5545.

Bolt, M. (2015) *Crisis to Insurrection: Notes on the Ongoing Collapse*. New York: Minor Compositions.

Boltanski, L. (2004) *Distant Suffering: Morality, Media and Politics*. Cambridge: Cambridge University Press.

Boltanski, L. and Eve Chiapello, E. (2007) *The New Spirit of Capitalism*. London: Verso.

Böröcz J. and Sarkar, M. (2017) The Unbearable Whiteness of the Polish Plumber and the Hungarian Peacock Dance around "Race." *Slavic Review* 76(2): 307–3014.

Boukala, S. (2014) Waiting for Democracy: Political Crisis and the Discursive (Re)Invention of the "National Enemy" in Times of "Grecovery." *Discourse and Society* 25(4): 483–499.

Bourdieu, P. (2010) *Distinction*. Abington: Routledge.

Bozatzis, N. (2016) Cultural Othering, Banal Occidentalism and the Discursive Construction of the "Greek Crisis" in Global Media: a Case Study. *Suomen Anthropologi* 41(2): 47–71.

Bramall R. (2013) *The Cultural Politics of Austerity Past and Present in Austere Times*. Houndmills. Basingstoke: Palgrave Macmillan.

Brevini, B. (2017) "When Neoliberal Ideology is not Enough: Post-Truth Politics and Australian Mining Debates" paper presented at CSAA 2017, Cultures of Capitalism Conference, Massey University Wellington, December.

Buchowski, M. (2006) The Specter of Orientalism in Europe: From Exotic Other to Stigmatized Brother. *Anthropological Quarterly* 79(3): 463–482.

Buck-Morss, S. (1987) Semiotic Boundaries and the Politics of Meaning: Modernity on Tour-a Village in Transition. In: Raskin, M.G. and Bernstein, H.J. (eds) *New Ways of Knowing: the Sciences, Society and Reconstructive Knowledge*. New York: Rowman, Littlefield, 200–236.

Buck-Morss, S. (1991) *The Dialectics of Seeing: Walter Benjamin and the Arcades Project*. Cambridge: The MIT Press.

Buck-Morss, S. (1992) Aesthetics and Anaesthetics: Walter Benjamin's Artwork Essay Reconsidered. *October* 62: 3–41.

Buck-Morss, S. (2002) *Dreamworld and Catastrophe, the Passing of Mass Utopia in East and West.* Cambridge Massachusetts, and London England: The MIT Press.

Büscher, B. and Fletcher, R. (2017) Destructive Creation: Capital Accumulation and the Structural Violence of Tourism. *Journal of Sustainable Tourism* 25(5): 651–667.

Caffentzis, G. (2013) *In Letters of Blood and Fire: Work, Machines, and the Crisis of Capitalism.* New York: Common Notions.

Cafruny, A. and Magnus R. (2016) *The European Union and Global Capitalism: Origins, Development, Crisis.* Houndmills: Palgrave.

Calhoun, G. (1996) Introduction: Habermas and the Public Sphere. In: Calhoun, G. (ed.) *Habermas and the Public Sphere.* Cambridge, Massachusetts, and London, England: The MIT Press, pp. 1–48.

Carah, N. and Louw, E. (2015) *Media and Society: Production, Content and Participation.* London: Sage.

Carastathis, A. (2014) Is Hellenism an Orientalism? Reflections on the Boundaries of "Europe" in an Age of Austerity. *Critical Race and Whiteness Studies* 10(1): 1–17.

Carpentier, N. and De Cleen, B. (2007) Bringing Discourse Theory into Media Studies: The Applicability of Discourse Theoretical Analysis (DTA) for the Study of Media Practices and Discourses. *Journal of Language and Politics* 6(2): 265–293.

Carpentier, N. (2011) *Media and Participation: a Site of Ideological-Democratic Struggle.* Bristol: Intellect.

Carpentier, N. (2017) *The Discursive-Material Knot: Cyprus in Conflict and Community Media Participation.* New York: Peter Lang Publishing.

Chakravartty, P. and Shiller, D. (2010) Neoliberal Newspeak and Digital Capitalism in Crisis. *The International Journal of Communication* 4: 670–692.

Chibber, V. (2013) *Postcolonial Theory and the Specter of Capital.* London: Verso.

Chibber, V. (2018) Why We Still Talk About the Working-Class. Available (consulted 21 August 2018) at: https://www.jacobinmag.com/2017/03/abcs-socialism-working-class-workers-capitalism-power-vivek-chibber/.

Chouliaraki, L. and Fairclough, N. (2005) *Discourse in Late Modernity, Rethinking Critical Discourse Analysis.* Edinburgh: Edinburgh University Press.

Chun, C. W. (2017) *The Discourses of Capitalism: Everyday Economists and the Production of Common Sense.* Oxon: Routledge.

Couldry, N. (2010) *Why Voice Matters: Culture and Politics after Neoliberalism.* London: Sage.

Crouch, C. (2004) *Post Democracy.* London: Polity.

Crouch, C. (2011) *The Strange Non-Death of Neoliberalism.* London: Polity.

Crouch, C. (2013) From Defensive to Assertive Social Democracy. Available (consulted 25 November 2016) at: https://www.socialeurope.eu/book/re-no-1-from-defensive-to-assertive-social-democracy/#.

Curran, J. (2003) *Media and Power.* London and New York: Routledge.

Dahlberg, L. (2014) Capitalism as a Discursive System? Interrogating Discourse Theory's Contribution to Critical Political Economy. *Critical Discourse Studies* 11(3): 257–271.

Dahlgren, P. (2009) *Media and Political Engagement: Citizens, Communication and Democracy*. Cambridge: Cambridge University Press.

Dahlgren, P. (2013) *The Political Web: Media Participation and Alternative Democracy*. Houndmills: Plagrave MacMillan.

Dalakoglou, D. and Poulimenakos, G. (2018) Airbnbizing Europe: Mobility, Property and Platform Capitalism. Available (consulted 14 May 2019) at: https://www.opendemocracy.net/can-europe-make-it/dimitris-dalakoglou-giorgos-poulimenakos/airbnbizing-europe-mobility-property-and

Dardot, P. and Laval, C. (2014) *The New Way of the World: On the Neoliberal Society*. London: Verso.

Davies, W. (2014) *The Limits of Neoliberalism; Authority, Sovereignty and the Logic of Competition*. London: Sage.

Davis, M. (2017) *Late Victorian Holocausts: El Niño Famines and the Making of the Third World*. London: Verso.

De Angelis, M. (2004). Separating the Doing and the Deed: Capital and the Continuous Character of Enclosures. *Historical Materialism* 12(2): 57–87.

De Cleen, B., Glynos, J. and Mondon, A. (2018) Critical Research on Populism: Nine Rules of Engagement. *Organization* 25(5): 649–661.

Dean, J. (2002) *Publicity's Secret: How Technoculture Capitalizes on Democracy*. Ithaca and London: Cornell University Press.

Dean, J. (2009) *Democracy and Other Neoliberal Fantasies: Communicative Capitalism and Left Politics*. Durham & London: Duke University Press.

Dean, J. (2009b) Politics without Politics. *Parallax* 15(3): 20–36.

Dean, J. (2012) *The Communist Horizon*. London: Verso.

Dean, J. (2016) *Crowds and Party*. London: Verso.

Dean, J. (2017) Crowds and Publics. *Stasis* 5(1): 196–247.

Debord, G. (1977) Society of the Spectacle. Available (consulted 19 October 2017) at: https://www.marxists.org/reference/archive/debord/society.htm.

Deleuze, G. and Guattari, F. (1977) *Capitalism and Schizophrenia: Anti-Oedipus*. Athens: Rappa.

Deleuze, G. and Guattari, F. (2003) *Kafka: Towards a Minor Literature*. Minneapolis: University of Minnesota Press.

Deleuze, G. and Masoch, L.V-S. (2006) *Masochism: Coldness and Cruelty, and Venus in Furs*. New York: Zone Books.

Demertzis, N. (2006) Emotions and Populism. In: Clarke, S. et al. (eds.) *Emotion, Politics and Society*. London: Palgrave Macmillan, 103–122.

Derber, C. and Magrass, Y. (2016) *Bully Nation: How the American Establishment Creates a Bullying Society*. Lawrence: University Press of Kansas.

Diken, B. (2009) Radical Critique as a Paradox of Post-Political Society. *Third Text* 23(5): 579–586.

Dimitriou, S. (2016) *Κοινωνική Εξέλιξη και Σχέσεις Δύναμης* (*Social Evolution and Power Relations*). Athens: Alexandreia.

Doudaki, V. (2015) Legitimation Mechanisms in the Bailout Discourse. *Javnost, the Public* 22(1): 1–17.

Doudaki, V. (2018) Discourse of Legitimation in the News: The Case of the Cypriot Bailout. In: Carpentier, N. and Doudaki, V. (eds) *Cyprus and its Conflicts: Representations, Materialities, and Cultures*. London: Berghahn, 142–162.

Douzinas, C. (2013) *Philosophy and Resistance in the Crisis, Greece and the Future of Europe*. London: Polity.

Doxiadis, K. (2016) *Προπαγάνδα* (*Propaganda*). Athens: Nisos.

Dörre, K. Lessenich, S. and Hartmut, R. (2015) *Sociology, Capitalism, Critique*. London: Verso.

Durand, C. (2017) *Fictitious Capital: How Finance Is Appropriating Our Future*. London: Verso.

Dyrberg, T.B. (1997) *The Circular Structure of Power*. London: Verso.

Dyrberg, T.B. (2005) Radical and Plural Democracy: In Defence of Right/Left Public Reason. In: Tønder, L. and Thomassen, L. (eds) *Radical Democracy: Politics Between Abundance and Lack*. Manchester: Manchester University press, 167–184.

Efsyn (2018). *Δέσμευση Απέναντι στους Εργαζόμενους* (Commitment to the Workers). Available (consulted 7 November 2018) at: http://www.efsyn.gr/arthro/desmeysi-apenanti-stoys-ergazomenoys.

Efsyn (2018) "*Το Eurogroup Πρέπει να γίνει πιο Δημοκρατικό*" ("The Eurogroup Must Become More Democratic"). Available (consulted 18 August 2018) at: https://www.efsyn.gr/arthro/eurogroup-prepei-na-ginei-pio-dimokratiko.

Elliot, L. (2016) Austerity Policies Do More Harm than Good, IMF Study Concludes. Available (consulted 3 June 2016) at: https://www.theguardian.com/business/2016/may/27/austerity-policies-do-more-harm-than-good-imf-study-concludes.

Ellul, J. (1973) *Propaganda: the Formation of Men's Attitudes*. New York: Vintage Books.

Ellul, J. (2008) *The Metamorphosis of the Bourgeois*. Thessaloniki: Nissides.

Endnotes (2010) Issue 2: Misery and the Value Form. Available (consulted 6 June 2018) at: https://endnotes.org.uk/issues/2.

Enikos, (2012) *Άδωνις: Όποιος δεν Προσαρμόζεται, Πεθαίνει* (Adonis: Whoever Doesn't Adjust, Dies). Available (consulted 21 October 2018) http://www.enikos.gr/politics/101186/adonisopoios-den-prosarmozetai-pethainei.

Entman, R.M. (1993) Framing: Toward Clarification of a Fractured Paradigm. *Journal of Communication* 43(4): 51–58.

Eriksson G. (2015) Ridicule as a Strategy for the Recontextualization of the Working-class. *Critical Discourse Studies* 12(1): 20–38.

Ervedosa C. (2017) The Calibanisation of the South in the German Public "Euro crisis" Discourse. *Postcolonial Studies* 20(2): 137–162.

Eurostat (2009) 79 Million EU Citizens Were at-Risk-of-Poverty in 2007, of Whom 32 Million Were also Materially Deprived. Available (consulted 17 October 2018) at: https://ec.europa.eu/eurostat/documents/3433488/5281381/KS-SF-09-046-EN.PDF/a710699c-8167-4ae8-87bc-26b71c91a74b.

Eurostat (2017) People at Risk of Poverty or Social Exclusion. Available (consulted 17 October 2018) at: https://ec.europa.eu/eurostat/statistics-explained/index.php/People_at_risk_of_poverty_or_social_exclusion.

Eurostat (2018) General Government Gross Debt. Available (consulted 23 August 2018) at: http://ec.europa.eu/eurostat/tgm/table.do?tab=table&plugin=1&language=en&pcode=sdg_17_40.

Fairclough, N. (2003) *Analyzing Discourse: Textual Analysis for Social Research*. London: Routledge.

Fairclough, N. and Fairclough, I. (2012) *Political Discourse Analysis*. London: Routledge.

Fanon, F. (2008) *Black Skin, White Masks*. New York: Grove Press.

Fekete, L. (2017) Flying the Flag for Neoliberalism. *Race and Class* 58(3): 3–22.

Feldner, H. & Vighi, F. (2015) *Critical Theory and the Crisis of Contemporary Capitalism*. New York: Bloomsbury.

Financial Times (2017). Dijsselbloem under Fire after Saying Eurozone Countries Wasted Money on "Alcohol and Women." Available (consulted 20 August 2018) at: https://www.ft.com/content/2498740e-b911-3dbf-942d-ecce511a351e.

Fisher, M. (2009) *Capitalist Realism: Is There No Alternative?* Ropley: Zero Books.

Fleisher, H. (2008) *Memory Wars: the Second World War in Contemporary Public History*. Athens: Nefeli.

Fokianaki, I. (2017) Documenting Documenta 14 Athens. Available (consulted 8 April 2018) at: http://www.metropolism.com/en/opinion/31387_documenting_documenta_14_athens.

Fokianaki, I. and Varoufakis, Y. (2017) "We Come Bearing Gifts" – iLiana Fokianaki and Yanis Varoufakis on Documenta 14 Athens. Available (consulted 08 April 2018) at: http://www.art-agenda.com/reviews/d14/.

Forchtner, B. (2014) Rhetorics of Judge-Penitence: Claiming Moral Superiority through Admissions of Past Wrongdoing. *Memory Studies* 7(4): 409–424.

Foucault, M. (2008) *The Birth of Biopolitics. Lectures at College de France, 1978–1979*. London: Palgrave McMillan.

Fouseki, K. and Dragouni, M. (2017) Heritage Spectacles: the Case of Amphipolis Excavations during the Greek Economic Crisis. *International Journal of Heritage Studies* 23(8): 742–758.

Fraser, N. (1996) Rethinking the Public Sphere: A Contribution to the Critique of Actually Existing Democracy. In: Calhoun, C. (ed) *Habermas and the Public Sphere*. Cambridge, Massachusetts, and London, England: The MIT Press, 109–142.

Fraser, N. (2017) Progressive Neoliberalism versus Reactionary Populism: A Choice that Feminists Should Refuse. *NORA – Nordic Journal of Feminist and Gender Research* 24(4): 281–284.

Fraser, N. and Honneth, A. (2003) *Redistribution or Recognition? A Political-Philosophical Exchange*. London: Verso.

Free, M. and Scully, C. (2016) The Run of Ourselves: Shame, Guilt and Confession in Post-Celtic Tiger Irish Media. *International Journal of Cultural Studies* 1–17 DOI: 10.1177/1367877916646470.

Fuchs, C., Schafranek, M., Hakken, D., and Breen, M. (2010) Capitalist Crisis, Communication, & Culture – Introduction to the Special Issue of *tripleC*. *tripleC* 8(29): 193–204.

Fuchs, C. (2014) Social Media and the Public Sphere. *tripleC* 12(1): 57–101.

Fuchs, C. (2015) *Reading Marx in the Information Age: a Media and Communication Studies Perspective on Capital Volume 1*. London: Routledge.

Fuchs, C. (2016) *Critical Theory of Communication: New Readings of Lukács, Adorno, Marcuse, Honneth and Habermas in the Age of the Internet*. London: University of Westminster Press.

Fuchs, C. (2017) *Social Media, a Critical Introduction, Second Edition*. London: Sage.

Fuchs, C. (2017b) Donald Trump: A Critical Theory-Perspective on Authoritarian Capitalism. *tripleC* 15(1): 1–72.

Galanopoulos, A. (2015) Για μια "Κανονική Χώρα": Η Βιοπολιτική Συμμόρφωση στον Σύγχρονο Ελληνικό Πολιτικό Λόγο (*For a "Normal Country": the Biopolitical Discipline in the Conteporary Greek Political Discourse*). Available (consulted 4 August 2018) at: https://www.researchgate.net/publication/305993501_Gia_mia_kanonike_chora_E_biopolitike_symmorphose_ston_synchrono_elleniko_politiko_logo.

García, Á.M. (2013) Haunted Communities: The Greek Vampire or the Uncanny at the Core of Nation Construction. In: Stasiewicz-Bieńkowska, A. and Graham K. (eds.) *Monstrous Manifestations: Realities and Imaginings of the Monster*. Inter-Disciplinary Press, 53–64.

Garner, S. (2010) *Racisms: an Introduction*. London: Sage.

Giddens, A. (1991) Mo*dernity and Self Identity: Self and Society in the Late Modern Age*. Stanford: Stanford University Press.

Giroux, H. (2008) *Against the Terror of Neoliberalism: Politics Beyond the Age of Greed*. Boulder: Paradigm.

Giroux, H. (2016) The Authoritarian Politics of Resentment in Trump's America. Available (consulted 15 November 2017) at: http://www.truth-out.org/opinion/item/38351-the-authoritarian-politics-of-resentment-in-trump-s-america.

Gkintidis, D. (2016) Docile Elites, Lumpen People, Spoiled Country: Some Preliminary Reflections on the Cultural and Moral Analysis of Capitalist Asymmetry in Post-War Greece. Available (consulted 4 August 2018) at: https://www.ceeol.com/search/article-detail?id=479378.

Gkintidis, D. (2018) European Funds and the Hermeneutics of the Capitalist Crisis: Insights from Within the Greek State. *PoLAR: Political and Legal Anthropology Review* 41(1): 142–159.

Glynos, J. and Howarth, D. (2007) *Logics of Critical Explanation in Social and Political Theory*. London, New York: Routledge.

Glynos J. and Savvas V. (2016) Ideology as Blocked Mourning: Greek National Identity in Times of Economic Crisis and Austerity. *Journal of Political Ideologies* 21:3: 201–224.

Golding, P. (2017) Citizen Detriment: Communications, Inequality, and Social Order. *International Journal of Communication* 11: 4305–4323.

Goodman, E. (2015) Noam Chomsky: Austerity Is Just Class War. Available (consulted 24 November 2016) at: http://www.alternet.org/economy/noam-chomsky-austerity-just-class-war.

Graeber, D. (2011) *Debt: The First 5000 Years*. New York: Melville House Publishing.

Graham, C. and Silke, H. (2017) Framing Privatisation: The Dominance of Neoliberal Discourse and the Death of the Public Good. *TripleC* 15(2): 796–815.

Greek Reporter (2015) French Tourists Deny to Pay Ticket at Greek Archaeological Site Because "France Offered Loans to Greece." Available (consulted 4 August 2018) at: http://greece.greekreporter.com/2015/07/19/french-tourists-deny-to-pay-ticket-at-greek-archaeological-site-because-france-offered-loans-to-greece/.

Greek Reporter (2016) German Tourist in Crete to Taxi Driver: "I Don't Have to Pay You because Greece Owes Germany Money." Available (consulted 4 August 2018) at: http://greece.greekreporter.com/2016/08/20/german-tourist-in-crete-to-taxi-driver-i-dont-have-to-pay-you-because-greece-owes-germany-money/.

Gumpert, M. (2017) Beware of Greeks Bearing Gifts: Metaphors as Viruses in Discourses on the Greek Crisis. *Journal of Greek Media & Culture* 3(1): 31–51.

Habermas, J. (1992) *The Structural Transformation of the Public Sphere: Inquiry into a Category of Bourgeois Society*. Cambridge: Polity.

Habermas, J. (2012) *The Crisis of the European Union: A Response*. Cambridge, Polity.

Hadjimichalis, C. (2011) Uneven Geographical Development and Socio-Spatial Justice and Solidarity: European Regions after the 2009 Financial Crisis. *European Urban and Regional Studies* 18(3): 254–274.

Hall, S., Critcher, C., Jefferson, T., Clarke, J. and Roberts, B. (1978) *Policing the Crisis: Mugging, the State, Law and Order*. London: McMillan Press.

Hall, S. (1992) Race, Culture, and Communications: Looking Backward and Forward at Cultural Studies. *Rethinking Marxism* 5(1): 10–18.

Hall, S. (2003) *Representation: Cultural Representations and Signifying Practices*. London: Sage.

Hall, S. (2011) The Neoliberal Revolution. *Cultural Studies* 25(6): 705–728.

Hamilakis, Y. (2015) Eternal Debts and Occult Economies: The Archaeo-Politics of the Contemporary Crisis. Available (consulted 30 October 2017) at: https://coursecast.soton.ac.uk/Panopto/Pages/Viewer.aspx?id=a70788c0-2b51-474e-8a19-1a67771ea658.

Hamilakis, Y. (2016) Some Debts Can Never Be Repaid: The Archaeo-Politics of the Crisis. *Journal of Modern Greek Studies* 34(2): 27–64.

Harjuniemi, T. (2018) Reason over Politics: The Economist's Historical Framing of Austerity. *Journalism Studies*. Available (consulted 25 June 2018) at: https://doi.org/10.1080/1461670X.2018.1423633.

Harkins, S. and Lugo-Ocando, J. (2016) How Malthusian Ideology Crept into the Newsroom: British Tabloids and the Coverage of the Underclass. *Critical Discourse Studies* 13(1): 78–93.

Harvey, D. (2005) *A Brief History of Neoliberalism*. Oxford: Oxford University Press.

Harvey, D. (2010) *The Enigma of Capital and the Crises of Capitalism*. London: Profile Books.

Harvey, D. (2014) *Seventeen Contradictions and the End of Capitalism*. Oxford: Oxford University Press.

Heer, H., Manoschek, W., Pollak, A. and Wodak, R. (eds) (2008) *The Discursive Construction of History: Remembering the Wehrmacht's War of Annihilation*. Houndmills: Palgrave McMillan.

Herman, E. and Chomsky, N. (1988) *Manufacturing Consent, the Political Economy of the Mass Media*. New York: Pantheon Books.

Hill, A. (2005) *Reality TV: Audiences and Popular Factual Television*. London and New York: Routledge.

Hirschman, A.O. (1991) *The Rhetoric of Reaction: Perversity, Futility, Jeopardy*. London: the Belknap Press.

Ho, K. (2009) *Liquidated: An Ethnography of Wall Street*. Durham and London: Duke University Press.

Howarth, D. (2018) Marx, Discourse Theory and Political Analysis: Negotiating an Ambiguous Legacy. *Critical Discourse Studies*, DOI: 10.1080/17405904.2018.1457550.

Hudis, P. (2018) Racism and the Logic of Capitalism: A Fanonian Reconsideration. *Historical Materialism*. Available (consulted 31 May 2018) at: http://www.historicalmaterialism.org/articles/racism-and-logic-capitalism.

INE-GSEE (2018) Annual 2018 Report for the Greek Economy and Employment. Available (consulted 25 August 2018) at: https://gsee.gr/?p=35483.

Info-war.gr (2015) Πως τα ΜΜΕ της Διαπλοκής Χρηματοδοτήθηκαν για να Γίνουν οι Ερπύστριες της «Τρόικας» (How the Corporate Media Were Financanced to Become the Troika's Crawlers). Available (consulted 27 September 2018) at: https://info-war.gr/πως-τα-μμε-της-διαπλοκής-χρηματοδοτήθ/.

Info-war.gr (2015b) Το Ποτάμι: Οι Φτωχοί Κάνουν Λάθος Επιλογές (To Potami: The Poor Make Wrong Choices). Available (consulted 8 April 2018) at: https://info-war.gr/το-ποτάμι-οι-φτωχοί-κάνουν-λάθος-επιλο/.

Information (2015) Den Græske Krise Er Selvforskyldt (The Greek Crisis Is Self-Inflicted). Avalable (consulted 20 May 2019) at: https://www.information.dk/debat/2015/03/graeske-krise-selvforskyldt.

Jacobsson, D. and Ekström, M. (2016) Dismantling Discourses: Compassion, Coping and Consumption in Journalistic Representations of the Working-Class. *Critical Discourse Studies* 13 (4): 379–396.

Jacobsson, D. (2016) Business Elite Competition or a Common Concern? *Journalism Studies*. Available (consulted 25 June 2018) at: http://dx.doi.org/10.1080/1461670X.2016.1164615 accessed 30/4/2016.

Jacobsson, D. (2016b) *Bruised by the Invisible Hand: A Critical Examination of Journalistic Representations and the Naturalization of Neoliberal Ideology in Times of Industrial Crisis*. Doctoral Dissertation, Department of Journalism, Media and Communication, University of Gothenburg.

Jameson, F. (2007) *Archaeologies of the Future: The Desire Called Utopia and Other Science Fictions*. London: Verso.

Jameson, F. (2015) *The Ancients and the Postmoderns: On the Historicity of Forms*. London: Verso.

Jameson, F. (2016) *An American Utopia: Dual Power and the Universal Army*. London: Verso.

Jeffries, S. (2016) *Grand Hotel Abyss: The Lives of the Frankfurt School*. London: Verso.

Jessop, B. (2004) Critical Semiotic Analysis and Cultural Political Economy. *Critical Discourse Studies* 1(2): 159–174.

Jessop, B. (2012) Recovered Imaginaries, Imagined Recoveries: A Cultural Political Economy of Crisis Construals and Crisis-Management in the North Atlantic Financial Crisis. Available (consulted 10 June 2016) at: http://speri.dept.shef.ac.uk/wp-content/uploads/2012/07/Bob-Jessop-Recovered-Imaginaries-Imagines-Recoveries-A-cultural-political-economy-of-crisis-construals-crisis-management-in-the-North-Atlantic-Financial-Crisis-549KB.pdf.

Johanssen, J. (2017) Immaterial Labour and Reality TV: The Affective Surplus of Excess. In: Briziarelli, M. and Armano, E. (eds) *The Spectacle 2.0: Reading Debord in the Context of Digital Capitalism*. London: University of Westminster Press, 197–208.

Jones, O. (2016) *Chavs: The Demonization of the Working Class*. London: Verso.

Jørgensen, M.W. & Phillips. L. (2006) *Discourse Analysis as Theory and Method*. London: Sage.

Kalyvas, S. (2015) *Modern Greece: What Everyone Needs to Know*. Oxford: Oxford University Press.

Kaplan, R.L. (2012) Between Mass Society and Revolutionary Praxis: The Contradictions of Guy Debord's Society of the Spectacle. *European Journal of Cultural Studies* 15(4): 457–478.

Karavasilis, L. (2017) Perceptions of "Populism" and "Anti-populism" in Greek Public Discourse during the Crisis: The case of the website "Anti-news." *Politik* 20(4): 58–70.

Kathimerini (29/03/2018). *Οι Πρωτοπόροι που Επένδυσαν στην Καινοτομία εν μέσω Κρίσης* (The Pioneers Who Invested in Innovation in the Midst of the Crisis). Available (consulted 7 April 2018) at: http://www.kathimerini.gr/956281/article/oikonomia/epixeirhseis/oi-prwtoporoi-poy-ependysan-sthn-kainotomia-en-mesw-krishs.

Keep Talking Greece (2017) IMF Thomsen: Unemployment in Greece will return to pre-crisis levels in 2038. Available (consulted 08 October 2018) at: http://www.keeptalkinggreece.com/2017/01/19/imf-thomsen-unemployment-in-greece-will-return-to-pre-crisis-levels-in-2038/.

Kellner, D. (2003) *Media Spectacle*. London: Routledge.

Kellner, D. (2004) Spectacle and Media Propaganda in the War on Iraq: A Critique of U.S. Broadcasting Networks. *Cultural Studies ↔ Critical Methodologies* 4(3): 329–338.

Kellner, D. (2016) *American Nightmare: Donald Trump, Media Spectacle, and Authoritarian Populism*. Rotterdam: Sense Publishers.

Keramidiotis, G. (2008) *Τι Σημαίνει να Ζείς: Καπιταλιστική Κρίση* (What it Means "To Live": Capitalist Crisis). Available (consulted 30 October 2017) at: http://www.youtube.com/watch?v=lUTsPXFWUD4&feature=related.

Kioupkiolis, A. (2014) Towards a Regime of Post-political Biopower? Dispatches from Greece, 2010–2012. *Theory, Culture & Society* 31(1): 143–158.

Klein, N. (2007) *The Shock Doctrine: The Rise of Disaster Capitalism*. New York: Metropolitan Books.

Klein, U. (1998) Tabloidized Political Coverage in *Bild-Zeitung*. *The Public* 5(3): 79–93.

Koliopoulos, J. and Veremis. T. (2003) *Greece, the Modern Sequel: From 1831 to the Present*. London: Hurst and Company.

Kompatsiaris P. and Mylonas Y. (2015) The Rise of Neo-Nazism and the Web: Social Media as Platforms for Racist Discourses in the Context of Greek Economic Crisis. In: Fuchs, C. and Trotier, D. (eds) *Social Media, Politics and the State: Protest, Revolutions, Riots, Crime, and Policing in the Age of Facebook, Twitter and YouTube*. London: Routledge, 109–130.

Kompatsiaris, P. (2017) Whitewashing the Nation: Racist Jokes and the Construction of the African "Other" in Greek Popular Cinema. *Social Identities* 23(3): 360–375.

Kompatsiaris, P. (2017b). *The Politics of Contemporary Art Biennials: Spectacles of Critique, Theory and Art*. New York and Abingdon: Routledge.

Konstantinidis, C. and Vlachou, A. (2016) Appropriating Nature in Crisis-Ridden Greece: The Rationale of Capitalist Restructuring, Part 1. *Capitalism Nature Socialism*. Available (consulted 11 June 2018) at: http://dx.doi.org/10.1080/10455752.2016.1264002.

Konstantinidis, C. and Vlachou, A. (2016) Appropriating Nature in Crisis-Ridden Greece: Deepening Neoliberal Capitalism, Part 2. *Capitalism Nature Socialism*. Available (consulted 11 June 2018) at: http://dx.doi.org/10.1080/10455752.2016.1264712.

Kosma, Y. (2015) Οριενταλιστικές Αναπαραστάσεις στον Κινηματογράφο: Το Παράδειγμα της Ταινίας Γάμος αλά Ελληνικά (Orientalist Representations in Cinema: The Case of "My Big Fat Greek Wedding"). In: Kioupkiolis, A., Pechtelidis, Y. and Kosma, Y. (eds) *Θεωρία του Λόγου: Δημιουργικές Εφαρμογές* (*Discourse Theory: Creative Applications*). Athens: Dardanos-Gutenberg, 41–81.

Kostopoulos, T. (2005) *Η Αυτολογοκριμένη Μνήμη: Τα Τάγματα Ασφαλείας και ο Μεταπολεμικός Εθνικισμός* (*The Self-Censored Memory: The Security Battalions and Post-War Nationalism*). Athens: Filistor.

Kotz, David M. (2009) The Financial and Economic Crisis of 2008: A Systemic Crisis of Neoliberal Capitalism. *Review of Radical Political Economics* 41(3): 305–317.

Kouki, H. (2014) European Crisis Discourses: the Case of Greece. In: Murray-Leach, T. (ed) *Crisis Discourses in Europe: Media EU-phemisms and Alternative Narratives*. Civil Society and Human Security Research Unit London School of Economics and Political Science, June 2014, 16–20.

Kousouris, D. (2014) *Δίκες των Δοσίλογων 1944–1949* (*Collaborationists' Trials, 1944–1949*). Athens: Polis.

Labrianidis L. and Pratsinakis, M. (2017) Crisis Brain Drain: Short-Term Pain/Long-Term Gain? In: Tziovas, D. (ed) *Greece in Crisis: the Cultural Politics of Austerity*. London, New York: I.B.Tauris, 87–106.

Laclau, E. and Mouffe, C. (1985) *Hegemony and Socialist Strategy, Towards a Radical Democratic Politics*. London: Verso.

Laclau, E. (1996) *Emancipations*. London: Verso.

Lapavitsas, C., Bratsis, P., Kouvelakis, S., and Balibar, E. (2010) The Greek Crisis: Politics, Economics, Ethics. *Journal Of Modern Greek Studies* 28: 293–309.

Lapavitsas, C. et al. (2012) *Crisis in the Eurozone*. London: Verso.

Lasch, C. (1979) *The Culture of Narcissism*. New York, London: W. W. Norton & Company.

Lazzarato, M. (2009) Neoliberalism in Action: Inequality, Insecurity and the Reconstitution of the Social. *Theory, Culture & Society* 26(6): 109–133.

Lefebvre, H. (2014) *Critique of Everyday Life*. London: Verso.

Lentin, A. and Titley, G. (2011) *The Crises of Multiculturalism: Racism in a Neoliberal Age*. London: Zed Books.

Lindekilde, L. (2014) The Mainstreaming of Far-Right Discourse in Denmark. *Journal of Immigrant & Refugee Studies* 12: 363–382.

Liptak, K. (2017) Once-critical Greek PM Praises Trump over "Common Values". Available (consulted 20 October 2017) at: http://edition.cnn.com/2017/10/17/politics/president-donald-trump-alexis-tsipras-greece-evil/index.html.

Littler, J. (2017) *Against Meritocracy: Culture, Power and Myths of Mobility*. London: Routledge.

Lorey, I. (2015) *States of Insecurity*. London: Verso.

Losurdo, D. (2011) *Liberalism, a Counter-History*. London: Verso.

Losurdo, D. (2016) Stalin and Hitler: Twin Brothers or Mortal Enemies? *Crisis & Critique* 3(1): 32–47.

Löwy, M. (2009) Capitalism as Religion: Walter Benjamin and Max Weber. *Historical Materialism* 17(1): 60–73.

Lukacs, G. (2001) *History and Class Consciousness*. Athens: Odysseas.

Lyle S.A. (2008) (Mis)Recognition and the Middle-class/Bourgeois Gaze: A Case Study of Wife Swap. *Critical Discourse Studies* 5(4): 319–330.

Maesse, J. (2018) Austerity Discourses in Europe: How Economic Experts Create Identity Projects. *Innovation: The European Journal of Social Science Research* 31(1): 8–24.

Maesse, J. (2018b) Discursive Marxism: How Marx Treats the Economy and what Discourse Studies Contribute to It. *Critical Discourse Studies*. Available (consulted 20 June 2018) at: https://doi.org/10.1080/17405904.2018.1457548.

Marcuse, H. (2009) *Negations: Essays in Critical theory*. London: MayFly.

Martin, J. (2015) The Colonial Origins of the Greek Bailout. Available (consulted 2 July 2018) at: https://imperialglobalexeter.com/2015/07/27/the-colonial-origins-of-the-greek-bailout/.

Marvaka, L. and Papatheodorou, V. (2012) Forgiving Siemens: Unraveling a Tangled Tale of German Corruption in Greece. Available (consulted 25 August 2018) at: https://corpwatch.org/article/forgiving-siemens-unraveling-tangled-tale-german-corruption-greece.

Marx, K. (1990) *Capital: Critique of Political Economy, Vol. 1*. London: Penguin.

Marx, K. (1992) *Early Writings*. London: Penguin.

Marx, K. and Engels, F. (2004) Manifesto of the Communist Party. Available (consulted 4 August 2018) at: https://www.marxists.org/archive/marx/works/1848/communist-manifesto/.

Matvejević, P. (2013) *Between Exile and Asylum: An Eastern Epistolary*. Zagreb: vbz.

Matza, T. (2018) *Shock Therapy: Psychology, Precarity and Well-Being in Postsocialist Russia*. Durham and London: Duke University Press.

Mazower, M. (2001) *Inside Hitler's Greece: The Experience of Occupation, 1941–44*. New Heaven and London: Yale University Press.

McChesney, R. (2009) *The Political Economy of Media. Enduring Issues, Emerging Dilemmas*. New York: Monthly Review Press.

McGuigan, J. (1996) *Culture and the Public Sphere*. London and New York: Routledge.

McRobbie, A. (2016) *Be Creative*. London: Polity.

Mentinis, M. (2013) The Entrepreneurial Ethic and the Spirit of Psychotherapy: De-politicisation, Atomization and Social Selection in the Therapeutic Culture of the "Crisis." *European Journal of Psychotherapy & Counselling* 15 (4): 361–374.

Mercille, J. (2013) The Role of the Media in Fiscal Consolidation Programmes: The Case of Ireland. *Cambridge Journal of Economics* 38(2): 281–300.

Michailidou, A. (2017) Twitter, Public Engagement and the Eurocrisis: More than an Echo Chamber? In: Barisione, M. and Michailidou, A. (eds) *Social Media and European Politics: Rethinking Power and Legitimacy in the Digital Era*. Houndmills: Palgrave Macmillan, 241–266

Mihaljevic D. (2017) The Contradictions of European Capitalism: An Interview with Joachim Becker – Part 1. Available (consulted 1 August 2017) at: http://www.criticatac.ro/lefteast/the-contradictions-of-european-capitalism-an-interview-with-joachim-becker-part-i/.

Mikelis, K. (2016) Neocolonial Power Europe? Postcolonial Thought and the Eurozone Crisis. *French Journal for Media Research* 5: 1–17.

Mikelis, K. and Dimitrios, S. (2017) Hierarchies, Civilization, and the Eurozone Crisis: The Greek Financial Crisis. In: Marangos, J. (ed.) *The Internal Impact and External Influence of the Greek Financial Crisis*. Houndmills: Palgrave Macmillan, 125–142.

Milech, T. (2013) *Ο Τόπος του Εγκλήματος: Γερμανία, η Ανοικεία Πατρίδα* (*The Crime Scene: Germany, the Uncanny Motherland*). Athens: Thyrathen/Epilogi.

Mirzoeff, N. (2011) *Right to Look: A Counterhistory of Visuality*. Durham: Duke University Press.

Mitralexis, S. (2017) Studying Contemporary Greek Neo-Orientalism: The Case of the "Underdog Culture" Narrative. *Horizons of Politics*, 8(25): 125–149.

Mosco, V. (2009) *The Political Economy of Communication, 2nd Edition*. London: Sage.

Mouffe, C. (2000) Deliberative Democracy or Agonistic Pluralism? Available (consulted 4 August 2018) at: https://www.ihs.ac.at/publications/pol/pw_72.pdf.

Mouzelis, N. (1979) *Modern Greece: Facets of Underdevelopment*. London and Basingstoke: The Macmillan Press Ltd.

Mouzelis, N. (1996) The Concept of Modernization: Its Relevance for Greece. *Journal of Modern Greek Studies* 14(2): 215–227.

Mylonas, Y. (2009) *Discursive Struggles on the "War on Terror": Politics, Crisis and Representation*. København: Københavns Universitet.

Mylonas, Y. (2012) Media and the Economic Crisis of the EU: The "Culturalization" of a Systemic Crisis and Bild-Zeitung's Framing of Greece. *triplec* 10(2): 646–671.

Mylonas, Y. (2012b) Reinventing Political Subjectivities: Studying Critical Documentaries on the War on Terror. *Social Semiotics* 22(4): 353–374.

Mylonas, Y. (2012c) Discourses of Counter-Islamic-Threat Mobilization in Post 9/11 Documentaries. *Journal of Language and Politics* 11(3): 405–427.

Mylonas, Y. (2013) The Emergence of Political Subjectivity in "Non-Political" Terrains; Conscientious Objection to the Military Service in Pre-Crisis Greece. *Subjectivity* 6(3): 320–348.

Mylonas, Y. (2014) Crisis, Austerity and Opposition in Mainstream Media Discourses of Greece. *Critical Discourse Studies* 11(3): 305–321.

Mylonas, Y. (2015) Austerity Discourses in "Der Spiegel" Journal, 2009–2014. *triplec* 13(1): 248–269.

Mylonas, Y. (2017) Liberal Articulations of the "Enlightenment" in the Greek Public Sphere. *The Journal of Language and Politics* 16(2): 195–218.

Mylonas, Y. (2017b) Social Media as Propaganda Tools: The Greek Conservative Party and National Elections. In: Barisione, M. and Michailidou, A. (eds) *Social media and*

European Politics: Rethinking Power and Legitimacy in the Digital Era. Houndmills: Palgrave Macmillan, 193–218.

Mylonas, Y. (2017c) Witnessing Absences: Social Media as Archives and Public Spheres. *Social Identities* 23(3): 271–288.

Mylonas, Y. (2017d) Book Review: Patricia Anne Simpson and Helga Duxies (eds), Digital Media Strategies of the Far Right in Europe and the United States. Lanham, MD: Lexington Books, 2015. *Media, Culture and Society* 39(2): 301–303.

Mylonas, Y. (2018) Constructions of the Opposition to "Structural Adjustment Reforms" in the German Mass Media. *Journal of Political Ideologies* DOI: 10.1080/13569317.2018.1449575.

Mylonas, Y. (2018b) Discursive Articulations of the Cypriot Economic Crisis in Greek Media. In: Carpentier, N. and Doudaki, V. (eds) *Cyprus and its Conflicts: Representations, Materialities, and Cultures*. London: Berghahn, 268–289.

Mylonas, Y. (2018c) Race and Class in German Media Representations of the "Greek Crisis." In: Basu, L. Schifferes, S. and Knowles, S. (eds) *Austerity and the Media: Comparative Perspectives*. London & New York: Routledge, 140–154.

Mylonas, Y. (2018d) The "Greek Crisis" as a Middle-Class Morality Tale: Frames of Ridicule, Pity and Resentment in the German and the Danish Press. *Continuum: Journal of Media and Cultural Studies* 32(6): 770–781.

Mylonas Y. and Kompatsiaris P. (2013) "Πολιτισμικές Ερμηνείες" της "Ελληνικής Κρίσης Χρέους": Όψεις του Νεοφιλελεύθερου Λόγου στον Ελληνικό Δημόσιο Χώρο (Culturalist Explanations of the Crisis in the Greek Public Sphere). In Pleios, G. (ed) *Η Κρίση και τα ΜΜΕ (The Crisis and the Media)*. Athens: Papazisis, 387–419.

Mylonas Y. and Kompatsiaris P. (2019) Trolling as Transgression: Culture Wars and Subversive Affirmations Against Neoliberal Austerity. *International Journal of Cultural Studies* (forthcoming).

Mylonas, Y. and Noutsou, M. (2018) The "Greferendum" in the Danish Daily Press. *Race and Class* 59(3): 51–66.

Naftemporiki, 2017. *Κυριάκος Μητσοτάκης: Αξιοκρατία Παντού, Αξιολόγηση Παντού* (Kyriakos Mitsotakis: Meritocracy Everywhere, Evaluation Everywhere). Available (consulted 1 March 2018) at: http://www.naftemporiki.gr/story/1232089/kur-mitsotakis-aksiokratia-pantou-aksiologisi-pantou.

National Herald (2017) Schaeuble Says He Saved Greece, Deserves Statue. Available (consulted 10 January 2018) at: https://www.thenationalherald.com/173022/schaeuble-says-saved-greece-deserves-statue/.

Negt, O. and Kluge, A. (2016) *Public Sphere and Experience*. London: Verso.

Nikolopoulou, A. and Cantera, L.M. (2016) "Exceptional," "Normal" or a "Myth"? The Discursive Construction of the "Crisis" by Greek Employees. *Discourse & Society* 1–17 DOI: 10.1177/0957926516651364.

Noys, B. (2010) *The Persistence of the Negative: A Critique of Contemporary Continental Theory*. Edinburgh: Edinburgh University Press.

OECD (2017) Hours Worked (indicator). Available (consulted 4 August 2018) at: https://www.oecd-ilibrary.org/employment/hours-worked/indicator/english_47be1c78-en.

Ojala, M. and Harjuniemi, T. (2016) Mediating the German Ideology: Ordoliberal Framing in European Press Coverage of the Eurozone Crisis. *Journal of Contemporary European Studies* 24(3): 414–430.

Ong, A. (2006). *Neoliberalism as Exception: Mutations in Citizenship and Sovereignty*. London: Duke University Press.

Papadimitriou, D. and Zartaloudis, S. (2015) European Discourses on Managing the Greek Crisis: Denial, Distancing and the Politics of Blame. In: Karyotis, G. and Gerodimos, R. (eds) *The Politics of Extreme Austerity: Greece in the Eurozone Crisis*. Houndmills & New York: Palgrave Macmillan, 34–45.

Papathanassopoulos, S. (2015) European Media Views of the Greek Crisis. In: Schifferes, S. and Roberts, R. (eds) *Financial Crises: Comparative and Historical Perspectives*. London and New York: Routledge, 103–118.

Pelt, M. (2006) *Tying Greece to the West: US-West German-Greek Relations 1949-1974*. Copenhagen: Museum Tusculanum Press.

Pentaraki, M. (2018) Austerity Common Sense and Contested Understandings of the Austerity Measures Within a Leadership of a Professional Association of Social Workers. *European Journal of Social Work* DOI: 10.1080/13691457.2018.1435507.

Pfeifer, M. (2016) Cinema in the Age of Austerity: On the Representation of Debt in Greek Cinema. Available (consulted 16 February 2017) at: http://filmiconjournal.com/blog/author/37/moritz-pfeifer.

Phelan, S. (2014) *Neoliberalism, Media and the Political*. New York: Palgrave McMillan.

Platonov, A. (2013) *Soul, and Other Stories*. London: Vintage.

Pleios, G. (2013) Τα Μ.Μ.Ε. Απέναντι στην Κρίση (The Media Facing the Crisis). In Pleios, G. (ed) *Η Κρίση και τα Μ.Μ.Ε. (The Crisis and the Media)*. Athens: Papazisi, 87–134.

Polanyi, K. (2001) *The Great Transformation: The Political and Economic Origins of Our Time*. Boston: Beacon Press.

Politico.eu (2017) Jeroen Dijsselbloem: "It Feels Like I Commited a War Crime" Available (consulted 18 August 2018) at: http://www.politico.eu/article/jeroen-dijsselbloem-it-feels-like-i-committed-a-war-crime/.

Potter, J. (2011) *Representing Reality: Discourse, Rhetoric and Social Construction*. London: Sage.

Poulantzas, N. (1979) *Classes in Contemporary Capitalism*. London: Verso.

Poulantzas, N. (1979b) *Fascism and Dictatorship*. London: Verso.

Poulantzas, N. (2000) *State, Power, Socialism*. London: Verso.

The Press Project. (2017) *Μητσοτάκης: η Κοινωνική Ισότητα Είναι Ενάντια στην Ανθρώπινη Φύση* (Mitsotakis: Social Equality is Against the Human Nature). Available (consulter 21 October 2018) at: https://www.thepressproject.gr/article/116872/Mitsotakis-I-koinoniki-isotita-einai-enantia-stin-anthropini-fusi.

Prime Minister Press Office (2010) Meeting with Dominique Strauss-Kahn. Statements Tuesday December 7, 2010. Available (consulted 18 March 2017) at: http://primeminister.gr/english/2010/12/07/meeting-with-dominique-strauss-kahn-statements/.

Prozorov, S. (2009) *The Ethics of Post-Communism: History and Social Praxis in Russia.* New York: Palgrave McMillan.

Rancière, J. (1992) Politics, Identification, and Subjectivization. *October* 61: 58–64.

Rancière, J. (2006) *Hatred of Democracy.* London: Verso.

Rancière, J. (2007) *On the Shores of Politics.* London: Verso.

Rear, D. (2013) Laclau and Mouffe's Discourse Theory and Fairclough's Critical Discourse Analysis: An Introduction and Comparison. Available (consulted 25 October 2018) at: https://www.academia.edu/2912341/Laclau_and_Mouffe_s_Discourse_Theory_and_Faircloughs_Critical_Discourse_Analysis_An_Introduction_and_Comparison.

Resigl, M. and Wodak, R. (2001) *Discourse and Discrimination: Rhetorics of Racism and anti-Semitism.* New York: Routledge.

Reuters (2012) Greece Plans "Special Economic Zones" to Boost Growth. Available (consulted 25 August 2018) at: https://www.reuters.com/article/us-greece-economy-zones-idUSBRE87R09820120828.

Roberts, J. (2015) *Revolutionary Time and the Avant-Garde.* London: Verso.

Rodgers, L. & Stylianou, N. (2015) How Bad Are Things for the People of Greece? Available (accessed 25 August 2018) at: https://www.bbc.com/news/world-europe-33507802.

Roediger, D. (2017) *Class, Race and Marxism.* London: Verso.

Roos, J. (2018) Why the Debt Deal with the EU is Bad for Greece. Available (consulted 25 June 2018) at: https://www.aljazeera.com/indepth/opinion/debt-deal-eu-bad-greece-180624082950318.html.

Roos, J. (2018b) Ten Years on, the Crisis of Global Capitalism Never Really Ended. Available (consulted 02 October 2018) at: https://roarmag.org/essays/lehman-brothers-fallout-financial-crisis/.

Roos, J. (2019) *Why not Default? The Political Economy of Sovereign Debt.* New Jersey: Princeton University Press.

Rosanvallon, P. (2011) *The Society of Equals.* Harvard: Harvard University Press.

Ross, G. (2016) Austerity and New Spaces for Protest: The Financial Crisis and Its Victims. In: Ancelovici, M. Dufour, P. and Nez, H. (eds) *Street Politics in the Age of Austerity: From the Indignados to Occupy.* Amsterdam: Amsterdam University Press, 43–66.

Ross, K. (2008) *The Emergence of Social Space: Rimbaud and the Paris Commune.* London: Verso.

Ross, K. (2009) Democracy for Sale. In G. Agamben et al., *Democracy in What State?* New York: Columbia University Press, pp. 82–99.

Routhier, D. and Bolt, M. (eds) (2015) *Kapitalisme som Religion: Walter Benjamin, Robert Kurz, Giorgio Agamben.* Copenhagen: Forlaget Nebula.

Said, E. (2003) *Orientalism*. London: Penguin.
Saldaña, J. (2009) *The Coding Manual for Qualitative Researchers*. London: Sage.
Salem, S., and Thompson, V. (2016) Old Racisms, New Masks: On the Continuing Discontinuities of Racism and the Erasure of Race in European Contexts. *Nineteen Sixty Nine: An Ethnic Studies Journal* 3(1). Available (consulted 23 May 2017) at: http://escholarship.org/uc/item/98p8q169.
Schäfer, A. and Streeck, W. (2013) Introduction: Politics in the Age of Austerity. In: Schäfer, A. and Streeck, W. (eds) *Politics in the Age of Austerity*. Cambridge: Polity Press, 1–25.
Schou, J. (2016) Ernesto Laclau and Critical Media Studies: Marxism, Capitalism, and Critique. *tripleC* 14(1): 292–311.
Schwab, K. and Sala-i-Martín, X. (2016) The Global Competitiveness Report 2016–2017. Available (consulted 21 September 2018) at: http://www3.weforum.org/docs/GCR2016-2017/05FullReport/TheGlobalCompetitivenessReport2016-2017_FINAL.pdf.
Sennett, R. (1998) *The Corrosion of Character: The Personal Consequences of Work in the New Capitalism*. New York and London: W.W. Norton & Company.
Sennett, R. (2006) *The Culture of Late Capitalism*. Yale: Yale University Press.
Sepos, A. (2016) The Centre–Periphery Divide in the Eurocrisis: A Theoretical Approach. In: Magone, J.M. Laffan, B. and Schweiger, C. (eds) *Core-Periphery Relations in the European Union, Power and Conflict in a Dualist Political Economy*. London & New York: Routledge, 35–55.
Sevastakis, N. (2004) Κοινότοπη Χώρα: Οψεις του Δημοσιου Χωρου και Αντινομιες Αξιων στη Σημερινη Ελλαδα (*Banal Country: The Public Space and Antinomies of Values in Contemporary Greece*). Athens: Savalas.
Shi, C.C. (2018) Defining My Own Oppression: Neoliberalism and the Demands of Victimhood. *Historical Materialism* 26(2): Identity Politics. Available (consulted 25 June 2018) at: http://www.historicalmaterialism.org/articles/defining-my-own-oppression.
Shklovsky, V. (2015) Art, as Device. *Poetics Today* 36(3): 151–174.
Siamanta, Z.D. (2017) Building a Green Economy of Low Carbon: The Greek Post-Crisis Experience of Photovoltaics and Financial "Green Grabbing." *Journal of Political Ecology* 24: 258–276.
Simopoulos, K. (2002) *Η Διαφθορά της Εξουσίας* (*The Corruption of Authority*). Athens: Piroga.
Sindorf, S. (2013) Symbolic Violence in the Online Field: Calls for "Civility" in Online Discussion. *The Fibreculture Journal* 22: 193–214.
Skeggs, B. (1997) *Formations of Class and Gender: Becoming Respectable*. London: Sage.
Skeggs, B. (2003) *Class, Self, Culture*. London: Routledge.

Skeggs, B. and Wood, E. (2012) *Reacting to Reality Television: Performance, Audience and Value*. London & New York: Routledge.

Slobodian, Q. (2018) *Globalists: the End of Empire and the Birth of Neoliberalism*. Cambridge: Harvard University Press.

Smith, H. (2017) Alexis Tsipras: "The Worst is Clearly Behind Us." Available (consulted 16 February 2018) at: https://www.theguardian.com/world/2017/jul/24/alexis-tsipras-the-worst-is-clearly-behind-us.

Sommer, M. (2014) European Crisis Discourses: The Case of Germany. In: Murray-Leach, T. (ed) *Crisis Discourses in Europe: Media EU-phemisms and Alternative Narratives*. Civil Society and Human Security Research Unit London School of Economics and Political Science, June 2014, 15.

Soules, M. (2015). *Media, Persuasion and Propaganda*. Edinburgh: Edinburgh University Press.

Stavrakakis, Y. (1999) *Lacan and the Political*. London: Routledge.

Stavrakakis, Y. (2013) Dispatches from the Greek Lab: Metaphors, Strategies and Debt in the European Crisis. *Psychoanalysis, Culture & Society* 18: 313–324.

Stavrakakis, Y. and Katsampekis, G. (2014) Left-wing Populism in the European Periphery: the Case of SYRIZA. *Journal of Political Ideologies* 19(2): 119–142.

Stavrakakis, Y. and Katsampekis, G. (2018) The Populism/Anti-Populism Frontier and its Mediation In Crisis-Ridden Greece: From Discursive Divide to Emerging Cleavage? *Eur Polit Sci*. Available (consulted 16 May 2018) at: https://doi.org/10.1057/s41304-017-0138-3.

Stolze, T. (2000) A Displaced Transition: Habermas on the Public Sphere. In Hill, M. and Montag, W. (eds) *Masses, Classes and the Public Sphere*. London: Verso, 146–156.

Streeck, W. (2014) *Buying Time: The Delayed Crisis of Democratic Capitalism*. London: Verso.

Streeck, W. (2016) *How Will Capitalism End?* London: Verso.

Streinzer, A. (2018) "Let Them Be Screwed by the Troika!" Blame, Shame and Ambivalent Pro-Troika Social Critique in Greece. Available (consulted 26 June 2018) at: http://ksa.univie.ac.at/fileadmin/user_upload/i_ksa/PDFs/Vienna_Working_Papers_in_Ethnography/vwpe07.pdf.

Stubbs, P. (2017) Slow, Slow, Quick, Quick, Slow: Power, Expertise and the Hegemonic Temporalities of Austerity. *Innovation: The European Journal of Social Science Research*, DOI: 10.1080/13511610.2017.1415806.

Sum, N.-L. and Jessop, B. (2013) *Towards a Cultural Political Economy: Putting Culture in its Place in Political Economy*. Cheltenham & Northampton: Edward Elgar.

Ta Nea (2017) Γ. Παπανδρέου: *Ο Ελληνικός Λαός Θα Πλήρωνε πολύ Βαρύτερα ένα «Όχι» στο Πρώτο Μνημόνιο* (The Greek People Would Pay a Harder Toll to a 'No' to the First Memorandum). Available (consulted 4 August 2018) at: http://www.tanea.gr/news/politics/article/5449635/g-papandreoy-o-ellhnikos-laos-tha-plhrwne-poly-barytera-ena-oxi-sto-prwto-mnhmonio/.

Taguieff, P.A. (2010) *Conspiracy Theories: Esoterism, Extremism*. Athens: Polis.
Theodoropoulou, S. and Watt, A. (2015) An Evaluation of the Austerity Strategy in the Eurozone: Was the First Greek Bailout Programme Bound to Fail? In: Karyotis, G. and Gerodimos, R. (eds) *The Politics of Extreme Austerity: Greece in the Eurozone Crisis*. Houndmills & New York: Palgrave Macmillan, 71–90.
Toscano, A. (2010) *Fanaticism: On the Uses of an Idea*. London: Verso.
Tracy, J.F. (2012) Covering "Financial Terrorism." *Journalism Practice* 6(4): 513–529.
Traverso, E. (2016) *Left-Wing Melancholia: Marxism, History, and Memory*. New York: Columbia University Press.
Traverso, E. (2017) *The New Faces of Fascism*. Athens: Ekdoseis tou Eikostou Protou.
Triantafyllou, S. and Ioakeimoglou, I. (2007) *For the Flag and the Nation*. Athens: Melani.
Triantafyllidou, A. Gropas, R. and Kouki, H. (2013) Introduction: is Greece a Modern European Country? In: Triantafyllidou, A. Gropas, R. and Kouki, H. (eds) *The Greek Crisis and European Modernity*. London: Palgrave Macmillan, 1–24.
Tsavdaroglou, C. Petrakos, K. and Makrygianni, V. (2017) The Golden "Salto Mortale" in the Era of Crisis. *City* DOI: 10.1080/13604813.2017.1331563.
Tsoukalas, C. (2012) *Ελλάδα της Λήθης και της Αλήθειας Από τη Μακρά Εφηβεία στη Βίαια Ενηλικίωση* (*Greece of Oblivion and Truth: From a Prolonged Adolescence to a Violent Maturation*). Athens: Themelio.
Tziovas, D. (2017) Introduction. In: Tziovas, D. (ed) *Greece in Crisis: the Cultural Politics of Austerity*. London, New York: I.B.Tauris.
Urry, J. (2002) *Consuming Places*. London: Routledge.
Van Dijk, T.A. (1991) *Racism and the Press*. London: Routledge.
Van Dijk, T. (2006) Ideology and Discourse Analysis. *Journal of Political Ideologies* 11(2): 115–140.
Van Dijk, T. (2008) *Discourse and Power*. New York: Palgrave Macmillan.
Van Leeuwen, T. (2008) *Discourse and Practice: New Tools for Critical Discourse Analysis*. Oxford: Oxford University Press.
Van Vossole, J. (2016) Framing PIGS: Patterns of Racism and Neocolonialism in the Euro Crisis. *Patterns of Prejudice* 50(1): 1–20.
Vardis, A. and Dalakoglou, D. eds. (2011) *Revolt and Crisis in Greece: Between a Present Yet to Pass and a Future Still to Come*. London: AK Press and Occupied London.
Varoufakis, Y. (2011) *Κρίσης Λεξιλόγιο* (*Crisis Vocabulary*). Athens: Potamos.
Varoufakis, Y. (2017) *Adults in the Room: My Battle with the European and American Deep Establishment*. London: Bodley Head.
Vasudevan, R. (2009) Dollar Hegemony, Financialization and the Credit Crisis. *Review of Radical Political Economics* 41(3): 391–304.
Vetta, T. (2014) The Political Economy of Greece: a Brief History, 1945–2013. Available (consulted 02 October 2018) at: https://www.academia.edu/36163683/The_Political_Economy_of_Greece_a_brief_history_1945-2013.

Vetta, T. (2017) The Habits of the Heart: Grassroots "Revitalization" and State Transformations in Serbia. In: Lashaw, A. Sampson, S. and Vannier, C. (eds) *Cultures of Doing Good: Anthropologists and NGOs*. University of Alabama Press, 56–74.

Vila, P.S. and Peters, M. (2016) The Privatizing Industry in Europe. Available (consulted 17 July 2016) at: https://www.tni.org/files/publication-downloads/tni_privatising_industry_in_europe.pdf.

Vincent, A. (2010) *Modern Political Ideologies*. Chester: Wiley-Blackwell.

Voglis, P. (2002) *Becoming a Subject: Political Prisoners during the Greek Civil War*. New York-Oxford: Berghahn.

Volkskrant. (2015) Griekenland Heeft Dictatuur Nodig (Greece Needs Dictatorship). Available (consulted 7 June 2018) at: https://www.volkskrant.nl/columns-opinie/griekenland-heeft-dictatuur-nodig~bfe425a5/.

Watt, H. (2014) Greece Sues for 7 Billion Euros over German Submarines that Have Never Sailed. Available (consulted 9 October 2018) at: https://www.telegraph.co.uk/news/worldnews/10895239/Greece-sues-for-7-billion-euros-over-German-submarines-that-have-never-sailed.html.

Weber, J. (1996) *Πρόσωπα από την Αντίσταση: Μνήμη Θανάτου, Μνήμη Ζωής* (*Faces from the Resistance: Memory of Death, Memory of Life*). Athens: Agra.

Wendling, A.E. (2012) *The Ruling Ideas: Bourgeois Political Concepts*. Lanham: Lexington Books.

Williams, R. (2015) *Politics and Letters, Interviews with the New Left Review*. London: Verso.

Wodak, R. and Boukala, S. (2015) European Identities and the Revival of Nationalism in the European Union, a Discourse Historical Approach. *Journal of Language and Politics* 14(1): 87–109.

Wood, E.M. (1995) *Democracy Against Capitalism: Renewing Historical Materialism*. Cambridge: Cambridge University Press.

Wood, E.M. (1999) The Politics of Capitalism. Available (consulted 9 October 2018) at: https://monthlyreview.org/1999/09/01/the-politics-of-capitalism/.

Wood, E.M. (2017) *The Origins of Capitalism, a Longer View*. London: Verso.

Wren, K. (2001) Cultural Racism: Something Rotten in the State of Denmark? *Social and Cultural Geography* 2(2): 141–162.

Wright, E.O. (2015) *Understanding Class*. London: Verso.

Yılmaz, F. (2016) *How the Workers Became Muslims: Immigration, Culture, and Hegemonic Transformation in Europe*. Michigan: University of Michigan Press.

Yurchenko, Y. (2018) *Ukraine and the Empire of Capital: From Marketization to Armed Conflict*. London: Pluto Press.

Žižek, S. (2006) The Antinomies of Tolerant Reason: A Blood-Dimmed Tide is Loosed. Available (consulted 30 May 2018) at: http://www.lacan.com/zizantinomies.htm.

Žižek, S. (2010) A Permanent Economic Emergency. *New Left Review* 64: 85–95.

Žižek, S. (2011) *Living in End Times*. London: Verso.

Index

Acceleration
   logic   57, 58, 81, 217
   of production and consumption   xiv
   of unemployment   48
Accumulation
   and austerity   78, 192
   capitalist process of   9, 30, 56–59
   and comprador bourgeoisie   177
   and creative destruction   62
   and debt   68, 80
   and default   77
   through dispossession   56, 68, 78, 81, 173
   and economic restructuring   79, 85
   and the Greek debt crisis   168
   and ideology   92
   neoliberal   43
   and non-western periphery   185
   post-Fordist   16
   primitive/primary   78, 80–82, 84, 174, 220
Activation   104, 111, 217
Adorno, Teodor   27, 122
   and Horkheimer, Max   27, 127, 140, 141, 147, 150
Affect
   and bourgeois ideology   177
   disaffection   207
   and fantasmatic logics   17
   and representation   145, 172
   and shaming   108, 119
Affective Modalities   46, 158–160
Ahmed, Sara   21–23, 46, 134, 159, 160
Ancient Greece   3, 24
   antiquity   26, 96, 134–139
Antagonism   14, 123, 145, 184
Apocalypse
   and capitalism   221–223
   and Habermas   192
   and media representations   47
   metaphors   196, 222
   myth   195
   and mythopoetic legitimation   188, 191
   and politics of exception   185

Badiou, Alain   98, 186, 214, 215, 225, 226
Bauman, Zygmunt   23, 27, 32, 33, 74, 125, 147, 179
Benjamin, Walter   xiv, 86, 88, 90
Biopolitics
   and austerity   46, 104
   biopolitical governance   43, 70
   and competition   42
   and discipline   223
   and hegemony   97, 111, 112
   and liberal crisis discourse   149
   and spectacle   108, 111
   and welfare   172
Bourdieu, Pierre   37, 154
Bourgeoisie   xiii, 4, 9, 13n, 16, 27, 30, 35–39, 42, 46, 56, 57, 61, 62, 77, 81, 89–91, 119, 131, 136, 139, 140, 148, 154, 156, 158–160, 165, 167, 174–181, 193, 203, 205, 209, 211, 214, 215, 218–221
Buck-Morss, Susan   26, 28, 39, 88, 90, 91, 125, 136, 153, 196, 208–211, 214
Bullying   96, 97, 122, 157

Capital   24, 26, 32, 35, 37–39, 41, 49
   cultural   22, 23, 37, 38, 89, 140, 155
   financial   58, 66–68, 72, 194
   social   37, 140, 155
Capitalist Center (Core)   3, 7, 11, 17, 30, 41, 46, 49, 52, 53, 65, 69–74, 76, 85, 95, 107n, 139, 143, 176, 186, 204, 207, 220, 222
Carpentier, Nico   5, 14, 15, 18, 46, 88, 104, 114, 115, 119, 173
Chains of equivalence   17, 115, 149, 157
Class
   middle   12, 13n, 17, 23, 30, 32, 34, 35, 37n, 39, 46, 84, 96, 100, 105, 121, 131, 138, 139, 152–159, 171, 172, 175, 216, 217, 220, 221
   working   xii, 2, 7, 13n, 17, 28, 30–32, 35–40, 46, 56, 73, 84, 90, 97, 106, 110, 111, 143, 152, 154–156, 158, 163–166, 170, 172, 174, 176, 177, 179–182, 200, 214, 216, 217, 219, 220, 226

Colonial   3, 11, 21, 22, 23, 25, 28, 46, 70, 73, 95, 125, 136, 146, 156, 167, 210, 214, 217, 219, 224
Commodification
  of the common   81
  and the Greek crisis in the media   46, 134
  of the lifeworld   59, 186
  and mediatisation   105
  and neoliberalism   88
  and Othering   46, 120, 132, 134
Commodity   35, 38, 57, 60, 61, 64, 67, 88, 90, 106, 134, 135, 141
  fetish   23, 28, 90, 106, 121, 128, 134–136, 174, 208
Competition
  acceleration and growth   58
  and biopolitics   46, 111
  and deregulation   64
  as destructive   213
  and the EU   73, 74, 150
  and the Euro   53
  and the free market   59, 60
  and global neoliberalism   44, 153, 174
  and human nature   78
  In the media   95
  and oligopolies   70
  and rewards   221
  and social mobility   152
  state protection of   42
  and Western capital   26
  winner and losers   157, 158
Confession   34, 35
Conspiracy   192–194
Consumerism   2, 3, 9, 23, 38, 43, 61n, 68, 78, 100, 106, 121, 134–136, 139, 164, 172, 178, 179, 186, 211, 220, 221
Control   xiv, 21, 35, 39, 42, 53, 54, 59, 61n, 65, 69, 70, 80, 81, 92, 93, 99, 105, 106, 131, 148, 157, 178, 189, 197, 204, 210, 220
Corruption
  culture   114, 149
  Greek   52, 85, 166
  high corruption   124
  as media spectacle   108, 109
  and Othering   121
  petty corruption   122, 141, 167
  revelation   166
  systemic   10
Creditor   xiii, 28, 29, 49, 52, 55, 63, 71, 78, 100, 142, 162, 168, 171, 190, 201, 216
Crisis
  1970's Oil Crisis   30, 40, 42, 56, 63, 78
  economic   1, 3–6, 16, 18–20, 23, 40, 42, 43, 46, 48, 49, 56, 58, 63, 64, 67, 74, 87, 94, 102, 109–111, 114, 135, 149, 166, 168, 177, 183–185, 191, 193, 209, 216, 221, 222, 225, 226
  environmental   xiv, xvi, 4, 6, 57, 48, 81, 82, 103, 222
  political   48, 56, 77, 218
  social   4, 215
Culturalization
  analysis   114
  of the Greek Crisis   120, 121, 133, 152, 215
  and Othering   28

Dean, Jodi   34, 40, 45, 87, 91, 92, 98, 183, 194, 204, 212
Debt
  and austerity   2, 45, 103, 195, 211
  and bankrupt Greeks   134
  and the Bank System   172
  and bourgeois morals   193, 199
  and colonialism   73
  and compounding   59
  and consolidation state   76–84
  and democracy   225
  and entitlement   148, 165, 170
  European   189, 200
  and Eurozone periphery   6, 74
  and expropriation   143, 168, 199
  and finance   66–68
  German War Debts to Greece   26n, 125, 127, 133
  Greek   xiii, 11n, 48–55, 94–98, 187
  and Greek anti-austerity politics   190
  Greek debt of 1823   25
  and Greek psyche   132
  Greek sovereignty   26
  and guilt   86, 173, 184
  and nationalist resentment   141, 142, 161
  in orientalist representations of Greece   128, 135, 139
  Public Recapitalization of Greek Debt   191
  and recession   217

INDEX

and ridicule   169, 196
securing the debt   192
two notions of Greek debt   28, 29
Debtor   71, 142, 165
Default   49, 68
Deleuze, Giles   138
and Guattari, Felix   xii, xiv, 213, 226
Democracy   xiii, 3, 8, 12n, 18, 21, 32, 40, 41, 43–45, 56, 60n, 65, 73, 74, 80, 90, 96, 99, 110, 124, 133, 134, 139, 150, 155, 176, 179, 186, 192, 194, 203, 204, 210, 211–213, 222–226
Anti/non democratic   20, 40, 47, 85, 98, 204–206, 212, 216, 219, 225
Discipline   34, 42, 44, 61, 62, 71, 97, 180, 217, 220

Enlightenment   13n, 21, 27, 37n, 133, 134, 177, 178, 205–209
Eschatology   187, 221
Eurocentrism   24, 47
Exception
    capitalist growth as historical   63
    cultural   115, 219
    exceptional events   9, 185, 221
    exceptional individual   36, 38, 178
    exceptional solidarity   224
    Greece as   xi, 49, 55, 95, 100, 131, 182, 202, 207, 211
    Greek crisis as   100, 122, 123
    politics of   47, 55, 183–186, 221
    propaganda   98
    state of   186
Exclusion
    economic   32, 90, 140, 153, 156–158
    media   18, 98, 178
    from public sphere   89, 90, 95, 130
    semantic   19
    social   37n, 48, 131, 181
    and social rights   172
Extreme Center   199, 211

Fascism
    and anticommunism   218
    antifascism   25n, 74
    austerity and crisis   4
    and authoritarian capitalism   209
    and capitalism in crisis   147
    and folk community   39

Greek collaborationism   125
and liberalism   9
media legitimation of   211
micro-fascisms xii
and modern Greece   3
and Western-centrism   214

Gaze
    ironic   159
    racial   22, 23
    and spectacle   106
    spiteful   175
    tourist   136
    upper/middle class   46, 121, 153–157, 220
    Western/Occidental   26, 137, 148, 149, 219
German Occupation of Greece   3, 125–128
Globalization   73, 183, 193, 194
Growth   6, 9, 39, 41, 42, 49, 52, 55–59, 62, 63, 65, 66, 69, 71, 72, 78, 79, 95, 106, 109, 162, 179, 190, 193, 198, 211, 217

Hall, Stuart   22, 43n, 110, 172
Harvey, David   41, 42, 45, 49, 56–59, 62, 63, 66, 67, 78, 81, 85, 86, 172, 178, 194, 207, 216, 217
Hegemony   92, 93, 111
    and anachronisms   214
    and biopolitics   112
    and the bourgeoisie   176, 177, 181
    and capitalist restructuring   184
    class   17, 35, 37, 85, 105, 152, 176, 220
    and common sense   195
    counter   101–104, 129, 148, 154, 191, 200–204, 211, 212, 226
    cultural   21, 183
    and democracy   225
    and Europe   132
    and events   215
    German   146, 193
    Greek crisis narrative   46, 47, 133, 137
    hegemonic crisis and austerity narrative   19, 54, 111, 128, 138, 163, 164, 185, 188, 193, 208
    hegemonic interventions   119, 120
    and identity   114, 136
    liberal-conservative   24
    and media   87, 215–218
    neoliberal   20, 40, 45, 109, 213

Hegemony (cont.)
    and Othering   23, 115, 159
    and propaganda   98, 99, 110
    reactionary   179, 180
    and recontextualisation   122
    and self-blaming   97
    and spectacle   160
    and the tax payer   172
    temporalities of   123, 196
    and universality   130
Holocaust   21, 27, 147, 148

Identity
    bourgeois   177, 219, 220
    Classical Greek   109
    culturalist construction of Greece   115, 119
    and cultural racism   22, 23
    and Discourse Theory   14, 16–19, 46
    European   76, 119, 130
    and hegemonic crisis construction of Greece   114, 121
    and ideology   92
    and individualism   33, 34
    liberal civic   177
    of Modern Greece   26
    national   166, 218
    and nominalisations   144
    North/West   136
    orientalism and Greece   29
    post modernism   31
    and social movements   27
    winner/loser   157, 158
    working class   38n, 155, 172
Imperialism   3, 26, 29, 69, 71, 146, 194, 214, 219
Individualism   9, 33, 36, 38, 64, 104, 105, 112, 122, 136, 157, 158, 181, 207, 208, 211
    individualisation   33, 34, 38, 39, 91
Interdiscursivity   18, 109, 121, 122, 146
Intertextuality   18, 102, 122, 142
Investment   36, 49, 58, 61, 62, 66, 67, 78, 79, 82, 83, 86, 140, 198

Laclau, Ernesto   15–17, 46, 114, 115, 119, 130, 176, 209
Lefebvre, Henri   106, 227
Legitimacy
    of austerity   xii, xiii, 3, 94, 97, 185, 191, 216, 221

    authoritative   102, 131, 139, 160, 162–164, 195
    and CDA   19, 114, 188
    class   16, 34, 90, 152, 154, 156, 167, 177
    and consensus   92, 215
    and cultural imperialism   26, 28
    delegitimation   42, 91, 110, 127, 192, 202, 203
    democratic   xii, 146
    and the dismantling of welfare   158
    and entitlement   100, 209
    and the EU   77
    of expropriation   168
    and finance   37
    and Germany   146, 201
    and media   1, 104
    moral   144, 146
    and mythopoesis   122, 123, 172
    and neoliberalism   65, 96
    political   17
    and popular sovereignty   42, 44
    and racism   21
    and rhetorical topoi   19
    semantic   114
    See also (Fascism, media legitimation of)

Marcuse, Herbert   8, 9, 39, 147
Market
    capitalist   4, 32, 33, 193, 213
    and competition   58, 157
    and consumerism   179
    cross-border activity   53
    and democracy   74–77
    financial   11, 36, 48, 66–68, 170, 188, 189, 211
    free   8, 22, 60, 64, 186, 210
    Greece and financial markets   54, 80, 103, 198–201
    and hegemony   92, 103
    ideology   xii, 63, 111, 141, 150
    labor   93, 202
    liberalism   9
    market-friendly policies   79
    media   1, 91, 95, 99
    and meritocracy   152
    In Michel Foucault   58
    and neoliberal politics   40–46, 73, 181, 219–225
    and the periphery   26, 69–71

INDEX

pre-capitalist 59, 59n
and primitive accumulation 81, 82, 85, 168
and the public sphere 88, 110, 194
self-regulating 65
society 157–159
structural violence 153
and wealth distribution 12
Marx, Karl 38, 56, 60, 227
class analyses 31, 32, 178
fictitious capital 67
and Franz Fanon 29
Guy Debord 106
heterogeneous Marxism 16
Marxian analysis of crisis 5
Marxism and Antonio Gramsci 93
Marxism and Negt and Kluge 90
Marxism and Robert Kurz 185
Marxist-Anarchist 175
and primitive accumulation 78, 80
Media Framing 15, 154
austerity 192, 197
class 156–160
and commodity culture 88, 121
devices 162
economic 94
the European periphery 71, 73
the Eurozone crisis 97–99
exoticisation 131
Germany 195
Greek crisis 115, 163, 181
nationalism 170
opposition 200, 206
orientalist 120, 132
protests 101
spectacle 106, 187
Meritocracy 150–152, 177
Migration
anti-immigration policies 10
modern Greek 84
and multiculturalism 22
and occidentalism 24
Minorities xiv, xv, 44, 204
Minor Literature 226
Mobility
and competition 152
in late modernity 33
social group 111

and structural insecurity 174
upward social 122, 177
MOU 11n, 12n, 49, 54

Narcissism 100, 128
bourgeois 221
and liberal publics 100
nationalist 131, 140, 141, 143, 152, 159
and spectatorship 128
West/North 138
Nationalism 113
and the Amphipolis excavation 113
and anti-migration 10
and Bild 11, 171
and class xii, 17, 110
and crisis representations 95, 170
identification 46
and indignation 145, 160
and insecurity 175
and internationalism 4
and neoliberalism 185, 211
and Othering 120
and populism 201
rise of Western and German 147n, 148
Samaras, Antonis 24n
and victimisation of Germany 144, 172
and WWII reparations 134
See also (Narcissism)
Nazi
Germany 74, 124–127, 138, 144–147, 214n
Golden Dawn xiv, 13n, 210, 211
Merkel as 142, 144
propaganda 2
Nodal Points 17, 115, 139, 171, 208
Nominalisations 19, 114
and authority 170, 201
and class reduction 165, 174
and common sense 193
and counter hegemony 201
and cultural Othering 121, 130, 131, 136, 205
and national homogeneity 144–146, 208
and universality 133

Occidentalism
and class 28, 139
common sense 119, 120
culture 24
and Europe 205

Occidentalism (cont.)
    and Greece   29, 132
    ideas   100
    Othering   22
    self   130
    See also (Gaze, Racism)
Ordoliberalism
    austerity   7
    European   64, 73
    German   7, 75, 143
    market freedom   76
    ordoglobalism   64
Orientalism   24, 130, 216, 217
    and class   158, 181
    and consumer culture   135
    and essentialism   114, 151
    in film   108
    and Greece   27–29, 107, 115
    and Greece as Europe's Other   120, 121, 129, 140, 187
    as myth   205
    Oriental Schism   123
    self-orientalisation   13n, 29, 97, 132, 133, 177, 208
    See also (Framing, Gaze, Racism, Stereotypes, Topoi)

Particularist   75, 215
Post Politics   39, 40, 164, 180, 206
Poverty
    and austerity   182
    and culture   114
    depoliticising   169
    in Greece   48
    and Greek crisis representation   148, 159, 168
    and Greek identity   121
    populism   12n, 152, 206
    and shame   6, 166
    and welfare   42
Privatisations
    and bailout loans   xiii
    and debt   28
    and neoliberalism   85, 95, 199
    of public assets   49, 59, 64, 77, 82, 198
    and shock therapy   211
Proletarian
    and destruction   62
    experience   90, 226
Proletarianisation

    and debt   78
    and land grabbing   178
    and primitive accumulation   80, 82
Propaganda
    corporate   99
    crisis and austerity   104
    and exceptional events   98, 215
    and hegemony   87, 97, 99, 110, 111
    Herman and Chomsky   99, 103
    and liberal democracy   215
    and mass media   45
    and myths   100
    and spectacle   110, 225
Publicity
    and Bild   134
    commercially driven   91, 92
    detournement   225
    and the Documenta   110
    European taxpayer   173
    and exclusion   95
    Greek crisis   xi–xiii, 2, 164, 168, 188
    of human suffering   169
    and nationalism   170
    negative   96, 97
    and ritualized communication   218
    spectacular   109, 160, 198
    and transparency   89
Public sphere
    and austerity   114
    and communicative capitalism   91
    and consensus   92
    and critique   194
    European   95, 139
    and exclusion   xiii
    Greece in North/West   218
    Greek   7, 101, 102, 109, 210, 217
    Habermasian   88, 89
    mainstream   154, 218, 227
    national   3, 7, 8
    notion   87, 110
    and phantasmagoria   88
    proletarian   90

Racism   21, 114
    and class   21, 30, 219
    cultural   11, 20, 22, 125
    and denmark   7, 140
    as disciplinary technology   181
    in Domenico Losurdo   21, 210
    and German nationalism   147

INDEX

identity and far-right politics 16
Jan Fleishenhauer 144
in late modernity 23
and meritocracy 151
and Nazi Germany 126
and neoliberalism 10, 153, 219
neoracism 46, 129
and orientalisation of Greece 96, 219
and orientalism 29
racist gut feelings xii
and sexism 9, 131, 139
to the southerners 11
and war 154
and western centrism 25, 138
Rancière, Jacques 39, 40, 43, 44, 226
Realism
  austerity as realist 174
  capitalist 221
  and conformity 146
  and conservativism in the EU 7
  and the Greek media 205, 206
  Habermas 89
  and ordoliberalism 143, 184
  politics 40, 47
  politics of exception 184
  and Syriza in Berlingske 175
  understanding of the crisis 200
Religion 9, 25
  capitalism as 85, 86
  and cultural racism 125, 129
  political 45
Resentment
  democratic 204
  Europe's resentment 126
  Greek resentment 132
  liberal 160
  narratives of 95
  nationalist 145, 170
  psychological 97
  sociological 170
  upper-class 177
Rhetorical topoi 19–20
  argumentative 185, 192
  and Classical Greece 128, 134
  culturalist common sense 114
  finance and expert authority 200
  lifestyle 131
  orientalist 130, 133
  and spectacle 106
  stereotypes 120

Ridiculisation
  and affective modalities 160
  and class gaze 46
  of the Greek Referendum 202
  and irony 166
  and loath 172
  of the loser 159
  of Tsipras 175
  of Varoufakis 94
Ritual 139
  media rituals 134, 218
  ritualistic representation of Greece 139, 148

Second World War
  and the European periphery in its aftermath 72, 185
  and German responsibility 146, 147
  and Greece 36n, 30, 84, 125
  and neoliberalism 43, 216
  and post democracy 40
  and post-war growth 63, 79
  and victimisation of Germany 146
Sexism 26, 131, 139
Shaming
  and bullying 96
  and cultural stereotypes 95
  and hegemony 111
  and humor xii
  and reality TV 108
  and trauma 97
  the working class 166, 181, 214
Skeggs, Beverly 22, 30–35, 100, 106, 108, 154, 155, 158, 160, 166, 167, 181
Socialism
  and capitalist propaganda 99
  and counter-hegemonic politics 212
  and democratism 40n
  ex-socialist states 30
  and George Papandreou Jr. 48, 101
  in Kathimerini 210
  and liberalism 8
  New socialist politics 47, 226
  as nihilism 64
  and orientalism 24
  post-socialist transition 210
  socialist and Communist Parties 42, 198
  socialist block 72, 74, 110, 211
  socialist movements 9, 89
  socialist vision 174, 227

Socialism (cont.)
   and Syriza   176
   and Tsipras   175
Spectacle
   crisis and austerity   46, 188
   and critical arts   110
   and diffused audiences   106
   and digital media   91
   disciplinary   111
   in Douglas Kellner   105, 107
   Greek crisis   xiii, 2, 217
   and Guy Debord   106, 225
   heritage, Amphipolis   109
   mainstream media   87, 108
   Olympic Games   94
   omnipresent   107
   and Othering   132, 218
   and phantasmagoria   88
   and sensualisation   203
   See also (Apocalypse, Propaganda, Hegemony, Sexism)
Spite   98, 170
   bourgeois   175
   and racism   210
   spiteful publicity   160, 174, 218
   See also (Gaze)
Stavrakakis, Yannis   15, 24, 95, 201, 206
Stereotypes   xi, 114
   consumer culture   134–136, 156, 185
   culture, race and class   1, 3, 46, 141, 169, 218
   gender   131
   Greek   95, 108
   orientalist   120, 139
   southerners   224
   tourist   96
Streeck, Wolfgang   6, 13n, 45, 49, 53, 56, 59n, 63, 72, 74–79, 201, 204
Surplus Value   61, 68, 81

Taxation
   and economic freedom   42
   increase for the poor   62, 77, 84
   Pierre Moscovici   224
   and precarity   181
   progressive   31
   reduction for the wealthy   64, 78, 79
   tax evasion   108, 109

Technocracy
   and austerity   52
   and class interests   17
   and crisis explanations   1, 20, 23, 44, 102, 215–217
   and European identity   149, 150
   and governance   40, 41, 198
   and the IMF   103
   jargon of   120, 128, 224
   neoliberal   80
   and PIIGS   73
   and populists   201
   and post-politics   180, 183, 184
   and revolution   208, 209
   unelected technocrats   11n, 225
Tourism   55n, 136
   austerity and Airbnb   82
   development and economic growth   72, 109, 140
   experience   136, 137, 139, 165
   French tourists   219
   German tourists   125, 214n, 219
   Greeks living as tourists   136
   northern petty-bourgeois   139
   as peaceful invasion   136
   and popular culture   100, 108, 121
   and popular culture and consumption   135, 156, 218
   the tourist and liquid modernity   23, 33
   tourist industry   3, 46, 55
   See also (Stereotypes)
Troika   11n
   and austerity   104, 190, 195
   and bailout loans   54, 98
   and Dominique Strauss Kahn   101
   and mass media   103
   and memorandums   49, 191
   and politics of exception   55
   and Poul Thompsen   48
   and rescue mechanism   186
   and sovereignty   209
   and structural adjustment reforms   81, 84
   and Syriza's succumbing   104, 179

Ukraine   4, 218
Universal
   bourgeois ideology   39

capitalism and liberal democracy   110
capitalism as universally beneficial   75
competition norm   42
Europe as a universalist sublime   130
and Fukuyama   205
growth   6
and Habermas   89
homo economicus   160
liberal values   133
middle-class experience   34
redistribution   32
standards of excellence   141
Western self   144
Western values   132
world safety   146

Utopia
   capitalist market   222
   communist   223
   in decline   45
   imagination and politics   226
   liberal   204

War
   of annihilation   125, 128, 147
   reparations   26n, 125, 126, 133, 134, 147, 214
   See also (Second World War)
Wehrmacht   126n, 127, 133
Wood, Ellen Meksins   12, 32, 35, 37n, 38n, 45, 58–60, 167, 193

www.ingramcontent.com/pod-product-compliance
Lightning Source LLC
Chambersburg PA
CBHW071152070526
44584CB00019B/2761